ROBERT BROWNING

**Studies in Eighteenth- and Nineteenth-Century Literature**

*General Editors*

Andrew Sanders, Professor of English, University of Durham

*Published titles*

*Forms of Speech in Victorian Fiction* Raymond Chapman
*Henry Fielding: Authorship and Authority* Ian A. Bell
*Language and Relationship in Wordsworth's Writing: Elective Affinities* Michael Baron
*Utopian Imagination and Eighteenth-Century Fiction from* Robinson Crusoe *to* Rasselas Christine Rees
*Robert Browning* John Woolford and Daniel Karlin

# ROBERT BROWNING

John Woolford
and
Daniel Karlin

LONDON AND NEW YORK

**Longman Group Limited**
Longman House, Burnt Mill,
Harlow, Essex CM20 2JE, England
*and Associated Companies throughout the world.*

*Published in the United States of America*
*by Longman Publishing, New York*



First published 1996

ISBN 0 582 096146 CSD
ISBN 0 582 096138 PPR

**British Library Cataloguing-in-Publication Data**

A catalogue record for this book is
available from the British Library

**Library of Congress Cataloging-in-Publication Data**

Woolford, John.
Robert Browning / John Woolford and Daniel Karlin.
p. cm. -- (Studies in eighteenth- and nineteenth-century literature)
Includes bibliographical references and index.
ISBN 0-582-09613-8 (pbk.). -- ISBN 0-582-09614-6 (cased)
1. Browning, Robert, 1812-1889. 2. Poets, English--19th century--Biography. I. Karlin, Daniel, 1953- . II. Title. III. Series.
PR4231.W66 1996
821'.8--dc20
[B] 95-44055
CIP

Set by 7 vv in 10/12 Goudy
Produced by Longman Singapore Publishers (Pte) Ltd.
Printed in Singapore

# Contents

# *Preface*

What unifies this study, and defines its position in contemporary critical debates, is its focus on context. We are both old enough to remember New Criticism, and to have participated in the critical discussions which have followed its decline since the 1960s. We are both conscious of the recent emergence of feminist, rhetorical and New Historical schools of criticism after the negative formalisms of the 1970s and 1980s. And we welcome their rehabilitation of context as a legitimate and urgent subject. A writer is someone who writes at a particular time, in a particular place, and under specific cultural conditions. Whether the work which emerges from these conditions can be understood outside them as an absolute aesthetic result is a matter for debate, but the debate must be an informed one. This book, therefore, engages with the many contexts – biographical, historical, intellectual – from which Browning's work emerged, and attempts to show how such contexts help to shape his characteristic forms and subjects.

Chapters 1 and 2 describe the nature of Browning's poetry. Chapter 1 reconstructs his process of composition, how the poetry came into being; chapter 2 describes Browning's characteristic forms and language. Chapters 3 and 4 are concerned with the immediate biographical frameworks within which Browning functioned. Chapter 3 details his family and early friendships, chapter 4 the role of love and marriage in both his life and his poetry. Chapters 5 and 6 move out to the wider contexts of politics (chapter 5) and philosophy (chapter 6). At no point, however, do we divorce these contexts from the poetry itself. While describing Browning's process of composition, chapter 1 illustrates Browning's acknowledgement (whether angry, ironic, or tolerant) that composition must *be* a process, conducted in a series of stages during which its originating impulse may be occluded rather than realised. In chapter 2 the context is the great Romantic debate over the nature and function of poetic language, which shapes

Browning's choice of form – the dramatic monologue – and the contention of two voices, one demotic and democratic, one 'poetic' and elevated, in his characteristic verbal texture. Chapter 3 takes the personal relationships – in particular with his parents and with his friend Alfred Domett – which were crucial for Browning's poetic and personal self-definition in the early years, and by examining their reflection in the poetry shows their actual ambivalence. Chapter 4 considers Browning's view of sexual love before and after his marriage, in the light of a conflict (further explored in chapter 6) between egotistic and altruistic impulses, and the ambivalence – in life and in poetry – with which Browning viewed both his own marriage and marriage in general. Chapter 5 explores parallel ambivalences in Browning's political attitudes, attempting to explain his apparent loss of radical enthusiasm in later years as his displacement of political debate onto wider social and historical arguments. Finally, chapter 6 summarises the complex philosophical positions within which all these shifting and contradictory impulses are held. If there is a unifying motif it is the idea of 'independence', Browning's fierce commitment to self-autonomy, and the compromises and conflicts which assail that principle when it encounters other things and other people.

This book is designed for use by all students of Browning. To non-specialists it offers an account of him in the form not of a primer – very good primers already exist – but of a series of topics which lead to the heart of his work. To specialist scholars it offers both a considerable body of new research, and our latest thoughts on a writer we have both worked on for many years. We have not attempted to homogenise our contributions: differences of view and overlaps of interest have been allowed to stand where we have felt that they helpfully illustrate the collision and/or convergence of our approaches. Daniel Karlin takes the biographical and stylistic topics which characterise his previous work (chapters 2, 3 and 4); John Woolford has concentrated upon the cultural and intellectual context in which Browning wrote (chapters 1, 5 and 6). While we would hesitate to call the result a mini version of *The Ring and the Book*, the analogy is a useful one: each of us examines the 'book' of Browning from a differing viewpoint, and each has then broken down that viewpoint into three different angles of approach.

While ranging widely across Browning's writings, we have made a short-list of poems which, in our opinion, are characteristic of him and merit lengthy discussion, and have consciously selected the majority of our illustrations from them. A list of these poems will be found on pp. x–xi. We also provide a chronology of Browning's life and a summary of Browning scholarship.

We are grateful to the following individuals and institutions for permission to quote from unpublished material in their possession or to which they hold copyright: Mr John Murray; the Pierpont Morgan Library, New York; the Beinecke Library of Yale University; and the Armstrong Browning Library at Baylor University. In the compilation of our Chronology, we have made extensive use of the chronologies in volumes 5 and 6 of the Longman series Foundations of Modern Britain: Eric J. Evans, *The Forging of the Modern State* (1991) and Keith Robbins, *The Eclipse of a Great Power* (2nd edn 1994).

Parts of chapter 1 derive from an essay in *Browning Society Notes* and a paper given at a conference at Liverpool University in July 1994; part of chapter 3 derives from a lecture given at Birkbeck College, London, in July 1994 for the University of London Extra-Mural Summer School. We would like to thank the following for help and advice: Sylvia Adamson, John Baker, Philip Kelley, Steve McGarty, John Maynard, Pat O'Shea, Joe Phelan, Robert Renton, Matthew Reynolds, Eugenia Sifaki, Kian Soheil, and Herbert F. Tucker.

John Woolford
Daniel Karlin

# *List of works principally discussed*

## 1. Long Poems

*Pauline* (1833)
*Sordello* (1840)
*Pippa Passes* (1841)
'The Flight of the Duchess' (*Dramatic Romances and Lyrics*, 1845)
'Bishop Blougram's Apology' (*Men and Women*, 1855)
'Mr. Sludge, "the Medium" ' (*Dramatis Personae*, 1864)
*The Ring and the Book* (1868–9), esp. books 7, 8, and 11
*Red Cotton Night-Cap Country* (1873)

## 2. Other Poems

'Johannes Agricola' [later 'Johannes Agricola in Meditation'] (first publ. in *Monthly Repository*, 1836, then *Dramatic Lyrics*, 1842)
'My Last Duchess' (*Dramatic Lyrics*, 1842)
'Soliloquy of the Spanish Cloister' (*Dramatic Lyrics*, 1842)
'Waring' (*Dramatic Lyrics*, 1842)
'England in Italy' [later 'The Englishman in Italy'] (*Dramatic Romances and Lyrics*, 1845)
'Italy in England' [later 'The Italian in England'] (*Dramatic Romances and Lyrics*, 1845)
'The Lost Leader' (*Dramatic Romances and Lyrics*, 1845)
'Love Among the Ruins' (*Men and Women*, 1855)
'Fra Lippo Lippi' (*Men and Women*, 1855)
'Childe Roland to the Dark Tower Came' (*Men and Women*, 1855)
'How It Strikes a Contemporary' (*Men and Women*, 1855)
'Andrea del Sarto' (*Men and Women*, 1855)
'Old Pictures in Florence' (*Men and Women*, 1855)
'Cleon' (*Men and Women*, 1855)
'Two in the Campagna' (*Men and Women*, 1855)

'One Word More' (*Men and Women*, 1855)
'Dîs Aliter Visum' (*Dramatis Personae*, 1864)
'May and Death' (*Dramatis Personae*, 1864)
'Thamuris marching . . .' (extract from *Aristophanes' Apology*, 1875)
'A Forgiveness' (*Pacchiarotto* [etc.], 1876)

## 3. Prose

The letters exchanged between Browning and EBB during their courtship, 1845–6

*Essay on Shelley* [i.e. 'Introductory Essay' to *Letters of Percy Bysshe Shelley*, 1852]; extracts reprinted in Appendix A

The exchange of letters about *Men and Women* between Browning and Ruskin, 1855 (reprinted in Appendix B)

# *Abbreviations*

*The following abbreviations are used throughout the text.*

| | |
|---|---|
| ABL MS | Manuscript in Armstrong Browning Library, Baylor University, Waco, Texas |
| *PMLA* | *Proceedings of the Modern Languages Association of America* |
| *TLS* | *Times Literary Supplement* |

Elizabeth Barrett Browning is referred to throughout as EBB.

# *Note on Texts*

Texts and titles of poems are those of first publication, following the policy of our Longman Annotated English Poets edition; where titles vary considerably, the later form is given in square brackets and separately indexed.

Quotations from the Brownings' correspondence follow the text of Kelley up to the most recent available volume (vol. xii, to May 1846). In the case of Browning's correspondence with EBB, this means that some quotations are referenced to Kintner, whose text is less reliable than Kelley's; we have corrected some readings from MS.

Both Browning and EBB, in letters and poems, make use of a two-point ellipsis (. .) which corresponds sometimes to a dash, sometimes to a three-point ellipsis in modern punctuation. The appearance of the two-point ellipsis does not, therefore, indicate a gap in the text.

# CHAPTER 1
# *Composition and influence*

In this chapter I shall reconstruct as much as possible of Browning's process of composition. This is not merely a technical exercise. It raises large questions about what goes into a work, where that work comes from, how it is drafted, what happens when it appears in print, and what the poet then feels or does about it when revising it for republication; the exercise also involves scrutiny of the influences in play at any given stage of this process. Such enquiries raise major theoretical issues, the most fundamental of which implies all of them. What is a work? When, during the process of its production, does a poem become itself? Naturally the answer to this question will differ for different writers, and where evidence of how the author went about making his works is lacking, it cannot be answered. Where such reconstruction *is* possible, as it is for most post-Renaissance writers, we have the practical task of tracking the compositional process; and where, as in the case of Browning, we confront an author who had a *theory* of composition, further questions come into play, most obviously: Does his theory correspond to his practice? What follows is an attempt to answer all these questions for him individually, but without neglecting the general issues which his particular case raises.

## Browning's theory of composition

Browning's theory of composition involves an uncompromising commitment to originality. It is set out in the following statement in his *Essay on Chatterton* (1842):

> Genius almost invariably begins to develop itself by imitation. It has, in the short-sightedness of infancy, faith in the world: and its object is to compete with, or prove superior to, the world's already recognised idols, at their own performances and by their own methods. This done, there grows up a faith in itself: and, no longer taking the performance or method of another for granted,

> it supersedes these by processes of its own. It creates, and imitates no longer. Seeing cause for faith in something external and better, and having attained to a moral end and aim, it next discovers in itself the only remaining antagonist worthy of its ambition, and in the subduing [sic] what at first had seemed its most enviable powers, arrives at the more or less complete fulfilment of its earthly mission. (Woolford and Karlin: ii 484)

The first two stages of this schema are straightforward. Juvenile poets imitate earlier writers because they know no better, or in a spirit of emulation or, more kindly, because they are learning their craft. With the arrival of maturity they shake off this dependence, cease to imitate, and begin to create for themselves. Up to this point Browning's theory shadows the general Romantic rejection of the more imitative aesthetic of the eighteenth century. At a more personal level, it seems to reflect the fierce commitment to personal independence which he felt in life, and his ambivalence about *all* relationships which seemed to threaten this: mother–son in Part iii of *Pippa Passes*, father–son in book xi of *The Ring and the Book*, friend–friend in 'Italy in England', all seem to menace a personal freedom which at the poetic level appears as absolute originality.[1]

But Browning perceives a further stage in which 'genius', as a result of acquiring 'a moral end or aim', sets about 'subduing what had at first seemed its most enviable powers'. This is a complication about which I will say at this stage only that it constitutes an attempt to combine a commitment to empathy with self-regard. What it means in practical terms is a good deal less clear, and will have to emerge from my discussion of Browning's compositional methods.

What does Browning mean by 'imitation'? Most obviously, he means imitation of earlier literary works, what we would now call 'influence'. He suggests a rationale for his aversion to being influenced in the case of Jules the sculptor in *Pippa Passes*.[2] In the fourth and final episode – the confrontation between the Bishop and the wicked Intendant – the Bishop reads out a letter he has received from Jules, whom we last saw at the end of the second episode, smashing his own statues. In his letter, Jules explains to the Bishop, who has apparently been his patron to date, that

1. For more on the poems mentioned, and on the topic of family and friends in Browning's poetry, see Chapter 2.

2. For a summary of the plot of *Pippa Passes*, see Chapter 4, p. 116.

> 'He never had a clearly conceived Ideal within his brain till today. Yet since his hand could manage a chisel, he has practised expressing other men's Ideals – and in the very perfection he has attained to he foresees an ultimate failure – his unconscious hand will pursue its prescribed course of old years, and will reproduce with a fatal expertness the ancient types, let the novel one appear never so palpably to his spirit: there is but one method of escape – confiding the virgin type to as chaste a hand, he will paint, not carve, its characteristics . . .' (iv 45–53)

This implies not only that the 'Ideal' cannot be directly represented but that since any skill in a creative medium inevitably reflects 'other men's Ideals' he will never be able to do more than 'reproduce with a fatal expertness the ancient types'; he proposes to evade the seductions of competence by transferring his efforts into a medium of which he knows nothing.

In a letter to a friend, Browning extended this repudiation of influence to include history. Mrs FitzGerald had apparently asked a friend of hers about the historical original of the protagonist of 'Jochanan Hakkadosh' (*Jocoseria*, 1883), a request which, when she communicated it to Browning, provoked in him something close to anger:

> you begin by asking of a friend 'Who Jochanan was': why, *nobody* . . . the poem *tells* you *who* he was, what he was, where he lived, and why he was about to die: what more do you want? . . . all the other stories are told at just as much length as is requisite for the purpose, and years of study of dictionaries and the like would make the student learned enough in another direction but not one bit more in the limited direction of the poem itself. I say all this because you imagine that with more learning you would 'understand' more about my poetry – and as if you would somewhere find it already written – only waiting to be translated into English and my verses: whereas I should consider such an use of learning to be absolutely contemptible: for poetry, if it is to deserve the name, ought to create – or re-animate something – not merely reproduce *raw* fact taken from somebody else's book. (17 Mar. 1883, McAleer 1966: 156–7)

Browning's theory of originality demands that the poem be totally independent not only of literary influence but of history too. Mrs FitzGerald had innocently assumed that Jochanan must have been a real historical character, only to be told that such an expectation is misguided: if the poet is original, we should look to the poem for such information, for there is none elsewhere. No such person as 'Jochanan Hakkadosh' ever existed; Browning invented him; and he belongs therefore exclusively to Browning, or more precisely to the poem 'Jochanan Hakkadosh'.

I distinguish 'Browning' from 'the poem' because Browning's theory of originality includes a rejection of any direct relation between the two. He was extremely reluctant to admit anything approaching a biographical interpretation of his work. In 'At the "Mermaid"' (*Pacchiarotto*, 1876), Shakespeare is made to say: 'Here's my work: does work discover / What was rest from work – my life?' and to answer that it is: 'Blank of such a record' (ll. 17–18, 25). Of course, Shakespeare had been a prime example of what the *Essay on Shelley* defines as the 'objective poet', and Browning had there claimed that while the biography of such a poet gave no insight into his poetry, this was not true of the 'subjective' sort.[3] But in another 1876 poem, 'House', he denies the public any such access to *his* personal life:

> No: thanking the public, I must decline.
> A peep through my window, if folks prefer;
> But, please you, no foot over threshold of mine!
>
> (ll. 10–12)

The obvious objection to this theory is that it is ridiculous. Any literary work must reflect the literary tradition, must bear some relation to the writer's life, must derive in some way from his or her historical moment. And the edginess of Browning's tone in many of these comments suggests that he knew that he was advancing an impossible claim. Indeed there is a significant qualification in his

3. It may be objected that when potential biographers asked him for details about the life of EBB, in his own terms a subjective poet *par excellence*, he invariably refused; but the reason seems in this case to relate more to emotional hurt than to a denial in principle of the link between life and art. He wrote to Isa Blagden, one of his and EBB's closest friends in their Florence years, about the activities of such biographers: 'what I suffer in feeling the hands of these blackguards . . . what I undergo with their paws in my very bowels, you can guess & God knows!' – adding that in the particular case he would make every effort to 'stop the scamp's knavery – along with his breath' (19 Jan. 1863, McAleer 1951: 149).

comment to Mrs FitzGerald when he writes that 'poetry, if it is to deserve the name, ought to create – or re-animate something'. What exactly does he mean by 're-animate', and why introduce such a dangerous concession? The obvious answer is that he was uneasily aware that many of his poems seem to derive from history in precisely the sense he said they shouldn't: what is *The Ring and the Book* if not a historical reconstruction? or 'Fra Lippo Lippi'? or 'Andrea del Sarto'? Browning introduces 're-animate' in order to distinguish such cases from 'imitation', 'reproduc[ing] *raw* fact taken from somebody else's book', but it is at first sight a distinction without a difference, especially when we note Browning's defence to Julia Wedgwood of the historical accuracy of *The Ring and the Book* (Curle: 158–9). The case of *Red Cotton Night-Cap Country* (1873) is even more striking, in that this poem was built up out of newspaper accounts of a contemporary *cause célèbre*: indeed, Browning originally planned to use the real names of the participants, and only changed them when the legal problems of doing so were pointed out to him.[4] It would be difficult to be much more historical than that.

So we turn to Browning's compositional practice aware of strains, if not contradictions, in his theory which make his actual procedures especially interesting. The following account will argue that Browning's theory of originality did in fact influence his practice, but in a special and rather complex sense. For though he is certainly one of the most original of English poets, every stage of his process of composition reflects external influences: his poetry is not (no poetry could possibly be) as autonomous as he would have preferred. But a series of strategies makes such dependence seem always to be departing, to be disappearing through a door which is just about to close behind it.

## Conceptions

Browning was in fact prepared to admit some – though not much – external influence on the conception of some – though not many – poems. In a letter to F.J. Furnivall of 15 Apr. 1883, he claimed that 'The

4. The poem was actually set up in proof with the real names of persons and places: Antoine Mellerio (changed to Léonce Miranda), Anna de Beaupré (changed to Clara de Millefleurs), etc. For a full list, see Pettigrew and Collins: ii 987–8.

Flight of the Duchess' 'originally all grew out of this one intelligible line of a song that I heard a woman singing at a bonfire on Guy Faux night when I was a boy – "Following the Queen of the Gypsies, O!" ' (Peterson 1979: 71). This is pretty grudging. The source is pushed as far back into the past as it will go ('when I was a boy'), it is oral rather than written ('a woman singing'), and it is no more than a 'line' from a work whose remainder is 'unintelligible' (and presumably forgotten). Browning emphasised his own independence by denying that he had read the well-known ballad 'Johnny Faa' (or 'The Gypsy Laddie') before writing his own poem, even though it has the same story as 'The Flight of the Duchess' and could indeed have been what he had heard the 'woman singing'. Other poems have similarly vestigial sources. The title of 'Childe Roland to the Dark Tower Came' is a line from *King Lear*; but it comes from one of Edgar's mad ('unintelligible') ballad fragments (note again the 'oral' aspect) which superficially contributes nothing to the play itself. At the end of *Sordello* Browning reports (or possibly imagines) hearing an Italian peasant boy 'singing . . . some unintelligible words' which represent 'All that's left / Of the Goito lay' (vi 860–6) – that is, the song which launched Sordello's career. Again the 'source' of the poem is in itself oral and 'unintelligible', throwing into relief the magnitude of the creative effort which 'develops' it. In cases where a source is more obviously pressing, Browning reverses this process, shrinking his own poem to a fragment on the verge of becoming 'unintelligible' to its source. In 'Artemis Prologuizes' the speaker recapitulates the story of Euripides' *Hippolytus*, but Browning claimed (in a note which appears in proof but not in the published text) that the poem was 'nearly all retained of a tragedy I composed, much against my endeavour, while in bed with a fever two years ago . . . when I got well, putting only thus much down at once, I soon forgot the remainder' (cited in Woolford and Karlin: ii 206). The obvious source in Euripides is superseded by a self-generated but lost source in Browning himself ('a tragedy I composed') of which the poem we have remains a tantalising fragment. It is the same with historical sources. Browning could hardly deny that many of his poems were in some sense historical, but he normally refused to be specific, commenting that 'How They Brought the Good News from Ghent to Aix', for example, reflected 'merely [a] general impression of the characteristic warfare and besieging which abounds in the Annals of Flanders', and adding, in another letter, 'A film or two, even so slight as the above, may sufficiently support a tolerably big spider-web of a story – where there is ability and good will enough to look most at the main fabric in the middle' (*TLS*, 8 Feb. 1952, p. 109). Similarly at the end of his description of the first conception of 'The Flight of the Duchess' he told Furnivall: 'From so slender a twig of fact can these little singing birds start themselves for a flight to more or less distances' (Peterson 1979: 71).

He made similar comments on poems which were, or were taken to be, based on real people. In later years, he was constantly being asked whether he had had Wordsworth in mind when he wrote 'The Lost Leader', a poem of 1845 containing a violent attack on an unnamed poet, and replied along the lines of this letter to the Rev. A. Grosart: 'I *did* in my hasty youth presume to use the great and venerable personality of Wordsworth as a sort of painter's model; one from which this or the other particular feature may be selected and turned to account'; but, he claims, he had had no intention of 'portraying the entire man': 'though I dare not deny the original of my little poem, I altogether refuse to have it considered as the "very effigies" of such a moral and intellectual superiority' (24 Feb. 1875, Hood: 166–7). Here he both admits and denies that he meant Wordsworth: admits it, in saying that he used him 'as a sort of painter's model', but denies that he has done more than incorporate a few scattered features of Wordsworth's personality and career into an essentially fictitious portrait.

## Between conception and draft

So the conception of a Browning poem may owe something to previous literature, history, or someone he knows, but in his opinion very little. Is this really the case?

In 1843, Richard Henry Horne wrote round to various acquaintances, including Browning and EBB, for help with his work *A New Spirit of the Age*, a survey of the major authors of the day. EBB actually co-wrote several essays with Horne. Browning offered epigraphs for some chapters, including the one on Wordsworth, for which he suggested a passage from *Paradise Lost* (x 441–54), adding at the end a sarcastic comment of his own:

> He, thro' the midst unmarked,
> In show plebeian angel militant
> Of lowest order, passed: and from the door
> Ascended his high throne which, under state

Of richest texture spread, at the upper end
Was placed in regal lustre. Down awhile
He sat, and round about him saw unseen.
At last, as from a cloud, his fulgent head
And shape star-bright appeared, or brighter, *clad*
*With what permissive glory since his Fall*
*Was left him, or false glitter.* All amazed
At that so sudden blaze, the *Stygian throng*
*Bent their aspect.* (As Jeffrey does in the reprint of his review of
the Excursion: this is too good a bit, I fear: take the kinder side
of the matter and give him some or all of your own fine sonnet.)[5]

Unsurprisingly, Horne did not use this passage, though he did adopt Browning's suggestions for other writers. Its application is specifically to Wordsworth's acceptance of the Poet Laureateship in the same year, and the widespread kow-towing which this prompted even in former enemies such as Jeffrey, who had written a notoriously savage review of *The Excursion* on its first appearance in 1814. Browning regarded this 'enthronement' as the symbolic finale of Wordsworth's renunciation of radicalism and acceptance of the existing political order, and the enthronement of Satan in this passage satirically mimes and undermines Wordsworth's elevation. That Satan appears 'in show plebeian angel militant' makes a particularly apt parallel to Wordsworth's original commitment to 'low and rustic life'.[6]

'The Lost Leader', written (probably) in the same year, evidently alludes to this passage from *Paradise Lost*. Here is the poem:

I.

Just for a handful of silver he left us,
   Just for a ribband to stick in his coat –
Got the one gift of which fortune bereft us,
   Lost all the others she lets us devote;
They, with the gold to give, doled him out silver,
   So much was their's who so little allowed:
How all our copper had gone for his service!
   Rags – were they purple his heart had been proud!

5. Cited in Woolford and Karlin: ii 176. We have not corrected Browning's quotation from Milton, which omits l. 444.

6. For more on the political aspect of Browning's attitude to Wordsworth, see Chapter 5, pp. 161–2.

We that had loved him so, followed him, honoured him,
  Lived in his mild and magnificent eye,
Learned his great language, caught his clear accents,
  Made him our pattern to live and to die!
Shakespeare was of us, Milton was for us,
  Burns, Shelley, were with us, – they watch from their graves!
He alone breaks from the van and the freemen,
  He alone sinks to the rear and the slaves!

II.

We shall march prospering, – not thro' his presence;
  Songs may excite us, – not from his lyre;
Deeds will be done, – while he boasts his quiescence,
  Still bidding crouch whom the rest bade aspire:
Blot out his name, then, – record one lost soul more,
  One task unaccepted, one footpath untrod,
One more devils'-triumph and sorrow to angels,
  One wrong more to man, one more insult to God!
Life's night begins: let him never come back to us!
  There would be doubt, hesitation and pain,
Forced praise on our part – the glimmer of twilight,
  Never glad confident morning again!
Best fight on well, for we taught him, – come gallantly,
  Strike our face hard ere we shatter his own;
Then let him get the new knowledge and wait us,
  Pardoned in Heaven, the first by the throne!

The darkness of the Miltonic Hell becomes the darkness brought about by Wordsworth's recantation ('Life's night begins'), and the false dawn of Satan's emergence from the 'cloud' which envelops him becomes the 'glad confident morning' which Wordsworth's action has made irrecoverable. To that extent, Browning recruits Milton into his denunciation of Wordsworth, Milton's self-appointed inheritor. At the same time, however, he goes beyond Milton. If Wordsworth is initially Judas, as the 'handful of silver' must indicate, then his potential redemption and elevation to the place of 'first' by God's 'throne' performs a monumental act of forgiveness, especially if, as the language implies, that position makes him equivalent to Christ. Browning adopts Milton's image of the throne to which Satan ascends, but then questions Milton's unappeasable militancy by transferring the throne to heaven and invoking the 'new knowledge' (the New Testament, as morally superior to the Old) which allows the redemption (of Wordsworth and by extension other lost souls) to become imaginable. The fact that Milton was Wordsworth's favourite poet makes this sequence of inversions particularly ironic.

This poem, then, intertwines a genealogy from Milton with a genealogy from Browning's personal life, but inverts both and thereby transcends the influences it admits.

Another, more complex case is 'The Flight of the Duchess' (1845). The narrator tells how, when he found an old Gypsy woman mesmerising his Duchess, his first instinct was to stop her, and why he didn't:

> For it was life her eyes were drinking
> From the crone's wide pair unwinking,
> Life's pure fire received without shrinking,
> Into the heart and breast whose heaving
> Told you no single drop they were leaving–
> Life, that filling her, past redundant
> Into her very hair, back swerving
> Over each shoulder, loose and abundant,
> As her head thrown back showed the white throat curving,
> And the very tresses shared in the pleasure,
> Moving to the mystic measure,
> Bounding as the bosom bounded.
>
> (ll. 540–51)

This is the central passage of the whole poem: if it is true, then the Duchess is redeemed rather than degraded by what follows it, her flight from her husband, and if not, not. Its literary origins lie in Coleridge's 'Kubla Khan':

> The shadow of the dome of *pleasure*
> Floated midway on the waves;
> Where was heard the mingled *measure*
> From the fountain and the caves . . .
> I would build that dome in air,
> That sunny dome! those caves of ice!
> And all who heard should see them there,
> And all should cry, Beware! Beware!
> His flashing *eyes*, his floating *hair*!
>
> (ll. 31–4, 46–50; my italics)

The motif of ecstasy ('pleasure') expressed rhythmically ('measure') through 'eyes' and 'hair' is complemented by Browning's modulation for these particular lines into the octosyllabics of 'Kubla Khan'. EBB noted in another passage an echo of Coleridge's 'Christabel',[7] and a motif which appears near the beginning of the poem alludes to his 'Youth and Age':

> I was born the day this present Duke was –
> (And O, says the song, ere I was old!)
> In the castle where the other Duke was–
> (When I was happy and young, not old!)
> (ll. 32–5)

Here are the relevant stanzas of Coleridge's poem:

> Verse, a breeze mid blossoms straying,
> Where Hope clung feeding, like a bee –
> Both were mine! Life went a-maying
> With Nature, Hope, and Poesy,
> When I was young!
>
> . . .
>
> Flowers are lovely; Love is flower-like;
> Friendship is a sheltering tree;
> O! the joys, that came down shower-like,
> Of Friendship, Love and Liberty,
> Ere I was old!
> (ll. 1–5. 18–22)[8]

7. In her critical notes on the poem, EBB praised 'the description of the crone with her eyes slinking back to the pits . . & the soul sinking in the body like a sword sent home to its scabbard! – it is very striking & forceful: & does not remind me of parts of Christabel to its own disadvantage as to originality – which you always have, you know, by the right divine' (cited Woolford and Karlin: ii 328). She was probably thinking of 'Christabel' ll. 583–5: 'A snake's small eye blinks dull and shy; / And the lady's eyes they shrunk in her head, / Each shrunk up to a serpent's eye.'

8. The fact that this echo appears so near the beginning of Browning's poem suggests that its influence extends to its first line: 'You're my friend', which would fit a poem whose subject could certainly be described as 'Friendship, Love, and Liberty'. For the element of irony in the shadowy friendship between the narrator and his listener, see Chapter 3, pp. 98–9.

Two important characteristics of these echoes need to be noted. They are all of passages in which Coleridge laments the loss of creative inspiration. And, even more than in the case of 'The Lost Leader', they are *inverse* echoes, inasmuch that in Browning's poem they involve or imply the *recovery* of power or inspiration.

In 'Youth and Age' Coleridge whimsically laments the loss of youth, but Browning's speaker echoes him only to go on to recall *his* youth and its formative event with haunted intensity, recovering the form and content of earlier experience to an extent that Coleridge declares impossible. 'Kubla Khan' too is about the loss of creative power. Its speaker develops his final vision of the inspired poet not as an actuality, but a forfeited possibility:

> A damsel with a dulcimer
> In a vision *once* I saw:
> It was an Abyssinian maid,
> And on her dulcimer she played,
> Singing of Mount Abora.
> *Could I* revive within me
> Her symphony and song,
> To such a deep delight '*twould* win me,
> That with music loud and long,
> I *would* build that dome in air . . .
> (ll. 37–46: my italics)

In Browning's poem, the Duchess receives inspiration like an electric charge from the Gypsy (equivalent to Coleridge's 'damsel'), and moves outside the boundaries of the poem towards the primal 'life' of which she speaks.

Confirmation of this revisionary relation to Coleridge emerges from Browning's account of his composition of this poem. Unusually for his work, it was first published in an incomplete state, ll. 1–215 appearing in *Hood's Magazine* in April 1845, the entire poem in *Dramatic Romances and Lyrics* in November of the same year. Browning wrote to EBB to explain that the *Hood's* portion was

> only the beginning of a story written some time ago, and given to poor Hood in his emergency at a day's notice, – the true stuff and story is all to come . . . (3 May 1845, Kelley: x 201)[9]

9. The allusion is to the last illness of the poet and essayist Thomas Hood, during which many friends and literary acquaintances made unpaid contributions to his journal, *Hood's Magazine and Comic Miscellany*. Browning contributed six items between June 1844 and April 1845.

More details emerge in a later letter to Frederick Furnivall:

> There was an odd circumstance that either mended or marred the poem in the writing – I fancied the latter at the time. As I finished the line – which ends what was printed in Hood's Magazine as the First Part – "and the old one – you shall hear!" I saw from the window where I sat a friend opening the gate to our house – one Captain Lloyd – whom I jumped up to meet, judging from the time of day that something especially interesting had brought him, – as proved to be the case, for he was in a strange difficulty. This took a deal of discussing, – next day, other interruptions occurred, and the end was I lost altogether the thing as it was in my head at the beginning . . . some time afterwards, I was staying at Bettisfield Park in Wales, and a guest, speaking of early winter, said "the deer had already to break the ice in the pond" – and a fancy struck me, which, on returning home, I worked up into what concludes the story . . .
> (15 Apr. 1883, Peterson 1979: 70–1)

This explanation clarifies that Browning composed the first part of the poem up to the point of his interruption by 'one Captain Lloyd', probably in the summer of 1842; in September 1842 he stayed at Bettisfield Park (the Flintshire home of Sir John Hanmer, a politician and poet whose work he admired) and resumed the poem, carrying it forward to an unspecified point; when he was asked to contribute something to *Hood's Magazine* he sent the first episode.[10]

The intensity with which Browning recalled the details of his compositional hiatus recalls Coleridge's explanation of the incompleteness of 'Christabel' and 'Kubla Khan'. The latter case is especially striking. 'Kubla Khan' too, according to Coleridge's preface, was begun on the basis of an isolated sentence (from Purchas's *Pilgrimage*), and interrupted by a visitor (the legendary 'person from Porlock'), after which he found that 'all the rest had passed away like the images on the surface of a stream into which a stone has been cast'. Coleridge concludes,

> Yet from the still surviving recollections in his mind, the Author has frequently purposed to finish for himself what had been originally, as it were, given to him.

10. In another letter, he confirms that 'I gave them [i.e. Hood's] as much as I could transcribe at a sudden warning' (1 July 1845, Kelley: x 286).

The fact that Coleridge never accomplished this purpose means that the incident could represent for Browning an image of creative impasse, and there is evidence that during the early 1840s, after the disastrous reception of *Sordello*, he experienced just such a faltering of creative purpose. The interrupted composition of 'Flight' was preceded by another abortive project, his attempt to write a sequel to Euripides' *Hippolytus*, which petered out into a Prologue, 'Artemis Prologuizes', for which Browning wrote the apologetic note already mentioned (p. 6). It was followed by another, a poem based on the story of Saul and David in 1 *Samuel* xvi 14–23, which breaks off abruptly and was published as 'Part the First' in *Dramatic Romances and Lyrics*. It is suggestive that all are about death or illness, and each anticipates but none reaches its cure. The biblical Saul is troubled by 'an evil spirit'. Hippolytus at the end of Euripides' play is torn to pieces by his own horses as a result of his father's curse. The original episode of 'The Flight of the Duchess' ends with these lines:

> So the little Lady grew silent and thin,
>    Paling and ever paling,
> As the way is with a hid chagrin;
>    And the Duke perceived that she was ailing,
> And said in his heart, " 'Tis done to spite me,
> "But I shall find in my power to right me!"
> Don't swear, friend – the Old One, many a year,
> Is in Hell, and the Duke's self . . . you shall hear.
> (ll. 208–15)

Both the other two poems cut off at a similar point, 'Artemis Prologuizes' with Artemis awaiting the resuscitation of Hippolytus at the hands of Aesculapius, 'Saul' with David awaiting the similar outcome of *his* therapy, the restoration of Saul to his normal mind.

Browning's account of how he came to compose 'Artemis Prologuizes' suggests an analogy between the situation of the victim-figures in these poems and himself:

> Yes, I had another slight touch of something unpleasant in the head which came on, one Good *Saturday*, as I sat reading the revise of 'Pippa Passes' – and my hair was cut off, but I soon got well: I wrote in bed such a quantity of that 'Hippolytus', of which I wrote down the prologue, but forgot the rest, though the resuscitation-scene which was to have followed, would have improved matters . . . (17 Oct. 1864, Curle: 102)

It is natural that Browning's illness – which I interpret as depressive – should suggest to him the subject of the slaughtered hero, and that his desire for cure should project itself as a planned 'resuscitation-scene'. The phrase 'my hair was cut off' suggests a further analogy with the biblical figure of Samson, another hero who endures humiliation and loss of strength, but recovers to further glory.

'Saul' was to be finished ten years later, and published in full in 1855; 'Artemis' was never finished. Uniquely in this group, 'The Flight of the Duchess' was completed by 1845, and Browning resumed it with a revision of Coleridge's account of how his vision of 'Kubla Khan' had 'passed away like the images on the surface of a stream into which a stone has been cast':

> Well, early in autumn, at first winter-warning,
> When the stag had to break with his foot, of a morning,
> A drinking-hole out of the fresh tender ice
> That covered the pond till the sun, in a trice,
> Loosening it, let out a ripple of gold,
> And another and another, and faster and faster,
> Till, dimpling to blindness, the wide water rolled:
> Then it so chanced that the Duke our master
> Asked himself what were the pleasures in season,
> And found, since the calendar bade him be hearty,
> He should do the Middle Age no treason
> In resolving on a hunting-party.
>
> (ll. 216–27)

The melancholy evanescence of Coleridge's poem inverts into the onrush of Browning's renewal of his, and the action which follows this *breaking of the ice* mirrors at the level of plot the sense of release which the image at once recognises and brings about: for the 'hunting-party' which comes into the Duke's head here will provide the opportunity for the Duchess's 'flight', a release equivalent to Browning's. In other words, the plot of 'The Flight of the Duchess' symbolised, or came to symbolise, a self-narrative of poetic deadlock and release, as is confirmed by the quiet pun in Browning's later description of its composition: 'From so slender a twig of fact can these little singing birds start themselves for a *flight* to more or less distances' (my italics). Coleridge's failure to renew *his* 'flight', recorded in his preface and repeated in Christabel's final paralysis and loss of speech, becomes the occasion for Browning's 'resuscitation' into creative energy, a resuscitation confirmed by his allusions to 'Kubla Khan' in the text after he resumed it.

So in this poem, Browning admits influence only to invert it; his account of its composition provides a practical illustration of his other strategy for sheltering his originality from outside influence, the claim that execution invariably betrays conception:

> It is an odd fact, yet characteristic of my accomplishings one and all in this kind, that of *the poem*, the real conception of an evening (two years ago, – fully) – of *that*, not a line is written, – tho' perhaps, after all, what I am going to call the accessories in the story are real though indirect reflexes of the original Idea, and so supersede properly enough the necessity of its personal appearance, – so to speak: but, as I conceived the poem, it consisted entirely of the Gipsy's description of the life the Lady was to lead with her future Gipsy lover – a *real* life, not an unreal one like that with the Duke – and as I meant to write it, all their wild adventures would have come out and the insignificance of the former vegetation have been deducible only – as the main subject has become now – of course it comes to the same thing, for one would never show half by half like a cut orange –
>
> (25 July 1845, Kelley: xi 3)

This account suggests that as soon as 'the real conception' submits to being 'written' it vanishes, to be replaced by something very close to its opposite ('reflexes of the original Idea'). He likewise describes *Luria* as 'clever attempted reproduction of what was conceived by another faculty, and foolishly let pass away' (22 Mar. 1846, Kelley: xii 168). Despite their negative character, these comments prevent a poem's execution from being understood as a simple continuation of his original conception, allowing the latter to remain original and/because unrepresented. He shelters his conception from scrutiny by declaring that it is not set down but transvested or inverted in the subsequent poem.

## 'Sundry jottings'

The next step would be to begin drafting, but I think we must identify a stage before this, a stage of purely mental elaboration of the original conception, recorded, if at all, in draft notes. He wrote to EBB of 'this darling "Luria" – so safe in my head and a tiny slip of paper I cover with my thumb!' (11 Feb. 1845, Kelley: x 70). It would be interesting to inspect that 'slip of paper', but here we encounter a difficulty: that Browning destroyed all, or nearly all such materials. His friend T.J. Wise found him making a bonfire of papers which probably included such items (Hood, p. xii); at any rate practically none survive, except where they were made in books which he was reluctant to destroy. But in such cases he ensured the privacy of his early thoughts by writing them in pencil which he then rubbed out with long, savage strokes, leaving only a few indecipherable dints to tantalise the unhappy editor.[11] In response to a request from a friend for 'the *very* original of a little poem of mine, – blots, scratches and so forth inclusive' he did send a manuscript of 'Hervé Riel' (now in the Pierpont Morgan Library, MA 10500), and it is one which certainly dates from an earlier compositional stage than usual, with plenty of emendations, rejected emendations and alternative readings. But equally certainly it is no first draft: headed 'Hervé Riel. by Robert Browning', dated at the end, and organised in numbered stanzas, it must have at least one and more probably two or three earlier drafts behind it.

One reason for this assumption is the probability that his earliest drafts were in prose. In a note on the MS of *Prince Hohenstiel-Schwangau, Saviour of Society* (1871), Browning referred to 'a little hand-breadth of prose' as its earliest state, and the Beinecke Library of Yale University holds a slip of paper which is clearly a fragment of a prose draft of *Red Cotton Night-Cap Country* (Gen. Mss. 111/[247]/800, Purdy-Hardy Collection). It is written in a tiny hand which is extremely difficult to decipher, and runs as follows:

> You white ?mass, – as you marched between the sheep and the goats, rod of guidance in hand, did you not indulge in some such satisfactory thought as this – Now, from the beginning of my career to this its close, I have managed men, friendly or inimical, as easily as those[.] Life is all – I was born in a hovel at Metz, – and in the domain here I shall "[sic] – conclude? Well, enough for the purpose of the simile: the silkworm will [ ] stop feeding and begin to spin its own thread, and be entombed in gold –

11. An example is the first draft of 'Home Thoughts, from the Sea', which he drafted inside the front cover of Bartoli's *De' simboli trasportati al morale*, a book which had strong personal associations for him (see chronology for 1887).

> whence awaking – what sort of a [ ] butterfly or plain moth – a painted lady or death's head – is past my conjecture: but

In the poem these elements appear almost in the order of this draft, but widely distributed. At ll. 821–903 the narrator gives an elaborate description of the character the draft refers to, Clara de Millefleurs, the mistress of his hero Léonce Miranda, introducing her in sedate procession with her dependents:

> Then four came tripping in a joyous flock,
> Two giant goats and two prodigious sheep . . .
> A rod of guidance marked the Châteleine,
> And ever and anon would sceptre wave . . .
> (ll. 883–4, 888–9)

These lines shadow the opening of the draft, but the monologue which follows does not appear. Clara's origins are referred to at ll. 1658 ff., but by the narrator, and she has become 'born at Sierck, / About the bottom of the Social Couch' (ll. 1660–1), a refinement upon the draft's 'hovel at Metz'. Her self-characterisation in the draft is likewise transferred to the narrator, who remarks with scientific detachment that she was

> Born, bred, with just one instinct, – that of growth:
> Her quality was, caterpillar-like,
> To all-unerringly select a leaf
> And without intermission feed her fill,
> Become the Painted Peacock, or belike
> The Brimstone-wing, when time of year should suit . . .
> (ll. 4036–41)

This passage paraphrases her comment in the draft that 'Life is all', and elaborates her comparison of herself to a silkworm, but meanwhile both elements have darkened into something not far from satire, a development confirmed in a second and later elaboration, the conclusion of the narrative:

> Though she have eaten her Miranda up,
> And spun a cradle-cone through which she pricks
> Her passage, and proves peacock-butterfly,
> This Autumn – wait a little week of cold!

> Peacock and death's-head-moth end much the same.
> And could she still continue spinning, – sure,
> Cradle would soon crave shroud for substitute,
> And o'er this life of her's distaste would drop
> Red-cotton-Night-cap-wise.
>
> (ll. 4221–9)

These developments suggest either that Browning's original intention was to provide a monologue for Clara de Millefleurs, or that his conception of a poem generally involved identifying with its characters and writing out their thoughts before deciding which of them should be represented in this manner in the final poem. Thus Miranda receives star treatment in the long monologue he is given at ll. 3287–591, but Clara's draft monologue is split up, dispersed and made over to the narrator who proceeds to elicit its ironies. Her comparison of herself to a silkworm, for example, seems to allude to a belief that after death she will be transmuted into something more beautiful, as the silkworm is transformed into a butterfly; but for the narrator, this image alludes to her supposedly having 'eaten her Miranda up' and as a reward already become the 'Peacock butterfly' which in the draft she imagines as her future shape; but in winter she will die like the butterflies, and the image is transformed into a commentary on her gaudy, paltry ambitions and the worthlessness of her existence.

It seems likely, therefore, that the 'tiny slip of paper' containing Browning's first thoughts for *Luria* was, if not a prose draft of this type, then a set of prose notes: *composition*, in the sense of a conversion of conception into verse, had not taken place at that stage.[12] The only surviving example of a slightly later stage of composition confirms this. During the 1850s Browning set about revising *Sordello*, which had had a disastrous reception on its first appearance in 1840 (see Chronology). Most of the additions he planned to make were recorded on separate sheets which he destroyed, but some pencil drafting survives in the copy of the first edition on which he worked. One passage runs as follows:

12. In a later letter to EBB, he referred again to this 'tiny slip of paper' in relation to the character of Domizia: 'I will try and remember what my whole character *did* mean – it was, in two words, understood at the time by "panther's-beauty" – on which hint I ought to have spoken! But the work grew cold, and you came between, and the Sun put out the fire on the hearth' (11 Feb. 1846, Kelley: xii 66).

'God concedes two sights to mortals – one of the whole work, the other of their own work, the first step'. In the version of the poem he published in 1863, this became:

> God has conceded two sights to a man –
> One, of men's whole work, time's completed plan,
> The other, of the minute's work, man's first
> Step to the plan's completeness . . . (v 85–88)

The relation of draft to published text is much closer here than in the *Red Cotton Night-Cap Country* example, suggesting that after his early prose notes Browning probably composed a running prose draft before turning to verse. It seems unlikely that at that moment '*the poem*' reappears, for prose and verse alike are forms of *language*, and language is the problem rather than the solution, as Sordello finds when he tries to make the transition from spinning fantasy-poems in his head to composing real poems for an audience. Browning compares this development to a warrior's equipping himself with armour in order to fight, but the analogy fails:

> Piece after piece that armour broke away
> Because perceptions whole, like that he sought
> To clothe, reject so pure a work of thought
> As language: Thought may take Perception's place
> But hardly co-exist in any case,
> Being its mere presentment – of the Whole
> By Parts, the Simultaneous and the Sole
> By the Successive and the Many.
> (ii 588–95)

What Sordello calls 'perceptions whole' are timeless, entire and therefore of a different kind from the 'language' in which he tries to capture them. At best, the latter would be an approximation, as a suit of armour only roughly follows the contours of the body beneath, affording protection at the price of clumsiness. But a 'perception' is nothing like a body, let alone a suit of armour, and language similarly breaks down under the impossible burden of embodying the disembodied. The relation of the poem to its 'perception' resembles that between God's 'Word' and human language as analysed by St Augustine:

> For your Word is not speech in which each part comes to an end when it has been spoken, giving place to the next, so that finally the whole may be uttered. In your Word all is uttered at one and the same time, yet eternally. If it were not so, your Word would be subject to time and change, and therefore would be neither truly eternal nor truly immortal. (Augustine: 259)

This distinction seems to underlie Browning's belittlement of the actual poem we read, by comparison to the 'Word' or 'perception' which hides behind it. Such near-blasphemous deification of poetic inspiration is characteristically Romantic, as when Coleridge calls the poetic imagination 'a repetition in the finite mind of the infinite I AM', but Browning's denial that what he imagines can ever be represented throws a shadow over such affirmations.

## Writing it down

Like Wordsworth, Browning intensely disliked the physical act of writing, and, again like Wordsworth, he frequently resorted to an amanuensis.[13] Before his marriage this role was performed by his sister Sarianna; after it, at least in the early years, his wife took it over, and the manuscript of *Christmas Eve and Easter Day* intertwines both their hands. It appears that this practice was then abandoned; at least, she comments to a correspondent that neither of them saw a line of their respective works until just before publication, and this is clearly the case with *Aurora Leigh*, as presumably also with *Men and Women*, published the year before.

But she had earlier played a much more crucial role, in that during the period of the courtship she had received, corrected and commented on most of the poems which make up *Dramatic Romances and Lyrics* (1845), and also the two plays published the following year, *Luria* and *A Soul's Tragedy*.[14] The manuscripts she commented on do not survive, but evidently Browning was unwilling also to destroy her notes, for he passed them to his son along with their love-letters. In fact, the love-letters, and the love which they record, constitute the most important dimension of Browning's reception of her criticisms,

13. 'I have no pleasure in writing myself – none, in the mere act . . . my heart sinks whenever I open this desk, and rises when I shut it' (to EBB 11 Mar. 1845, Kelley: x 121).

14. On this subject see also Chapter 4, pp. 142–50.

in that he accepted almost all of them, including one which she herself attempted to withdraw.[15] Clearly he wanted her hand in his poems, in anticipation of taking it in marriage.

Many, indeed most, of her comments concern his irregular rhythms, which she regularly tried to smooth down. In 'The Boy and the Angel', for example, Browning had originally written:

> Said Blaise, the listening monk, 'Well done;
> I doubt not thou art heard, my son;
>
> As if thy voice to-day
> Were praising God the Pope's great way . . .
> (ll. 11–14)

He altered the third line to 'As well as if thy voice to-day' at EBB's suggestion: she commented 'Not that the short lines are not good in their *place*'. The result is questionable. The meaning is slightly banalised by the change. For the 'boy' is about to be transformed into the Pope of whom 'Blaise, the listening monk' speaks, and discover the inferiority of a Pope's praise to his own, a development which is unnecessary if he is already heard 'as well as' the Pope. And the alteration sacrifices the pause after 'to-day' and the emphasis that this throws on the contemporaneity of this moment with the later moment when he praises God as Pope, a contemporaneity possible because 'With God a day endures alway, / A thousand years are as a day.' Lines 23–6 originally ran:

> In Heaven God said, 'Nor day nor night
> Brings one voice of my delight.'
>
> Then Gabriel, like a rainbow's birth,
> Spread his wings and sank to earth . . .

EBB suggested 'God said in Heaven' as 'a simpler & rather solemner intonation', sacrificing the contrast between 'In Heaven' and 'to earth' which is essential to the meaning of a poem whose whole point is the difference between heavenly and earthly 'praise' and the *superiority* of the latter. In other words, she urged stylistic orthodoxies without always considering what purpose Browning's original

15. This concerned line 512 of 'The Flight of the Duchess': see note in Woolford and Karlin: ii 318.

expression served. Her influence on 'The Laboratory' brings out the difference between her aesthetic and his in this respect. The opening of this poem originally ran:

> Now I have tied thy glass mask on tightly,
> May gaze thro' these faint smokes curling whitely,
> As thou pliest thy trade in this devil's-smithy,
> Which is the poison to poison her, prithee?

EBB commented:

> I object a little to your tendency . . which is almost a habit . . & is very observable in this poem I think, . . of making lines difficult for the reader to read . . see the opening lines of this poem. Not that music is required everywhere, nor in *them* certainly, but that the uncertainty of rhythm throws the reader's mind off the *rail* . . & interrupts his progress with you & your influence with him. Where we have not direct pleasure from rhythm, & where no peculiar impression is to be produced by the changes in it, we sh[d] be encouraged by the poet to *forget it altogether*, – should we not? (21 July 1845, Kelley: x 315–16)

Browning duly emended the first line to read: 'Now that I, tying thy glass mask tightly', which is certainly a little easier to scan (though Tennyson for one still found it 'a very difficult mouthful'), but her comment on the function of rhythm throws into relief the fact that he had no desire to make the reader 'forget it altogether': rather the reverse. For if, as we have seen, the written poem is intrinsically and necessarily inferior to its original conception, its execution must be ironised to prevent confusion between the two, and Browning commonly does this by burlesquing its literary status, whether by the use of grotesque rhymes, or, as at the beginning of 'The Laboratory', by refusing the seamless metrical flow that EBB preferred and advised (I owe this point to S.M. Adamson). The fact that the emended line is only a little less difficult to scan suggests continued reluctance to make entrance into the poem an easy matter. In one instance, the difference between them was so extreme as to cause him to reject her suggestion altogether. One passage in 'The Flight of the Duchess' describes how the Duchess receives the Duke's suggestion that she should participate in the stag-hunt:

Her eyes just lifted their long lashes,
As if pressed by fatigue even he could not dissipate,
And duly acknowledged the Duke's forethought,
But spoke of her health, if her health were worth aught . . .
(ll. 284–7)

EBB thought this 'beautiful', but pointed out that in the passage as a whole 'you make your Duchess's eyes acknowledge the Duke's forethought & speak of her health &c – as if such a Duke would be likely to understand that sort of speaking. The personal pronoun has been forgotten somehow. Just see if it has not.' Browning did not accept this suggestion because it reflected her failure to notice that the Duchess *never speaks* after her entry into the Duke's castle. She must not be compromised by the poem's language because in the poem as written she remains an elusive representation of the poem as originally conceived and lost (as she is 'lost' to the narrator on her departure).

## Ready for the printers

With the exception of *Christmas Eve and Easter Day*, surviving fair copy MSS of Browning's poems are written in his hand: they frequently also bear printer's marks. Few examples survive from his early career, but from *Dramatis Personae* onwards he carefully preserved them, and from 1871 he presented them to Balliol College, Oxford.

The state of these MSS varies considerably. Some, especially of shorter poems, are virtually clean, but others show extensive revision. It seems unlikely, though not impossible, that such revision actually represents drafting: the fact that inserted passages are already fully versified suggests that Browning first did his preliminary drafting on a loose sheet or in a notebook, and only when satisfied transferred the new passage into his MS. In the case of collections, it is intriguing that whereas revisions to short and medium-length poems are relatively light, those for long poems are often very much heavier: in *Dramatis Personae*, for example, 'Mr. Sludge "the Medium" ' has an average of one alteration per line, a proportion unapproached by any other poem. In all revisions, punctuational changes predominate, and it seems clear that Browning settled his wording before he thought out the more mechanical aspects of the text. In some instances, crucial features of punctuation were evidently added after the words themselves had been transcribed: in 'Caliban upon Setebos', for example, the apostrophes which mark omitted articles ("Sayeth', "Thinketh' for 'He sayeth', 'He thinketh') may well have been an afterthought. Like Wordsworth and Blake, Browning found punctuation difficult, and seems to have added it only when the drift towards publication became inexorable.

There are however many verbal changes in surviving holographs, and these give us considerable insight into this late stage of a poem's growth. But here we meet a complication. The obsessive privacy about his compositional procedures which led Browning to destroy all his early drafts reappears in his holographs as an anxiety to conceal superseded readings, which though in ink are carefully erased and then overwritten by the new reading: in some instances Browning nearly goes through the paper in his zeal to conceal. But while they often yield to patient scrutiny, the result is usually to make one wonder why he took (and gave!) so much trouble. For example, Sludge describes the effect on his listeners of his evocation of the ghost of a dead child (ll. 473–8):

MS

The little voice set lisping once again,
The tiny hand made feel for yours once more,
The poor lost image brought back, plain as dreams,
Which, if a careless word had chanced recall,
The usual cloud would cross your eyes, I think,
Your heart return the old tick, give the pang!

MS: cancelled readings

The little voice set *stammering once more*,
The tiny hand made feel for yours *again*,
The poor lost image brought back, plain as dreams,
Which, if a careless word had chanced recall,
The usual cloud would cross your *brow, you know*,
*And your heart sound the old tick, one pang more!*

These are hardly major changes, though they do make a difference. The swapping of 'once again' for 'again' at the ends of lines one and two was presumably prompted by the substitution of 'lisping' for 'stammering', a change which intensifies pathos but necessitates the addition of another syllable to the first line: the substitution of 'give the pang' for 'one pang more' has the reverse effect of reducing the melodrama of remembered loss. But there is also a more technical motive: the original draft had two lines ending in 'more', which is problematic in a blank verse poem. In a parallel case, Alfred Domett records how, when he read Browning a passage from *Paracelsus*, Browning objected to 'those rhyming endings "you" and "dew" in blank verse' (Horsman: 98), and he evidently combed his drafts for blunders of this kind. Similarly, he probably spotted the awkward near-homophony of 'brow . . . know', and after substituting 'eyes' for 'brow' decided to avoid the repeated sounds of 'usual . . . your . . . you' (in that order because 'your brow, I think' is unproblematic, suggesting that 'brow' was changed first). A similar aesthetic decision might have helped prompt the change of 'stammering' to 'lisping', which spaces out the alliteration ('set stammering' is replaced by 'little . . . lisping'). Not that alliteration is banned: the change of 'sound' to 'return' in the last line creates a new alliteration with 'tick', though again at a decent distance. (It is perhaps worth adding that the first edition text substitutes 'pay its pang', providing a further alliteration.)

Such decisions are of great interest at the aesthetic level, but no, or very few, different directions or even changes of emphasis are deducible from underlying readings, and the same can be said of interpolated lines and passages. There are plenty of these in some holographs, but they serve to explain or reinforce or amplify existing ideas rather than introduce new ones. In one passage in *Fifine at the Fair*, for example (beginning at l. 771), the speaker describes what he believes to be a sculpture by Michelagnolo of the Greek nymph Eidothee:

> out she stands, and yet stops short, half bold, half shy,
> Hesitates on the threshold of things, since partly blent
> With stuff she needs must quit, her native element.
> I think it is the daughter of the old man of the sea,
> Emerging from her wave, goddess Eidothee . . .

Browning inserted a new passage before the last two lines in the MS:

> her native element
> I' the mind o' the Master, – what's the creature, dear-divine
> Yet earthly-awful too, so manly-feminine,
> Pretends this white advance? What startling brain-escape
> Of Michelagnolo takes elemental shape?
> I think he meant the daughter of the old man o' the sea,
> Emerging from her wave, goddess Eidothee . . .

This settles an ambiguity in the original draft, in which the 'native element' of the image could be either the stone from which Michelangelo carved her, the seas from which, Venus-like, she emerges, or the imagination in which she grows into an ideal image: it is the latter, and by also changing 'I think it is the daughter' etc. to 'I think he meant the daughter' Browning stresses both the indeterminacy of the actual image, the pristine integrity of its original 'I' the mind o' the Master' and the effort which the beholder has to make to recover it from the illegible stone. As so often, conception defeats realisation, and in this instance the drafting process mirrors the meaning on which it works, rendering more explicit an image which is itself about what it means to become explicit.

## Proofs

At this point, a controversy begins. Is the final manuscript the true representation of the author's consolidated intention, and should that therefore be used as copy-text for an edition? For some authors this may be the case, but not Browning. The evidence suggests that he used the next stage of the poem's existence, its appearance in the form of proofs for correction and revision, as a further active stage of composition: 'I found my poem [*The Ring and the Book*] . . . might go to press & return to me with advantage in type, – there being still plenty to do, but nothing which needs stop the printing' (15 May 1868, Donner: 101).

What Browning means by 'return to me with advantage in type' is clarified in another letter referring to his composition of this poem:

> it has been a particularly weary business to write this whole long work by my dear self – I who used always to be helped by an amanuensis – for, I cannot clearly see what is done, or undone, so long as it is thru' the medium of my own handwriting . . . in print, or alien charactery, I *see* tolerably well . . .
>
> (1 Feb. 1868, Curle: 175)

The word 'alien' is surprisingly strong, and in company with the word '*see*' implies that in his 'own handwriting' Browning's poem was not visible to him as text, that its graphic character only became manifest when it became, like the work of the objective poet, 'projected from himself and distinct' ('Essay on Shelley', Appendix A, p. 245). But because relatively few proofs of Browning's works survive, and because those that do are often of problematic status, it is difficult to say anything more definite about this stage. It is likely that he often received several copies of a given set of proofs, marked up one for the printers, and gave others away without entering his canonical corrections, or removing any unadopted experimental readings they might contain.[16] In some instances, he received more than one set: *Dramatic Lyrics* is a case in point, and Kelley and Coley record both galleys and page proofs for parts of *The Ring and the Book*. Placing such fragmentary and anonymous texts in a genealogy is very difficult, as it seems probable that Browning intended it to be.

There is one instance where we have at least a record of his proof-changes for a whole volume, however: a copy of the first edition of *Men and Women*, now in the Huntington Library, on which proof-readings are recorded as variants. There is a startling number of them, and some are so radical as to suggest that in this instance at least proofs were indeed used as a stage of drafting. Because the authority of this text is bibliographically questionable, no particular reading can be relied upon; but most are intrinsically plausible, and in the absence of better examples it is worth noting one or two. The hypothesis that long poems arrived at this stage in a less finished state than short ones is confirmed by the very extensive revision to 'Bishop Blougram's Apology' as compared to the almost clean state of, for example, 'De Gustibus–' and 'Protus'. This is not, however, a fixed rule: 'Andrea del Sarto', a longish poem, is virtually unaltered while the very much shorter 'The Last Ride Together' is extensively revised. There is a tendency for revisions to be concentrated towards the ends of poems: the first four stanzas of 'Old Pictures in Florence', for example, have only three revisions, two of which are minor revisions of punctuational changes; the last four stanzas have twenty-three, and the last stanza is effectively rewritten. The text in proof was as follows:

So said, so done. That morning the scaffold
  Is broken away, and the long-pent fire
Like the golden hope of the world unbaffled
  Springs from its sleep, and up goes the spire –

16. An example is a bound proof of *Paracelsus*, now in Texas A&M University Library.

When with 'God and the People' plain for its motto,
  Thence the new tricolor flaps at the sky,
Why, to hail him, the vindicated Giotto
  Thanking God for it all, the first am I!

The first-edition text runs:

Shall I be alive that morning the scaffold
  Is broken away, and the long-pent fire
Like the golden hope of the world unbaffled
  Springs from its sleep, and up goes the spire–
As, 'God and the People' plain for its motto,
  Thence the new tricolor flaps at the sky?
Foreseeing the day that vindicates Giotto
  And Florence together, the first am I!

So eager is the proof for the revolution the poem anticipates that by a syntactic slide ('That morning . . . When . . . to hail him . . . the first am I') it is made actually to take place with Browning himself present as its 'first' celebrant. In the first-edition text this confidence is more qualified: the speaker asks 'Shall I be alive' when the event happens? and by separating off the last two lines syntactically and inserting the word 'Foreseeing' he positions it firmly in the future. At the same time Giotto, who originally was to participate alongside Browning in the festivities by 'Thanking God for it all', is pushed back into the past and replaced by 'Florence', which provides the cultural continuum between Giotto's past, Browning's present, and the future revolution. These revisions, segregating the temporalities which the original version enthusiastically merged, mark a cooling-off, not necessarily of Browning's political commitments, but of the naïvety of their expression: in a more general sense, he seems to be in the process of withdrawing from his poem as print crystallises it into a public object.

## Revision

I will venture to say, that no one but a pedant ever read his own works regularly through. They are not *his* – they are become mere words, waste-paper, and have none of the glow, the creative enthusiasm, the vehemence, and natural spirit with which he wrote them. When we have once committed our thoughts to

> paper, written them fairly out, and seen that they are right in the printing, if we are in our right wits, we have done with them for ever. (Hazlitt, 'Whether Genius is Conscious of its Powers?' *The Plain Speaker* [1826])

> had he printed the piece just as it stands, without any delay at all, – he would have at least done justice, in his own mind, to these conceptions of death and life and the intermediate possible state: the exhibition would have been both done and done with: he would have turned his attention to other subjects of thought and feeling, which, whether as congenial to him as the former, were at least new and unexpressed: whereas, he is prevented somehow from venting these, and so goes round and round them, ends in the exclusive occupation of his soul with them, – does not he? (Browning to Thomas Kelsall, 22 May 1868) [17]

> I was fain
> To efface my work, begin anew,
> ('James Lee', viii ['Beside the Drawing-Board'] 19–20)

Once a poem was printed, Browning seems to have completed the process of withdrawal by forgetting all about it. 'I never keep a copy of anything I write', he told a correspondent, Mrs Franklyn (16 Nov. 1877, ABL MS); to another, L.H. Courtney, he wrote:

> I have not looked at the poem . . . since it appeared in print – reserving that business for a future day . . . when the whole work will be carefully revised: at present I have the faintest memory concerning any particular part or passage of it. (14 May 1881, *TLS*, 25 Feb. 1909, p. 72)

Effectively, he *disowns* his poems once they are in print. The reason Browning gives for this – that it helps the process of revision – cannot be – is not said by him to be – the only one: other remarks confirm that he wanted to 'get rid' of a poem once it was 'done'; thus it becomes 'probably the last of the kind I shall care to write'; he is 'not likely to try anything of the sort again'. Of *The Ring and the Book* he

17. Browning alludes to *Death's Jest-Book*, by Thomas Lovell Beddoes. Most of Browning's correspondence with Beddoes' literary executor, Thomas Kelsall, is reprinted in Donner, including this letter (pp. 103–5), which we quote from the ABL MS. See also ch. 6, pp. 199, 216.

wrote, 'profoundly tired as I am of the whole business . . . I shall begin something else in a different way' (12 Feb. 1869, Curle: 179). Julia Wedgwood was baffled by what she found his deprecatory tone towards the poem; Browning responded: 'As to being "impatient with what has occupied me for years" – no: it is *done*; I occupy myself elsewhere, or else look elsewhither' (8 Mar. 1868, Curle: 196). Of *Sordello*, he had written in similar terms to Edward Dowden a few years earlier:

> I have a facility at forgetting my own things once *done*, and . . . in this case, I have put this particular poem away and behind me long ago – not at all meaning to undervalue it thereby, but because it is good husbandry of energy in an artist to forget what is behind and press onward to what is before.
> (5 Mar. 1866, Hood: 91–2)

This process is evidently connected to what Mrs Orr notes as a

> peculiarity in Mr. Browning's attitude towards his works: his constant conviction that the latest must be the best, because the outcome of the fullest mental experience, and of the longest practice in his art. (Orr 1891: 380–1)

Hence in response to a request for a sample of his work he wrote: 'I think the book shall be this one I am just engaged upon, which ought to be my best' (to L. Barrett, 17 Aug. 1886, Hood: 254). He preferred reading 'a man's *collected* works, of any kind, *backwards*'. To Carlyle he wrote:

> As I believe no man a real poet or genius of any sort who does not go on improving till eighty and over, I shall begin again and again as often as you set me right. (23 Jan. 1856, Hood: 44)

But though the word 'improving' seems to imply the neo-classical belief, most persuasively argued by Reynolds, that 'genius is an infinite capacity for taking pains', Browning's emphasis in these passages on the need to *begin again* contradicts the smooth progression by which a poet is conventionally supposed to 'mature'. It is a phrase he frequently uses. In the famous comparison between EBB's 'pure white light' and his own 'prismatic hues' (13 Jan. 1845, Kelley: x 22), he announces that he has 'begun' a work in her style: in his next letter he reiterates that he 'mean[s] to begin work in deep earnest, BEGIN – without affectation' (27 Jan. 1845, Kelley: x 44).[18] She clearly found this rather odd, remarking, 'when the author of "Paracelsus" & the "Bells & Pomegranates" says that he is only "going to begin," we may well (to take "the opposite idea" . . .) rejoice & clap our hands' (3 Feb. 1845, Kelley: x 53). Clearly, she felt that he was modestly disparaging his previous works, a reading which certainly fits the often self-deprecatory rhetoric of his letters to her. But Browning's remark to Dowden that in forgetting *Sordello* he was 'not at all meaning to undervalue it' implies that he did not consistently believe in continuous improvement, and in a note on *Paracelsus* he advanced a rather different explanation, arguing that since history consists of

> an eternal *succession* of consummations, rather than of a tendency to any *one* consummation . . . *success* should be looked for as obtainable *degree by degree*, each perfect in itself, not in *one* grand and conclusive attainment precluding further advance. (cited in Woolford and Karlin: i 109)

This suggests a revisionary attitude both to the literary tradition, and, in the context we are now considering, towards his own works. Finality, the appearance of an absolutely comprehensive work, would imply *cessation*, the impossibility of new ones. This must not be allowed to happen, and therefore Browning treats both his own and his precursors' works – say, *Paradise Lost* – as imperfect foreshadowings of the one on which he is now working. Revision of earlier works would imply the possibility of perfecting them, but this cannot – should not – be done.

This argument would mean that Browning should either not revise or only minimally revise his poems once published, and on the whole this is the case. Tennyson's wholesale changes of his 1830 and 1832 poems in 1842 outraged him, and although he *did* revise his own poems, he insisted that his changes were solely clarificatory. Thus when he was forced to acknowledge and reprint, in the *Poetical Works* of 1868, the anonymously published and long-suppressed early poem *Pauline*, he took pride in saying in a preface that 'no syllable is changed', even though 'good draughtmanship . . . and right

18. See Chapter 2, p. 50, for more on the contrast between 'pure white light' and 'prismatic hues'.

handling were far beyond the artist at that time'. The exceptions to this self-imposed rule belong principally to the 1840s, when under EBB's influence he made substantial revisions to the poems he had previously published: his attempt to rewrite *Sordello* formed part of this process. But he claimed in a letter to William Michael Rossetti that such revisions were 'purely additions, accretions, innestations, merely explanatory – I change *nothing*, but interpolate' (Rossetti: 218–19). And when it came to it, he was unable to complete the attempt, explaining in his preface to the version of *Sordello* he published in 1863: 'I lately gave time and pains to turn my work into what the many might, – instead of what the few must, – like: but after all, I imagined another thing at first, and therefore leave as I find it' – more or less what he said about *Pauline* in 1868. In 1863 he also withdrew many, though by no means all, of the changes he made to other poems in 1849.

But when he reissued *Pauline*, his first published poem, in his final collected edition, the *Poetical Works* of 1888–9, he took a slightly different course. He reprinted the preface he had written for the *Poetical Works* of 1868, and then added another:

> I preserve, in order to supplement it, the foregoing preface. I had thought, when compelled to include in my collected works the poem to which it refers, that the honest course would be to reprint, and leave mere literary errors unaltered. Twenty years' endurance of an eyesore seems more than sufficient: my faults remain duly recorded against me, and I claim permission to somewhat diminish these, so far as style is concerned, in the present and final edition where 'Pauline' must needs, first of my performances, confront the reader. I have simply removed solecisms, mended the metre a little, and endeavoured to strengthen the phraseology – experience helping, in some degree, the helplessness of juvenile haste and heat in their untried adventure long ago.

Here, with an audible wriggle, Browning justifies what amounts to a very considerable redrafting of an earlier poem, yet by saying 'my faults remain recorded against me' he in effect allows the *Pauline* of 1868 (as represented by its Preface, which he reprints) to remain in the public domain, rather than claiming that the revised version simply supersedes it. Such a gesture works against the implied teleology of speaking of the *Poetical Works* of 1888–9 as 'the present *and final* edition'. It is final in the sense that there will be no more after it, but not in the sense that it brings its contents to an apotheosis which can legitimately efface their earlier states.

If this were an isolated example, one might feel inclined to pass it by, but there are other cases of Browning publishing variant states of a poem which do not participate in a developmental sequence. His normal practice when revising already-published poems was to enter his revisions on a copy of the previous edition, but there is one notable exception to this rule. His volumes of selections seem to have been set from a variety of different earlier texts, even when in his most recent collected edition he had made revisions to the poems they contain. Conversely, he seems to have taken little or no account of changes made in selections when he revised a poem again for a subsequent collected edition. As a result, the selections in many instances provide a unique textual state or series of states, a line of descent quite separate from that provided in collections.[19]

This raises the question, which of these states represents the work? which should an editor use in a definitive edition? The most obvious answer, and the traditional one, is that because the poet uses drafts to improve the aesthetic execution of the poem, the final text is the best one. This is what Browning appears to claim in describing himself as having, in the 1888 *Pauline*, 'simply removed solecisms, mended the metre a little, and endeavoured to strengthen the phraseology'. It is this kind of explanation that nourishes the 'last-text' argument, by which it is supposed that the work is driven towards self-perfection by a process which always has that finality as its object. I have already noted, however, that Browning's preface to the final edition of *Pauline* effectively refuses to make this claim, and I do not think that all the changes he introduced in *Pauline* can be explained in such terms. Compare the versions shown in Example 1.1.

19. 'The Englishman in Italy', for example, was changed from alternating long and short lines to single long lines specifically for the volume of selections published in 1872, and remains in long lines in selected editions deriving from that text; but it remained in its original form in collected editions published in the same period.

**Example 1.1**

| *1833* | *1888* |
|---|---|
| Nought makes me trust in love so really, | Nought makes me trust some love is true, |
| As the delight of the contented lowness | But the delight of the contented lowness |
| With which I gaze on souls I'd keep for ever | With which I gaze on him I keep for ever |
| In beauty – I'd be sad to equal them; | Above me; I to rise and rival him? |
| I'd feed their fame e'en from my heart's best blood, | Feed his fame rather from my heart's best blood, |
| Withering unseen, that they might flourish still. | Wither unseen that he may flourish still. |
| * * * * | |
| Pauline, my sweet friend, thou dost not forget | Pauline, my soul's friend, thou dost pity yet |
| How this mood swayed me, when thou first wert mine, | How this mood swayed me when that soul found thine, |
| When I had set myself to live this life | When I had set myself to live this life, |
| Defying all opinion. | Defying all past glory. |

Replacing 'opinion' by 'past glory' disguises Browning's youthful embrace of Shelley's atheist, vegetarian, and millenarian socialist ideas. Removing the asterisks complements this change, smoothing the 'Romantic' fragmentariness of the text. The revisions also have the effect of first reducing the 'souls' whom the speaker refuses to 'equal' to a single figure, which can only be Shelley's, but then of deprecating his influence by changing 'thou dost not forget' to 'thou dost pity yet' (implying that his Shelley-worship was in some way inadequate), and finally of completing the renunciation by depriving Shelley of the word 'soul' and transferring it to the speaker and Pauline.

In order to explain this alteration, it is necessary to abandon the aesthetic criterion as the sole determinant of revision policy, and to rethink the drafting process as the product of other pressures. I shall begin from the historicist perspective already implied in my discussion of *Pauline*, by considering the possibility that revision may be influenced by changes in the political climate. 'The Lost Leader' was increasingly at odds, as Browning himself clearly felt, with his own growing respect for Wordsworth, especially in the years after the poet's death. Accordingly, the language of the poem in successive editions moderates from an invitation to Wordsworth to 'Strike our face hard ere we shatter his own' (1845: l. 30), to 'Aim at our heart ere we pierce through his own' (1849) to 'Menace our heart ere we master his own' (1863–88) – a progressive weakening of physical aggression. Other changes move in the same direction. In 1845, line 23 had run: 'One more devils'-triumph and sorrow to angels.' In 1849, and in subsequent editions, this became: 'One more triumph for devils and sorrow to angels.' This change eliminates an ambiguity that emerges if the original poem is read aloud: that Wordsworth's action could be the triumph of one more devil, i.e. that Wordsworth is himself *a* or even *the* devil, rather than simply the cause of the triumph *in* the devils (plural). All his collected works after that date retain this emendation.

It is therefore curious that the *Selections* of 1872 retains the original reading, and in fact intensifies it. The revised line runs: 'One more devil's triumph and sorrow to angels', making what had been an oral ambiguity in 1845 a visual one: the line in this state in no way debars the reader from assuming that Wordsworth is the devil in question. If the copy-text for this selection had been the first edition, this could have been a slip, but it seems in fact to have been the 1863 or 1868 version, since all other readings correspond to theirs, including for example the softened version of l. 30 ('Menace our heart ere we master his own'). The 1872 text mingles a reading derived from 1845 with others from the 1863 text, making it unique in the sequence of versions of 'The Lost Leader'.

An ideal reader encountering the 1872 version of 'The Lost Leader' would experience a kind of double vision, conscious on the one hand that the text mainly confirms the revisions which, as I have argued, offer a truce in the hostilities with Wordsworth, but on the other hand that the more truculent 1845 version symbolically survives as a kind of ghost behind the arras in the line intercalated from it. A similar process could be posited of the alterations to the text of *Pauline* which I examined earlier. I explained one of these as Browning's 'completing the renunciation [of Shelley] by depriving Shelley of the word "soul", which is transferred to the speaker and Pauline'. But this interpretation is only open to readers familiar with the earlier text, who then experience this intertextual transfer as the transformed ghost of the earlier one. The irony of depriving Shelley of this word, with all its sacramental associations, emphasises Browning's self-emancipation from Shelley, but does so only by intertextual allusion.

Another version of this kind of self-quotation might be argued for another of the alterations to this passage. I have noted that Browning replaces 'thou dost not forget' with 'thou dost pity yet' in the course of his strategy to deprecate Shelley's contribution. It is striking that the revised line *rhymes with the earlier one*. In fact, this is remarkably common in Browning's revisions to his blank verse poems, in particular those undertaken in his later years. It is not in itself surprising that this should happen. In revising a poem, the poet has the original text in front of him, and the first word to offer itself in substitution for a rejected reading might easily have some other relation to it than one of simple clarification, might assonate, alliterate, or, as here, rhyme with it. But in the context of my argument it becomes necessary to ask why such a relation should be retained, and I interpret these decisions as representing another, more attenuated form of intertextual quotation. The new version gets rid of an earlier reading, but allows it to persist within the new in the form of a reminiscent assonance, emphasising the change (by differing in meaning across a similarity of sound), but at the same time, and necessarily, keeping the earlier reading in play by the very same process. The text therefore remains mobile and unconsummated, as Browning's theory says it should.

# CHAPTER 2
# *Genre and style*

## GENRE

### Dramatic method

'O lyric Love!' begins one of the most famous passages of Browning's poetry, his invocation of EBB in *The Ring and the Book.* But it is an unusual moment.[1] Browning is not a lyric poet. He never wrote an ode, disliked the sonnet-form, has a mere handful of solitary effusions or meditations.[2] 'Home-Thoughts, from Abroad', one of his best-known poems, is in this sense one of his least typical. His poetry is primarily dramatic: it consists of a few stage plays and a multitude of dramatic poems of one kind or another.[3] The titles of his shorter

1. Only 9 of his poems begin with 'O' or 'Oh'; Shelley has 17, Tennyson 30, EBB 23.
2. Of Browning's 11 sonnets he included only 3 in his published volumes, the three slight 'illustrations' of Rabbinical legend which follow 'Jochanan Hakkadosh' (*Jocoseria*, 1883). He did not collect his best sonnets, notably 'The Names'. Among Browning's major works, I would count only 'Johannes Agricola' ['Johannes Agricola in Meditation'], 'Abt Vogler' and the 'Prologue' to *Asolando* as meditative lyrics, and 'Caliban upon Setebos' as a genuine soliloquy (a debate with the self).
3. Browning himself never used the term 'dramatic monologue'. The term seems to have been first used by George W. Thornbury in a collection of poems published in 1857 (Culler: 366) and first applied to Browning's poetry in William Stigand's review of *Dramatis Personae* in the *Edinburgh Review*, Oct 1864 (not, as Culler says, in a review of *The Ring and the Book* in 1869). Browning did distinguish between 'dramatic lyric' and 'dramatic romance', the former presenting an emotional or psychological state (e.g. 'The Laboratory', 'Two in the Campagna', 'A Toccata of Galuppi's') and the latter telling a story of action (e.g. 'Incident of the French Camp', 'The Flight of the Duchess', 'Childe Roland'). The two categories are present as 'Lyrics' and 'Romances' in his *Poetical Works* of

collections reflect this: *Dramatic Lyrics*, *Dramatic Romances and Lyrics*, *Dramatis Personae*, *Dramatic Idyls*. The most famous, *Men and Women*, does not have 'dramatic' in its title, but still implies a group of dramatic characters, a point which is made explicit in the 'extra' poem which concludes the volume, 'One Word More':

> Love, you saw me gather men and women,
> Live or dead or fashioned by my fancy,
> Enter each and all, and use their service,
> Speak from every mouth, – the speech, a poem.
> (ll. 129–32)[4]

The titles of individual poems often reflect this emphasis on character and dramatic speech: poems are named after their speakers ('Fra Lippo Lippi', 'Andrea del Sarto', 'Cleon', 'Mr Sludge, "the Medium" ', 'Martin Relph'), sometimes with a specific pointer to the dramatic situation ('Soliloquy of the Spanish Cloister', 'Artemis

---

1863, and as 'Dramatic Lyrics' and 'Dramatic Romances' in the *Poetical Works* of 1868 and 1888–9. See Woolford and Karlin: ii, Appendix A (pp. 463–9). Some of the poems included in either category don't fit ('How They Brought the Good News from Ghent to Aix' and 'The Confessional' are 'lyrics', while 'Time's Revenges' is a 'romance'), and the boundary between the two categories is in any case blurred by such poems as 'By the Fire-Side', 'Saul', 'Waring', 'The Last Ride Together', and 'A Grammarian's Funeral' (the first two are 'lyrics', the others are 'romances'). Browning defined the 'idyl' of *Dramatic Idyls* as 'a succinct little story complete in itself' (letter of 7 Oct. 1889, cited in Pettigrew and Collins: ii 1067).

4. If 'each and all' means what it says, then it includes the speakers of poems which have traditionally been regarded as strongly autobiographical – for example 'By the Fire-Side', 'The Guardian-Angel', and 'Two in the Campagna'. The case of 'The Guardian-Angel' is especially puzzling, since in the three concluding stanzas Browning all but names himself and his wife and does in fact name his close friend, Alfred Domett. Perhaps he is using *himself* as a persona, to whose feelings and ideas he is not (as a *poet*) committed; but this seems a rather desperate expedient, and I think it more likely that Browning wanted to insist on the uniqueness of 'One Word More' and was prepared to cut corners. For other comments by Browning on the dramatic nature of his work, see below, p. 48.

Prologuizes', 'A Woman's Last Word', 'Any Wife to Any Husband', 'Bishop Blougram's Apology').[5] In 'A Light Woman' Browning adopts a different tactic: the speaker reveals at the end that the person he has been confiding in is the poet himself:

> Well, any how, here the story stays,
> So far at least as I understand;
> And, Robert Browning, you writer of plays,
> Here's a subject made to your hand!

The poem cannot be 'Browning's', since it is spoken to him rather than by him. Indeed the text pretends not to be a poem at all, but a story told in conversation, which among other things illustrates the annoying habit that a writer's friends have of pressing their life-stories on him as suitable material; Browning's friend here hasn't even realised that Browning is no longer a 'writer of plays', having abandoned writing for the theatre ten years before.

Even when Browning declares that he is going to abjure the dramatic method for third-person narrative, as he does at the outset of *Sordello*, he cannot keep to the straight and narrow: the authorial voice keeps giving way to the voices of characters in the story or, even more significantly, splitting itself into more than one voice, staging a debate within the narrator-self which occupies half of book iii of the poem.[6] There are plenty of exciting stories in Browning, but most of them are told by participants and eye-witnesses, especially in his earlier work: 'Count Gismond', 'Incident of the French Camp', 'How They Brought the Good News from Ghent to Aix', 'The Flight of the Duchess', 'Italy in England', 'The Confessional', 'The Glove', all dating from 1845 or before.[7] 'Childe Roland to the Dark Tower

5. This is probably the reason why Browning changed some of his titles from their first-edition forms: 'The Tomb at St Praxed's', for example, became 'The Bishop Orders His Tomb at Saint Praxed's Church', which gives much more of a stage-direction to the reader.
6. See the notes to *Sordello* iii 574–994 in Woolford and Karlin: i 562–93.
7. There are exceptions, of course: 'The Statue and the Bust' in *Men and Women*, for example, 'Gold Hair' in *Dramatis Personae*, a number of the *Parleyings* (1887), for example the 'Parleying with Daniel Bartoli', and 'Beatrice Signorini' in Browning's last volume, *Asolando* (1889). These stories are all told by a narrator who is so close to the poet as scarcely to

Came' marks a crisis in this method, since Roland, who tells the story, ends up, like some of Edgar Allan Poe's narrators, in the apparently impossible position of surviving his own death in order to relate it. In later poems Browning experimented with narrative and dramatic frames: in 'Clive' (*Dramatic Idyls, Second Series*, 1880), for example, the core of the poem is a story told by the great Lord Clive, but it is relayed, in a way which anticipates Conrad and Kipling, by an obscure acquaintance of Clive's, who is trying to justify to his son his own life's lack of adventure and achievement. But the greatest example of such framing is of course *The Ring and the Book*, ten of whose twelve books consist of monologues by participants in the story, while the first and last books comprise an authorial prologue and epilogue.[8]

Browning's dramatic method is varied, or rather he works with a number of dramatic methods; there is certainly no such thing as an archetypal dramatic monologue which dominates the field. The formal criteria for 'pure' dramatic monologue usually include the presence of an implied listener or interlocutor, a dramatic situation which is inferred from what the speaker says but not stated directly, and the poem beginning in the middle of its action. 'Andrea del Sarto', for example, begins:

> But do not let us quarrel any more,
> No, my Lucrezia . . .

---

be distinguished from him except in purely formal terms. *Asolando* also has a cluster of short, anecdotal poems: 'Which?', 'The Cardinal and the Dog', 'The Pope and the Net', 'The Bean-Feast', 'Muckle-Mouth Meg'. Of the book-length poems, only *Red Cotton Night-Cap Country* (1873) and *The Two Poets of Croisic* (1878) would qualify as stories told by the poet as omniscient narrator, and in both cases the telling of the story is staged in a narrative frame. Dialogue-poems are even rarer in Browning: 'In a Gondola' (Dramatic *Lyrics*, 1842) is the only example before the appearance in a long poem, *La Saisiaz* (1878) of a dialogue between 'Reason' and 'Fancy' (ll. 405–524); then there is nothing before *Asolando*, which has the only other examples: 'Arcades Ambo', 'The Lady and the Painter', and 'Flute-Music, with an Accompaniment'. See also Chapter 4, p. 131 and n. 14.

8. Even in book xii there are several interpolations by characters in the story, some of whom we have met before (the two lawyers, for example), others of whom make cameo appearances (a Venetian envoy, the friar who gave Pompilia absolution).

Immediately the reader picks up clues as to what is going on, and what has been going on before the beginning of a poem; Browning uses this technique in numerous poems, and he is especially fond of opening lines in which the speaker's desire to grab the listener's attention doubles as the poet's desire to grab the reader's; three poems open with the arresting word 'Stop':

> Stop playing, poet! may a brother speak?
>
> Stop, let me have the truth of that!
>
> Stop rowing![9]

All the features of 'pure' dramatic monologue occur many times in Browning's work, but a list of poems in which they all occur would comprise only a fraction of it. This fraction would admittedly contain some famous poems ('My Last Duchess', 'Andrea del Sarto', and 'Mr Sludge, "the Medium" ', for example) but other, equally famous, poems would be left out: there is no implied listener in 'Childe Roland to the Dark Tower Came', the dramatic situation *is* stated in the opening lines of 'Caliban upon Setebos' (rather clumsily, too, as though Browning couldn't trust his readers to work it out), and 'A Grammarian's Funeral' opens with the start of a funeral procession and ends with its arrival at the cemetery. Even the commonest condition of all, that the poem should be *spoken*, is not universally fulfilled: 'An Epistle of Karshish', as its title implies, is a letter, and so is its companion-poem in *Men and Women* set in the early Christian period, 'Cleon'; 'A Death in the Desert' (*Dramatis Personae*) contains a long speech by St John, but it is a reported speech, transcribed in a parchment scroll.

The dramatic monologue cannot, then, be reduced to a set of generic rules; but it remains the case that Browning was principally concerned, as a poet, with the creation of dramatic speakers and dramatic situations. Many of his characters resemble him in this respect. Even where the speakers of poems are nominally alone, they often imagine an audience. The speaker of 'A Toccata of Galuppi's' addresses the composer whose music he has been playing, as does the

9. 'Transcendentalism' (*Men and Women*), 'Dîs Aliter Visum' (*Dramatis Personae*), 'Ponte dell' Angelo, Venice' (*Asolando*). To these we might add the opening of 'Popularity' (*Men and Women*): 'Stand still, true poet that you are.'

organist in 'Master Hugues of Saxe-Gotha'; but these examples pale beside that of Prince Hohenstiel-Schwangau. When the poem of that name opens, the prince (a portrait of Napoleon III) is apparently in exile in London after the downfall of his political career. He tells the story of his life to a sympathising woman. Only when the poem nears its end (after nearly 2000 lines) do we learn that this whole scene has been a fantasy: the prince is on his own in his palace in Hohenstiel-Schwangau, his political career is not yet over, and he is in fact debating whether to send a certain letter which will decide his fate. But he could not bear to reason it out on his own. He had to project a time and place in which he could recast soliloquy as dramatic monologue. Similarly, when Bishop Blougram wants to discomfit his interlocutor, Gigadibs, he does so by constructing an imagined speech by Gigadibs, set at some point in the future:

> I well imagine you respect my place
> (Status, *entourage*, worldly circumstance)
> Quite to its value – very much indeed
> –Are up to the protesting eyes of you
> In pride at being seated here for once –
> You'll turn it to such capital account!
> When somebody, through years and years to come,
> Hints of the bishop, – names me – that's enough –
> 'Blougram? I knew him' (into it you slide)
> 'Dined with him once, a Corpus Christi Day,
> All alone, we two – he's a clever man –
> And after dinner, – why, the wine you know, –
> Oh, there was wine, and good! – what with the wine . . .
> 'Faith, we began upon all sorts of talk!
> He's no bad fellow, Blougram – he had seen
> Something of mine he relished – some review –
> He's quite above their humbug in his heart,
> Half-said as much, indeed – the thing's his trade –
> I warrant, Blougram's sceptical at times –
> How otherwise? I liked him, I confess!'
> *Ché ch'é*, my dear sir, as we say at Rome,
> Don't you protest now! It's fair give and take;
> You have had your turn and spoken your home-truths –
> The hand's mine now, and here you follow suit.
>
> (ll. 25–48)[10]

10. This passage is finely analysed by Hugh Sykes Davies (pp. 12–14) from

By projecting a monologue within his own monologue, Blougram gives Gigadibs a phantom voice even as he effectively silences him on the occasion of his own overbearing speech. It is a tactic which fits Blougram's dramatic character, it matches the combination of burly swagger and urbane irony with which he treats Gigadibs throughout the poem, but it is also compulsive on the *poet*'s part; that is, Browning's poetry is filled with mimics, impersonators, ventriloquists, with characters whose speech consists of putting words into other people's mouths, for all the world as though they were poets or dramatists themselves. In 'Soliloquy of the Spanish Cloister' the jealous monk satirises Brother Lawrence's innocent prattle:

> At the meal we sit together:
>   *Salve tibi!* I must hear
> Wise talk of the kind of weather,
>   Sort of season, time of year:
> *Not a plenteous cork-crop: scarcely*
>   *Dare we hope oak-galls, I doubt:*
> *What's the Latin name for 'parsley'?*
>   What's the Greek name for Swine's Snout?
>
> (ll. 9–16)

In *The Ring and the Book*, Guido is visited in his death-cell by two old friends; he imagines them making capital of him after his execution:

> I use my tongue: how glibly yours will run
> At pleasant supper-time . . . God's curse! . . . to-night
> When all the guests jump up, begin so brisk
> 'Welcome, his Eminence who shrived the wretch!
> Now we shall have the Abate's story!'
>
> (xi 138–42)

The thought of life continuing after his own death is bound up for Guido with this social scene, with there being speakers and storytellers. His antagonist, the Pope, makes up his mind to confirm the death-sentence after a monologue in which he 'listens' to other,

---

the point of view of its 'representing the fluidity of a man's most intimate colloquy'; see my discussion of Browning's style in the second section of this chapter.

imagined voices, some of which he allows their own dignity and integrity (the voice of Euripides, for example, whose ghost challenges him from the classical past), others which he satirises and parodies, such as the collective voice of civil society, the 'instinct of the world', which demands that he spare Guido in the name of a false pity:

> 'Come, 'tis too much good breath we waste in words:
> The pardon, Holy Father! Spare grimace,
> Shrugs and reluctance! Are not we the world,
> Bid thee, our Priam, let soft culture plead
> Hecuba-like, "*non tali*" (Virgil serves)
> "*Auxilio*", and the rest! Enough, it works!
> The Pope relaxes, and the Prince is loth,
> The father's bowels yearn, the man's will bends,
> Reply is apt.'
>
> (x 2084–92)

The Pope imagines himself bullied, patronised, and taken for granted, but of course he has the last laugh: Virgil will *not* serve here, after all. The quotation comes from the *Aeneid*: as Troy falls, Hecuba persuades her husband, the aged King Priam, not to go out to fight: 'It is not aid like that [non tali auxilio], nor any armed defence, which is needed now' (ii 521–2). Priam would do better, Hecuba says, to cling to the altar and hope for mercy. It doesn't work: he's killed anyway. The Pope imagines 'the world' casting him as this enfeebled, weak-willed, and doomed old man, but by his very imagining of its speech, he pre-empts it and demonstrates his own mastery. Unlike Priam, he still has the authority and power to strike a blow; it is Guido who clings to the altar and is not spared.

The tendency of Browning's characters to dramatize the voices of others can make for a baffling complexity.[11] The most extreme example in a short poem is 'Dîs Aliter Visum' (*Dramatis Personae*, 1864). This poem is spoken by a woman to a man who has just informed her that, ten years before, he had been on the point of proposing marriage to her, but had not done so. Perhaps he uses the title phrase to her: 'to the gods it seemed otherwise', a tag from Virgil which is like a fatalistic shrug: 'it was not meant to be'; he is a famous

11. The complexity occasionally defeated his printers even before it affected his readers: there is a brain-bewildering example in *Sordello* iii 617–25 (see notes in Woolford and Karlin: i 567–9).

and learned poet, after all. Her reaction is swift and bitter. It is not 'the gods' who are to blame for missing an opportunity which might have proved their salvation, but his own emotional cowardice. She recalls not just the occasion, but what she now realises went through his mind as he hesitated and then failed to speak. Within *her* monologue, therefore, she projects *his* voice (the inner voice of his thoughts). But that is not all. The figure she projects – the man of ten years ago, debating within himself whether to ask her to marry him – is himself a dramatiser, who projects *her* voice, imagining what she would think if they did get married and it turned out badly; and, as though that were not enough . . . but here is the passage at its most complex:

> 'Then follows Paris and full time
>    For both to reason: "Thus with us!"
> She'll sigh, "Thus girls give body and soul
>    At first word, think they gain the goal,
> When 'tis the starting-place they climb!
>
> ' "My friend makes verse and gets renown;
>    Have they all fifty years, his peers?
> He knows the world, firm, quiet, and gay;
>    Boys will become as much one day:
> They're fools; he cheats, with beard less brown.
>
> ' "For boys say, *Love me or I die!*
>    He did not say, *The truth is, youth*
> *I want, who am old and know too much;*
>    *I'd catch youth: lend me sight and touch!*
> *Drop heart's blood where life's wheels grate dry!*
>
> 'While I should make rejoinder' – (then
>    It was, no doubt, you ceased that least
> Light pressure of my arm in yours)
>    ' "I can conceive of cheaper cures
> For a yawning-fit o'er books and men." '
>
> (ll. 71–90)

She imagines him thinking that if they were to marry, they would both regret it (she because of his age, he because of her excessive emotional demands); the way she imagines him thinking this is by him imagining what she would say; and what she imagines him imagining her saying consists, in part, of her version of what *he* ought to have said had he been honest with her – at which point single and double quotation marks give out and the printers have to resort to italics. When the single quotation marks in 1. 86 close and the parenthesis opens, it brings us back for a sharp instant to the 'present' in which the monologue is being spoken, and to the woman who speaks it: she remembers how the pressure of his arm relaxed, but only now can she reconstruct the thoughts which influenced that small gesture and appreciate its fatefulness.

With 'Dîs Aliter Visum' dramatic monologue reaches an apotheosis which is close to breakdown.[12] It is a sign that dramatic method, like civilisation, has its discontents. Browning had cultivated it since his earliest published poem, *Pauline*, but he did not do so with an express sense of pride or pleasure. On the contrary, he constantly described dramatic writing as *inferior* to lyric. Why should this have been so? The answer lies in the ideas about poetic creativity which govern Browning's work, ideas which, in turn, were generated by the pressure of his philosophical and political beliefs.[13]

## So many Robert Brownings

> Yet here comes one of those fatal ifs, the egoism of the man, and the pity of it. He cannot metempsychose with his creatures, they are so many Robert Brownings.

Eliza Flower's comment on *Pippa Passes* (cited Woolford and Karlin, ii, 17) is a familiar one in Browning criticism. Ruskin made exactly the same point, and about the same work, in a letter to Browning himself:

> I entirely deny that a poet of your real dramatic power ought to let *himself* come up, as you constantly do, through all manner of characters, so that every now and then poor Pippa herself shall speak a long piece of Robert Browning. (Appendix B, pp. 255–6)

12. In *Fifine at the Fair* (1872) the form does in fact break down, and, for the first time in Browning's work, the interlocutor in a monologue breaks the convention and speaks (first at l. 199, then ll. 254–6 and other places).

13. For more detail on some of these ideas, to which brief reference will be made in the next section of this chapter, see Chapter 6.

Ruskin's 'poor Pippa' puns on the idiom: poor Pippa to be forced to spout Browning, but especially so because Pippa is really, materially poor, a factory girl. The poet who asserted unequivocally that his poems were 'so many utterances of so many imaginary persons, not mine' ('Advertisement' to *Dramatic Lyrics*, 1842) stands accused of producing no more than 'so many Robert Brownings'. Compared to his vigorous rebuttals of Ruskin's other criticisms in this letter, Browning's reply on this point is curiously tentative:

> The last charge I cannot answer, for you may be right in preferring it, however unwitting I am of the fact. I *may* put Robert Browning into Pippa and other men and maids. If so, *peccavi* [I have sinned]: but I don't see myself in them, at all events. (Appendix B, p. 258)

He was more robust with a later critic, Julia Wedgwood, though her criticism was more charitably expressed. She complained about a passage in *The Ring and the Book* which she found too learned for its speaker:

> I should like to ask why you break down the dramatic framework so often in your characters? That passage about Justinian and the Pandects, for instance, is yours, and not Franceschini's. But you must have a distinct intention in this, and I can't help always enjoying it, it seems so characteristic of you – though it does seem to me an artistic defect. (Curle: 156)

Browning denied the particular charge and challenged Julia Wedgwood to substantiate the general one:

> Why is the allusion to Justinian *mine* and not the man's I give it to? The whole of his speech, as I premise, is untrue – cant and cleverness . . . but he was quite able to cant, and also know something of the Pandects, which are the basis of actual Italian law. What are the other escapes from dramatic propriety into my own peculiar self – do tell me that! (p. 161)

But in one sense the charge is impossible to answer, because it is true: Julia Wedgwood is quite right to say that Guido's speech at this point is *characteristic*, in the sense that all Browning's characters sound like Browning; a Browning poem is instantly recognisable as itself, and for a writer with so much surface Browning is surprisingly hard to imitate. In 'Within a Budding Grove', Proust remarks of the painter, Elstir:

> The particulars of life do not matter to the artist; they merely provide him with the opportunity to lay bare his genius. One feels unmistakably, when one sees side by side ten portraits of people painted by Elstir, that they are all, first and foremost, Elstirs. (Proust: i 910)

That Elstir is a fictitious painter makes the observation positively Browningesque; I imagine Browning enjoying the joke, but also taking it seriously. 'There they are, my fifty men and women', he tells EBB in 'One Word More'; there may be lots of them, but they are all *his*: 'Naming *me* the fifty poems finished' (ll. 1–2, my italics).[14] The multiplicity of Browning's characters are first and foremost characters in Browning; yet the multiplicity also matters, is in itself a formidable fact. There are two truths, then, about Browning's dramatic method, neither of which cancels the other out: that he is always himself, and that he is so in many guises: 'so many Robert Brownings'.

In his second letter to EBB, Browning was already keen to seize the low ground. 'Your poetry,' he declared, 'must be, cannot but be, infinitely more to me than mine to you' (13 Jan. 1845, Kelley: x 22). He was wrong, she replied:

> Why sh$^{d}$ you deny the full measure of my delight & benefit from your writings? I could tell you why you should not. You have in your vision two worlds – or to use the language of the schools of the day, you are both subjective & objective in the habits of your mind – You can deal both with abstract thought, & with human passion in the most passionate sense. (15 Jan. 1845, Kelley: x 26)

A month later, she repeated this praise of Browning's double vision, this time emphasising not subject matter but style:

> You have taken a great range – from those high faint notes of the mystics which are beyond personality . . to dramatic impersonations, gruff with nature, 'gr-r- you swine' . . .
> (17 Feb. 1845, Kelley: x 79)[15]

14. The syntax of ll. 1–2 is ambiguous; it allows this reading, but does not prescribe it.

15. EBB quotes the last line of 'Soliloquy of the Spanish Cloister'; the 'high faint notes of the mystic' probably refer to *Paracelsus*, especially Paracelsus's deathbed speech beginning at v 582.

The 'high faint notes of the mystics which are beyond personality' evidently belong to the 'subjective' world of 'abstract thought' while the 'dramatic impersonations, gruff with nature' belong to the 'objective' world of 'human passion'. Browning himself was later to deploy this opposition between subjective and objective poetry in the *Essay on Shelley*, but with a crucial variation in the meaning of the first term. In the *Essay*, the association of 'subjective' poetry with abstraction does not imply going 'beyond personality', but, on the contrary, the expression of pure personality, namely the poet's own:

> Not with the combination of humanity in action, but with the primal elements of humanity he [the subjective poet] has to do; and he digs where he stands, – preferring to seek them in his own soul as the nearest reflex of that absolute Mind, according to the intuitions of which he desires to perceive and speak. . . . He is rather a seer, accordingly, than a fashioner, and what he produces will be less a work than an effluence. That effluence cannot be easily considered in abstraction from his personality, – being indeed the very radiance and aroma of his personality, projected from it but not separated.
>
> (Appendix A, p. 247)

Shelley, in Browning's view, was such a poet, and so was EBB; but he himself was not. In his letter to her of 13 January 1845, he goes on to explain why her poetry *must* mean more to him than his to her:

> you *do* what I always wanted, hoped to do, and only seem now likely to do for the first time – you speak out, *you*, – I only make men & women speak, – give you truth broken into prismatic hues, and fear the pure white light, even if it is in me . . .

According to Browning, then, *all* his poetry consists of 'dramatic impersonations', including the 'high faint notes of the mystics'. None of it is the 'effluence' of his own personality, the 'pure white light' of self-consciousness; none of it is 'speaking out'. 'I never have begun, even, what I hope I was born to begin and end, – "R.B. a poem" ' (11 Feb. 1845, Kelley: x 69). EBB agreed: 'in fact, you have not written the R.B. poem yet – your rays fall obliquely rather than directly straight' (17 Feb. 1845, Kelley: x 79).

The terms 'effluence', 'radiance' and 'pure white light' take us straight to the Platonic idea of knowledge or truth as *inwardly* generated which so influenced Browning's intellectual life. In Chapter 6 (p. 196) we cite a passage of *Paracelsus* which directly bears on this point; and, as far as the opposition between dramatic and lyric forms is concerned, we can add the passage in his letter to EBB which immediately follows his declaration that he had not yet written 'R.B. a poem', and in which Browning describes the difficulty he feels he has in enabling his own 'imprison'd splendour' to 'dart forth':

> And, *next*, if I speak (and, God knows, feel) as if what you have read were sadly imperfect demonstrations of even mere ability, it is from no absurd vanity, tho' it might seem so – these scenes and song-scraps *are* such mere and very escapes of my inner power, – which lives in me like the light in those crazy Mediterranean phares I have watched at sea – wherein the light is ever revolving in a dark gallery, bright and alive, and only after a weary interval leaps out, for a moment, from the one narrow chink, and then goes on with the blind wall between it and you . . . the work has been *inside*, and not when, at stated times I held up my light to *you* – and, that there is no self-delusion here, I would prove to *you* . . . even by opening this desk I write on, and showing what stuff, in the way of wood, I *could* make a great bonfire with, if I might only knock the whole clumsy top off my tower!
>
> (11 Feb. 1845, Kelley: x 69–70)

The sense of imprisonment and frustration, of an almost physical bafflement, is palpable here; but there is also something odd about it, something which should alert us to a turn, a twist in the plot which the writer is unfolding. A lighthouse could not function with a steady, permanent beam; it would defeat the object, which is precisely to send out an intermittent, flashing signal. The conditions under which the light exists – the dark gallery, the weary interval, the narrow chink – are the only ones in which it can serve its purpose. And we should not forget what that purpose is: to illuminate, to warn, to save. These are not ignoble analogies for poetry.[16]

In the *Essay on Shelley* Browning wrote admiringly of Shelley's 'spheric poetical faculty', which had 'its own self-sufficing central light, radiating equally through immaturity and accomplishment, through many fragments and occasional completion' (Appendix A, p. 251). The word 'occasional' carries the sense of 'on occasion', but it

16. For other images of imprisoned creativity, see Chapter 4, pp. 143–4.

can also mean 'accidental, not essential to the main purpose'. To perceive Shelley's greatness, in other words, is not to evaluate the works he actually produced, but to worship the 'self-sufficing central light' of his genius. The dualism fostered by Platonic thought, and expressed in the Gnostic division of the cosmos into spiritual and material principles, results, when you apply it to poetry, in a contempt for actual poems (and the language of which they are composed), since these are the mere 'body' in which genius is forced reluctantly to clothe itself. But if genius, creative inspiration, 'radiate[s] equally through immaturity and accomplishment', why bother to accomplish anything at all?

The danger of poetic genius taking itself and its audience for granted can be articulated in the vocabulary of Platonic or Gnostic philosophy; it can also be articulated in another vocabulary equally close to Browning's experience, that of Protestant theology. Browning was well aware of extreme tendencies in Protestant thought: his father's library was filled with pamphlets, sermons, spiritual autobiographies, and histories of the religious controversies of the Reformation and beyond, which figure constantly in his work. One of his earliest dramatic monologues is spoken by a historical figure, Johannes Agricola, an early Protestant who founded the 'Antinomian' sect. Antinomianism is a perversely logical extension of Calvinist doctrine, and consists in the belief that the elect, those whom God has predestined for salvation, are exempt from the moral law: nothing they do or don't do can affect their ultimate salvation, since God has arbitrarily chosen them from all eternity. As Johannes says:

> I have God's warrant, could I blend
> All hideous sins, as in a cup, –
> To drink the mingled venoms up,
> Secure my nature will convert
> The draught to blossoming gladness fast . . .
> (ll. 33–7)

However, Browning is not so interested in the licence which Johannes' theology gives him to commit sin without penalty, as in the malign consequences it has for his view of other people. In a passage of grotesque brilliance, Johannes imagines himself in heaven, 'smiled on, full fed / With unexhausted blessedness' (ll. 41–2), an infant eternally suckling but with a devil's relish:

I gaze below on Hell's fierce bed,
   And those its waves of flame oppress,
Swarming in ghastly wretchedness,
Whose life on earth aspired to be
   One altar-smoke, – so pure! – to win
If not love like God's love to me,
   At least to keep his anger in . . .
And all their striving turned to sin!
Priest, doctor, hermit, monk grown white
   With prayer: the broken-hearted nun,
The martyr, the wan acolyte,
   The incense-swinging child . . . undone
Before God fashioned star or sun!

(ll. 43–55)

The damned are all, not surprisingly, Roman Catholic religious figures ('doctor' in l. 51 means 'doctor of the church', like Thomas Aquinas), but the point goes deeper than Johannes' local Protestant prejudice. His exalted belief in his own union with God has cut him off from humanity. Browning's satire on Antinomianism has a strong political edge: the poem was published in the *Monthly Repository* whose editor, Browning's 'literary father' W.J. Fox, was not only a Unitarian in religion but a radical in politics.[17] Egalitarian and democratic ideas, ideas of solidarity and community, depend crucially on empathy, on the willingness and ability to imagine other people. (This is especially true for those who, like Browning, come to such ideas from the privileged end of the social scale.) They also depend on the willingness to act, and to take responsibility for action. The 'striving' which Johannes scorns is one of Browning's talismanic words, summed up in the proverb he cites in the 'Epilogue' to *Asolando*, 'Strive and thrive'.[18] But Johannes conceives of himself as blessed with divine

17. Unitarians rejected the doctrines of the trinity and of the divinity of Christ, and were sceptical about the doctrines of original sin and eternal punishment. Their rationalism and belief in the goodness of human nature made them natural exponents of political reform. See also Chapter 5, pp. 160–1.

18. The words 'strive' and 'strife' occur 139 times in 55 poems by Browning. The eponymous speaker of 'Ixion' (*Jocoseria*, 1883) is representative: 'Strive, my kind, though strife endure thro' endless obstruction, / Stage after stage, each rise marred by as certain a fall!' (ll. 97–8). In the *Poetical Works* of 1888–9 Browning revised 'my kind' to 'mankind'.

inertia, divine irresponsibility:

> I lie – where I have always lain,
>   God smiles – as he has always smiled; –
> Ere suns and moons could wax and wane,
>   Ere stars were thundergirt, or piled
> The heavens . . . God thought on me his child,
> Ordained a life for me – arrayed
>   Its circumstances, every one
> To the minutest . . .
>
> (ll. 11–18)

This stasis of spirit, where nothing can 'wax and wane', where even the most majestic acts of creation are irrelevant, figures a poetry of utter self-absorption. Johannes is blazing away all right, without weary intervals or narrow chinks, but his 'self-sufficing central light' is, to use Milton's phrase, 'no light, but rather darkness visible'. Not surprisingly, therefore, Johannes is not speaking to anyone, except himself: he is his own dramatised listener.[19] Fear of becoming like Johannes, it might be argued, keeps Browning a dramatic poet, prevents him from yielding to the lyric self-expression he praised in the poetry of Shelley, of Tennyson, and of his wife. In the invocation to EBB from which I quoted at the beginning of this chapter, Browning pays his most intense and moving tribute to the faculty from which he had consciously alienated himself, but he makes it clear that he is not trying to emulate or adopt it. As against the image of the 'half-angel and half-bird', who 'braved the sun . . . And sang a kindred soul out to his face' (i 1391–5), an image which clearly links EBB to Shelley's skylark, is set the image of Browning himself as a 'wistful eagle' who dies with 'heaven, save by his heart, unreached'; and even that image sounds too grand, for Browning immediately adds: 'Yet heaven my fancy lifts to, ladder-like, – / As Jack reached, holpen of his beanstalk-rungs!' (i 1342–7). It is an undignified image; but perhaps we should remember that the first thing Jack stole from the giant and brought back to earth was his golden harp.

19. Browning emphasised this point when he revised the title in the *Poems* of 1849 to 'Johannes Agricola in Meditation'.

## STYLE: 'IS IT SINGING, IS IT SAYING?'[20]

Browning's style is vocal. His poems, like those of Donne, demand to be voiced: speakers predominate in Browning's work, pleading, hectoring, boasting, repenting, expiring. As we shall see, Browning's conception of voice is not uniform and does not follow a single creative pattern. There is a great division, a fault-line, running through Browning's poetics, a division which gives rise in his poetry to two voices, for which he himself used the terms 'saying' and 'singing'. But it is also the case that the voice for which Browning is best remembered is the first, the voice of 'saying', and we should begin by looking at how it works.

### The voice of saying

In the poems written in this style, Browning makes verse imitate, as far as possible, the diction, idioms, and rhythms of human speech, the speech which consists of ordinary words in their natural order of utterance. He stretched the metrical forms with which he worked (both in blank verse and rhyme) to the limit in order to do this, though he never broke them and never showed any interest in 'free' verse or prose poetry.[21] This practice of making verse imitate speech does not depend on subject, mood, or occasion; the speakers concerned can be happy or sad, subdued or exclamatory, their utterances can be ten lines long or a thousand. Browning's poetic voice imposes itself on a multitude of differing dramatic situations and psychological states:

> Ah, did you once see Shelley plain,
> And did he stop and speak to you?

> But do not let us quarrel any more,
> No, my Lucrezia . . .

> I will be quiet and talk with you,
> And reason why you are wrong . . .

20. The phrase is adapted from 'The Flight of the Duchess', l. 512. See the note on this line in Woolford and Karlin: ii 318.

21. The closest Browning comes to an irregular metre is his occasional use of variable stress in, e.g., the Gypsy's speech in 'The Flight of the Duchess' (ll. 567–689), where the influence of Coleridge is prominent: see Chapter 1, p. 10.

Now, don't sir! Don't expose me! Just this once!

I am just seventeen years and five months old . . .[22]

The purpose of this style is to give the impression that someone is 'simply' talking; the reader may not be taken in, but will be affected nonetheless, may even collude in the process, voicing the poem in such a way as to bring out its 'spoken' quality and subordinate its formal properties (rhyme, metre, structure, etc.). 'My Last Duchess' is written in couplets, and yet the 'natural' rhythm of the Duke's speech is at certain moments so strong that it seems to over-ride and dissolve the poem's versification:

She had
A heart . . how shall I say? . . too soon made glad,
Too easily impressed; she liked whate'er
She looked on, and her looks went everywhere.
. . .
She thanked men, – good; but thanked
Somehow . . I know not how . . as if she ranked
My gift of a nine hundred years old name
With anybody's gift.

(ll. 21–24, 31–34)

A combination of enjambement and the Duke's colloquial hesitation makes the rhymes 'had/glad' and, to a lesser extent, 'thanked/ranked' almost undetectable, certainly without rhetorical weight. The speaking voice in Browning is often modulated in this way in order to disguise, or off-set, the effects of metre and rhyme; not that rhyme and metre are unimportant, but that they are felt as pressure, as atmosphere, rather than as constitutive of expression (the contrast with Tennyson, again, is especially sharp). Such speakers seem to have fallen by accident into a metrical stream, the force of whose current they alternately acknowledge and resist.[23] And the current can be strong, as strong as the swinging couplets of 'Up at a Villa – Down in the City':

22. The openings of 'Memorabilia', 'Andrea del Sarto', 'Mr Sludge, "the Medium" ', part iv of 'James Lee' ('Along the Beach'), and book vii of *The Ring and the Book*.

23. See, for example, the moment in 'Mr Sludge, "the Medium" ', which is written in blank verse, when Sludge perpetrates an 'inadvertent' rhyme and comments: 'Bless us, I'm turning poet!' (l. 1184).

But bless you, it's dear – it's dear! fowls, wine, at double the rate.
They have clapped a new tax upon salt, and what oil pays
  passing the gate
It's a horror to think of. And so, the villa for me, not the city!
Beggars can scarcely be choosers – but still – ah, the pity, the
  pity!

(ll. 55–58)

or the jaunty quatrains of 'Soliloquy of the Spanish Cloister':

Oh, those melons! If he's able
  We're to have a feast; so nice!
One goes to the Abbot's table,
  All of us get each a slice.

(ll. 41–44)

Both these poems are ostentatiously metrical, and yet the speakers give the impression that, had they not been in a poem by Browning, they would still have spoken in the same way. For the speaker of the 'Soliloquy', in particular, the strongly marked rhymes seem to be part of his colloquial energy and not at all an external form imposed upon it. Browning is equally capable of subordinating the rhythms of a speaking voice to a metrical pattern, yet without diminishing this sense that verse is second nature to voice. Take, for example, these lines from 'Andrea del Sarto':

I dared not, do you know, leave home all day,
For fear of chancing on the Paris lords.
The best is when they pass and look aside;
But they speak sometimes; I must bear it all.

(ll. 144–7)

Apart from the first phrase (which replaces 'I did not dare, you know'), there is little to distinguish this from prose as far as the word order is concerned; but the rhythm is a different matter. Even written out as prose the strong segmentation of the lines reveals itself:

I dared not, do you know, leave home all day, for fear of chancing on the Paris lords. The best is when they pass and look aside; but they speak sometimes; I must bear it all.

End-stopping is the mark of Andrea's melancholy: there are only a handful of true enjambements in the whole poem, and most of the lines have the falling cadence which suggests not merely Andrea's failure but the pleasure he takes in it:

> There's the bell clinking from the chapel-top;
> That length of convent-wall across the way
> Holds the trees safer, huddled more inside;
> The last monk leaves the garden; days decrease
> And autumn grows, autumn in everything.
>
> (ll. 41–5)

The third line runs on syntactically from the second, but the enjambement is notional: the strong stress on 'Holds' ensures that the self-containment of the line is barely affected. Andrea's conversational phrasing ('There's the bell . . . That length of wall') is subordinated to a lyric self-absorption whose sign is 'the poetic' (alliteration, in this example, as well as rhythm).[24] And yet these 'poetic' features seem not to make Andrea's speech forced, but on the contrary to form part of its naturalness.

In many poems the colloquial style predominates because it is itself of the essence of the speaker's dramatic character.[25] Other examples

24. 'There's the bell' and 'That length of wall' are also characteristic of Andrea's use of demonstratives: 'There's what we painters call our harmony . . . This chamber for example – . . . that cartoon, the second from the door . . . Yonder's a work, now . . . That arm is wrongly put' (ll. 34, 53, 57, 103, 110). He points to things, to landscapes, to the actions of his wife and himself: 'To paint a little thing like that you smeared . . . My works are nearer heaven, but I sit here' (ll. 74, 87). The word 'here' brings together a general condition ('earthbound') and a particular situation ('here, in this room with you'). A similar combination is active, but to a quite different effect, in the passage from 'Bishop Blougram's Apology' discussed earlier (p. 43). Where Andrea stages a drama of defeated narcissism, Blougram uses 'here' to point towards the future, to control his interlocutor's own demonstrations: 'here, / I well imagine you respect my place . . . Are up to the protesting eyes of you / In pride at being seated here for once . . . The hand's mine now, and here you follow suit'.

25. The same reason would account for Browning's extensive use of technical vocabulary and professional jargon (e.g. medicine, music, law); but it is also true that Browning (like Kipling) delighted in such language for its own sake, as his comment on a particularly ripe legal document in *The*

(not coincidentally they are some of Browning's best-known works) include 'Fra Lippo Lippi', 'Bishop Blougram's Apology', and 'Mr Sludge, "the Medium" '. 'I was a baby when my mother died,' Lippi says, 'And father died and left me in the street' (ll. 81–2). He is rescued from the street, yet compulsively returns there : it is in the street that the watch finds him, and the street gives him his emotional and aesthetic language. His career as a painter begins in the margins of learned texts and sprawls outwards into the world:

> I drew men's faces on my copy-books,
> Scrawled them within the antiphonary's marge,
> Joined legs and arms to the long music-notes,
> Found nose and eyes and chin for A.s and B.s,
> And made a string of pictures of the world
> Betwixt the ins and outs of verb and noun,
> On the wall, the bench, the door.
>
> (ll. 129–35)

It is 'They, with their Latin' who denigrate his art (l. 242); Lippi's way of speaking, in its very vulgarity and matter-of-factness, is an intrinsic part of his protest at 'their' repressive learning and piety. Sludge, though a much less attractive character than Lippi, has the same linguistic grievance against his patrons and social superiors, expressed with a similar demotic relish. 'May I sit, sir?' he asks Hiram H. Horsefall, with mock-politeness, after agreeing to spill the beans about his career as a fraudulent medium:

> May I sit, sir? This dear old table, now!
> Please, sir, a parting egg-nogg and cigar!
> I've been so happy with you! Nice stuffed chairs,
> And sympathetic sideboards; what an end
> To all the instructive evenings! (It's alight.)
> Well, nothing lasts, as Bacon came and said!
> Here goes, – but keep your temper, or I'll scream!
>
> (ll. 76–82)

These lines do more than mark Sludge's characteristic tone of odious familiarity; they show the edge of his intelligence and resentment, his

---

*Ring and the Book* shows: 'I like and shall translate the eloquence / Of nearly the worst Latin ever writ . . .' (xii 794–5).

ability to discomfit the very man who apparently has the power to ruin him. The 'dear old table' is the one which Sludge has been rapping in order to deceive Horsefall, whose bourgeois respectability and gullibility are figured in the 'Nice stuffed chairs / And sympathetic sideboards'. The parenthesis, which shows Horsefall ministering to Sludge instead of beating him, fixes the scene with a single dazzling stroke of the poet's art and the speaker's impudence. Bishop Blougram, too, is a master of conversational idiom, which in his case represents not impudence but condescension and the exercise of power, as when he interrupts his extended metaphor of the voyage of life to give Gigadibs a taste of how the metaphor works in practice:

> You peep up from your utterly naked boards
> Into some snug and well-appointed berth
> Like mine, for instance (try the cooler jug –
> Put back the other, but don't jog the ice)
> And mortified you mutter . . .
>
> (ll. 130–4)

or when he disdains to remember the title of one of Verdi's operas:

> Like Verdi when, at his worst opera's end
> (The thing they gave at Florence, – what's its name?)
>
> (ll. 381–2)

or when he flicks a crumb of his intellect in Gigadibs' direction:

> Do you know, I have often had a dream
> (Work it up in your next month's article)
>
> (ll. 780–1)

In all these examples, Blougram knows what he is doing; he is *using* idiomatic speech in the active sense, rather than using it because he always talks like that.[26] Yet such speech is also in the grain of the man, is characteristic and constitutive. Moreover Blougram's style, and that of Fra Lippo Lippi and Mr Sludge, is one aspect of a conflict between different ways of perceiving and interpreting the world.

26. The effectiveness of Blougram's conversational asides may be judged by comparing them with their lacklustre equivalents in *Prince Hohenstiel-Schwangau* (e.g. ll. 255–61).

All three of these speakers see themselves as realists, as down-to-earthlings, as partisans of the here-and-now against the untenable illusions and attempts at transcendence of their fellow-men, whether masters or dupes (in the case of Sludge, both). Lippi's painting is founded on the premise that

> This world's no blot for us,
> Nor blank – it means intensely, and means good:
> To find its meaning is my meat and drink.
> (ll. 313–15)

It was the 'admonitions from the hunger-pinch' which, Lippi says, taught him 'the look of things' in the first place (ll. 125–6); the idiom 'my meat and drink' comes naturally to him, he reads the world through an appetite for its surfaces, 'The shapes of things, their colours, lights and shades' (l. 284). Instructed by his superiors that his

> business is not to catch men with show,
> With homage to the perishable clay,
> But lift them over it, ignore it all,
> Make them forget there's such a thing as flesh . . .
> (ll. 179–82)

Lippi retorts:

> Now, is this sense, I ask?
> A fine way to paint soul, by painting body
> So ill, the eye can't stop there, must go further
> And can't fare worse!
> (ll. 198–201)

So natural is the indignant exclamation in the first line that it takes a moment to realise the pun on 'sense', which means both 'common sense' and 'the faculty of physical sensation' (Lippi has already used 'sense' in opposition to 'soul' at l. 124). Lippi then takes the notion of elevation in art ('lift them over it') and, again using a popular turn of phrase, converts the vertical into a vulgar horizontal: 'must go further / And can't fare worse'.

For Blougram, too, plain speaking is the vehicle of a worldliness, a materialism, which he repeatedly launches against Gigadibs's unthinking idealism: 'your grand simple life, / Of which you will not realise one jot', as he puts it (ll. 82–3):

> The common problem, yours, mine, every one's,
> Is not to fancy what were fair in life
> Provided it could be, – but, finding first
> What may be, then find how to make it fair
> Up to our means – a very different thing!
> No abstract intellectual plan of life
> Quite irrespective of life's plainest laws,
> But one, a man, who is man and nothing more,
> May lead within a world which (by your leave)
> Is Rome or London – not Fool's-paradise.
>
> (ll. 87–96)

and again:

> We speak of what is – not of what might be,
> And how 'twere better if 'twere otherwise.
> I am the man you see here plain enough . . .
>
> (ll. 346–8)

This 'common problem' is a problem *common* to all human beings, but also a commonplace; the epithet threatens to become derogatory, if once the existence of a world which is *neither* 'Rome or London' *nor* 'Fool's-paradise' is acknowledged. And Blougram does acknowledge it; like Lippi and Sludge, he is haunted by what he has repudiated; on occasion he speaks in a different register, as when he argues that complete disbelief in God is as difficult to sustain as complete faith; but this 'high' speech is confused and flawed:

> Just when we are safest, there's a sunset-touch,
> A fancy from a flower-bell, some one's death,
> A chorus-ending from Euripides, –
> And that's enough for fifty hopes and fears
> As old and new at once as Nature's self,
> To rap and knock and enter in our soul,
> Take hands and dance there, a fantastic ring,
> Round the ancient idol, on his base again, –
> The grand Perhaps!
>
> (ll. 182–90)

Romantic pathos governs the images in the first three lines, which speak of transience and closure in nature, human life, and art as though they were all alike and belonged in Keats's 'Ode on

Melancholy'; then 'fifty hopes and fears', with Victorian briskness, 'rap and knock and enter in our soul', like spirits summoned by Sludge; finally the evocation of 'the ancient idol' shows that Blougram is abreast of current developments in religious anthropology which traced the links between Christianity and paganism.[27] The instability of the language here suggests that Blougram is more truly himself in the mask with which he confronts his opponent, that his declaration 'I am the man you see here plain enough' is truer than he would like to think.

Blougram's defence of living 'for this world now' is also a defence of the voice of 'saying', and is conducted in that voice; but it is not the voice that his interlocutor Gigadibs heeds. Blougram himself, as I pointed out earlier in this chapter, disappears from his own monologue, and it is Browning who, at the end of the poem, records that Gigadibs has emigrated to Australia, adding:

> there, I hope,
> By this time he has tested his first plough,
> And studied his last chapter of St. John.
> (ll. 1011–13)

The 'last chapter of St. John' may be either the last chapter of St John's gospel, or the last chapter of *Revelation*, both of them among Browning's favourite books of the Bible.[28] The last chapter of St John's Gospel concerns the third and final appearance of the risen Jesus to the disciples; the last chapter of *Revelation* tells of the 'river of water of life, clear as crystal, proceeding out of the throne of God and of the Lamb' (xxii 1). Neither in subject matter nor style are they concerned with 'this world now'. Gigadibs, we should note, has gone to Australia not to pursue a Utopian project but with 'settler's-implements'

27. Browning returned to this image in later poems, after he began spending his summer holidays in Brittany, where traces still remained of pre-Christian fertility rituals: see *Fifine at the Fair*, 2022 ff. and *The Two Poets of Croisic*, 89 ff.

28. The full title of *Revelation* is *The Revelation of St John the Divine*. The traditional identification of John the author of *Revelation* with the John who wrote the fourth gospel was already being questioned by biblical scholarship in Browning's day, but Browning accepted it, at any rate for poetic purposes: see 'A Death in the Desert' (*Dramatis Personae*, 1864).

(l. 1010); his feet will be on the ground, but the spirit which guides him will nevertheless be exalted and apocalyptic. It is this spirit which governs the second voice of Browning's poetry, the voice of 'singing', dissident, devious, ineradicable; subversive of common speech, suggestive of transcendence. Without this radical opposition, Browning's colloquial style would lose half its force; but the opposition was there from the beginning, and Browning found the quarrel between singing and saying in the very roots of his poetic identity.

## Genius and the common man

As with so much else in Browning's career as a writer, the conflict between 'saying' and 'singing', between the two voices of his poetry, derives from a conflict within Romanticism, in this case from the dispute over poetic language between Wordsworth and Coleridge. In the preface to *Lyrical Ballads*, Wordsworth argued

> that not only the language of a large portion of every good Poem, even of the most elevated character, must necessarily, except with reference to the metre, in no respect differ from that of good Prose, but likewise that some of the most interesting parts of the best Poems will be found to be strictly the language of Prose, when Prose is well written.[29]

This argument is not simply technical; in the next paragraph Wordsworth links it explicitly to a radical humanist aesthetic:

> I do not doubt that it may be safely affirmed, that there neither is, nor can be, any essential difference between the language of Prose and metrical composition. We are fond of tracing the resemblance between Poetry and Painting, and, accordingly, we call them sisters; but where shall we find bonds of connection sufficiently strict to typify the affinity betwixt metrical and Prose composition? They both speak by and to the same organs; the bodies in which both of them are clothed may be said to be of the same substance, their affections are kindred, and almost identical, not necessarily differing even in degree; Poetry sheds no tears 'such as Angels weep', but natural and human tears; she

29. The text is that of the 1805 edition (Mason: 67).

> can boast of no celestial ichor that distinguishes her vital juices from those of Prose; the same human blood circulates through the veins of them both. (Mason: 68–9)

Wordsworth directs his allusions principally against Milton: it is Satan in *Paradise Lost* who sheds 'tears such as angels weep' (i 620), and when he is wounded 'A stream of nectarous humour issuing flowed / Sanguine, such as celestial spirits may bleed' (vi 332–3).[30] And it is Milton who, in the invocation to book ix of the poem, seeks an 'answerable style' for his epic from his muse, Urania, his 'celestial patroness' (ll. 20–1). Wordsworth renounces a centuries-old tradition of the poet as *vates* or seer, uttering divinely-inspired oracles in an 'answerable style', a style whose first requirement is that it *differ* from 'natural and human' language. On the contrary, the poet is (in the preface's most famous phrase) 'a man speaking to men', and the word 'speaking' is not the least important part of this formula.

In *Biographia Literaria*, Coleridge ridicules Wordsworth's assertion that the language of poetry should be that of 'real life', and that a poem should sound as far as possible like someone (anyone, that is, but the divinely-inspired poet) talking.[31] And, citing a passage from 'The Thorn' as evidence that the best of Wordsworth's poetic language is in fact elevated and sublime even where it purports to be 'the language of ordinary men', Coleridge 'reflect[s] with delight how little a mere theory, though of his own workmanship, interferes with the processes of genuine imagination in a man of true poetic genius'. These phrases – 'genuine imagination' and 'true poetic genius' – go to the heart of the matter; for Coleridge the poet is not 'a man speaking to men' but a philosopher or prophet, possessed of 'the highest and intuitive knowledge as distinguished from the discursive, or, in the

30. The word 'ichor' glances at Homer as well as Milton; Satan's wound is modelled on that of Ares, the god of war, in *Iliad* v 339.

31. Coleridge takes the first lines of 'The Last of the Flock' as a 'chance' example: 'In distant countries I have been, / And yet I have not often seen / A healthy man, a man full grown, / Weep in the public roads, alone', and rewrites them as they would really have been spoken by a 'rustic' narrator: ' "I have been in a many parts far and near, and I don't know that I ever saw before a man crying by himself in the public road; a grown man I mean, that was neither sick nor hurt," etc. etc.'

language of Wordsworth, "The vision and the faculty divine" ' (ch. xii, Watson: 139).[32] Wordsworth would admit only differences of degree, not of kind, between the poet and the common run of humanity:

> the Poet is chiefly distinguished from other men by a greater promptness to think and feel without immediate external excitement, and a greater power in expressing such thoughts and feelings as are produced in him in that manner. But these passions and thoughts and feelings are the general passions and thoughts and feelings of men. And with what are they connected? Undoubtedly with our moral sentiments and animal sensations, and with the causes which excite these; with the operations of the elements and the appearances of the visible universe; with storm and sunshine, with the revolutions of the seasons, with cold and heat, with loss of friends and kindred, with injuries and resentments, gratitude and hope, with fear and sorrow. These, and the like, are the sensations and objects which the Poet describes, as they are the sensations of other men, and the objects which interest them. The Poet thinks and feels in the spirit of the passions of men. How, then, can his language differ in any material degree from that of all other men who feel vividly and see clearly? It might be *proved* that it is impossible. But supposing that this were not the case, the Poet might then be allowed to use a peculiar language when expressing his feelings for his own gratification, or that of men like himself. But Poets do not write for Poets alone, but for men. Unless therefore we are advocates for that admiration which depends upon ignorance, and that pleasure which arises from hearing what we do not understand, the Poet must descend from this supposed height, and, in order to excite rational sympathy, he must express himself as other men express themselves. (Mason: 78–9)

It is hard to see that the object of a poem like 'Kubla Khan' is to 'excite rational sympathy'. Coleridge's poetics are based on the opposite principle to Wordsworth's: on the difference in kind between the poet and 'other men', on poetry as the product of 'the philosophic imagination, the sacred power of self-intuition' (ch. xii, Watson: 139). In an elaborate figure, which intentionally, I think, recalls a

32. The quotation is from *The Excursion* i 79. Coleridge uses it again, with even more ironic force, in the passage from ch. xviii just quoted.

Wordsworthian landscape, Coleridge argues for the existence of a special and privileged class of beings, exactly the class to which Wordsworth denied that poets belonged:

> The first range of hills that encircles the scanty vale of human life is the horizon for the majority of its inhabitants. On its ridges the common sun is born and departs. From them the stars rise, and touching them they vanish. By the many even this range, the natural limit and bulwark of the vale, is but imperfectly known. Its higher ascents are too often hidden by mists and clouds from uncultivated swamps which few have courage or curiosity to penetrate. To the multitude below these vapors appear, now as the dark haunts of terrific agents on which none may intrude with impunity; and now all a-glow with colors not their own, they are gazed at as the splendid palaces of happiness and power. But in all ages there have been a few who, measuring and sounding the rivers of the vale at the feet of their furthest inaccessible falls, have learnt that the sources must be far higher and far inward; a few who even in the level streams have detected elements which neither the vale itself nor the surrounding mountains contained or could supply.
>
> (ch. xii, Watson: 137–8)

Coleridge's scorn for the 'common sun' which shines on 'the multitude below', and his corresponding exaltation of the 'few' who dare the 'higher ascents' translates into scorn of common language, the speech of ordinary people being as ill-adapted to transcendent vision as it is well-adapted to 'the general passions and thoughts and feelings of men'.[33]

Browning's poetic style is the product, not of a choice between these two opposed notions of poetry, but of a ceaseless and unstable conflict between them.[34] It figures in his poetry as a conflict between speech and song, associated respectively with Wordsworth and Coleridge. As 'a man speaking to men', the poet uses not just the vocabulary and syntax of common language, but its form as well, which is one reason why there are so many speakers in Browning's

33. 'A Grammarian's Funeral' takes up the theme of genius and the imagery of ascent, and is purportedly chanted by a chorus of students.

34. It is arguable that this conflict is in fact present in both Wordsworth's and Coleridge's own poetry, but this does not affect the argument here.

poetry. Speech is the medium of 'men and women' (Browning's most famous collection is not called 'ladies and gentlemen') and suggests the poet's appeal, with all the word implies of humility and fellowship, to 'the general passions and thoughts and feelings of men'. But song is the most ancient form of poetry: poets began as singers, as bards, and the figure persisted long after poetry ceased literally to be sung or chanted. By Browning's time the 'singer' was either very high and famous (the prophetic bard with his lyre) or very low and anonymous (the ballad-monger), but in either case could claim a prestige which was specifically denied to colloquial speech, the middle class of literary language. Not surprisingly, therefore, though Browning's poetry is famous for its speakers, the first poet in his work, the narrator of *Pauline*, consistently describes himself as a singer,[35] the second, Sordello, is a minstrel who sings his own compositions, and the pattern continues throughout his work. Its most potent manifestation comes towards the end of *Aristophanes' Apology* (ll. 5182–258) in a poem recited (or chanted) by Aristophanes, which is known to Browning critics by its first two words, 'Thamuris marching'.[36] Thamyris was a legendary Thracian bard who boasted that he could defeat the Muses in a singing-contest, for which they blinded him and took away his gift of song. Homer tells his story briefly in the *Iliad* (ii 594–600), and Milton also names him with honour in *Paradise Lost* (iii 35). In 'Thamuris marching', the bard is represented as advancing, confident of victory, towards his fatal contest with the Muses, through a landscape of incandescent beauty, his perception of it matched by his lyric power. The poem is written in the same *terza rima* as Shelley's *The Triumph of Life*, with a comparable intensity of vision and utterance. There is nothing like it in Browning except 'Childe Roland to the Dark Tower Came', of which it is undoubtedly, as Harold Bloom remarks, a 'conscious revision', its 'landscape of joy' a 'deliberate point-by-point reversal of Childe Roland's self-made phantasmagoria of ordeal-by-landscape' (Bloom and Munich: 144–5). But Bloom is wrong, I think, to read the poem in isolation from its context. It is true that Browning wrote it

35. See, for example, ll. 17, 77, 126, 252, 258, 376.

36. The name is more usually Thamyris; Browning's spelling of Greek names attempts a more phonetic rendering than the traditional forms; for his defence of this practice, see his Preface to the *Agamemnon* (1877).

separately and pasted it into its position in the manuscript of *Aristophanes' Apology*; but after all, that is what he did with it. Unlike the beautiful 'Spring Song' ('Dance, yellows and whites and reds') which was originally published as a separate poem and subsequently incorporated into 'Parleying with Gerard de Lairesse' (ll. 426–34), 'Thamuris marching' was never published separately, and indeed never finished as a complete poem in itself. It resembles *The Triumph of Life* not only in form and rhetorical energy, but in being a fragment; it resembles 'Childe Roland' in breaking off just before a moment of defeat which may also be read as a moment of triumph; but it resembles neither Shelley's poem nor Browning's own in being *performed* by a dramatic speaker. Aristophanes tells the story as an apologia for his *own* art, which is deliberately not that of the transcendent singer. The intensity of the verse is rhetorical in this sense: it represents Aristophanes' desire for the kind of creative power which he attributes to Thamuris, and simultaneously suggests that this power carries too high a price. A speaker enfolds and encloses the song, and the figure of the singer, in a gesture of yearning but also of renunciation. Thamuris reaches and grasps his heaven, in which the qualities of the world exchange themselves in blissful abandon:

> Say not the birds flew! they forbore their right –
> Swam, revelling onward in the roll of things.
> Say not the beasts' mirth bounded! that was flight –
>
> How could the creatures leap, no lift of wings?
> Such earth's community of purpose, such
> The ease of earth's fulfilled imaginings, –
>
> So did the near and far appear to touch
> I' the moment's transport, – that an interchange
> Of function, far with near, seemed scarce too much . . .
> (ll. 5218–26)

But it *is* too much, and this is what Aristophanes knows: he shows Thamuris attaining an unfathomably ironic immortality, struck blind and dumb in a pose of inspiration:

> Thamuris, marching, let no fancy slip
> Born of the fiery transport; lyre and song
> Were his, to smite with hand and launch from lip –

Peerless recorded, since the list grew long
Of poets (saith Homeros) free to stand
Pedestaled mid the Muses' temple-throng,

A statued service, laureled, lyre in hand,
(Ay, for we see them) – Thamuris of Thrace
Predominating foremost of the band.
(ll. 5236–44)[37]

The 'moment's transport' and the 'fiery transport' both figure the poet's daemonic energy, which expresses itself in motion ('Thamuris *marching*') and in the *mobility* of the natural world, so that fixed properties are loosened and freed, and the barriers of separate identity are dissolved. But how does Thamuris end up? His 'transport' is imaged as fixity, as ultimate stasis; with cruel wit Aristophanes says that he is 'free to stand / Pedestaled'; he epitomises the violent overthrow of poets who 'smite with hand and launch from lip'. Aristophanes concludes his recital with Thamuris's 'outburst / Of victory' (ll. 5251–2), but breaks off before he can be implicated in the terrible reply to the bard's challenge:

Here I await the end of this ado:
Which wins – Earth's poet or the Heavenly Muse. . . .

But song broke up in laughter. 'Tell the rest,
Who may! *I* have not spurned the common life,
Nor vaunted mine a lyre to match the Muse
Who sings for gods, not men! Accordingly,

37. The phrase 'foremost of the band' may well allude to Wordsworth – a poet who also marched through a good deal of landscape in his day, and who would figure here not as 'a man speaking to men' but as the exponent of what Keats called the 'egotistical sublime'. 'Foremost of the band' occurs twice in the 1850 text of *The Prelude*, which Browning certainly read: once in book x (l. 570), when Wordsworth meets a group of travellers and the 'foremost of the band' tells him the thrilling news of Robespierre's death; and once, even more significantly, in book xiv, when Wordsworth describes climbing Snowdon with a companion and their guide, 'And I, as chanced, the foremost of the band' (l. 34); the great vision of the moonlit 'sea of hoary mist' immediately follows. If Wordsworth is saved, in Browning's eyes, from Thamuris's fate (and it is not certain that he is saved) it may be because his vision is itself followed by *reflection*. But this is too complex a topic to pursue here.

> I shall not decorate her vestibule –
> Mute marble, blind the eyes and quenched the brain,
> Loose in the hand a bright, a broken lyre!
> – Not Thamuris but Aristophanes![']
>
> (ll. 5257–66)

It would be too simple to say that Browning sees himself here as Aristophanes/Wordsworth, embracing 'the common life' and its poetic language; what he has done is to stage the conflict between this Wordsworthian impulse and the transcendent or Coleridgean side of his poetry, its claim to divine origin and warrant, to special insights and privileges, its lofty attitude towards its readers. Twenty years before *Aristophanes' Apology* Browning had written to Ruskin: 'A poet's affair is with God, to whom he is accountable, and of whom is his reward; look elsewhere, and you find misery enough' (Appendix B, p. 258). After all he, too, 'sings for gods, not men'.

In writing thus to Ruskin Browning was paraphrasing the description of the poet in 'How It Strikes a Contemporary' (recently published in *Men and Women*):

> Did the man love his office? frowned our Lord,
> Exhorting when none heard – 'Beseech me not!
> Too far above my people, – beneath Me!
> I set the watch, – how should the people know?
> Forget them, keep Me all the more in mind!'
> Was some such understanding 'twixt the Two?
>
> (ll. 66–71)

The poet's 'contemporary', who claims he 'could never write a verse' (l. 114), is the speaker of the poem, one of the most 'colloquial' in Browning (in fact, it would be a good candidate for the poem least like 'Thamuris marching' in all his work). The speaker represents the poet as the reverse of poetic or even bohemian in appearance and habits, and he does this in language which implies that he, himself, is a plain man using plain speech. Yet what this plain man speaks is verse. 'How It Strikes a Contemporary' is song masked as speech; its speaker passionately affirms the poet's transcendent status and destiny, in language which apparently denies it. The speaker describes the poet as an acute observer of life in terms which have nothing Coleridgean about them:

He stood and watched the cobbler at his trade,
The man who slices lemons into drink,
The coffee-roaster's brazier, and the boys
That volunteer to help him turn its winch.
He glanced o'er books on stalls with half an eye,
And fly-leaf ballads on the vendor's string,
And broad-edge bold-print posters by the wall.
He took such cognisance of men and things,
If any beat a horse, you felt he saw;
If any cursed a woman, he took note;
Yet stared at nobody, – they stared at him,
And found, less to their pleasure than surprise,
He seemed to know them and expect as much.
(ll. 23–35)[38]

Why should the artist here be a poet rather than a novelist or a painter? The speaker's own language is as prosaic as Wordsworth could wish, devoid of a single figure of speech; the syntax, with the sole exception of line 34, is utterly plain.[39] Yet the speaker has not done with the theme of watching. At the end of the poem the poet-observer becomes the subject of the speaker's speculative gaze:

I'd like now, yet had haply been afraid,
To have just looked, when this man came to die,
And seen who lined the clean gay garret's sides
And stood about the neat low truckle-bed,
With the heavenly manner of relieving guard.
(ll. 99–103)

The poet watching 'the cobbler at his trade' has become a poet who dies watched over by angels, or by the spirits of other great poets, in a transformation of the scene of mourning in Shelley's *Adonais*; watched

38. The poet's observant eye here is both like and unlike that of Fra Lippo Lippi (see ll. 112–26) and the Roman police spy described by Sludge (ll. 519–43). The passage also uncannily foreshadows Browning's discovery of the Old Yellow Book on a market-stall in Florence (see *The Ring and the Book* i 33 ff.).

39. Even the omission of 'that' before 'If' in lines 31 and 32 and 'He' in line 35 (nominally required by 'such' in line 30) is more of a colloquial feature than a poetic device.

also by the supposedly unpoetic speaker, whose poetic imagination in fact creates this scene of triumph and transcendence.[40]

Wordsworth at Coleridge's service? The poem's colloquial style may carry a message of divine provenance, but the irony cuts both ways; the message has to be smuggled in, disguised as its opposite, because if it appeared in its own guise it would not be accepted. It might be rejected, or ridiculed, or simply not believed, as the speaker does not believe reports of the poet's hidden wealth:

> I found no truth in one report at least –
> That if you tracked him to his home, down lanes
> Beyond the Jewry, and as clean to pace,
> You found he ate his supper in a room
> Blazing with lights, four Titians on the wall,
> And twenty naked girls to change his plate!
> Poor man, he lived another kind of life
> In that new, stuccoed, third house by the bridge,
> Fresh-painted, rather smart than otherwise!
> (ll. 72–80)

In one sense the speaker misses the point here. He is wrong to find 'no truth' in the 'report', if the 'truth' be understood metaphorically; the poet may indeed conceal, beneath his respectable bourgeois exterior, just such a life of luxury and erotic excess, the life of the imagination; if you 'tracked him to his home', the place of his inner being, you might find the singer of *Pauline* who 'ne'er sung / But as one entering bright halls, where all / Will rise and shout for him' (ll. 77–9). But the poet lives his daily, visible life in the house of speech. So does Browning. What we *hear* in 'How It Strikes a Contemporary' is the speaker's urbane, worldly chat; like Molière's Monsieur Jourdain in reverse, he speaks verse without knowing it.[41]

40. Compare the poets whom Aprile sees in a vision at the point of death (*Paracelsus* ii 594–90), and the 'lost adventurers', the 'peers' whom Childe Roland similarly sees gathered to witness his death (ll. 194–201).

41. *Le Bourgeois Gentilhomme* II iv: '[M. Jourdain:] What? when I say: "Nicole, bring me my slippers, and give me my night-cap," is that prose? [Philosophy Teacher:] Yes, Sir. [M. Jourdain:] Good heavens! For more than forty years I have been speaking prose without knowing it.'

# CHAPTER 3
# *Family, friendship, fame*

## FAMILY

### Browning's family

Browning was born into a warm and supportive family, materially well-off, socially middling, emotionally stable; he received an extensive if irregular education, had the freedom to travel, and was able to choose and sustain a literary career funded by his parents until he was thirty-four years old (after which it was funded by his wife).[1] He spoke of his parents with admiration and affection; in 'Development', a poem in his final collection, *Asolando*, Robert Browning Sr appears to be an ideal father, both wise and playful; it is likely that the 'lady' of 'The Flower's Name' (*Dramatic Lyrics*, 1842), whose 'lightest footfall' is 'treasured', is a homage to his mother. Browning repeatedly emphasised to EBB both how devoted his parents were to him, and how independent of them he was: 'since I was a child I never looked for the least or greatest thing within the compass of their means to give, but given it was, – nor for liberty but it was conceded, nor for confidence but it was bestowed' (12 June 1846, Kintner: ii 775). Browning is not being quite accurate here – he had clashed with his mother in particular over his adolescent rejection of her strict Nonconformist religion, and he admitted elsewhere to EBB that he had had to fight 'many good battles' to get his parents to accept the 'absolute independence' which he enjoyed, and 'which, if I had it not, my heart would starve and die for' (16 Sept. 1845, Kelley:

1. The Brownings lived almost entirely off EBB's income (earned and unearned) until 1857, when they received a legacy of £11,000 from their friend John Kenyon. Browning did not begin to earn significant amounts of money from the sale of his books until the late 1860s. For an outline of Browning's family history, see the Chronology; the best full account in both social and psychological terms is in Maynard, especially Chapters 3 and 4.

xi 82). But of course he had a particular motive in making much of his 'liberty' to EBB; hers might be constrained by her tyrannical father, his was not: 'What earthly control can they have over me? They live here, – I go my own way, being of age and capability' (*ibid.*). He was explicit in another letter about what he called the 'involuntary contrast' which he was driven to make between the behaviour of her father and his, and he added a revealing parenthesis about his mother:

> if I went with this letter downstairs and said simply 'I want this taken to the direction to-night – and am unwell & unable to go – will you take it now?' My father would not say a word, – or rather would say a dozen cheerful absurdities about his 'wanting a walk', 'just having been wishing to go out' &c – At night he sits studying my works – illustrating them (I will bring you drawings to make you laugh) – and *yesterday* I picked up a crumpled bit of paper . . . 'his notion of what a criticism on this last number ought to be, – none, that have appeared, satisfying him!' – So judge of what he will say! – (And my mother loves me just as much more as must of necessity be –)
>
> (18 Jan 1846, Kelley: xii 2–3)[2]

Whereas Mr Barrett oppresses his children, Mr Browning is his son's servant and one-man fan club; to this we might add that for many years Browning's sister, Sarianna, was his amanuensis, making fair copies of his poems.[3] Still, the mother's love *necessarily* exceeds that of even the fondest father; Browning's relationship with his mother was so close, he told EBB, that he suffered sympathetically when she was ill, and vice versa:

> My mother continues indisposed. The connection between our ailings is no fanciful one. A few weeks ago when my medical adviser was speaking about the pain and its cause . . my mother

2. The 'last number' to which Browning refers is *Dramatic Romances and Lyrics* (recently published in November 1845), the seventh 'number' or volume of *Bells and Pomegranates*, the series in which Browning published his work between 1841 and 1846.

3. Browning later made oblique amends to Sarianna by his depiction, in *The Two Poets of Croisic*, of a clever sister who actually writes her brother's poems.

> sitting by me . . he exclaimed 'Why, has anybody to search far for a cause of whatever nervous disorder you may suffer from, when *there* sits your mother . . whom you so absolutely resemble . . I can trace every feature &c &c'
>
> (22 Aug. 1846, Kintner: ii 986)

At this point some doubts may begin to creep in about the idealisation of Browning's home. Something is not quite right about the way 'pain' and 'mother' are associated in the phrase 'the pain and its cause . . . my mother sitting by me'; and the continuation of this letter strengthens this suspicion:

> '. . I can trace every feature &c &c' To which I did *not* answer – 'And will anybody wonder that the said disorder flies away, when there sits my Ba, whom I so thoroughly adore.'
>
> Yes, there you sit, Ba!
>
> And here I kiss you, best beloved, – my very own as I am your own. (pp. 986–7)

Erotic reciprocation ('my very own as I am your own') replaces the domination of inheritance, in which 'every feature' is determined; it may also be that one kind of sexual love drives out another, the son's desire for the mother being a 'disorder'; she sits by him like a consort whose place the rival queen usurps. Browning had more than one reason for staying at home as long as he did, but it seems likely that one of the main reasons was that he could not bear to leave his mother. Nevertheless when the time came he did leave her; left her decisively and for ever (he did not see her before her death in 1849), and borrowed £100 from his father to make the trip.

There are other cracks in the picture of Browning's ideally tolerant and supportive family. Browning was cleverer than his parents, cleverer than his sister, cleverer than the minister of his local church (one of whose lengthy sermons so maddened him as a boy that he gnawed the top of his pew). In the sketch of his father which he gives in the letter just quoted, his father's intellectual subservience is manifest: he studies and illustrates his son's works, his own writing figures as a 'crumpled bit of paper'; his drawings are *amusing*. After his father's death, Browning both praised and excused him to Isa Blagden: 'So passed away this good, unworldly, kind hearted, religious man, whose powers natural & acquired would have so easily made him a notable man, had he known what vanity or ambition or the love of money or social influence meant' (McAleer 1951: 240–1). It is convenient for the famous to admire the obscure for the good qualities which have kept them in obscurity; Browning doesn't say which of the bad qualities his father lacked had motivated *him* to become a 'notable man'. Browning also associates this idea of his father being an essentially secondary figure, even a bit of a clown, with a defective taste in art; in one of his earliest letters to Elizabeth Barrett he mentions finding a print of 'Polidoro's perfect Andromeda along with "Boors Carousing by Ostade", – where I found her, – my own father's doing, or I would say more' (26 Feb. 1845, Kelley: x 99); in another letter he does say more:

> There was always a great delight to me in this prolonged relation of childhood almost . . nay, altogether – with all here. My father and I have not one taste in common, one artistic taste . . in pictures, he goes, 'souls away,' to Brauwer, Ostade, Teniers . . he would turn from the Sistine Altar piece to these, – in music he desiderates a tune 'that has a story connected with it,' whether Charles II's favorite dance of 'Brose and butter' or . . no matter, – what I mean is, that the sympathy has not been an intellectual one . . (13 Aug. 1846, Kintner: ii 960)

The 'prolonged relation of childhood' emphatically does not include what we often think of as one of its main features, namely the subordination of the child's intellect and judgement to those of its parents. What Browning means is that he continued to be cherished and provided for, like a giant nestling, while claiming to soar as he pleased in skies beyond his parents' scope. 'I have been accustomed,' he went on in this letter, 'by pure choice, to have another will lead mine in the little daily matters of life'; the life of the mind was another matter. Browning's passionate attachment to his home did not in the slightest preclude his sense of himself as an alien figure there: he left home in the sense of intellectual emancipation long before he left for Italy with EBB. How, then, does the family figure in his poetry?

## The family in Browning

A young man contemplates suicide through the length of the night, a dark night of the soul; then he realises that the dawn has come, it is Sunday, and from his window he can see people going to church:

One walked between his wife and child,
With measured footfall firm and mild,
And now and then he gravely smiled.

The prudent partner of his blood
Leaned on him, faithful, gentle, good,
Wearing the rose of womanhood.

And in their double love secure,
The little maiden walked demure,
Pacing with downward eyelids pure.

These three made unity so sweet,
My frozen heart began to beat,
Remembering its ancient heat.

Whatever you might think of these lines, one thing is immediately obvious: they couldn't possibly be by Browning; not unless they were surrounded by some blackly comic irony, such as the fact that, unbeknownst to the speaker, the grave smiler has a knife under his cloak, the prudent partner is having an affair with the vicar, and both are planning to sell the little maiden to the white slave trade. In Tennyson's poem ('The Two Voices', published in 1842) it never occurs to the speaker that what he sees from the window may not be the truth; such an idea has no weight in the poem's design. On the other hand, the scene is a powerful emblem of what he desires; there is irony in the poem after all, but it is not located where Browning would locate it. It is not *dramatic* irony, but part of the representation of a complex psychological state.

Here is a scene from *The Ring and the Book* with figures similar in some respects to those in 'The Two Voices': it begins with a young mother fondly discussing her new-born baby with her doting parents:

Six days ago when it was New Year's-day,
We bent above the fire and talked of him,
What he should do when he was grown and great.
Violante, Pietro, each had given the arm
I leant on, to walk by, from couch to chair
And fireside, – laughed, as I lay safe at last,
'Pompilia's march from bed to board is made,
Pompilia back again and with a babe,
Shall one day lend his arm and help her walk!'
Then we all wished each other more New Years.

. . .
Oh what a happy friendly eve was that!
And, next day, about noon, out Pietro went –
He was so happy and would talk so much,
Until Violante pushed and laughed him forth
Sight-seeing in the cold, – 'So much to see
I' the churches! Swathe your throat three times!' she cried,
'And, above all, beware the slippery ways,
And bring us all the news by supper-time!'
He came back late, laid by cloak, staff and hat,
Powdered so thick with snow it made us laugh,
Rolled a great log upon the ash o' the hearth,
And bade Violante treat us to a flask,
Because he had obeyed her faithfully,
Gone sight-see through the seven, and found no church
To his mind like San Giovianni – 'There's the fold,
And all the sheep together, big as cats!
And such a shepherd, half the size of life,
Starts up and hears the angel' . . .

(*The Ring and the Book* vii 220–9, 249–66)

A string of keywords denote the values of home and family: *New Year's-day*, *couch*, *chair*, *fireside*, *safe*, *babe*, *happy*, *friendly*, *laughed*, *supper-time*, *hearth*, *flask*, *faithfully*. The scene has the artful simplicity of a genre painting, a tender domestic interior, lit by the fire and with the figures grouped in 'natural' poses. The parents support their child, whose own child in turn will one day support her: the family thus projects itself into the future. The warmth and safety of the interior contrast strongly with the hostile 'cold' and 'slippery ways' of the outside world, which must nevertheless be confronted. But its negative or threatening elements are countered both by laughter ('pushed and laughed him forth / Sight-seeing in the cold . . . Powdered so thick with snow it made us laugh') and by the mock-adventure of Pietro's journey and safe return. Pietro goes *out* to visit the local churches and report on their Christmas decorations; he goes *in* to the churches; what he sees is the representation of an *outdoor* scene (the angel appearing to the shepherds); yet what this scene suggests is the domestic security from which he has come and to which he will return: 'There's the fold, / And all the sheep together, big as cats!' A religious image crowns and validates the image of secular comfort and contentment; you might expect the angel to announce 'God's in his heaven – / All's right with the world!'

But just as Pippa sings these words outside a house of murder and adultery, so the scene in *The Ring and the Book* is an ironic confection: Pompilia is speaking from her death-bed, projecting a simulacrum of happiness which is not only about to be shattered but fake in some of its essential parts. Pietro and Violante are not Pompilia's parents; the childless Violante bought Pompilia from a prostitute and passed her off as her own, and not out of maternal sentiment either: she and Pietro needed an heir to secure a property in which Pietro had otherwise only a life-interest. Sold by her natural mother, Pompilia was then sold a second time by Violante, who married her to Count Guido Franceschini at the age of thirteen; when the parents fell out with their son-in-law, they revealed the secret of their daughter's birth, and sued Guido for the return of the dowry! Pompilia's 'babe' is of disputed parentage (either the legitimate child of the loathsome Guido, or the fruit of an adulterous liaison with the handsome priest Caponsacchi) and is not, in any case, in the house at all, but in hiding, taken away from his mother 'two days after he was born . . . for fear his foe should find' (ll. 46–8). There is even a nightmarish twist to the image of the shepherd and the angel:

> 'And such a shepherd, half the size of life,
> Starts up and hears the angel' – when, at the door,
> A tap: we started up: you know the rest.
> (ll. 265–7)

The tap at the door is Guido's, come with his accomplices to murder Pompilia and her putative parents; they are wolves in shepherd's clothing. Though in Guido's case there are additional motives of sexual hatred and revenge, the root cause is again money: by murdering his wife and parents-in-law, and subsequently taking custody of the child, Guido hopes to secure all the property in the case at one fell swoop.

Greed, social climbing, lust, and violence are the frame of Pompilia's family life. When Guido takes her to his family home in Arezzo, she finds a *ménage* which the Pope describes as a den of evil creatures, 'Huddling together in the cave they call / Their palace . . . All alike coloured, all descried akin / By one and the same pitchy furnace' (x 870–1, 876–7). Guido's mother, 'The gaunt grey nightmare in the furthest smoke' (l. 910), is especially stigmatised: 'Unmotherly mother and unwomanly / Woman, that near turns motherhood to shame, / Womanlinesss to loathing' (ll. 912–14). The Gothic extremity of the Pope's language may be suspect, but this is only one of the ways in which Guido's home life in Arezzo is depicted. Several speakers in the poem, including Guido himself, comment on the demeaning shifts to which the impoverished nobleman was reduced in order to keep up appearances, and one of Guido's fiercest resentments against Pietro and Violante was their broadcasting of the shameful and ridiculous details of his penny-pinching lifestyle, 'The petty nothings we bear privately / But break down under when fools flock around' (iv 644–5). Life in Arezzo was not just a nightmare, but a nightmare in reduced circumstances.

Pompilia's family is a fraud, and Guido's is melodramatically dysfunctional; but Browning doesn't stop there. 'Normal' family life is the subject of one of the poem's most satirical depictions, that of the lawyer Archangelis, Guido's defence counsel:

> The jolly learned man of middle age,
> Cheek and jowl all in laps with fat and law,
> Mirthful as mighty, yet, as great hearts use,
> Despite the name and fame that tempt our flesh,
> Constant to that devotion of the hearth,
> Still captive in those dear domestic ties!
> (i 1131–6)

Archangelis himself puts the case for 'those dear domestic ties' in ways which Browning presumably intended to make many of his middle class readers shift uncomfortably in their seats:

> Let others climb the heights o' the court, the camp!
> How vain are chambering and wantonness,
> Revel and rout and pleasures that make mad!
> Commend me to home-joy, the family board,
> Altar and hearth! These, with a brisk career,
> A source of honest profit and good fame,
> Just so much work as keeps the brain from rust,
> Just so much play as lets the heart expand,
> Honouring God and serving man, – I say,
> These are reality, and all else, – fluff,
> Nutshell and naught, – Thank Flaccus for the phrase!
> (viii 48–58)[4]

4. 'Flaccus' is a common term for the Roman poet Horace (Quintus

Behind this home-loving respectability is a selfishness as predatory, soulless, and cynical as Guido's; the dominant note in Archangelis's monologue is greed, the dominant imagery that of food and appetite. The murder trial itself is a 'crusty case' which he is going to 'triturate full soon / To smooth Papinianian pulp' (ll. 12–14);[5] but it is Guido whom the fat, jovial Archangelis devours, just as surely as Mr Vholes, the cadaverous and vampiric lawyer in *Bleak House*, devours his client Richard Carstone, all for the sake of his three daughters and his father who is 'dependent on him in the Vale of Taunton'.[6] Archangelis is particularly castigated for his son-worship – unlike Pompilia, who utters the most soaring and lyrical sentiments about her child without any implication of irony. But then, Pompilia's maternal passion is almost wholly idealised, since she dies three weeks after giving birth to her son and had only had physical possession of him for two days. Little Giacinto, on the other hand, is a thoroughly socialised individual, his father's namesake, prospective partner and successor, a smart lad who knows his Latin and can crack a joke at Guido's execution (xii 333–56).[7] Archangelis drafts his defence of Guido on

---

Horatius Flaccus); he is presumably invoked as the apostle of moderation, the 'golden mean' of *Odes* II x. But the actual quotation is from *Satires* II v and has a very different connotation: it is a satire on legacy-hunting, in which the con-man is advised to befriend old rich suitors in the law-courts with the words: 'I know the mazes of the law; I can defend a case. I will let anyone pluck out my eyes sooner than have him scorn you or rob you of a nutshell. This is my concern, that you lose nothing, and become not a jest' (ll. 34–7). Needless to say this applies to Archangelis's exploitation of his client.

5. 'Triturate' means grind (here, chew); Archangelis means that he is going to resolve the difficult aspects of Guido's defence with the skill of Papinianus, one of the most famous jurists of imperial Rome.

6. See ch. xxxix, where the motif of cannibalism is explicitly evoked: reform of the law is opposed on the grounds that it would put 'respectable' lawyers like Vholes out of busines, 'As though, Mr. Vholes and his relations being minor cannibal chiefs, and it being proposed to abolish cannibalism, indignant champions were to put the case thus: Make man-eating unlawful, and you starve the Vholeses!'

7. In some disturbing ways the relationship between father and son, particularly the father's anxious pride at his son's scholarly attainments, reminds you of Browning's relationship with his own son, also named

his son's birthday, and throughout his monologue he looks forward to the 'yearly lovesome frolic feast' (viii 20) which will reward his day's work; and part of the entertainment will be to see little Giacinto play his father:

> Rogue Hyacinth shall put on paper toque,
> And wrap himself around with mamma's veil
> Done up to imitate papa's black robe . . .
> And call himself the Advocate o' the Poor,
> Mimic Don father that defends the Count,
> And for reward shall have a small full glass
> Of manly red rosolio to himself . . .
> (ll. 1752–60)

The red wine is figuratively Guido's blood, which Archangelis imbibes with professional relish. His love for his son consumes every other human or humane feeling; in the end it is as perverse a form of self-love as any that Guido displays.

Guido himself makes great play of his desire to be reunited with his son – in his first monologue, that is, when he is still fighting for his life in court. 'Give me – for last, best gift, my son again,' he snivels;[8] if he is released, he and his son will 'Go forward, face new times, the better day' (v 2026, 2036). You can imagine Archangelis suggesting this as the line to take. But in his second monologue, in his death cell, Guido gives the lie to Archangelis's sentiment. Even if he did get out alive, he remarks, he would have little to look forward to: 'How sad and sapless were the years to come . . . Where's my second chance?' (xi 1820, 1844). Then he remembers the child:

> Ay, but the babe . . . I had forgot my son,
> My heir! Now for a burst of gratitude! . . .

---

after himself. In book xii we are told that Gaetano, Pompilia's child, has been lost sight of: he is given the ambiguous, open-ended fate of a Romantic orphan, like Pippa; the fate of little Giacinto, like that of Robert Wiedemann Barrett Browning (his name encloses those of Browning's wife and mother) is pre-eminently worldly.

8. For a wife-murderer this is an injudicious choice of phrase, because 'Heaven's last best gift', according to Adam in *Paradise Lost*, was Eve (v 19).

Old, I renew my youth in him, and poor
Possess a treasure, – is not that the phrase?
Only I must wait patient twenty years –
Nourishing all the while, as father ought,
The excrescence with my daily blood of life.
(ll. 1845–53)

Guido's universe is bounded by self: he cannot conceive of his son as his own flesh and blood except in the sinister sense of a devouring parasite. The idea of replicating himself in his son has no meaning for him, since it will not be literal; *he, himself* will not be renewed, but drained of life. Guido then imagines two possible outcomes of this process: in one the son will prove himself worthy of the father, and will therefore ironically displace him:

Why, here's my son and heir in evidence,
Who stronger, wiser, handsomer than I
By fifty years, relieves me of each load, –
Tames my hot horse, carries my heavy gun,
Courts my coy mistress . . .
(ll. 1856–60)

Not surprisingly, what the son usurps is specifically the father's masculine energy, figured as the ability to master horses, guns and women. But even this is preferable to the second possible outcome, which is that the son will prove *incapable* of truly succeeding the father, so that all the father's effort of nourishing him with his 'daily blood of life' will have been for nothing:

But grant the medium measure of a man,
The usual compromise 'twixt fool and sage,
– You know – the tolerably-obstinate,
The not-so-much-perverse but you may train,
The true son-servant that, when parent bids
'Go work, son, in my vineyard!' makes reply
'I go, Sir!' – Why, what profit in your son
Beyond the drudges you might subsidize,
Have the same work from at a paul the head?
(ll. 1877–85)[9]

9. A paul is an Italian coin of very small value.

Guido has muddled his biblical quotation: the 'true son-servant' (in Matthew xxi 28–32) is not the one who *says* 'I go, sir', and who then doesn't, but the one who says 'I will not', and who then does. Since Guido has been saying one thing and doing another all his life, the slip is typical of him, but what is equally typical is his literal reading of the son as servant. Either the son will master the father, or the father will master the son; but in the latter case, the bond of obedience will be *no more than* that between an employer and his 'drudges'. Jesus's parable of the son who does his father's will has not only been inverted, but emptied of love.

The family in *The Ring and the Book*, then, is a site of deceit, corruption, violence, and greed; marital, parental, and filial relationships are endorsed only when they are figurative, as in the 'marriage' of Pompilia and Caponsacchi, or the Pope's spiritual adoption of Pompilia as his daughter.[10] How typical a view is this in Browning's poetry as a whole? Thoroughly, is the answer. Family life gets a poor showing in Browning's work from its earliest period. In *Sordello* the family is Mafia-like, exacting loyalty and causing tragic conflict; the young Sordello encounters the ancestral line of the Ecelins in an ominous Gothic tapestry:

> see him lurk
> ('Tis winter with its sullenest of storms)
> Beside that arras-length of broidered forms
> On tiptoe, lifting in both hands a light
> Which makes yon warrior's visage flutter bright
> – Ecelo, dismal father of the brood,
> And Ecelin, close to the girl he wooed
> – Auria, and their Child, with all his wives
> From Agnes to the Tuscan that survives,
> Lady of the castle, Adelaide . . .
>
> (i 452–61)

The generations are at war, as the old gangster Ecelin II tells his consigliere, Taurello Salinguerra:

10. For another instance of surrogacy, linked with the idea of escape from the family, see the discussion of 'Italy in England' below, pp. 94–8. Surrogacy is not always a good thing, however: in 'The Confessional', the speaker pointedly refers to the priest who betrays her as 'the father'.

> God help me! for I catch
> My children's greedy sparkling eyes at watch –
> He bears that double breastplate on, they say,
> So many minutes less than yesterday!
> (ii 875–8)

This is the same look that the Bishop of St Praxed's catches in the eyes of the 'nephews' gathered around his deathbed, who 'hope / To revel down my villas', whose 'eyes . . . glitter like your mother's for my soul', and who have 'stabb'd me with ingratitude' (ll. 64–5, 104–5, 111). The *dénouement* of the plot of *Sordello* hinges on the discovery that Sordello is Taurello's long-lost son, but this is no fairy-tale ending; on the contrary, the opportunity offered to Sordello (which involves both reunion with a kingly father and marriage to a princess) is simultaneously a satanic temptation to abandon his political beliefs and collude in the founding of a tyrannical dynasty. Sordello rejects his sonship and dies in an apotheosis of neo-adolescent rebellion: he too stabs Taurello with ingratitude, though he is right to do so. In *Pippa Passes* another Italian Bishop candidly reflects on his own family history to Maffeo, the wicked Intendant who is trying to blackmail him by threatening to reveal the skeletons in the family cupboard:

> Maffeo, my family is the oldest in Messina, and century after century have my progenitors gone on polluting themselves with every wickedness under Heaven: my own father . . . rest his soul! – I have, I know, a chapel to support that it may: my dear two dead brothers were, – what you know tolerably well: I, the youngest, might have rivalled them in vice, if not in wealth, but from my boyhood I came out from among them, and so am not partaker of their plagues. (iv 98–105)

It is perhaps a little unrealistic of the Bishop to portray his escape from his polluted family in these terms; after all, there is a long tradition in such families of making one of the sons a priest precisely so that he can support a chapel for the souls of the others. Moreover, the Bishop's duel with the wicked Intendant doesn't end on this high-minded note: the Bishop has enough of the gangster left in him to be tempted by the Intendant's bribe and to make it necessary for him, too, to be redeemed by Pippa's song.[11] 'Coming out from among them'

11. This is much clearer in the first edition, where the Bishop replies explicitly to the Intendant's offer to get rid of Pippa: see Woolford and Karlin: ii 98 (ll. 210–11 and notes).

is a feature of Browning's heroes, but so is 'partaking of their plagues'. Fra Lippo Lippi has escaped from the street where he starved as a child, but his art and language are street-wise and his appetites are undiminished; the critics who disparage his painting are in a direct line of descent from his 'Aunt Lapaccia' who 'trussed [him] with one hand' and dragged him off 'By the straight cut to the convent' to make a monk of him (ll. 88–91). Andrea del Sarto has 'come out from among' his family not in a morally good sense but in quite the opposite:

> My father and my mother died of want.
> Well, had I riches of my own? you see
> How one gets rich! Let each one bear his lot.
> They were born poor, lived poor, and poor they died:
> And I have laboured somewhat in my time
> And not been paid profusely. Some good son
> Paint my two hundred pictures – let him try!
> (ll. 249–55)

Andrea manages, with characteristic ingenuity, both to despise his parents for their lack of get-up-and-go and to pity himself for not having made more out of his Romantic flight from his origins. Yet these origins ('del Sarto' means 'tailor's son') persist in his workshop aesthetic: Andrea has 'laboured' to produce his 'two hundred pictures', and the sweat and quantity matter (as they do also to Browning: 'There they are, my fifty men and women', he tells his wife; in this as in many other ways 'One Word More' is the 'answer' to 'Andrea del Sarto'). It is no accident that earlier in the poem Andrea draws on a painting with a piece of chalk, which both tailors and painters use (l. 195); in the desperate bargains he strikes with Lucrezia he is a tragic and ridiculous cuckold, but also a tradesman:

> To-morrow, satisfy your friend.
> I take the subjects for his corridor,
> Finish the portrait out of hand – there, there,
> And throw him in another thing or two
> If he demurs; the whole should prove enough
> To pay for this same Cousin's freak. Beside,
> What's better and what's all I care about,
> Get you the thirteen scudi for the ruff.
> (ll. 233–40)

Of course Lucrezia's lover is her cousin; poor Andrea's troubles are all in the family. (But cousins are like that, in Browning; several of his sexual intrigues feature them.[12]) Families are hard to get away from: the lovers in 'In a Gondola' drift along, indulging fantasies of escape 'farther than friends can pursue' (l. 65),[13] and lamenting 'Must we, must we *Home*?' (l. 125); all the time they are being tracked by the sinister 'Three' (probably the woman's husband and brothers, though the relationships are never precisely stated) who catch up with them at the end. The excuse which the 'heroine' of 'The Statue and the Bust' makes to herself for not eloping with her lover is doubly a sign of weakness:

> 'I fly to the Duke who loves me well,
> Sit by his side and laugh at sorrow
> Ere I count another ave-bell.
>
> ''Tis only the coat of a page to borrow,
> And tie my hair in a horse-boy's trim,
> And I save my soul – but not to-morrow' –
>
> (She checked herself and her eye grew dim) –
> 'My father tarries to bless my state:
> I must keep it one day more for him.[']
> (ll. 70–78)

12. The cousin-as-lover reappears in book ii of *The Ring and the Book*, whose speaker, 'Half-Rome', addresses an interlocutor whose cousin is making advances to his (Half-Rome's) wife; in the same poem, jolly Canon Conti, who points out Pompilia to Caponsacchi at the theatre, is Guido's cousin: 'Is not she fair? 'T is my new cousin,' said he: / The fellow lurking there i' the black o' the box / Is Guido, the old scapegrace: she's his wife, / Married three years since: how his Countship sulks!' (vi 413–16). In 'Count Gismond' the speaker is an orphan (rather a self-pitying and self-serving one) whose wicked cousins, jealous of her beauty, plot her downfall by getting Count Gaulthier to accuse her of unchastity. 'In a Balcony' has a love-triangle of the Queen, her cousin Constance, and Norbert; the young man in *The Inn Album* is engaged to his cousin, who is the friend of an older woman with whom he is infatuated.

13. 'Friends' means 'family, relatives', a connotation still active in 1842, when the poem was written; Browning uses the term in a letter to EBB about her own family's possible objections to their marriage: 'For your friends . . . whatever can be "got over," whatever opposition may be rational, will be easily removed, I suppose' (23 Oct. 1845, Kelley: xi 135).

Her eye grows dim with sentiment, but also with moral blindness, the inability to perceive truly and act on that perception: 'I fly to the Duke who loves me well.' Tears for her father mean that she will never 'laugh at sorrow'. (Let's not waste ours on the old boy: like the Count in 'My Last Duchess', he is selling his daughter into a loveless marriage.)

This example prompts the question of whether the bad family in Browning is to be identified with patriarchy. We need to distinguish here between the depiction in stories of bad fathers, and an ideological assault on the principle of fatherhood itself, with its connotations of social privilege and authority. In *Sordello* Taurello lays his 'iron arms' on his new-found son's 'shrinking shoulders' (*Sordello* v 863–4); but his oppressive love might be countered by that of the affectionate, nurturing, playful father in 'Development'. Neither of these examples carries a general symbolic import. Browning does express dislike of some aspects of patriarchy (in the feminist sense): for example the 'execrable policy of the world's husbands, fathers, brothers, and domineerers in general', as he put it in a letter to Elizabeth Barrett (4 Sept. 1846, Kintner: ii 1044), meaning in this instance the policy of cultivating female docility. Women resist men and behave violently in his work and are admired for it: Pompilia attacks Guido with his own sword in *The Ring and the Book*, and Beatrice Signorini, in the poem of that name, rips to shreds the painting in which her husband commemorates an infidelity he dared not actually commit. But both of these examples are heavily qualified by context; Pompilia herself draws attention to the exceptional nature of her action (vii 1591 ff). The argument between Balaustion and Aristophanes in *Aristophanes' Apology* could be viewed as an argument between a feminist and a male chauvinist, but the positions of both are so riven with contradictions as to make such a reductive interpretation practically untenable. Little in Browning's work suggests that he had the kind of doubts about fatherhood articulated in, say, his wife's poem *Aurora Leigh*; men have no monopoly of power within the family, which may rest with women (and in some cases with children); what counts is that the exercise of such power is almost always malevolent.

The oppressive family is associated in Browning with other institutions and collectives, other structures of authority – social, political, religious, artistic – which limit or actively suppress individual freedom, creativity, and sexual passion. The family is like the 'world' in the wonderful short poem 'Respectability', the 'sponsor' of 'plighted troth' and the enemy of 'warmth and light and bliss', and the world is such a family, the abode of constraint, hypocrisy, and censorship, as it is in *Paracelsus*, 'Fra Lippo Lippi', 'Youth and Art' and many other poems. Escape from the family's worldliness, and the world's familial plot, becomes paramount in Browning's art and takes multiple imaginative forms, from literal escape (the Duchess in 'The Flight of the Duchess') to symbolic rejection and the embrace of death (by Sordello and, arguably, by Pompilia). In *Paracelsus* we meet the hero as adolescent genius, rejecting his 'friends' Festus and Michal – Betty Miller is surely right to see their names as substitutes for those of Father and Mother (Miller: 4) – rejecting his teachers, rejecting wholesale the wisdom of the past; the tradition of knowledge itself is like a stifling home which the impatient teenager can't wait to leave. The same impatient figure 'bursts out' of the little chapel 'Into the fresh night-air again' at the opening of *Christmas Eve* (though he will find his way back in the end); he becomes visible, too, in 'England in Italy', whose speaker leaves behind, literally and symbolically, the family with whom he is lodging near Sorrento in order to ascend a mountain and experience a transcendent vision.

In order to illustrate in detail this preoccupation with escape from the family I want to look closely at an episode of *Pippa Passes* and at 'Italy in England', both of which concern Italian revolutionary politics. In the introductory section of *Pippa Passes* Pippa yearns for different kinds of love, arranged on an ascending scale: mere physical passion is the lowest kind, sexual love fully realised in marriage is better, parental love even better than that, and religious love best of all.[14] Parental love ranks high because, Pippa believes, it 'lap[s you] round from the beginning; / As little fear of losing it as winning' (*Intro*. 128–9). The example of filial bliss which Pippa cites is that of a youth, Luigi, and his mother, whom she has noticed 'communing' regularly towards evening in a little turret on the outskirts of Asolo. The orphaned Pippa associates this relationship with erotic and fertile nature, 'each to each imparting sweet intents . . . as brooding bird to bird' (ll. 134–5), and imagines herself as happy as Luigi must be, 'cared about, kept out of harm / And schemed for, safe in love as with a charm' (ll. 136–7).

14. For a detailed study of this scale of love, see the first section of Chapter 4 (pp. 116–18).

The words 'schemed' and 'charm', however, carry possible negative meanings, and when we actually meet Luigi and his mother in part iii of the drama these negative meanings become fully apparent. Far from 'communing', Luigi and his mother are quarrelling, and over a very traditional topic of dispute between parents and children, namely politics. Admittedly the topic takes a rather melodramatic form, since Luigi, an ardent supporter of Italian liberation from the Austro-Hungarian Empire, plans to assassinate the Austrian emperor, and his mother is trying to persuade him not to. She tries first by argument: questioning the justification for extreme action, casting aspersions on the revolutionary leaders who have inspired Luigi to do the deed but haven't the courage to undertake it themselves, drawing attention to the practical difficulties of killing a well-protected ruler, and pointing out that he has little chance of escaping alive. Luigi has a satisfactory answer to all these points (satisfactory to himself, at any rate), trumping his mother's fear for his safety by declaring that he *intends* to die, since he has already lived life to the full (if it were possible to kick a fictional character in the backside, Luigi would be a leading candidate, though even he can't quite match the sculptor Jules, in part ii of the drama, for priggish self-regard). Whatever we may think of Luigi, however, as far as the argument goes the drama endorses him: as we point out in Chapter 5, this is one of a number of works in which Browning clearly supports the assassination of tyrants. At the same time there is something ill-minded about Luigi's exalted, lyrical determination to become a killer and die himself. He knows that his mother thinks he is mad; his idea of murder and self-sacrifice is bound up with a strained, super-refined aestheticism:

> I can give news of earth to all the dead
> Who ask me: – last year's sunsets and great stars
> That had a right to come first and see ebb
> The crimson wave that drifts the sun away –
> Those crescent moons with notched and burning rims
> That strengthened into sharp fire and there stood
> Impatient of the azure – and that day
> In March a double rainbow stopped the storm –
> May's warm, slow, yellow moonlit summer nights –
> Gone are they – but I have them in my soul!
>   *Mother*. (He will not go!)
>   *Luigi*. You smile at me – I know
> Voluptuousness, grotesqueness, ghastliness

Environ my devotedness as quaintly
As round about some antique altar wreathe
The rose festoons, goats' horns, and oxen's skulls.
(iii 73–87)

In the image of the 'crimson wave that drifts the sun away' (one of Browning's most accurate pastiches of Shelley) Luigi figures both his deed and his fate: royal power ebbs on a tide of blood, but the 'sun' of kingship is also the 'son' whose life will be so langorously given.[15] Luigi's Romantic enthusiasm for death is disturbing, but even more disturbing is his neo-Romantic knowingness: the way he reads his own behaviour through a further symbol, matching the terms with an obsessive concern for precision: voluptuousness with roses, grotesqueness with goats' horns, ghastliness with oxen's skulls. In fact Luigi's mother's smile, and her aside, do not mean what Luigi thinks: she believes that his language is a sign of unreality, of make-believe, and that his enterprise will remain a fantasy. Mother and son, whom Pippa believes to be 'communing' so intimately, are at extreme opposite points, each discreditably blind to the other. Nevertheless Luigi's mother nearly succeeds in tempting him to stay by playing the sex card:

*Mother.* Why go to-night?
Morn's for adventure. Jupiter is now
A morning-star . . . I cannot hear you, Luigi!
*Luigi.* 'I am the bright and morning-star,' God saith –
And, 'such an one I give the morning-star!'
The gift of the morning-star – have I God's gift
Of the morning-star?
*Mother.* Chiara will love to see
That Jupiter an evening-star next June.
*Luigi.* True, mother. Well for those who live June over.
Great noontides – thunder storms – all glaring pomps
Which triumph at the heels of June the God
Leading his revel thro' our leafy world.
Yes, Chiara will be here –
*Mother.* In June – remember
Yourself appointed that month for her coming –

15. The cadence of the line recalls that of a line in 'My Last Duchess', also connecting sunset and declining power: 'The dropping of the daylight in the West' (l. 26).

*Luigi.* Was that low noise the echo?
*Mother.* The night-wind.
She must be grown – with her blue eyes upturned
As if life were one long and sweet surprise –
In June she comes.
*Luigi.* We are to see together
The Titian at Treviso – there again!

[*Without* ] A King lived long ago,
In the morning of the world . . .

(iii 144–64)

The passage resonates to a clash of symbols. Luigi's mother speaks of the planet Jupiter, the royal planet; when Jupiter becomes an evening star it will be associated with 'June the God', a pagan deity of power and pleasure, or 'glaring pomps' and 'revel'; like Milton's Comus, June offers sexual pleasure in the 'leafy world' of physical sensation. Luigi desires Chiara, whose name means 'bright', but he also sees himself as 'the bright and morning-star'.This image is from *Revelation*, and refers to Jesus: 'I am the root and the offspring of David, and the bright and morning star' (xxii 16). The saviour is self-authored: Jesus, son of God, is also God the father; Luigi, too, would like to be both root and offspring. No wonder that he and Chiara were going to see the 'Titian at Treviso': Titian symbolised luxuriant sexuality for Browning,[16] but this particular Titian also speaks of mother-love, since it is a fresco of the Annunciation (the moment at which the son authors himself). The voice from 'without', that is, from outside, is that of Pippa, who 'passes' at this precise moment singing her song, a song which begins with an image of 'the morning of the world': morning rescues Luigi from evening and from his mother, who was offering Chiara to him like a pimp ('She must be grown . . .'). Yet the rescue is ambivalent,

16. See, for example, Browning's second letter to EBB in which he praises 'Titian's Naples Magdalen' for 'that heap of [golden] hair in her hands' (13 Jan. 1845, Kelley: x 22); in his poetry, see 'Any Wife to Any Husband' ll. 77–8, and especially Guido in *The Ring and the Book*: 'Give me my gorge of colour, glut of gold / In a glory round the Virgin made for me! / Titian's the man, not Monk Angelico . . .' (xi 2117–19). Titian is also associated with paintings of the pagan god Jupiter's amorous adventures, in 'Filippo Baldinucci on the Privilege of Burial', ll. 397–403.

like the others which follow Pippa's passing in the other scenes of the drama. Luigi rushes off after Pippa's song, leaving his mother literally speechless (the scene closes without her saying another word); in a sense he has borrowed Pippa's voice to shut her up. Pippa's song, which tells of a mythological utopia, fittingly prompts Luigi to take flight, to escape the 'leafy world' and pre-empt his sexual nature. Anything, even his fantasy of pure murder and ideal justice, is better than staying at home with mother.

Like Luigi, the speaker of 'Italy in England' (later called 'The Italian in England', and first published in *Dramatic Romances and Lyrics*, 1845) is an Italian nationalist; when the poem opens he is in exile in England, telling a group of fellow patriots the story of his escape from the Austrians. His monologue is a distraction from the 'business' of the meeting, as the speaker apologetically remarks at the end of the poem; as with so many of Browning's characters, he is compulsively revisiting a particular memory, a 'spot of time' to use Wordsworth's phrase, a site of repressed (but irrepressible) feeling.

The speaker begins his story by relating how, on the run from the Austrian authorities, he hid in a ruin which had been a haunt of his childhood:

> I made six days a hiding-place
> Of that dry green old aqueduct
> Where I and Charles, when boys, have plucked
> The fire-flies from the roof above,
> Bright creeping thro' the moss they love.
> – How long it seems since Charles was lost!
>
> (ll. 6–11)

Childhood's pastoral innocence is 'lost' because Charles has become a traitor to the nationalist cause; the aqueduct is 'dry' in more senses than one, and can offer the speaker no permanent shelter; in l. 17 it is a 'recess', where he lies thinking of 'Charles's miserable end', by l. 41 it has become a 'crypt', a place of death.[17] Driven out by hunger, the speaker risks asking a peasant woman for help, and at first thinks of concocting a story which would disguise his real identity:

17. Compare the 'maple-panelled room' in the castle of Goito in *Sordello*, also described as a 'crypt'; Sordello's mother is buried there, and he himself will be laid in her 'font-tomb' (i 389–442, v 773–7, vi 629–31). For further comment on the speaker's friendship with Charles, see p. 99.

I had devised a certain tale
Which, when 'twas told her, could not fail
Persuade a peasant of its truth;
This hiding was a freak of youth;
I meant to give her hopes of pay,
And no temptation to betray.
But when I saw that woman's face,
Its calm simplicity of grace,
Our Italy's own attitude
In which she walked thus far, and stood,
Planting each naked foot so firm,
To crush the snake and spare the worm –
At first sight of her eyes, I said,
'I am that person on whose head
'They fix the price because I hate
'The Austrians over us . . .'
(ll. 51–66)

Instead of condescending to the woman as an ignorant and venal peasant, the speaker idealises her as a statuesque emblem of Italy itself, as Britannia represents Great Britain. The woman is also associated with Eve, the general mother, and with the Virgin Mary. In *Genesis*, God curses the serpent who tempts Eve and says: 'I will put enmity between thee and the woman, and between thy seed and her seed; it shall bruise thy head, and thou shalt bruise his heel' (iii 15); in Christian tradition the serpent is identified with the devil and the curse is fulfilled when, as Milton puts it, 'Jesus son of Mary second Eve, / Saw Satan fall like lightning . . . Whom he shall tread at last under our feet' (*Paradise Lost* x 183–90). The speaker refuses to be the serpent who offers this Eve any 'temptation to betray', and he also refuses to speak to her as a sexual being, though sexual desire is implicit in everything he says about her. After he has instructed her on how to get a message to the underground network which will help him to escape, he says:

'Then come back happy we have done
'Our mother service – I, the son,
'As you the daughter of our land!'
(ll. 85–7)

While waiting for his escape to be arranged, the speaker continues to hide in the aqueduct, where the woman visits him and talks to him about herself:

we conferred
Of her own prospects, and I heard
She had a lover – stout and tall,
She said – then let her eyelids fall,
'He could do much' – as if some doubt
Entered her heart, – then, passing out,
'She could not speak for others – who
Had other thoughts; herself she knew:'
And so she brought me drink and food.
(ll. 91–9)

Poor Giovanni (let's call him)! – handsome, perhaps, but with no revolutionary fire in his belly; and, as the French proverb says, 'the absent are always in the wrong'. His potency – 'He could do much' – is devalued by his evidently doing nothing; she turns from him to nourish another man. The speaker, who cannot admit his own desire, must denigrate its appearance in another and transmute it, in himself, to a feeling of brotherly solidarity. At the moment of parting, he is impelled to kiss her, to touch her, but kiss and touch are not allowed a sexual meaning:

at last arrived
The help my Paduan friends contrived
To furnish me: she brought the news:
For the first time I could not choose
But kiss her hand and lay my own
Upon her head – 'This faith was shown
'To Italy, our mother; – she
'Uses my hand and blesses thee!'
She followed down to the sea-shore;
I left and never saw her more.
(ll. 101–10)

The speaker and the woman he loves are both members of a family constituted by a figure of speech: Italy, their 'mother', will not behave as Luigi's mother behaves, but will always foster and bless them; the price for this, however, is the severance of connection with any real family, and, since families are constituted not by speech but by sex, it is sexuality itself which must be rejected. The traditional figure of the abandoned woman on the sea-shore, watching her faithless lover sail away, shadows the pious and uplifting scene the speaker wants to depict; as we wipe the tear from our eye, we might wonder what the mute woman thought of it all.

The speaker is haunted by what he has left behind, and yearns to go back: the latter part of the poem is taken up with his fantasy of return. But this fantasy, too, carries a price: without quite realising what he is doing, the speaker contradicts his earlier notion of Italy. Returning to Italy would mean returning to 'his father's house' (l. 131), where he would be unwelcome: his brothers 'live in Austria's pay' and have 'disowned' him (ll. 133–4), and his 'early mates' are 'turning wise' and finding the usual excuses for political inaction: 'So, with a sullen "All's for best," / The land seems settling to its rest' (ll. 135–44). This is an implicitly critical view of 'the land'; yet what has happened to 'our land', the perennially noble mother, of which the speaker and the woman were the son and daughter? The speaker is alienated from his own family, but instead of Italy being an ideal surrogate, it seems to be *like* his family, acquiescing in Austrian rule and disowning him twice over. If he went back, therefore, it would be for something other than the national cause:

> I think, then, I should wish to stand
> This evening in that dear, lost land,
> Over the sea the thousand miles,
> And know if yet that woman smiles
> With the calm smile – some little farm
> She lives in there, no doubt – what harm
> If I sate on the door-side bench,
> And, while her spindle made a trench
> Fantastically in the dust,
> Inquired of all her fortunes – just
> Her children's ages and their names,
> And what may be the husband's aims
> For each of them – I'd talk this out,
> And sit there, for an hour about,
> Then kiss her hand once more, and lay
> Mine on her head, and go my way.
>
> So much for idle wishing – how
> It steals the time! To business now!
>
> (ll. 145–62)

Italy is 'that dear, lost land' not simply because the speaker is exiled from his homeland, but because it is the site of a lost love. The fearless and patriotic woman of the earlier episode gives way to a sentimentalised matron, who married the other chap and settled down (instead of carrying on with her promising career as a revolutionary). We can be sure that 'the husband's aims' for his children do not include turning them into radical freedom-fighters; indeed the speaker does not want that, all trace of politics is expunged from his desire, which is now frankly sexual and domestic. When he imagines kissing her hand and laying his hand on her head, no grand pious words accompany these gestures as they did in the earlier episode; they belong rather to a renunciation-scene familiar from sentimental poetry and fiction. The speaker catches himself out, and brusquely brings his 'idle wishing' to an end; but after all he has had his wish: for better or worse, he has escaped from what he truly desired. Perhaps it is only in looking back, in the act of memory, that he can express this desire and name it in the moment of its dissolution.

## FRIENDSHIP'S DOUBLE FACE

'You're my friend,' says the old huntsman who narrates 'The Flight of the Duchess', in the very first line of the poem; and again, near the end of his story:

> You're my friend –
> What a thing friendship is, world without end!
> (ll. 833–4)

But he doesn't mean it, and nor does Browning. The 'friend' in this poem is like the wedding-guest in 'The Rime of the Ancient Mariner', whom the speaker seizes upon as a means of unburdening his memory: in fact he is even more anonymous and silent than in Coleridge's poem; all we can deduce about him is that he is, in fact, unlikely to be the huntsman's friend in the sense of knowing him well, because he is a stranger to the region.[18] After rhapsodising about friendship for another ten lines, the huntsman says:

> I have seen my Lady once more,
> Jacynth, the Gypsy, Berold, and the rest of it,
> For to me spoke the Duke, as I told you before;
> I always wanted to make a clean breast of it,
> And now it is made . . .

18. The huntsman describes the Duke's domain, and talks about the character of the local gypsies, in terms which imply that his interlocutor is unfamiliar with them (ll. 6–31, 350–6).

It is not only the 'clean breast' that has been made, but the story. The 'friend' has been an unwitting accessory to an act of 'making' (which is, as Browning points out in the *Essay on Shelley*, the root meaning of 'poetry').[19] The huntsman's 'friend' might reasonably complain that he had been taken advantage of under a false title. Other 'friends' in Browning have similar cause for complaint, even, as we shall see, friends who migrate into his poetry from 'real life'.

## Charles

Let us return to the 'dry green old aqueduct' where the speaker of 'Italy in England' played as a boy with his friend, Charles. Now Charles is 'lost' (l. 11), in the sense of being a 'lost leader': he has betrayed the revolutionary cause; later the speaker remarks that after (and because of) this betrayal 'nothing could convince / My inmost heart I had a friend' (ll. 116–17). There is an association between the 'inmost heart' and the 'dry green old aqueduct': they are both conduits of feeling; and feeling originates, as it does in Wordsworth, in childhood and in natural magic: the aqueduct is lit by fire-flies 'Bright creeping thro' the moss they love' (l. 10). Browning was to return to this scene of childhood in 'After', the poem which is paired with 'Before' in *Men and Women*. 'Before' is a justification of the morality of duelling, spoken not by one of the duellists but by a third party, who is speaking just before the duel takes place. 'After' is spoken by the survivor, who has killed his opponent. From spectator to participant, from wordy argument to laconic feeling: the speaker of 'After' looks the corpse of his opponent in the face, and reveals to us that the two were childhood friends:

> Ha, what avails death to erase
>    His offence, my disgrace?
> I would we were boys as of old,
>    In the field, by the fold –
> His outrage, God's patience, man's scorn
>    Were so easily borne.
>
> (ll. 11–16)

The speaker of 'Before' begins: 'Let them fight it out, friend!' But his 'friend' is merely his interlocutor, the term is no more than a form of

19. See Appendix A, p. 245.

familiar address; the real friendship is, or was, between 'them'; and this friendship was founded in pastoral, 'In the field, by the fold'. The 'fold' is a site of innocence, and is also associated with poetry: 'For we were nursed upon the self-same hill, / Fed the same flock; by fountain, shade, and rill,' says the shepherd in Milton's *Lycidas*. In the paradise of childhood things may be 'easily borne' which cannot be suffered in adulthood. What are these things? 'His outrage, God's patience, man's scorn': the last refers to the social stigma which results from turning the other cheek (it is Christian not to avenge an injury, but we actually despise people who don't for being either cowards or weaklings). The speaker transposes all this into childhood and imagines bearing it, because in childhood the bond of love has not yet given way to the bond of rivalry.

For the secret, the scandal of 'After' is the suppression of a voice, the voice of the 'other' who is killed, as the voice of Lycidas is suppressed in the poem to which he gives no more than his name. In each case it is the survivor who speaks, and from a position of authority opened to him by the other's death. The speaker of 'Italy in England' is also a survivor; the 'loss' of Charles turns out after all to be a kind of death. The last lines of 'After' have a chilling connotation of triumph:

> I stand here now, he lies in his place –
>   Cover the face.

The symbolic geometry of the long line is expressed in a matter-of-fact statement which balances physical and metaphysical oppositions: 'I stand/he lies', 'here now/in his place'; the difference between 'I' and 'he' obliterates the 'we' of 'we were boys', the distance between 'here' and 'his place' dismembers the intimacy of field and fold. The explosive short line which concludes the poem is an imperative whose energy flows from what has just been realised.

Elegy has a double face: the voice of mourning is also the voice of celebration: 'I stand here now'. Charles, who is lost in 'Italy in England', is lost once more in the short poem 'May and Death' (*Dramatis Personae*, 1864) which Browning wrote in memory of his cousin, James Silverthorne:

1.

I wish that when you died last May,
   Charles, there had died along with you
Three parts of spring's delightful things;
   Ay, and, for me, the fourth part too.

2.

A foolish thought, and worse, perhaps!
   There must be many a pair of friends
Who, arm in arm, deserve the warm
   Moon-births and the long evening-ends.

3.

So, for their sakes, be May still May!
   Let their new time, as mine of old,
Do all it did for me: I bid
   Sweet sights and sounds throng manifold.

4.

Only, one little sight, one plant,
   Woods have in May, that starts up green
Save a sole streak which, so to speak,
   Is spring's blood, spilt its leaves between, –

5.

That, they might spare; a certain wood
   Might miss the plant; their loss were small:
But I, – whene'er the leaf grows there,
   Its drop comes from my heart, that's all.

May was Browning's birth-month (hence, I think, the choice of the phrase 'Moon-births' in l. 8), so the joining of May with death is especially poignant for him. As for the Silverthornes, they were associated with Browning's deepest feelings and experiences: not only was James one of the two witnesses at Browning's wedding, but his mother, Browning's aunt, had paid for the publication of *Pauline* in 1833. And Browning signals his own status as a *poet*-mourner by the use of internal rhyme, which, as John Woolford points out, pervades *Dramatis Personae* and constantly draws attention to poetic artifice (Woolford 1988: 161–2); though in this poem the effect is one of quiet pathos and not, as it is elsewhere, of Byronic satire and self-display. The plant with the bloody streak is usually identified as the spotted persicaria (*Polygonum persicaria*), which by tradition grew beneath the Cross and was spotted by Christ's blood, but Browning could also have been thinking of wood-sorrel (*Oxalis acetosella*), which flowers in spring and one of whose names is 'Alleluia', because it was associated with the Easter liturgy and was 'a sign of delight' (Grigson: 110). He was probably also thinking of the many myths which identify particular plants with the blood of dying gods or the mortals whom they loved – Hyacinth, for example, who was loved by Apollo and whose story is one of the best known in Ovid's *Metamorphoses*. In 'May and Death' the poet both affirms and denies his own creative power. He pronounces and then retracts his curse on the spring as though he had the power to enforce it, as though he were indeed a god who could magnanimously 'bid / Sweet sights and sounds throng manifold'; at the same time he asks for the obliteration of the sign of his own divinity, the plant whose 'drop comes from my heart'. We return here to the 'inmost heart' of the speaker of 'Italy in England', and to his association of friendship with enclosure, with erotic privacy, and with loss and death. We return also to the speaker of 'After', who yearns for the time 'of old', the same phrase Browning uses here (l. 10). It is as though, in the figure of his childhood friend, Browning condensed an image of love, of poetic rivalry, of grief, and of fierce creative pleasure. 'Its drop comes from my heart, that's all': the phrase which ends the poem is indeed conclusive; it signs off, it chooses the moment to fall silent which is the truest mark of the power to speak.

## Waring

What became of James Silverthorne looks back to an earlier metamorphosis of one of Browning's closest personal friends. 'Waring' begins with some famous lines, famous enough, at any rate, to be in most books of quotations:

> What's become of Waring
> Since he gave us all the slip,
> Chose land-travel or seafaring,
> Boots and chest, or staff and scrip,
> Rather than pace up and down
> Any longer London-town?

The original of Waring was Browning's friend Alfred Domett, who emigrated to New Zealand in 1842. This fact alone emphasises the difference between real and fictional person: put the question 'What's become of Domett?' and you would have got a simple answer, 'Gone to New Zealand', whereas the whole point of the poem is not knowing. Had Browning wanted to name Domett directly he would have done so, as he did later in 'The Guardian-Angel', where he calls him 'Alfred, dear friend' (l. 37). Nevertheless it was Domett who inspired the poem, which cannot be understood without some knowledge of Browning's friendship with him.

It was a friendship founded on common social and geographical ground. Domett was Browning's age, the son of an ex-naval officer and shipping merchant who had settled in Camberwell; and Browning's family, on both sides, had extensive connections in the worlds of shipping and banking. The Domett household was described as 'bright, unconventional, if somewhat rough', a place 'with a lively atmosphere of freedom' (cited Horsman: 2). Like Browning, Domett was a precocious maker of verses, 'Mingling and mangling bits of rhymes / And changing each a thousand times', as he describes himself at the age of fourteen.[20] After an unprofitable year or two at Cambridge, and the unsuccessful publication of his first volume of poetry in 1833, Domett travelled to North America, and on his return took up the law as his profession. But there is always a sense of restlessness about him. In his American journal he wrote that he travelled 'to destroy *ennui* rather than ignorance' (cited Horsman: 5). This is not languid, *fin-de-siècle* boredom, but, so to speak, real boredom, a talented young man's frustration with pre-ordained social conditions. It was a feeling with which Browning acutely sympathised, and which 'Waring' records and explores; but here the difference between Browning and Domett is as striking as the resemblance. Like Domett, Browning grew up in a family and social class which expected him, after however indulgent an early start, to take up a regular and respectable profession – the law, shipping, banking, the diplomatic service. As late as the eve of his marriage Browning was protesting to Elizabeth Barrett that she had only to say the word and he would secure gainful employment at the drop of a hat rather than remain an unremunerated poet living off her unearned income; but his protestation was rhetorical, and she knew it. Like Domett,

20. 'A Reverie', ll. 3–4; dated 1825 and published in *Poems* (1833).

Browning felt *ennui*, but unlike Domett he was a genius and chose the internal exile of poetry. It is too simple to say that Browning's choice of poetry as a profession was made easy for him by the fact that he lived at home until he was thirty-four, and that his father paid for the publication of all his volumes before *Men and Women* except the first, *Pauline*, and that, as we have seen, was paid for by his aunt, Mrs Silverthorne. All this is true, but it is also true that in this period Browning wrote *Sordello*, which alone would justify half a lifetime's parasitism. *Sordello* contains one of the most searching and fascinating accounts of the discovery of poetry as a vocation, a life's work. Alfred Domett had no such vocation. Yet Domett, too, had a surprise in store for Browning and everyone else.

Though Browning and Domett shared many social and even family connections, their own friendship began rather late, when they were both in their middle twenties. They probably knew each other slightly by around 1835; they belonged to an informal association known to its members as 'the Set' or 'the Colloquials', who met in each other's houses to discuss literature and politics and because they liked each other's company. By the time *Sordello* was published in 1840 the friendship was much closer, and it grew rapidly into the closest relationship Browning was ever to have with another man apart from the closest of all, that with the French critic Joseph Milsand. But Milsand's friendship, exceptional and enduring as it was, was founded on his recognition of Browning's writing. It was an article on Browning in the *Revue des Deux Mondes* in 1851 which brought them together. Browning's friendship with Domett did not endure in the same way, as we shall see, but it was founded in different circumstances and for its brief duration had, I think, a greater intensity. It was a friendship of two young men who each had something savage about them, something unforgiving in the way they looked at their surroundings. The spirit of Carlyle – caustic, indignant, delighting to hate, mocking and melancholic – broods over 'Waring', or at least over the first section of the poem, as it does over Tennyson's 'Locksley Hall', published in the same year, and Browning's friendship with Domett was born, I think, under Carlyle's star.

Domett's surprise was to take flight. In November 1841 he was called to the Bar, and shared chambers with a friend of his and Browning's, Joseph Arnould. Steady respectable middle-class life loomed before him. In April 1842 he emigrated to New Zealand, suddenly, almost without warning. His farewell note to Browning gives a vivid impression of the swiftness with which he upped and left:

> Dear Browning –
> I return your books with many thanks – I need not assure you of my love nor that my wishes for all good for you will be as lasting as life. God bless you for ever – *Write* (to *the world*) – & to me at New Zealand. Say goodbye for me to your family – I have no time to call –
>
> Yrs ever
> Alfred Domett
> (30 Apr. 1842, Kelley: v 325)

It was not a completely crazy decision or destination, in the sense that Domett had family links with the New Zealand Company from whom he purchased a plot of land in Nelson, and one of his own cousins was already established there. But it was still a radical break, a plunge into uncertainty, and it struck Browning into an immediate response. He obeyed both parts of Domett's injunction, and linked them together. He did indeed write to Domett personally, a series of letters which lasted, significantly perhaps, until his marriage in 1846; but he also wrote to the world, in the form of 'Waring'. The poem was composed rapidly, probably in the summer of 1842, and included in *Dramatic Lyrics*, published in November of the same year.

Domett's flight was a surprise; but in one sense Browning had anticipated it, because it tallied so closely with his own feelings. Two years before he had written to Domett:

> Don't you feel a touch of the *vagabond*, in early spring-time? How do the lines go –
>
> ηλιβατοιξ υπο χευθμϖσι γενοιμαν
> ινα με πτεφουσσαν οφνιν
> θεοξ εν πταναιξ αγελαισι θειη –
> αφθειην δε επι ποντιον,
> χυμα ταξ Αδφιηναξ αχταξ,
> Ηφιδανου θ' 'υδϖφ.
>
> and so would you, I fancy –)
> (23 Mar. 1840, Kelley: iv 262)[21]

21. 'Under the arched cliffs O were I lying, / That there to a bird might a God change me, / And afar mid the flocks of the winged things flying, / Over the swell of the Adrian sea / I might soar – and soar, – upon poised wings dreaming, / O'er the strand where Eridanus' waters be . . .'

The lines which Browning quotes are from a chorus of Euripides' *Hippolytus*: they speak of Romantic flight and the yearning for metamorphosis, in ways which strongly foreshadow the last section of 'Waring'. Browning clearly saw in Domett a kindred spirit of restlessness and desire, but when he wrote his poem he subjected his friend to a metamorphosis in opposition to his own. After all, Euripides' lines would be at home in Keats or Coleridge: Browning's flight and self-transformation are those of the poet of 'Ode to a Nightingale' or 'Kubla Khan', and the god who touches him is Apollo, the god of poetry and presiding deity of *Sordello*.[22]

What Domett actually did, and what Browning made of what he did, are fascinatingly distinct. If the real Domett resembles anyone in Browning's poetry, it is the journalist Gigadibs, who, at the end of 'Bishop Blougram's Apology', is seized by a 'sudden healthy vehemence' and emigrates to Australia with 'settler's-implements, enough for three'. Though Browning, along with several of Domett's other close friends, fully expected him to return within a few years, and indeed exhorted him to do so, Domett stayed for thirty years and attained high office in the new colony, including a brief period as Prime Minister. One of his appointments was that of Commissioner of Crown Lands in Hawke's Bay, which is why the town of Napier has streets named after Browning, Tennyson, and Carlyle. He returned to England in 1872, and published his long poem *Ranolf and Amohia, a South-Sea Day-Dream* about which *The Sunday Times* proclaimed: 'We are justified in hailing this as the New Zealand epic.' Actually *Ranolf and Amohia* is not that bad, though it is over-long and over-lush; Tennyson shrewdly commented that Domett 'only want[ed] limitation to be a very considerable poet', but the want was severe and was never supplied. New Zealand owes its national library to Domett's energies, but not its national literature. And what Domett achieved in New Zealand was not fame, but distinction, as in the phrase 'distinguished

---

(transl. A.S. Way, 1912, Loeb Classical Library edition). The version by P. Vellacott (Penguin Classics, 1953) is even more Coleridgean: it has 'Where the lost waters of Eridanus flow deep / Down to an unknown sea'.

22. Browning had just sent *Sordello* to Domett; the letter quoting Euripides was written in response to a letter of Domett's (now lost) offering some criticisms of Browning's poem.

public servant', that mainstay of obituaries. When he returned to England in 1872 it was to retirement – busy, prosperous, honoured even, in the award of a knighthood in 1880 – but it was not to fame. That belonged to Browning, and it belonged to him because he, and not Domett, had taken flight not in the sense of escape but of soaring, 'upon poised wings dreaming, / O'er the strand where Eridanus' waters be'. And Browning's relationship with Domett in the 1870s, which can be followed in Domett's diary of those years, was everything which the early friendship was not: it was *cordial* and *hearty*, but neither man's heart was really in it. Nearly three years after Domett left, Browning wrote to him with his strongest exhortation yet to come home, and added: 'You will find no change . . . in this room, where I remember you so well, I turned my head, last line, to see if it was *you* came up with hat above the holly hedge' (23 Feb. 1845, Kelley: x 88). But when Domett did come back, thirty years later, and called at Warwick Crescent, Browning was out.

Browning's impulse, on Domett's departure, was to identify himself with it, or rather to identify it with his own desire; and this desire is centred on poetry. In his first letter, written when Domett was still on board ship, he urged Domett to write to him, in the following terms:

> Begin at the beginning – tell me how you are, where you are, what you do and mean to do – and to do in *our* way: for live properly *you cannot* without writing – and to *write* a book now, will take one at least the ten or a dozen years you portion out for your stay abroad. I don't expect to do any real thing till then: the little I, or anybody, can do as it is, comes of them *going to New Zealand* – partial retirement and stopping the ears against the noise outside – but all is next to useless – for there is a creeping magnetic assimilating influence nothing can block out. When I block it out, I shall do something. Don't you feel already older (in the wise sense of the word –) farther off – as one 'having a purchase' against us? What I meant to say was – that only in your present condition of life, so far as I see, is there any chance of your being able to find out . . what is wanted, and how to supply the want when you precisely find it. I have read your poems – you can do anything – and (I do not see why I should not think – ) *will* do much. I will, if I live.
>
> (22 May 1842, Kelley: v 355–6)

Browning is torn between literal and metaphorical readings of Domett's journey: on the one hand, 'going to New Zealand' is a metaphor for the 'partial retirement' in which poetry must be written, but on the other hand he needs to assure his friend that he has gained an actual advantage by going to a place which is really, physically remote, there to realise his ambitions. But in either case, two things are clear from this passage. First, Browning unequivocally associates Domett with himself as a poet: '*our* way' is the way of writing, and specifically the writing of poetry. Domett has gone abroad to 'find out what is wanted, and how to supply the want', but he is prophet as well as merchant; he is looking not just for materials to fill a gap in the market (to give people what they *want*) but for vision and inspiration (to give people what they *lack*). Browning's own idea of poetry, and his own ambition, are finely caught here, and also the nature of his feelings for Domett, the desire to attribute to him the highest conceivable motive for his action. And second, it is society and, it seems, literary society in particular, which threatens the poet and from which he must escape. Browning feels his creativity stifled by the 'creeping magnetic assimilating influence' of contemporary culture which 'nothing can block out', and he *knows*, without having to reflect on it, that Domett must feel the same; and here, I think, whatever the wrongness of Browning's estimate of Domett's literary talent, he is drawing on shared experience, on a real interchange of ideas. In the same way, Browning and Domett agreed on the impoverishment or frivolity of the contemporary literary scene. 'Sir L. Bulwer has published a set of sing-songs', Browning informed Domett shortly after his departure; 'I read two, or one, in a Review – & thought them abominable . . . here, every thing goes flatly on . . . our poems &c are poor child's play' (13 July 1842, Kelley: vi 33). 'We are dead asleep in literary things,' he wrote in another letter, 'and in great want of a "rousing word" (as the old puritans phrase it) from New Zealand or any place *out* of this snoring dormitory . . . don't leave off ploughing, for *poetry* will come of *that*! Here the vilest mill goes round & round . . . and outside the dry dust track is a strip of sand, and beyond, – your country' (15 May 1843, Kelley: vii 124–5). This letter echoes the already-published 'Waring', where 'this old world' is described as 'sound asleep', and Waring himself is exhorted in the same terms as Domett:

contrive, contrive
To rouse us, Waring! Who's alive?
Our men scarce seem in earnest now:
Distinguished names, but 'tis, somehow,
As if they played at being names
Still more distinguished, like the games
Of children. Turn our sport to earnest
With a visage of the sternest!
(ll. 194–201)

Yet the combination of these things – high literary ambition, a low opinion of contemporary literature, and the desire for 'partial retirement' from the world – is represented in Waring with more ambivalence than Browning allowed to show in his letter to Domett, though traces of it are to be found there too. This ambivalence is most strongly felt in the motives which are attributed to Waring for his sudden disappearance, in the structure of the poem, and in the master-stroke of its ending.

In Waring Browning created a figure of fierce, but suppressed ambition. The narrator of the poem describes his friend as an unrecognised genius – or at any rate, someone who felt himself to be an unrecognised genius – who is not valued by his friends (the narrator among them) because he has not actually produced any visibly impressive work:

He was prouder than the Devil:
How he must have cursed our revel!
Ay and many other meetings,
Indoor visits, outdoor greetings,
As up and down he paced this London,
With no work done, but great works undone,
Where scarce twenty knew his name.
(ll. 22–8)

In these 'Indoor visits, outdoor greetings' we can recognise the meetings of the 'Set' or 'Colloquials' to which both Browning and Domett belonged. The 'revel' which the narrator mentions refers to a supper party on the eve of Waring's disappearance:

I left his arm that night myself
For what's-his-name's, the new prose-poet
That wrote the book there, on the shelf –
How, forsooth, was I to know it
If Waring meant to glide away
Like a ghost at break of day!

(ll. 15–20)

There's the rub: Waring is not 'the new prose-poet', but feels superior to him, and, now that he is gone, the narrator realises how he should have behaved. Rather than praising the finished work of the 'distinguished names' of the day, he should have praised his friend's 'Stray-leaves, fragments, blurs and blottings', the embryonic signs of genius rather than the actual productions of mediocrity:

Oh, could I have him back once more,
This Waring, but one half-day more!
Back, with the quiet face of yore,
So hungry for acknowledgement
Like mine! I'd fool him to his bent!
Feed, should not he, to heart's content?
I'd say, 'to only have conceived,
Your great works, tho' they never progress,
Surpasses all we've yet achieved!'
I'd lie so, I should be believed.
I'd make such havoc of the claims
Of the day's distinguished names
To feast him with, as feasts an ogress
Her sharp-toothed golden-crowned child!

(ll. 80–93)

That last extraordinary image, taken from 'Little Thumb', one of Perrault's fairy tales, vividly expresses both Waring's 'hunger for acknowledgement', and the narrator's urge to satisfy it. Waring has vanished because the narrator did not 'fool him to his bent' about the value of his non-achievements. Had he done so, the narrator says, it would have been a lie, yet in the rest of this first section of the poem he seems fully to endorse Waring's claims to greatness. First he imagines Waring having all sorts of exotic adventures, beginning with an oriental and imperial fantasy worthy of Rider Haggard –

Who, of knowledge, by hearsay,
Reports a man upstarted
Somewhere as a God,
Hordes grown European-hearted,
Millions of the wild made tame
On a sudden at his fame?
In Vishnu-land what Avatar?
(ll. 102–8)

Then he imagines that Waring has not left at all, and that he is simply waiting, in the 'partial retirement' of which Browning wrote to Domett, to unfold his masterpiece, whether of painting, or music, or great acting, or political satire, or poetry. What differentiates these fantasies from the narrator's earlier scepticism about Waring's claim to be an unacknowledged genius is precisely that they are fantasies, and that their playful hyperbole tells us not to take them seriously. The image of Waring as a general in the Russian army, stepping over the 'Kremlin's pavement' with 'five other Generals / That simultaneously take snuff' (ll. 111–14) belongs to this burlesque mode, as does the image of him covering 'Some garret's ceiling, walls and floor, / Up and down and o'er and o'er' with 'something great in fresco-paint' (ll. 148–50). What Browning does take seriously, however, is not Waring's fantasy future, but his boyhood's past, a past which, I believe, belonged to Browning as much as to Domett. If there is a thread of autobiography in the poem, it is here that it comes out, in Browning's wonderful version of pastoral, as the narrator imagines Waring leaving his hiding-place in London:

Then down he creeps and out he steals
Only when the night conceals
His face; in Kent 'tis cherry-time,
Or, hops are picking; or, at prime
Of March, he steals as when, too happy,
Years ago when he was young,
Some mild eve when woods grew sappy
And the early moths had sprung
To life from many a trembling sheath
Woven the warm boughs beneath,
While small birds said to themselves
What should soon be actual song,
And young gnats, by tens and twelves,
Made as if they were the throng

That crowd around and carry aloft
The sound they have nursed, so sweet and pure,
Out of a myriad noises soft,
Into a tone that can endure
Amid the noise of a July noon,
When all God's creatures crave their boon,
All at once and all in tune,
And get it, happy as Waring then,
Having first within his ken
What a man might do with men,
And far too glad, in the even-glow,
To mix with the world he meant to take
Into his hand, he told you, so –
And out of it his world to make,
To contract and to expand
As he shut or oped his hand.

(ll. 153–82)

The young Waring is both like and unlike the creatures he sees in the 'prime of March'. He is like them in being in a state of promise, a state of becoming and make-believe. Like the small birds, he is saying to himself what will 'soon be actual song'; like the 'young gnats', he 'makes as if' he already possessed in its fulness the 'boon' which is due to him as one of 'God's creatures'. Browning is remembering Keats here: but Keats's 'wailful choir' of 'small gnats' figure as mourners in the 'Ode to Autumn', whereas Browning's are celebrants of spring and harbingers of the 'July noon' of utter fulfilment. But the young Waring is also and crucially unlike these inhabitants of the world of nature, for his happiness is identified not with this 'July noon' itself but with the moment of its anticipation. In the 'noise of a July noon', Browning states, 'all God's creatures crave their boon . . . *And get it*'; and *when* they achieve their utmost desire, they are as happy as Waring was *then*, that is not when he grasped his bliss, but when it came 'first within his ken'. And Waring's anticipated bliss is the bliss of power, of creative and destructive energy: not to be one of God's creatures, but to be like God himself, taking the world and remaking it in his image, allowing it 'To contract and to expand / As he shut or oped his hand'.

The young Waring's greatest happiness, therefore, is located not at the moment when his desire is fulfilled, but at the moment when that desire is at its most intense. The older Waring's silence, his inability to produce actual works to justify his genius, is related to this condition. His glorious future is behind him; it was in his boyhood imagination that he truly possessed his genius. 'Oh, Waring, what's to really be?' asks the narrator (l. 183), yearning for his friend to perform an impossible feat, to match promise with performance, when one has in fact pre-empted the other. Moreover, the ironic action of time means that Waring now experiences not the bliss of potentiality but the continually unsatisfied 'hunger for acknowledgement'. For you can't have it both ways: fame is the reward not of saying things to yourself, but of 'actual song'. The narrator remembers Waring blushing with repressed emulation as he, the narrator, praised 'some stupendous . . . Penman's latest piece of graphic' (ll. 51–6), but it is Browning, through all the burlesque, who is really the 'stupendous penman', who reaps where the likes of Waring disdained to sow. Browning wanted to believe that Domett had gone to New Zealand to follow *our way*, to write poetry, but he knew well enough, I think, that almost the reverse was the case, that Domett had gone not because he was a poet but because he was not one. 'Waring' is the poem of this knowledge, tender towards its subject, but also ruthlessly clear-sighted.

What, then, has 'become of Waring'? The second section of the poem offers this failed or occluded genius an extraordinary consolation, a lyric afterlife, suffused with romantic colour and movement, but one which is also a condition of irredeemable exile. Waring, it seems, has been spotted by a friend of his and the narrator's – not as a white god in the exotic east, but as a boatman on the Adriatic:

I

When I last saw Waring . . .'
(How all turned to him who spoke –
You saw Waring? Truth or joke?
In land-travel, or sea-faring?)

II

'We were sailing by Triest,
Where a day or two we harboured:
A sunset was in the West,
When, looking over the vessel's side,
One of our company espied
A sudden speck to larboard.
And, as a sea-duck flies and swims
At once, so came the light craft up,
With its sole lateen sail that trims

And turns (the water round its rims
Dancing, as round a sinking cup)
And by us like a fish it curled,
And drew itself up close beside,
Its great sail on the instant furled,
And o'er its planks a shrill voice cried,
(A neck as bronzed as a Lascar's)
"Buy wine of us, you English Brig?
Or fruit, tobacco and cigars?
A Pilot for you to Triest?
Without one, look you ne'er so big,
They'll never let you up the bay!
We natives should know best."
I turned, and "just those fellows' way,"
Our captain said, "The 'long-shore thieves
Are laughing at us in their sleeves."

III

'In truth, the boy leaned laughing back;
And one, half-hidden by his side
Under the furled sail, soon I spied,
With great grass hat, and kerchief black,
Who looked up, with his kingly throat,
Said somewhat while the other shook
His hair back from his eyes to look
Their longest at us; and the boat,
I know not how, turned sharply round,
Laying her whole side on the sea
As a leaping fish does; from the lee
Into the weather cut somehow
Her sparkling path beneath our bow;
And so went off, as with a bound,
Into the rose and golden half
Of the sky, to overtake the sun,
And reach the shore like the sea-calf
Its singing cave: yet I caught one
Glance ere away the boat quite passed,
And neither time nor toil could mar
Those features: so I saw the last
Of Waring!' – You? Oh, never star
Was lost here but it rose afar!
Look East, where whole new thousands are!
In Vishnu-land what Avatar?

(ll. 204–57)

Waring has not become a white god in the east, like Conrad's Lord Jim (incidentally I wouldn't be surprised to find that Conrad knew Browning's poem); it seems clear that we are meant to take the narrator's denial at the end as wishful thinking. Nor, on the other hand, has Waring dwindled into ordinary success, as Alfred Domett was to do. What has become of Waring is this 'half-hidden' figure, a royal exile with his 'kingly throat' and his laughing young companion, with whom he has 'gone native' in dress and occupation. Browning had written grandly to Domett about finding out what people wanted and supplying it; Waring is neither stupendous penman nor merchant prince but ' 'long-shore thief', offering his countrymen 'wine, tobacco and cigars' in place of poetry. Yet this apparent failure is also a triumph, symbolised by the 'rose and golden' sunset into which Waring vanishes, this time for good. The poetry which Waring will never now write has passed into the poetry of his movement and of the movement of his boat, which, like the sea-creatures it resembles, inhabits its element without restlessness or anxiety. The 'light craft' or craft of light follows a 'sparkling path' which leads it to 'overtake the sun' and reach a 'singing cave': in these images Waring's ambition of worldly fame is both commemorated and finally abandoned.

# CHAPTER 4
# *Love and marriage*

## LOVE

### *Pippa Passes* and the hierarchy of love

On the morning of New Year's Day, a young factory girl, Pippa, wakes up to her single annual holiday. She decides to spend the day wandering around the little Italian town of Asolo and neighbouring Possagno, 'passing' by four sites associated with the four happiest people she knows, and whom she would like to be. The first of these sites is the 'shrub-house' of the villa owned by her employer, old Luca Gaddi, where Luca's young wife, Ottima, has her rendezvous with her lover, Sebald. The second is the house in Possagno where Jules, a young sculptor, will bring home his newly-wed bride, the beautiful Phene. The third is a ruined turret on the outskirts of Asolo to which young Luigi and his mother stroll in their evening walks together.[1] The fourth is the palace of the local ruler, who has just died, and where his brother, a Bishop, is staying to wind up his affairs and pray for his soul. Pippa wistfully imagines being in turn Ottima, Phene, Luigi, and the Bishop. The drama's four main scenes take place at the four sites, each of which is further identified with a time of day: the Ottima–Sebald scene takes place in the morning, the Jules–Phene scene at noon, the scene between Luigi and his mother in the evening, and the scene between the Bishop and his late brother's Intendant (the manager of his estate) at night. The climax of each scene is Pippa's 'passing', during which she sings a song which, without her knowledge, radically changes the course of events.

The strong structure of *Pippa Passes* suggests a hierarchy of love, with sexual passion at the bottom and divine love at the top. Maternal love ranks above both kinds of sexual love, licit and illicit; as Pippa puts it (in lines added to the text in the *Poems* of 1849):

1. This scene is examined in detail in Chapter 3 (pp. 90–4).

'Lovers grow cold, men learn to hate their wives, / And only parents' love can last our lives'.[2] What should we make of this ascending scale of love, and does the rest of Browning's poetry endorse it?

The first thing we should take into account is that the hierarchy is put forward by a dramatic character, Pippa, whose assumptions about the happiness of the figures she envies are, to put it mildly, a little off-target. (Ottima and Sebald have just murdered Luca; Phene is a prostitute who has been married to Jules as a result of a cruel hoax; Luigi and his mother are quarrelling over Luigi's intention to go off and assassinate the Austrian Emperor; and the Bishop has come to arrest the Intendant for, among other things, blackmailing his late brother by threatening to reveal the true identity of Pippa herself – who, in true fairy-tale fashion, turns out to be the lost heiress of the family estate.) In formal terms, therefore, *Pippa Passes* is divided between Pippa's fantasy and the reality which the dramatist, Browning, presents us with, a reality which is denied to Pippa herself. For though she passes by each enclosed space in turn, her being on the outside means that she cannot see what is going on inside. We, by contrast, are shown this inner reality, whose ironic reflection on Pippa's naïvety and idealism might then imply that the drama constituted a critique of her fantasy. Yet the fantasy has power: Pippa's passing affects the people who hear her songs, though in ways which themselves compound the problem. In two cases – the Ottima–Sebald scene and the scene between Luigi and his mother – the effect of Pippa's passing seems to be not to confirm that sexual passion or maternal love are good, but to reject them: Sebald rejects Ottima and commits suicide out of guilt and remorse, Luigi breaks free from his mother and dedicates himself to his project of assassination. In the other two scenes, the effect of Pippa's passing is to restore love to its ideal state: Jules, whom his enemy Lutwyche intended to degrade and destroy by tricking him into marrying a prostitute, realises that Phene is devoted to him heart and soul, and escapes with her to live (presumably) happily ever after; while the Bishop, whom the Intendant had almost persuaded to agree to what is effectively the murder of Pippa herself, comes to his senses and behaves with the integrity with which she credited him in the first place.

2. Added between ll. 129 and 130 of the first edition; ll. 163–4 of the text of the final collected edition, the *Poetical Works* of 1888–9.

We might simply conclude that Pippa is right about married and divine love, which are intrinsically good and can therefore be redeemed if they fall into error, and wrong about sexual passion and mother-love, which are intrinsically and irredeemably perverse. But here another consideration comes in. Pippa the fantasist is also a surrogate for Browning the poet (her singing itself proves this), and the motivation for her 'passing' in the first place is also love. In fact it is Pippa's kind of love, and not any of the four kinds she describes, which binds the structure of the drama together, explains its formal division into 'outside' and 'inside' views of events, and is itself the subject of the work's ironic attention.

Pippa's love consists of self-projection. In the *Defence of Poetry* Shelley had argued for the moral value of empathy: 'The great secret of morals is love; or a going out of our own nature, and an identification of ourselves with the beautiful which exists in thought, action, or person, not our own' (Brett-Smith: 33). To this we may add Keats's account, in a letter to Richard Woodhouse which Browning may have known, of 'the poetical Character':

> A Poet is the most unpoetical of any thing in existence; because he has no Identity – he is continually in for – and filling some other Body – The Sun, the Moon, the Sea and Men and Women who are creatures of impulse are poetical and have about them an unchangeable attribute – the poet has none . . .
>
> (27 Oct. 1818, Rollins: i 387)[3]

But the principle of empathy is double-edged. 'Love' in Shelley's sense can be humble, selfless, devotional; or it can be aggressive,

3. This letter was not published until 1848, in Richard Monckton Milnes's *Life, Letters, and Literary Remains of John Keats* (i 221–3); but Browning had known Milnes since the mid-1830s (Orr 1891: 83), when Milnes was already collecting 'unpublished productions' of Keats from a wide circle of Keats's friends (see Milnes's preface, vol. i, pp. ix–xi). Browning's admiration for Keats dated from the same period in the late 1820s when he discovered Shelley. In addition to Milnes, Browning knew several other people in Keats's circle, among them Leigh Hunt and the painter Joseph Severn. For parallels in *Sordello* with another unpublished Keats letter, see Woolford and Karlin: i 440 and 606–7. Both Shelley's maxim from the *Defence of Poetry* and Keats's view of the 'poetical Character' are further discussed in Chapter 6 (p. 218).

self-serving, tyrannical. The sinister turn is arguably present in Shelley's own language:

> A man, to be greatly good, must imagine intensely and comprehensively; he must put himself in the place of another and of many others; the pains and pleasures of his species must become his own . . . Poetry enlarges the circumference of the imagination by replenishing it with thoughts of ever new delight, which have the power of attracting and assimilating to their own nature all other thoughts, and which form new intervals and interstices whose void for ever craves fresh food.

To put yourself in another's place may be a mode of sympathy, but it may equally be a mode of usurpation. The openness of the imagination looks rather devouring by the end of that last sentence; perhaps the imagination cannot be trusted so far. In *Sordello* the 'circumference of the imagination' posits itself as infinite, and the result is impotence and self-undoing.

There are other and opposite difficulties. The desire to be or become another person, to be 'continually in for – and filling some other body', may be a form of self-love, or it may be a form of self-hatred. Loss of self and union with the divine is traditionally a goal of religious mysticism (both Western and Oriental), but it is also a source of terror, equivalent to death and in some cases symbolic of it. The religious aspect of loss of self is easily translatable into other contexts: 'God' may figure as a political cause, as 'the people', as 'Art', or as any abstraction which threatens, like a combination of Moloch and the Royal Mint, to devour the individual's identity, melt it down and reissue it as a token indistinguishable from the other currency in circulation.

Looked at in this light, the 'unpoetical' Pippa's self-imaginings – as adulteress, bride, son, and priest – are aspects or emanations of the principle of desire itself. No wonder these emanations turn out to be full of irony and self-contradiction: like parent like child. This ambivalence about desire goes back a long way in Browning, as far back as *Pauline*, whose narrator's self-consciousness is 'linked . . . to self-supremacy' and to 'a principle of restlessness / Which would be all, have, see, know, taste, feel, all' (ll. 273, 277–8);[4] it shapes the conception of Paracelsus and Sordello, and of numerous other

4. For more detailed comment on this passage, see Chapter 6 (p. 202).

characters in Browning's work, protean in form but consistent as a primary element of both his psychology and his poetics.

Pippa's imagination is playful, but it is also aggressive. Her passion for the natural world, which is the subject of the drama's opening lines, is in part a passion to exercise power over it. When she sees a sunbeam reflected on the ceiling of her room from water which she splashes into her basin, she crows over its prismatic dance:

> You fool-hardy sunbeam – caught
> With a single splash from my ewer!
> You that mocked the best pursuer,
> Was my basin over-deep?
> One splash of water ruins you asleep
> And up, up, fleet your brilliant bits
> Wheeling and counterwheeling,
> Reeling, crippled beyond healing –
> Grow together on the ceiling,
> That will task your wits!
>
> (*Intro*. 49–58)

The violence of Pippa's language here – flight, capture, maiming, mockery – is an aspect of her imaginative power, an energy that undoes and destroys in order to create.[5] It is a version of Shelley's famous lines in *Adonais* – 'Life, like a dome of many-coloured glass, / Stains the white radiance of Eternity' (ll. 462–3) – without the concluding phrase in the next line, which Browning, like many other readers, conveniently forgets: 'Until Death tramples it to fragments.' Or rather he does not forget it, but transfers it to the shattered sunbeam's 'brilliant bits': Pippa's 'single splash' (like the splash of a painter's brush on a white canvas) causes both death and life, an explosion of energy into a state 'beyond healing'.

In the *Poems* of 1849 Browning revised a couple of lines which made Pippa's desiring self seem too scandalous. Keats, in the same letter from which I quoted above, insists that the 'poetical Character . . . has as much delight in conceiving an Iago as an Imogen'; this loss of ethical determinacy is a result of its having no authentic

5. In ch. xiii of *Biographia Literaria*, Coleridge defines the 'secondary imagination' as the power which 'dissolves, diffuses, dissipates, in order to re-create . . . It is essentially *vital*, even as all objects (*as* objects) are essentially fixed and dead.'

identity of its own. Pippa's first fantasy is of being like the adulteress Ottima, and in the first edition the lines read:

> Up the hill-side, thro' the morning,
> Love me as I love!
> I am Ottima, take warning . . .
> (*Intro.* 83–5)

In 1849 they read as follows:

> See! Up the Hill-side yonder, through the morning,
> Some one shall love me, as the world calls love:
> I am no less than Ottima, take warning!

The revised text of *Pippa Passes* contains many such blunders;[6] some were retracted in later editions, but not this one. The new line 83 is merely leaden, but lines 84–5 are worse: they are pusillanimous. Pippa's bold appropriation of sexual passion is hedged with prim qualifications; the suggestion that her own desire *matches* that of Ottima ('Love me as I love') is cut out. Yet the whole thrust of the drama is towards such a conclusion. At the very end, in a passage which Browning did not revise in this way, Pippa returns to her room and sums up her day:

> I have just been Monsignor!
> And I was you too, mother,
> And you too, Luigi! . . .
> And I was Jules the sculptor's bride,
> And I was Ottima beside,
> And now what am I? – tired of fooling!
> (iv 269–76)

Pippa recounts her day in reverse order, returning from night to morning, ending where she began, with Ottima. To her question in line 276 she can give only an evasive answer. What she *is*, in herself, is not a matter of desire but escape. To put it another way, desire is a mode of escape, as it is for other apparently self-forgetting characters,

6. For an account of the revisions, and Browning's later attitude to them, see Woolford and Karlin: i 102 and ii 7. For more comment on Browning's revisions generally, see Chapter 1 (pp. 29–37).

and not just in Browning's work. I am thinking of an episode early in Dickens's *Bleak House*, where Esther Summerson, a character who resembles Pippa in being a poor orphan who does not know the secret of her birth, and who is famously modest and devoted to others, goes to sleep after comforting Caddy Jellyby; and she too looks back on the episodes of a crowded day:

> By degrees, the poor tired girl fell asleep; and then I contrived to raise her head so that it should rest on my lap, and to cover us both with shawls. The fire went out, and all night long she slumbered thus before the ashy grate. At first I was painfully awake, and vainly tried to lose myself, with my eyes closed, among the scenes of the day. At length, by slow degrees, they became indistinct and mingled. I began to lose the identity of the sleeper resting on me. Now it was Ada; now, one of my old Reading friends from whom I could not believe I had so recently parted. Now, it was the little mad woman worn out with curtseying and smiling; now, some one in authority at Bleak House. Lastly, it was no one, and I was no one.
>
> (ch. iv, penultimate paragraph)

The parallelism between Caddy and Esther is suggested by the repetition of key phrases: 'By degrees . . . by slow degrees'; 'tried to lose myself . . . began to lose the identity'. Esther's loving nature draws Caddy to herself; but who is Esther, herself? All we know of her self is that it pains her, that she 'vainly tries to lose [herself] among the scenes of the day'; she too, like Pippa, is a shape-changer. Is she 'some one in authority at Bleak House', since she narrates half the novel? But if she is, she is truly 'no one'; like Keats's poet, she is annihilated in the act of creation.

The 'love' which impels the poet to project his own identity into that of another person has, therefore, two dark sides to it: the desire for power, and the fear of loss. But we should not forget that it has also an aspect of generosity and humankindness. In *Pippa Passes* each episode concludes with an act of altruism, of self-forgetting: Jules devotes himself to Phene, Luigi sacrifices himself in the cause of Italian freedom, the Bishop chooses justice above self-interest or the interest of the Church. I have kept the first episode till last, because it is the most surprising and the most complex. There the act of altruism comes from the passionate, vengeful, sin-loving sensualist, Ottima. Sebald's righteous indignation at Ottima's corruption is the overt moral consequence of Pippa's song, but after all Pippa does not identify with Sebald, but with Ottima. What happens to Ottima? She changes from tyrant to supplicant: from the dominatrix who commands Sebald to crown her as his 'queen, [his] spirit's arbitress' (i 211) to the lover who pleads with God on his behalf (her last words, and the last words of the scene, are 'Not me – to him oh God be merciful!' (i 276)). Her love for him desires no return:

> Lean on my breast . . not as a breast; don't love me
> The more because you lean on me, my own
> Heart's Sebald.
>
> (i 268–70)

Leaning is associated in other Browning poems with loving dependency: the narrator of *Pauline*, for example, addressing Christ, describes himself as 'leaning on thy bosom, proudly less' (l. 852), an image which itself goes back to 'the disciple whom Jesus loved', who leans on Jesus' bosom at the Last Supper (*John* xiii 23). Ottima, like Christ, loves Sebald unconditionally, gratuitously (her breast is neither sexual nor maternal), yet he is her own, she owns him, he is in her heart. Ottima gives herself away, but simultaneously recuperates her power: it is her speech, her voice, which sounds the last note of love.

## Climbing-plants and propping-trees

The 'Flight of the Duchess', in the poem of that name, is a flight from lovelessness to love. The Duchess escapes from her (possibly impotent, certainly inadequate) husband, leaving him to enjoy his unhealthy relationship with his mother, at the instigation of an old Gipsy woman who enchants her with a vision of freedom and sexual pleasure: 'Henceforth be loved as heart can love, / Or brain devise, or hand approve!' (ll. 616–17). But there is a choice to make between two kinds of love: 'Art thou the tree that props the plant, / Or the climbing plant that takes the tree[?]' (ll. 623–4). And the Gipsy elaborates this idea in a passage which EBB singled out for praise in the critical notes which she wrote on the poem when she saw it in manuscript:

Shall some one deck thee, over and down,
Up and about, with blossoms and leaves?
Fix his heart's fruit for thy garland crown,
Cling with his soul as the gourd-vine cleaves,
Die on thy boughs and disappear
While not a leaf of thine is sere?
Or is the other fate in store,
And art thou fitted to adore,
To give thy wondrous self away,
And take a stronger nature's sway?
(ll. 636–45).[7]

Love means either worshipping or being worshipped, absorbing another's life or surrendering one's own, according to whose is the 'stronger nature'. Although the process involves the symbolic death or annihilation of one identity, the Gipsy does not, apparently, mean to suggest that one 'fate' is better than the other. 'Not a power of life but we'll employ / To satisfy thy nature's want', she tells the Duchess (ll. 621–2); and this 'want' may be for either kind of love.

It may be asked why things should be so ordered. The Gipsy anticipates the question:

If any two creatures grew into one,
They would do more than the world has done;
Tho' each apart were never so weak,
Yet vainly thro' the world should ye seek
For the knowledge and the might
Which in such union grew their right:
So, to approach, at least, that end,
And blend, – as much as may be, blend
Thee with us or us with thee,
As climbing-plant or propping-tree,
Shall some one deck thee . . .
(ll. 626–36)

These lines relate the division between the two kinds of love to Browning's belief in the necessary imperfection of human life (not just

7. The passage struck EBB as an 'infinitely beautiful revivification' of the proverbial figure of the elm and the vine: see Woolford and Karlin: ii 323–4, and for an account of EBB's comments on 'The Flight of the Duchess' in general, which she wrote during the late spring and summer of 1845, see Karlin 1985: 92–4.

in love but in art, religion, politics, morals). The perfect union of two human beings (restoring a primordial unity, perhaps, as in Aristophanes' myth of the origins of love in Plato's *Symposium*) would transcend the limits of human possibility; it would be like seeing, or becoming, God, attaining absolute forms of knowledge and power which the human condition itself disallows. Since we cannot love as perfect equals, it follows that even the best forms of human love will always, necessarily, involve an imbalance of power.[8]

There is a close analogy to this idea in the *Essay on Shelley* in which Browning represents the division between 'objective' and 'subjective' poetry in the same terms as the division between the two kinds of love. You can imagine a perfect union of objective and subjective qualities in the same creative mind, just as you can imagine a perfect union of lovers: there is no reason, Browning says, 'why these two modes of poetic faculty may not issue hereafter from the same poet in successive perfect works'; but it remains true that 'A mere running-in of the one faculty upon the other, is, of course, the ordinary circumstance . . . while of the perfect shield, with the gold and the silver side set up for all comers to challenge, there has yet been no instance' (Appendix A, p. 248). It seems clear that 'there has yet been no instance' is a form of 'there never will be': perfect poetry, like perfect love, would be too much for the world to contain.

The analogy is not an accidental one. Objective poetry, whose culminating form is drama, is in one sense the *product* of unselfish love, by which the poet 'gives his wondrous self away' to the people he evokes; while subjective poetry, whose culminating form is lyric, subdues all external phenomena to 'the stronger nature's sway'. Like all oppositions in Browning, this one is mobile, unstable, forever collapsing on itself but always taking shape again. 'The Flight of the Duchess' is itself a good example of this process, as is a poem it closely resembles in some respects, 'The Pied Piper of Hamelin'. The old Gipsy and the Piper both offer ecstatic visions of freedom and escape, and both leave behind a figure who is excluded from bliss, yet whose exclusion is paradoxically desirable, because it enables him to become

8. For more on Browning's attitude to the problem of power in sexual relationships, see Chapter 5 (pp. 177–81).

a storyteller.[9] The old huntsman's narrative in 'The Flight of the Duchess' *secretes* the Gipsy's vision: we gain access to her rapture through his 'poor version' of it, spoilt by 'stammering' (ll. 697–8), but this is the only access we can have. The huntsman is the 'objective' poet of the poem and the Gipsy the 'subjective'; and whereas the huntsman loves the Duchess with painful, inferior, inarticulate devotion, the Gipsy is a figure of regal authority, presence, and language. When the Duchess is on the point of leaving, the huntsman can only 'stammer' his love:

> . . . I ventured to remind her,
> I suppose with a voice of less steadiness
> Than usual, for my feeling exceeded me,
> – Something to the effect that I was in readiness
> Whenever God should please she needed me, –
> (ll. 763–7)

My *feeling exceeded me*: not just 'I was too moved to speak steadily' but literally, 'my love was greater than my self': the huntsman gives himself away to the Duchess here (he gets a lock of hair in return); he will spend the rest of his life re-creating, re-presenting, the (absent) object of his desire: her flight (an escape, also a soaring: he compares her several times to a bird) motivates his language of love. But when the Gipsy mesmerises the Duchess, the huntsman witnesses the opposite of his 'stammering' declaration:

> For it was life her eyes were drinking
> From the crone's wide pair unwinking,
> Life's pure fire received without shrinking,
> Into the heart and breast whose heaving
> Told you no single drop they were leaving –
> Life, that filling her, past redundant
> Into her very hair, back swerving
> Over each shoulder, loose and abundant,
> As her head thrown back showed the white throat curving,

9. In fact 'The Pied Piper of Hamelin' has two such figures, the rat who, 'stout as Julius Caesar', swims across the river and 'lived to carry . . . To Rat-land home his commentary' (ll. 116–20), and the poor lame child who could not keep up with the other children, and against whom 'The door in the mountain side shut fast' (l. 224).

And the very tresses shared in the pleasure,
Moving to the mystic measure,
Bounding as the bosom bounded.
(ll. 540–51)

The huntsman witnesses an act he cannot perform himself (no more than can the Duke, his master), the giving of sexual pleasure; the Duchess's 'loose and abundant' hair is a common sign in Browning of female pleasure (behind the word 'abundant' shimmers the ghost of the word 'abandoned'), and the scene here answers that in 'Porphyria', where Porphyria's unbinding of her hair so threatens her lover that he strangles her with it.[10] The Gipsy's action has a physical effect, but the medium of it is her look; her 'stronger nature's sway' shows itself not in physical but mental force. Her energy literally animates, gives a soul to, the Duchess's being, by means of a 'mystic measure' to which the poor narrator has no access. Yet the Gipsy's poem of 'Life's pure fire' is not accessible to us, either, except through the huntsman's reporting of it. Browning intended it otherwise, but found he was unable to write the poem in the voice of lyric love. 'Of *the poem*,' he told EBB, 'not a line is written . . . as I conceived the poem, it consisted entirely of the Gipsy's description of the life the Lady was to lead with her future Gipsy lover' (25 July 1845, Kelley: xi 3). The Gipsy's seduction of the Duchess results in her flight, but the huntsman's devotion to her results in 'The Flight of the Duchess'.[11]

## 'Infinite passion'

A huntsman-Gipsy, who both carried the Duchess off and remained behind, would represent an impossible transcendence of human conditions. Both love and poetry desire such transcendence, but must face its impossibility; this helps to explain why so many of Browning's love poems are dramatic representations of failure, inadequacy, or death. Again and again this note is struck, whether in poems written before, during, or after Browning's own romance and marriage. Of the fifty poems of *Men and Women* (excluding 'One Word More', which is a special case), twenty-three are (wholly or in one important respect)

10. See Karlin 1993: 214–16 for further discussion of this point.

11. See Chapter 1 (pp. 10–16) for further comment both on the passage from the poem and Browning's account of its composition.

love poems, and of these only one, 'Women and Roses', is 'about' love or sexuality in the abstract; the others are all about relationships, more or less particularised. Table 4.1 shows in the first column the poems in which relationships are successful; in the second the poems in which they are not.[12]

**TABLE 4.1 Love poems in *Men and Women***

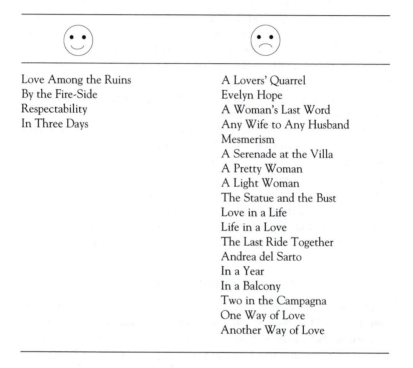

| ☺ | ☹ |
|---|---|
| Love Among the Ruins | A Lovers' Quarrel |
| By the Fire-Side | Evelyn Hope |
| Respectability | A Woman's Last Word |
| In Three Days | Any Wife to Any Husband |
| | Mesmerism |
| | A Serenade at the Villa |
| | A Pretty Woman |
| | A Light Woman |
| | The Statue and the Bust |
| | Love in a Life |
| | Life in a Love |
| | The Last Ride Together |
| | Andrea del Sarto |
| | In a Year |
| | In a Balcony |
| | Two in the Campagna |
| | One Way of Love |
| | Another Way of Love |

The poems in which relationships are unhappy, or unfulfilled, or perverse, outnumber the positive poems by more than 4 to 1. In Browning's next collection, *Dramatis Personae*, the proportions are

12. The judgement of 'success' is generous to some poems, such as 'Love Among the Ruins' (see Chapter 5, pp. 175–6), but for the purpose of the exercise I have taken the poems more or less at their word. 'In a Balcony' remains a problem case; I read the outcome as tragic (for the Queen) and fatal (for Norbert and Constance).

virtually the same: of six poems about relationships, only one, 'Confessions', the shortest and slightest, is positive; the others ('James Lee', 'The Worst of It', 'Dîs Aliter Visum', 'Too Late', and 'Youth and Art') are poems of profound unhappiness and frustration. The openings of these poems set their tone:

Beautiful Evelyn Hope is dead!

Let's contend no more, Love,
Strive nor weep –

My love, this is the bitterest . . .

So far as our story approaches the end,
Which do you pity the most of us three?

I said – Then, dearest, since 'tis so,
Since now at length my fate I know,
Since nothing all my love avails,
Since all my life seemed meant for, fails . . .

But do not let us quarrel any more,
No, my Lucrezia; bear with me for once . . .

Never any more
While I live,
Need I hope to see his face
As before.

Ah, love, but a day,
And the world has changed!
The sun's away,
And the bird's estranged;
The wind has dropped,
And the sky's deranged:
Summer has stopped.

Would it were I had been false, not you![13]

The circumstances vary from the everyday to the extreme, from the detailed to the quasi-abstract, from the present to the past; the range of tone is similarly wide, from the plain mournfulness of James Lee's

13. 'Evelyn Hope', 'A Woman's Last Word', 'Any Wife to Any Husband', 'A Light Woman', 'The Last Ride Together', 'Andrea del Sarto', 'In a Year', 'James Lee', 'The Worst of It'.

wife to the Gothic exaltation of Evelyn Hope's mad middle-aged lover, claiming a spiritual affinity with her beyond the grave. The quarrel between Andrea del Sarto and Lucrezia is a rich period piece, with no expense spared in the location and costumes; 'A Woman's Last Word' has no stage props at all, not so much as a hint of the characters' names, ages, or the reason for their quarrel. The chatty speaker of 'A Light Woman', who confides his little human conundrum to Browning himself, is answered by the despairing bleakness of the woman who speaks 'In a Year', apparently to no one but herself.

Yet if we look at the circumstances which govern these poems, one factor recurs: a wrongness in the nature of things, a flaw or gap, a refusal to communicate or fit, of which the failure of particular lovers to find fulfilment is only an instance. As the speaker in 'By the Fire-Side' puts it:

> If you join two lives, there is oft a scar,
>   They are one and one, with a shadowy third;
> One near one is too far.
>
> (ll. 228–30)

In this rare instance the join is perfect: the 'bar' between the lovers is 'broken', and they are 'mixed at last / In spite of the mortal screen' (ll. 233–5). Another, and disturbing, form of this perfect union occurs in 'Love Among the Ruins', where the lovers 'rush' together and 'extinguish sight and speech / Each on each' (ll. 71–2). Most of Browning's lovers never manage even this violent overcoming. Their language is filled with images of frustration and thwarted desire. 'Yet one thing, one, in my soul's full scope, / Either I missed or itself missed me', says the speaker of 'Evelyn Hope' (ll. 45–6). 'Where does the fault lie? what the core / Of the wound, since wound must be?' asks the speaker of 'Two in the Campagna' (ll. 39–40). His assurance that 'wound *must* be' is shared by Andrea del Sarto: 'In this world, who can do a thing, will not – / And who would do it, cannot, I perceive' (ll. 136–7). And his sense of puzzlement is shared by the speaker of 'In a Year':

> Was it something said,
>   Something done,
> Vexed him? was it touch of hand,
>   Turn of head?

Strange! that very way
  Love begun.
I as little understand
  Love's decay.
    (ll. 9–16)

The speaker of 'Evelyn Hope' is driven to imagine an after-life in which his lack will be healed; the wife in 'Any Wife to Any Husband' fails in her desperate attempt to persuade herself that her husband will remain faithful to her after her death, and her final exclamation is like a gush of blood from the 'core of the wound':

What did I fear? Thy love shall hold me fast
Until the little minute's sleep is past
  And I wake saved. – And yet, it will not be!
    (ll. 124–6)

What these speakers cannot reconcile is a gap between the ideal and the actual. It is a dualism with a long intellectual history, whose extreme development is the Gnostic idea of an irreconcilable warfare in the cosmos between spirit and matter. In his later work Browning was to explore this opposition overtly, signposting it in *Red Cotton Night-Cap Country*, for example, with the subtitle 'Turf and Towers', staging a dialogue between 'Fancy' and 'Reason' in *La Saisiaz* (ll. 405–524), and subtitling his last volume, *Asolando*, 'Fancies and Facts'. In *Men and Women* and (though to a lesser extent) *Dramatis Personae* he still had faith in his readers.[14]

14. For more on Gnosticism, see Chapter 6 (p. 196, n.8). In Chapter 2 (p. 41, n.7) I comment on the rarity of dialogue-poems in Browning; it is significant that a cluster of them occurs in *Asolando*, where the opposition between 'fancy' and 'fact' is more deliberately thematised. The desire to make things clear partly accounts for the emergence in Browning's work of the 'structured collection', represented not just by *Dramatis Personae* but by the revised, 12-poem *Men and Women* in the *Poetical Works* of 1863, and of which *The Ring and the Book* is a development; on this topic see Woolford 1988, esp. chs 2 and 4. Browning's crucial moment of disillusion in the capacity of his readers to follow him came in the aftermath of *Men and Women*: see the exchange of letters with Ruskin reproduced in Appendix B, esp. p. 258.

'All poetry [is] a putting of the infinite into the finite,' Browning wrote to Ruskin; but 'Thrusting in time eternity's concern' brings Sordello to grief (i 566). Yet this 'putting' and 'thrusting' are acts of love: the gap between ideal and real is a necessary condition of love (and of art). The speaker of 'Two in the Campagna', in the definitive statement of this paradox in Browning's poetry, says to his beloved:

I would I could adopt your will,
  See with your eyes, and set my heart
Beating by yours, and drink my fill
  At your soul's springs, – your part, my part
In life, for good and ill.

No. I yearn upward – touch you close,
  Then stand away. I kiss your cheek,
Catch your soul's warmth, – I pluck the rose
  And love it more than tongue can speak –
Then the good minute goes.

Already how am I so far
  Out of that minute? Must I go
Still like the thistle-ball, no bar,
  Onward, whenever light winds blow,
Fixed by no friendly star?

Just when I seemed about to learn!
  Where is the thread now? Off again!
The old trick! Only I discern –
  Infinite passion and the pain
Of finite hearts that yearn.

(ll. 41–60)

In the first of these stanzas, the balance between aggression and surrender is perfectly poised: the speaker is willing the surrender of his will, satisfying himself by a complete merging of that self with another, to the extent that the formula 'for good *and* ill' implies that he actively wants bad experiences as well as good to guarantee the authenticity of his desire. But of course the very perfection of this wish ensures that it will not be fulfilled: the word 'No' shears off the possibility like the blade of a guillotine. The next stanza is ruled not by 'and' but by 'then', not by merging but by separation: 'touch you close, / Then stand away . . . Then the good minute goes.' In the third stanza the mode of desire ('I would I could') is replaced by despairing questions, and in the last stanza the speaker seems lost in pathos and self-pity.

But in the final three lines something odd happens. The grammar of 'Only I discern' means that, though he has experienced the frustration he describes many times before, *this time* he has been able to 'discern' something which he had previously failed to grasp. In order to find out what this something was, we need to go back to the beginning of the poem:

> I wonder do you feel to-day
>    As I have felt, since, hand in hand,
> We sat down on the grass, to stray
>    In spirit better through the land,
> This morn of Rome and May?
>
> For me, I touched a thought, I know,
>    Has tantalised me many times,
> (Like turns of thread the spiders throw
>    Mocking across our path) for rhymes
> To catch at and let go.
>
> Help me to hold it . . .
>
> (ll. 1–11)

There are two *threads*, two actions of *touching*, *tantalising*, *catching*, and *letting go* in the poem, one of them to do with sexual union – 'I touch you close . . . catch your soul's warmth . . . the good minute goes . . . Where is the thread now?' – and the other to do with a 'thought', an idea, which turns out to be that which the speaker 'discerns' at the end: 'Infinite passion, and the pain / Of finite hearts that yearn'. He sees and understands not just his own suffering, but its ground and principle. This painful knowledge he *does* catch, and what he loses as a lover he gains as a poet. It is almost as if the failure of the sexual relationship has been staged for that purpose, so that the speaker cheats the very fate he suffers; and he does so alone, for though the woman 'helps him to hold it' he is left at the end (in the other meaning of 'Only I') alone with his vision.

# MARRIAGE

## Browning's marriage

### 'My perfect wife'

Two myths about Browning's marriage are current. The first, and still the dominant and popular one, is the myth of an ideal union: it circulates in gifte shoppe editions of *Sonnets from the Portuguese* (and in the use of Sonnet xxii ['When our two souls stand up erect and strong'] in the marriage scene of *Love Story*), in snippeted quotations from 'By the Fire-Side' (the title of this section is from l. 101), 'One Word More' and the 'O lyric Love' lines in *The Ring and the Book*, and in the preservation of sacred relics and sites. The Armstrong Browning Library at Baylor University, which has the world's largest and most important collection of manuscripts and printed books by both the Brownings, and which displays and gives scholars access to this material, is in one respect a professional research institution; it is also a shrine, with a memorial chapel dedicated to the Brownings, whose centrepiece is a life-cast of their clasped hands by the American sculptor Harriet Hosmer.[15] In Florence, Casa Guidi, where the Brownings lived for much of their married life, is being lovingly restored with, in some cases, the Brownings' own furniture and possessions. The process of embalming began early. In her very first letter to Browning, dated 14 May 1864, Julia Wedgwood disparaged her own grief at the imminent death of her brother by writing: 'Your own unparalleled loss must dwarf in comparison every other separation' (Curle: 23).[16] Why must it? Because, she wrote in a later letter, Browning had been privileged to cohabit with a spirit. Speaking of the 'paganism' which 'casts its shade over the thoughts of the lost', she wrote:

15. The cast was made in Rome in 1853 (Carr: 92).

16. She repeated the point in a letter of 5 Nov. 1868, after Browning had told her of the death of EBB's sister Arabel: 'I am so grieved to hear you have lost any one [who] belonged to your beloved one. But the world can hardly grow emptier to you than it was when she left it' (p. 150).

> I know that it does not fall upon *your* grave and that for you there has only been a working dress laid aside, precious to you, but not precious to the wearer. This has been your rare privilege, that you had the wearer, and not as most of us, only the garment. I do not mean that there is not the infinite in every soul, but so few of us can reach it – we see nothing but the pattern on the veil! (p. 116)

I wonder how Browning felt at being told in what the 'privilege' of his marriage consisted. But Julia Wedgwood had not done. When she read the first two volumes of *The Ring and the Book* (that is, books i–vi, concluding with Caponsacchi's monologue but not including Pompilia's), she wrote complaining that Browning had exaggerated the 'atmosphere of meanness and cruelty' in the story, that there was 'an absolute superfluity of detail in the hideous portraits', and that even Caponsacchi's language was too coarse: 'Might not his speech have been free from Swift-like metaphor?' (pp. 154–5). Her rebuke was directly linked to her view of Browning's marriage:

> I feel sometimes tempted to be indignant with you for this, because it seems to me you are so bound to give us this which we need. Do you know what an exceptional experience yours has been? . . . love, to most of us, is quite as much the discipline, as the refreshment, of life. We would give our lives for those whose presence is a continual scourge to our taste, or we watch hungrily for the footsteps of those of whose lives we can only think with a blush. Or we deliberately choose companions – perfectly satisfactory to a part of our nature perhaps, but utterly unresponsive to so much, that the joint life seems a starved poor mutilated thing. Does not almost every marriage illustrate some form of this dislocation? But your love had not to split itself up into gratified taste in one direction and exercised severance in another, and intellectual sympathy in a third. One channel held them all.
>
> Did you not thereby contract this debt to us to give some intellectual translation of your experience, and make us feel that love is the principal thing in this world, and the world beyond[?]. (pp. 155–6)

The demand in that last paragraph could hardly be plainer, and it was strengthened by Julia Wedgwood's belief that an 'intellectual translation of experience' was exactly what EBB herself had given in

*Sonnets from the Portuguese*.[17] Browning finds himself coerced not just personally by the idealisation of his marriage, but in terms of his writing. The terms of Julia Wedgwood's description leave no room for stress or gaps: she insists on wholeness and fulness, on an 'exceptional' (and therefore exemplary) union.[18]

Julia Wedgwood may have relied principally on the Brownings' poetry for her view of their marriage; later commentators have had the love-letters as well, and at first sight it looks as though both Browning and EBB were active collaborators in building up the myth of a perfect, and unique, relationship. EBB, in particular, constantly disparages the ordinary notion of marriage, and the ordinary marriages that she witnessed among her friends and social circle:

> To see the marriages which are made everyday! worse than solitudes & more desolate! In the case of the two happiest I ever knew, one of the husbands said in confidence to a brother of mine . . . that he had 'ruined his prospects by marrying,' – & the other said to myself at the very moment of professing an extraordinary happiness, . . . 'But I should have done as well if I had not married *her*.' (21–4 Dec. 1845, Kelley: xi 259)

In a later letter she told Browning an anecdote from the other side of the gender barrier:

> When I was a child I heard two married women talking. One said to the other . . . 'The most painful part of marriage is the first year, when the lover changes into the husband by slow degrees.' The other woman agreed, as a matter of fact is agreed to. I listened with my eyes & ears, & never forgot it . . as you observe. It seemed to me, child as I was, a dreadful thing to have a husband by such a process. (6 July 1846, Kintner: ii 853)

Such observations vary from the humorous to the bleak, but always with the same implication. 'I *saw* a woman, once, burst into tears, because her husband cut the bread & butter too thick,' EBB told

17. 'I do not know any utterance that has the same sort of thrill in it as they have – not that others have not felt it, but it is rarely given to express and experience at once that sort of feeling. Generally the life and the art are two things; at least, it seems to me an exception when they are so much one as they were with her' (1 Nov. 1864, p. 112).

18. Browning himself had specifically told her that this was not the case: see below, p. 141.

Browning (18 Dec. 1845, Kelley: xi 245). Domestic discontent could take a less amusing turn, especially when the discontented party was a man:

> Did you ever observe a lord of creation knit his brows together because the cutlets were underdone, shooting enough fire from his eyes to overdo them to cinders . . . Did you ever hear of the litany which some women say through the first course . . low to themselves . . Perhaps not! – it does not enter into your imagination to conceive of things, which nevertheless *are*.
>
> Not that I ever thought of YOU with reference to SUCH – oh no, no! (7 Apr. 1846, Kelley: xii 221)

That last qualification is typical of many others in the correspondence: both Browning and EBB habitually exempt each other from the comic or tragic vices they observe in marriage. EBB's satirical glimpse of (presumably) her own father's behaviour at the dinner table belongs to a chain of allusions in the correspondence to the abuse of male power; when Browning first became aware of Mr Barrett's domineering temper, he commented on it by telling EBB an anecdote of how he had publicly denounced a brutal self-satisfied husband who bullied and humiliated his wife at a dinner-party (18 Jan. 1846, Kelley: xii 1–2). EBB was as blunt about 'the common rampant man-vices which tread down a woman's peace' as she was certain that Browning was free of them:

> Oh, I understand perfectly, how as soon as ever a common man is sure of a woman's affections, he takes up the tone of right & might . . & he *will* have it so . . & he *won't* have it so! I have heard of the bitterest tears being shed by the victim as soon as ever, by one word of hers, she had placed herself in his power. Of such are 'Lovers' quarrels' for the most part. The growth of power on one side . . & the struggle against it, by means legal & illegal, on the other. There are other causes, of course – but for none of them could it be possible for *me* to quarrel with *you* now or ever. (4 July 1846, Kintner: ii 844)

The topic of unhappy marriage extends from imbalances of power to cover the compromises and adjustments which follow after the 'lover has changed into the husband'. EBB feared all through the courtship that Browning would tire of her, and she also hated the thought that she and Browning might relapse into an 'ordinary' marriage:

> I believe that I never could quarrel with you; but the same cause would absolutely hinder my living with you if you *did* not love me. We could not lead the abominable lives of 'married people' all round – you *know* we could not – *I* at least know that *I* could not, & just because I love you so entirely.
>
> (2 July 1846, Kintner: ii 836)[19]

Browning was quick to respond:

> I feel altogether as you feel about the horribleness of married friends, mutual esteemers &c – when your name sounds in my ear like any other name, your voice like other voices, – when we wisely cease to interfere with each other's pursuits, – respect differences of taste &c &c, all will be over *then!*
>
> (3 July 1846, Kintner: ii 839)

But he was just as quick to deny the possibility, adding at once:

> I cannot myself conceive of one respect in which I shall ever fall from this feeling for you . . there never has been one word, one gesture unprompted by the living, immediate love beneath –

The absoluteness of both lovers' language in such exchanges ('I love you so *entirely*', 'I cannot . . . conceive of *one* respect') posits itself as a guarantee against inadequacy and failure, and matches the violence with which they stigmatise 'the abominable lives of "married people" all round' and 'the horribleness of married friends'. In addition, Browning offers the integrity of the past as an assurance for the future, as though *never has been* were equivalent to *always will be*. In all this the element of self-privileging is rather odious. We are used to artists claiming to be special, but when the artists are lovers and extend the claim to the quality of their love, implying that the rest of us have to make do (or, worse, are happy to make do) with an inferior article, their exalted self-opinion is a little hard to stomach.

Inevitably, therefore, a counter-myth has grown up around the Brownings' marriage. In her influential biography *Robert Browning: A Portrait*, published in 1952, Betty Miller argued that Browning did, indeed, tire of EBB: that all her fears of being a drag on his social and intellectual freedom proved true, that her faddishness and feminine

19. EBB wrote 'learn' first and then corrected it to 'lead'.

indulgence of their son, her political naïvety in hero-worshipping Napoleon III, and her gullibility about spiritualism, irritated and alienated her husband to the extent that his love for her was saved only by her timely death. In the winter of 1860–1, Browning is in vigorous middle age, while EBB is 'drawn and dessicated' with 'the air of a very aged child' (Miller: 213); six months later EBB is glad to die because '[she] knew, now, that nothing was lost: all that she valued was safe . . . now that she was to die, love would live' (p. 217).

The core of Miller's argument is that Browning found himself trapped by his own rhetoric. Throughout the courtship he claimed that he wanted nothing better than to submit his will entirely to hers: 'I should like to breathe and move and live by your allowance and pleasure', he wrote to her (23 Apr. 1846, Kelley: xii 272), and again, 'I wish your will to be mine, to originate mine, your pleasure to be only mine' (4 June 1846, Kintner: ii 757). When they were married, he found EBB willing to oblige – too willing, in fact. Miller quotes a letter in which Browning told EBB 'how much my happiness would be disturbed by allying myself with a woman to whose intellect, as well as goodness, I could *not* look up' (13 Aug. 1846, Kintner: ii 960), and suggests that this was exactly the position in which he found himself after the first years of marriage. Miller notices the preponderance of unhappy love poems in *Men and Women* (she deals with 'One Word More' by calling it a 'laboured' afterthought, hastily put in to redress the balance); she firmly identifies Browning with the disillusioned speaker of 'Two in the Campagna'. She also points to the bitterness of 'James Lee', the poem that opens *Dramatis Personae*, and quotes Browning's description of it to Julia Wedgwood: 'people newly-married, trying to realize a dream of being sufficient to each other, in a foreign land (where you can try such an experiment) and finding it break up – the man being tired *first*, – and tired precisely of the love' (Curle: 123).

Neither the myth of perfect union, nor the counter-myth of disenchantment, seems to me accurate or helpful. Browning's first biographer, Alexandra Sutherland Orr, in whom he confided more than any other person in the last two decades of his life, states forthrightly that 'the marriage was a hazardous experiment', in which 'the latent practical disparities of an essentially vigorous and an essentially fragile existence' eventually made themselves felt (Orr 1891: 147–8). But the risks of an experiment are just that: risks, not results. Orr acknowledges (and I believe that Browning himself is the source of her account here) that EBB's 'ailments were too radical for permanent cure, as the weak voice and shrunken form never ceased to attest' and that, after a remarkable period of recovery and renewal 'in the sunshine of her new life', she 'gradually relapsed, during the winters at least, into something like the home-bound condition of her earlier days'; but she does not conclude that either husband or wife felt that their marriage was a failure as a result:

> It became impossible that she should share the more active side of her husband's existence. It had to be alternately suppressed and carried on without her. The deep heart-love, the many-sided intellectual sympathy, preserved their union in rare beauty to the end. But to say that it thus maintained itself as if by magic, without effort of self-sacrifice on his part or of resignation on hers, would be as unjust to the noble qualities of both, as it would be false to assert that its compensating happiness had ever failed them. (pp. 148–9)

This seems to me a humanly persuasive account, which itself 'preserves the union' from those who seek either to promote it as a myth, or to debunk it. The same is true of the particular differences of opinion, the gaps and strains which we can discern over the years of the marriage: these undoubtedly qualify what the lovers claimed or expected during their courtship, but they do not amount to the kind of final estrangement depicted in 'James Lee'. Browning himself wrote on this point to Isa Blagden:

> α β γ δ ε χ ι There! Those letters indicate seven distinct issues to which I came with Ba, in our profoundly different estimates of thing and person: I go over them one by one, and must deliberately [and] inevitably say, on each of these points I was, am proved to be, right and she wrong. And I am glad I maintained the truth on each of these points, did not say, 'what matter whether they be true or no? – Let us only care to love each other.' (19 Sept. 1867, McAleer 1951: 282)[20]

20. The letters are Greek: alpha, beta, gamma, delta, epsilon, chi, iota. The seven issues cannot all be identified, but certainly include, as McAleer suggests, spiritualism, the role of Napoleon III in Italian politics, the upbringing of Pen, and the trustworthiness of a once-close friend, Sophie Eckley. McAleer suggests three other possibilities, one of which ('their own marriage, which EBB at first opposed') seems very unlikely.

It is fair to say that Browning had not written like this during the courtship: on one occasion, during a dispute with EBB over the morality of duelling, he wrote to her: 'I submit, unfeignedly, to you, there as elsewhere' (9 Apr. 1846, Kelley: xii 229), and it was she who had gently to remonstrate: 'you cannot, you know, – you know you cannot, dearest . . "submit" to me in an *opinion*, any more than I could to you, if I desired it ever so anxiously' (9 Apr. 1846, Kelley: xii 230). During the courtship Browning had a particular motive for wishing to insist that he *could* submit in this way;[21] but in their marriage he accepted her sensible and principled discrimination between love and judgement. And he developed his own version of it to Julia Wedgwood:

> it is so easy, wickedly easy, for people indifferent to each other never to quarrel: thence comes it that living in families tends to cretinize one – you find out early all about your fellows, love them always, but have no more curiosity about them, have no hope of improving them in any way, nor indeed desire it – they will *do* as they are: but you yourself will not do as you are, and if you wish another spirit to keep close by you while you go up higher, offences must come, and the wings get in the way of each other: how easily that must be seen by the bird that gets first to the height! Of course I was fortunate through the peculiarity of the relation: in that closeness there could be no misunderstanding: but had there been, I should care nothing about it now. (19 Aug. 1864, Curle: 63)[22]

Browning suggests that he and EBB could differ without 'misunderstanding', that is, without either of them assuming that the nature and quality of their love were threatened by particular disagreements. On the contrary: it is precisely because they are engaged in an emulative ascent, a joint effort to 'go up higher', that

21. See Karlin 1985: 150–1 for more on this point.

22. This passage is prefaced by an observation which Browning made in a mountain-pass in the Pyrenees, where he was staying at the time: 'I liked best of all a great white-breasted hawk I saw sunning himself on a ledge, with his wings ready'. The date of the letter is close to the start of composition of *The Ring and the Book*, and the images of the hawk and the 'bird that gets first to the height' clearly anticipate the invocation to EBB in that poem.

'offences must come'. The phrase derives from Jesus's words in *Matthew* xviii: 7: 'it must needs be that offences come; but woe to that man by whom the offence cometh!' Browning's quotation is characteristically revisionary: he disarms the 'woe', and converts conflict between lovers into a necessary condition of true love itself.

## EBB's influence on Browning's work[23]

In the courtship correspondence, Browning repeatedly told EBB that he wanted and intended his poetry to be influenced by her. He had strong motives for doing so both at the very outset of their friendship, when he wanted to establish her as his superior, and as the friendship developed into a love affair, when he wanted to counteract her perennial fear that she would be a burden to him or would bring him bad luck. Not only did he send her his work-in-progress as soon as he could manoeuvre her into agreeing to 'correct' it (a word she vigorously disputed), but when their marriage was decided he emphasised that this represented only the beginning of the process. 'I look forward to a real life's work for us both', he wrote to her: '*I* shall do all, – under your eyes and with your hand in mine, – all I was intended to do' (6 Feb. 1846, Kelley: xii 45). This is the first of a cluster of such statements in the period in which he was preparing for the press the last works he was to publish before marriage, *Luria* and *A Soul's Tragedy*: he seemed to himself to have reached a threshold beyond which a different kind of creative life awaited him. When he finished revising a batch of proof, he wrote to EBB:

> all my work (work!) – well, such as it is, it is done – and I scarcely care *how*. I shall be prouder to begin one day – (may it be soon! –) with your hand in mine from the beginning – *that* is a very different thing in its effect from the same hand touching mine *after* I had begun, with no suspicion such a chance could befall! (25 Mar. 1846, Kelley: xii 178)

Again, four days later: 'I seriously hope and trust to shew my sense of gratitude for what is promised my future life, by doing some real work in it, – work of yours, as thro' you' (29 Mar. 1846, Kelley: xii 187). And yet again, a week later, this time illustrating the point with a lengthy simile:

23. On the general question of influence in Browning's poetry, see Chapter 1, where EBB's influence is also discussed.

> I have told you, and tell you, and will tell you, my Ba, because it is simple truth, – that you have been 'helping' me to cover a defeat, not gain a triumph. If I had not known you *so far* THESE works might have been the *better*, – as assuredly, the greater works, I trust will follow, – they would have suffered in proportion! If you take a man from prison and set him free . . do you not probably cause a signal interruption to his previously all-ingrossing occupation, and sole labour of love, of carving bone-boxes, making chains of cherry-stones and other such time-beguiling operations – does he ever take up that business with the old alacrity? No! But he begins ploughing, building – (castles he makes, no bone-boxes now) – I may plough & build – but these, – leave them as they are!
>
> (1 Apr. 1846, Kelley: xii 201–2)

We usually associate the imagery of imprisonment with EBB, not Browning (the darkened room in Wimpole Street, the oppressive jailor-father), and though elements of the picture have become grossly distorted over time there is no doubt that EBB herself was in part responsible for it. 'I have done most of my talking by the post of late years – as people shut up in dungeons, take up with scrawling mottos on the walls', she wrote to him in her third letter (3 Feb. 1845, Kelley: x 51). And she stressed that her art had suffered: in another early letter she lamented that she 'had seen no Human nature' and 'had beheld no great mountain or river – nothing in fact', and went on:

> And do you also know what a disadvantage this ignorance is to my art. Why if I live on & yet do not escape from this seclusion, do you not perceive that I labour under signal disadvantages . . that I am, in a manner, as a *blind poet*?
>
> (20 Mar. 1845, Kelley: x 133)

EBB famously did 'escape' and 'live on', with Browning playing the role of liberator: 'lifting me from the ground and carrying me into life & the sunshine', as she wrote to him on the day after their marriage (13 Sept. 1846, Kintner: ii 1064). Yet in 'By the Fire-Side' (l. 101) the speaker calls his wife 'my Leonor', the character in Beethoven's opera *Fidelio* (subtitled 'Married Love') who rescues her husband from prison, and even if this poem is not straightforwardly autobiographical the persistence of the image of the wife as liberator is striking. Nor is Browning's self-image as a prisoner, practising a cramped, introverted, death-minded art, odd in itself; it matches other images of frustrated or blocked creativity in the correspondence with EBB, for example the image of the light imprisoned in the lighthouse which is discussed in Chapter 2 (p. 51). But there *is* something odd about the prospect of liberation itself.

In order to understand this oddness, we need to go back to another image of poetic limitation, applied to the poet Eglamor in *Sordello*. Sordello defeats Eglamor in a singing-contest and takes his place as Palma's minstrel, and Browning makes it clear that Eglamor's inferiority is not one of degree, but of kind:

> He, no genius rare,
> Transfiguring in fire or wave or air
> At will, but a poor gnome that, cloistered up,
> In some rock-chamber with his agate cup,
> His topaz rod, his seed-pearl, in these few
> And their arrangement finds enough to do
> For his best art.
>
> (ii 213–19)

The four primal elements of creation were traditionally arranged in an ascending order: earth, water, air, and fire. Eglamor is an earth-creature, a 'gnome', who works *in* the lowest element, imprisoned in his 'rock-chamber', and *with* this element, whose most precious forms still permit only 'arrangement' and not 'transfiguring'. The cup, the rod, and the seed are images of magical fertility, but they are literally turned to stone; Eglamor is trapped in his identity, and can transfigure neither his materials nor himself. He is what he is *intrinsically*: he is a gnome, not a genius, just as Sordello is a genius and not a gnome. If you took Eglamor out of his 'rock-chamber' he would not become any different; indeed the concept of setting him free is beside the point, since the rock-chamber is a metaphor of his *identity* and not his *situation*. In his letter to EBB, on the other hand, Browning represents himself as imprisoned not by nature but by circumstance; he claims, as it were, not to resemble Eglamor, but Chatterton, as Browning had described him in his 1842 essay,

> setting sometimes to work with the poorest materials; like any painter a fathom below ground in the Inquisition, who in his penury of colour turns the weather-stains on his dungeon wall into effects of light and shade, or outlines of objects, and makes the single sputter of red paint in his possession go far indeed!
>
> (Woolford and Karlin: ii 502–3)

The implication is clear: release the painter from the dungeons of the Inquisition, and he would make the most of great opportunities as he had of small.

Did Browning really think of himself as improvable in this way? There is a contradiction between what he says to EBB in the courtship correspondence, and almost everything else we know about his self-definition as an artist. Ten years after EBB's death, he wrote to Isa Blagden: 'the simple truth is that *she* was the poet, and I the clever person by comparison: remember her limited experience of all kinds, and what she made of it – remember, on the other hand, how my uninterrupted health & strength, & practice with the world have helped me' (McAleer 1951: 365). In this view Browning is no better off for his opportunities: he has not changed from being a 'clever person' to a 'poet', he is still a 'gnome', stuck in his rock-chamber, while EBB figures as a 'genius rare' who, like the painter in his dungeon, made the best of her 'limited experience'.[24]

What, then, does the evidence tell us about EBB's influence on Browning's poetry in the period of their courtship and marriage? The effort Browning made to write in a visionary, personal style, the style he admired in EBB and other 'subjective' poets, shows in *Christmas Eve and Easter Day*, the first new works he wrote after his marriage: these two dream-poems, autobiographical fictions in which Browning incorporates religious and philosophical speculation, are uneasy and abortive works, and Browning did not return to this mode until *La Saisiaz* in 1878, and then in a heavily qualified form. He told EBB that he wanted nothing better than to 'stoop of a sudden under and out of this dancing ring of men & women hand in hand' (26 Feb. 1845, Kelley: x 98); but in *Men and Women* the dance continues, and in 'One Word More' Browning explained that it must be so, that his creativity was inalienably dramatic: 'One Word More' itself is an exception, a unique event: 'Once, and only once, and for One only' (l. 60). If EBB was not to change the kind of poet Browning was, then what of her influence on his subject matter and style? Plenty of lines and passages in Browning's poems reflect his reading of EBB's work,

24. Unlike EBB herself, and almost every subsequent commentator, Browning does not seem to acknowledge that EBB's poetry improved as a result of her marriage to him, whether in terms of the wider personal and social experience it gave her, or of the influence of his own poetry on hers.

and his reflections on it: these lines from 'A Vision of Poets', for example, a poem of hers which he singled out for praise, certainly went into the rich mix of sources for 'Childe Roland':

> [He] with a deathly sickness, passed
> Beside the fourth pool and the last,
> Where weights of shadow were downcast
>
> From yew and alder and rank trails
> Of nightshade clasping the trunk-scales
> And flung across the intervals
>
> From yew to yew: who dares to stoop
> Where those dank branches overdroop,
> Into his heart the chill strikes up;
>
> He hears a silent gliding coil,
> The snakes strain hard against the soil,
> His foot slips in their slimy oil,
>
> And toads seem crawling on his hand,
> And clinging bats but dimly scanned
> Full in his face their wings expand.
> (ll. 163–77)

The image of the 'last leaf' in 'By the Fire-Side' (ll. 201–15) clearly alludes to the image of the leaf in EBB's 'The Weakest Thing'; the use of Giotto's unfinished campanile as a central metaphor in 'Old Pictures in Florence' is anticipated in EBB's *Casa Guidi Windows* (i 67–72); indeed the whole of 'Old Pictures in Florence' is a kind of pendant to *Casa Guidi Windows*, to which it pays homage by name in line 260. Examples could be multiplied, but they do not really differ from similar traces in Browning's poetry of his responsive reading of Tennyson, or Arnold, or Dickens. They show that EBB's poetry *affected* Browning, but not that it changed the direction or pattern of his creative life. Such a change did, however, take place, though not permanently, in Browning's style and tone.

As we have seen, Browning told EBB that the work he had begun before he knew her was incapable of real improvement; nevertheless, in the period of the courtship he took account of her criticisms of the poems of *Dramatic Romances and Lyrics* and the two plays *Luria* and *A Soul's Tragedy*, and a comparison of her notes on the manuscripts of these works with their published versions shows how closely Browning followed her advice.[25] He went further than this after they were married by undertaking a complete revision of all his published work for his first collected edition, the *Poems* of 1849.[26] Much of this revision consists of expansion and clarification (the former often caused by the latter). Like almost every other critic of Browning before or since, EBB found him unnecessarily obscure, elliptical and difficult: when she first saw *Pippa Passes* she joked to Mary Russell Mitford: ' "Pippa passes" . . comprehension, I was going to say!' (Kelley: v 75). She clearly saw Browning's revisions as they were being made: she wrote to Anna Jameson on 4 February 1847: 'Robert is very busy with his new edition, and has been throwing so much golden light into "Pippa", that everybody shall see her "pass" properly . . yes, and *sur*pass' (cited Miller: 136–7). And Browning agreed: 'The point which decided me to wish to get printed over again', he wrote to his publisher Edward Moxon, 'was the real good I thought I could do to *Paracelsus*, *Pippa*, and some others; good, not obtained by cutting them up and reconstructing them, but by affording just the proper revision they ought to have had before they were printed at all' (24 Feb. 1847, Hood: 14). Besides her concern with clarity of meaning and syntax, EBB persistently recommended Browning to smooth out his metre. In her notes on the poems of *Dramatic Romances and Lyrics* the word 'rhythm' occurs again and again, usually sounding the knell for some rough felicity; here too the 1849 text shows further signs of her influence.[27]

But EBB's influence on the style of the poems is only part of the story. In her first letter to Mary Russell Mitford about *Pippa Passes*, she criticised its obscurity, but also remarked: 'Was there any need for so

25. These notes may be found in the annotations of both Woolford and Karlin (vol. ii) and Jack *et al.* (vol. iv).

26. The only major omissions from this collection were *Pauline*, which Browning could not bear to acknowledge, *Strafford*, and *Sordello*, which he reserved for an even more ambitious and extensive rewriting (which, as it turned out, he was unable to accomplish). A prefatory note in the first volume states: 'The various Poems and Dramas have received the author's most careful revision.'

27. In 1845 EBB missed (probably because she saw it too late) the striking abruptness of the opening of 'Home-Thoughts, from the Sea': 'Nobly Cape St. Vincent to the north-west died away'; in 1849 Browning added a second 'nobly', regularising the metre and ruining the effect.

much coarseness?' Though her admiration for the work rather increased than diminished, it is likely that some of this original sentiment persisted and communicated itself to Browning; at any rate *Pippa Passes* in 1849 is not just longer and more explanatory, but more genteel: some of the original 'coarseness' (about sex, inevitably, but also about class) is toned down. This partly accounts for the trouble Browning took over the Jules–Phene episode, and in particular the figure of Phene herself, the prostitute whom Jules has been tricked into marrying. Example 4.1 shows the 1841 and 1849 versions of lines 105–17.

The 1849 version is clearer in its syntax: the 'if I do not try . . . it is to keep myself' clause replaces the 'I do not attempt . . . that I may keep myself' clause, making Phene more coherent but not necessarily more convincing; the change of a single letter (from 'bade' to 'made') lets her off the hook a bit, so that Natalia (her pimp) seems to bully her rather than persuade her to co-operate; the change of pronouns from 'you' to 'it' means that Phene talks more precisely about the effect of Jules's voice, but the precision is bought at the cost of a certain amount of human warmth. The change in order from 'altered . . . altering –' to 'altering – altered!' similarly makes Phene more logical but less natural: it looks as if Browning had momentarily forgotten that this is how people really think and speak, and were remembering only how they read and write. As for the added lines, they seem altogether incongruous. In 1841 Phene speaks; in 1849 she declaims, using an abstract vocabulary to discuss metaphysical distinctions. The simplicity and brevity of her lines in 1841 are equally a part of the realism of the scene and of its dramatic pace; in 1849 the scene pauses while Phene is given elevated and self-pitying sentiments to utter. From being a young, scared, ignorant working-class girl, she becomes a proto-Pompilia, genteelly vulnerable and yet trenchantly moral.

Browning came to distrust the general project of revision he undertook for the 1849 *Poems*; many revised lines and passages (though not the one just discussed) return to the first-edition reading in the *Poetical Works* of 1863, the first collection published after EBB's death. But EBB's influence went deeper and lasted longer than its local impact would suggest: for a decade after her death Browning continued to take pains to make himself clear and accessible to his readers, and to woo them with direct address, even if somewhat gruffly ('Well, British Public, ye who like me not' may not sound very

**Example 4.1**

*1841*

Oh, you . . what are you? – I do not attempt
To say the words Natalia bade me learn
To please your friends, that I may keep myself
Where your voice lifted me – by letting you
Proceed . . but can you? – even you perhaps
Cannot take up, now you have once let fall,
The music's life, and me along with it?
No – or you would . . we'll stay then as we are
Above the world –

Now you sink – for your eyes
Are altered . . . altering – stay – 'I love you,
love you,' –
I could prevent it if I understood
More of your words to me . . was't in the tone
Of the voice, your power?

*1849*

Oh, you . . what are you? – if I do not try
To say the words Natalia made me learn
To please your friends, it is to keep myself
Where your voice lifted me – by letting it
Proceed . . but can it? – even you perhaps
Cannot take up, now you have once let fall,
The music's life, and me along with that –
No – or you would . . we'll stay then as we are
– Above the world.
You creature with the eyes!
If I could look for ever up to them,
As now you let me, – I believe, all sin,
All memory of wrong done or suffering borne,
Would drop down, low and lower, to the earth
Whence all that's low comes, and there touch
and stay
– Never to overtake the rest of me,
All that, unspotted, reaches up to you,
Drawn by those eyes! What rises is myself,
Not so the shame and suffering; but they sink,
Are left, I rise above them – Keep me so
Above the world!
But you sink, for your eyes
Are altering – altered! –stay – 'I love you,
love you' . . .
I could prevent it if I understood
More of your words to me . . . was't in the tone
Or the words, your power?

endearing, but most readers of *The Ring and the Book* were probably too surprised at Browning acknowledging their existence to mind). Only with *Fifine at the Fair*, which he described as his 'most metaphysical and boldest' poem since *Sordello*, did he revert to type; and he was right, as he told Alfred Domett, to be 'very doubtful as to its reception by the public' (Horsman: 52–3). It is not without irony, and perhaps not without significance, that the subject of the poem is a husband's brilliant, prolonged, and perverse refusal to listen to his wife.

## Marriage in Browning

Marriage is one of the central topics of Browning's poetry. Of his twenty-one plays and long poems, three – *The Ring and the Book*, *Balaustion's Adventure*, and *Fifine at the Fair* – are founded on the relation between a husband and wife; in eight others – *Sordello*, *Pippa Passes*, *King Victor and King Charles*, *A Blot in the 'Scutcheon*, *Colombe's Birthday*, *A Soul's Tragedy*, *Red Cotton Night-Cap Country*, and *The Inn Album* – such a relation, actual or prospective, is crucial to the story. Of the shorter poems, 'My Last Duchess', 'The Flight of the Duchess', 'By the Fire-Side', 'Any Wife to Any Husband', 'Andrea del Sarto', 'James Lee', 'Too Late', 'Dîs Aliter Visum', 'The Worst of It', 'The Householder', 'A Forgiveness', 'Doctor –', and 'Beatrice Signorini' stand out; but you might immediately add a host of passages, stanzas, stray lines and phrases in poems where marriage is not a central concern, from the brilliant cameo of marital tension in the opening section of 'A Likeness' to the witty and cruelly apt cuckolding of De Lorge in the last lines of 'The Glove'; from the spirited evocation of 'my wife Gertrude', who 'laughs when you talk of surrendering' in the third of the 'Cavalier Tunes', to the stroke of tenderness at the climax of 'Hervé Riel', in which the heroic saviour of the French fleet requests nothing more as his reward than shore-leave to see his wife, 'whom I call the Belle Aurore' (l. 124).[28]

Such happy marriages, like happy lovers, are the exception in Browning's work. To take the three long works I mentioned: the central marital relationship of *The Ring and the Book* is characterised by deception, hatred, and violence; Balaustion, in *Balaustion's*

28. Browning may have been especially drawn to this detail because of EBB's *Aurora Leigh*.

*Adventure*, recites Euripides' *Alcestis* with her own running commentary on the abject cowardice of Admetus in allowing Alcestis to sacrifice herself on his behalf; in *Fifine at the Fair*, Don Juan's wonderful mind – quick, playful, speculative, bold – implicitly allies itself with his infidelity and mocks his wife's misery. Happiness is for the most part not a complex phenomenon, and Browning liked complexity; 'By the Fire-Side' is a rare example of a poem about faithful loving marriage whose psychology is as intricate as that, say, in 'A Forgiveness'. In his representation of unhappy or bad marriages there is little bias: infidelity is practised by both sexes, both dominate and exploit weak or helpless partners, both are capable of corruption. As usual, we should beware of assuming that Browning's own opinions coincide with those of his characters: 'Any Wife to Any Husband' suggests not that Browning believes that men are less constant than women, but that he believes that women believe it. There is as little 'Victorian' soppiness about marriage in Browning as there is unthinking misogyny; perhaps only 'Doctor –' counts as an example of the latter.[29]

An interest in marriage is not unusual in the period: it preoccupied novelists, of course, but also churchmen, social critics, and legislators.[30] Coventry Patmore's *The Angel in the House* (1854–1863) and George Meredith's *Modern Love* (1862) are only the most famous of a proliferation of poetic treatments: the *English Poetry Full-Text*

29. Satan complains to God about the proverb 'Stronger than Death is a Bad Wife'. God tells him to test its truth, so Satan comes to earth and marries. The dénouement of the story proves the proverb to be correct. It also proves that Browning couldn't tell Jewish jokes.

30. The Civil Marriage Act of 1836, many times amended in Browning's lifetime, is the foundation of modern practice in respect of the procedures of marriage; the Matrimonial Causes Act of 1857, also many times amended, is the foundation of modern practice in respect of divorce. The Married Women's Property Act was passed in 1870. For the social history of marriage in the period, see among others J.R. Gills, *For Better, For Worse* (Oxford: Oxford University Press, 1985), and L. Davidoff and C. Hall, *Family Fortunes: Men and Women of the English Middle Class 1780–1850* (London: Hutchinson 1987). A good deal of the material in L. Stone, *The Family, Sex, and Marriage in England 1500–1800* (New York 1977) and in A. Macfarlane, *Marriage and Love in England 1300–1840* (Oxford: Blackwell 1986) is still relevant to the period of the Brownings' marriage.

*Database* has over two hundred examples of poems with 'marriage', 'husband', or 'wife' in the title in the mid-nineteenth century alone.[31] What is surprising is to find the spirit of analysis and definition, which we might expect to flourish among the social critics and the legislators, active among the poets also. There are many Victorian poems *about* marriage, concerned with saying what it is, or should be. 'Right Marriage: elevation in communion, / The joy of perfect freedom, closest union', runs a complete poem by William Allingham; Letitia Landon (L.E.L.) takes a less sanguine view in her poem 'The Marriage Vow', which opens 'The altar, 'tis of death! for there are laid / The sacrifice of all youth's sweetest hopes'. It is hard to find anything in Browning like this, or like Robert Leighton's 'True Marriage':

> True marriage is two persons but one life;
>   Two brains one mind – the hour-glass and the sand,
> No grain of reservation – husband, wife –
>   One interest, hand in hand.

This is more like versified dogma than poetry; Browning's characters may say things like this, but narrative and dramatic context troubles and complicates our response to them. In *The Ring and the Book*, for example, the characters all repeatedly produce a whole series of conventional definitions of marriage, but virtually none of these definitions corresponds either to the character's own experience and beliefs, or to any view of the matter which we might attribute to the poem itself. Pompilia, at the beginning of her monologue, describes the emotional vertigo she felt when Pietro and Violante, whom she thought her parents, disowned her; and she goes on:

> So with my husband, – just such a surprise,
> Such a mistake, in that relationship!
> Everyone says that husbands love their wives,
> Guard them and guide them, give them happiness;
> 'Tis duty, law, pleasure, religion: well,
> You see how much of this comes true in mine!
> (vii 150–5)

31. Needless to say there must be many more poems about marriage than this; only two of Browning's, for example, 'Any Wife to Any Husband' and 'James Lee's Wife' (the revised title of 'James Lee') showed up in the title search. Poems which are about marriage, but which do not mention marriage in the title, are more likely to be narrative or dramatic.

Pompilia's naïvety exposes the gap between what 'everyone says' and what, in fact, everyone knows about marriage; but it is more than an instrument for detecting social hypocrisy, it is a *negation of social convention itself*. Pompilia is an absolutist, intolerant of any gap between language and meaning: in the end she is martyred for her intransigence. Whether the poem intends to beatify her for it is more problematic – as problematic as whether it intends to damn Guido for taking the opposite line, for assuming that marriage is nothing more than a transaction. In his first monologue, Guido argues that he followed the advice of his brother, Paul, and took his aristocratic title to market; and like Pompilia he is (or affects to be) naïve about the business:

> Now, Paul's advice was weighty: priests should know:
> And Paul apprised me, ere the week was out,
> That Pietro and Violante, the easy pair,
> The cits enough, with stomach to be more,
> Had just the daughter and exact the sum
> To truck for the quality of myself: 'She's young,
> Pretty and rich: you're noble, classic, choice.
> Is it to be a match?' 'A match,' said I.
> Done! He proposed all, I accepted all,
> And we performed all. So I said and did
> Simply.
>
> (v 413–23)

Guido's 'simplicity' consists in taking the social world as he finds it. For he is well aware of the objection to his action, indeed he voices it immediately with a parody of virtuous indignation:[32]

> As simply followed, not at first
> But with the outbreak of misfortune, still
> One comment on the saying and the doing – 'What?
> No blush at the avowal you dared buy
> A girl of age beseems your granddaughter,
> Like ox or ass? Are flesh and blood a ware?
> Are heart and soul a chattel?'

32. Browning's speakers habitually incorporate opposing voices in their own discourse: see Chapter 2, p. 44.

> Softly, Sirs!
> Will the Court of its charity teach poor me
> Anxious to learn, of any way i' the world,
> Allowed by custom and convenience, save
> This same which, taught from my youth up, I trod?
> Take me along with you; where was the wrong step?
> (ll. 423–35)

With sly wit, Browning makes Guido stumble over that last line, with its extra foot; but Guido has, too, a sharp eye for the hypocrisy of his critics, whose rebuke comes only after 'the outbreak of misfortune'. His idea of marriage as a social transaction, regulated by 'custom and convenience' and having nothing to do with romance, belongs to his dirty realism, his insistence on fact over fancy. Yet he discovers that the world will not stand for his honesty any more than it will stand for Pompilia's innocence. She will be destroyed for taking the world at face value ('Everyone says that husbands love their wives'), and he will be destroyed for refusing to do so.

The absolutism of both Guido and Pompilia is set against the norm of marriage as social partnership. The marriage of Pietro and Violante represents this norm, which is also associated with 'the modest middle class' to which they belong (ii 194): all the poem's speakers add touches to its composite portrait of the strong-minded, social-climbing wife and her weak, easy-going husband, a portrait whose psychology is as rooted in circumstantial detail as it would be in a novel by Dickens or Balzac. So, to a lesser extent, is the glimpse we get of the lawyer Archangelis's marriage: his affection for his 'good wife, buxom and bonny yet' (viii 25) is mixed up with the mercenary expectations he has of her family. Indeed, Archangelis concludes his monologue by linking his own marriage with that of Pietro and Violante: if his wife persuades her father to cancel a bequest to his nephew and transfer it to their son instead,

> The wife should get a necklace for her pains,
> The very pearls that made Violante proud,
> And Pietro pawned for half their value once . . .
> Her bosom shall display the big round balls,
> No braver should be borne by wedded wife!
> (ll. 1793–1800)

Archangelis and his wife are in partnership; conjugal affection is part of this partnership, but so is social pride and a comfortable indifference to the fate of those who slip up in the race of life. Archangelis and his wife take the place of Pietro and Violante, a successful bourgeois enterprise acquiring the assets of one that has been broken up.

Neither Guido nor Pompilia can come to terms with marriage as such a partnership, in which emotional and material interests are balanced; neither belongs to the social ground on which Pietro and Violante and Archangelis stand – Guido because he is noble in one sense, and Pompilia because she is noble in the other. Pompilia in particular is the heroine of a reverse fairy-tale, in that she is a foundling whose real social origin is not higher but lower than that of her putative parents; far from being a princess in disguise, she is the illegitimate daughter of a prostitute; yet *just as if she were of royal birth*, she grows up with hallmarks of beauty, virtue, and sensitivity which mark her out from her supposed class. Her nightmarish marriage to Guido is, in this sense, as extreme a sign of her specialness as the transcendent marriage which she imagines as its replacement. Towards the end of her monologue, she contemplates the impossibility of an earthly union with Caponsacchi, and makes that impossibility into a ground on which all human marriages are judged and found wanting:

He is a priest;
He cannot marry therefore, which is right:
I think he would not marry if he could.
Marriage on earth seems such a counterfeit,
Mere imitation of the inimitable:
In heaven we have the real and true and sure.
'Tis there they neither marry nor are given
In marriage but are as the angels: right,
Oh how right that is, how like Jesus Christ
To say that! Marriage-making for the earth,
With gold so much, – birth, power, repute so much,
Or beauty, youth so much, in lack of these!
Be as the angels rather, who, apart,
Know themselves into one, are found at length
Married, but marry never, no, nor give
In marriage; they are man and wife at once
When the true time is: here we have to wait
Not so long neither!

(vii 1821–38)

The biblical text to which Pompilia refers is *Matthew* xxii 30, and comes in reply to a trick question posed to Jesus by the Sadducees; it is far from supporting Pompilia's reading of it. Jesus says that people in heaven are like angels, but not that angels enjoy a superior kind of human sexuality. Perhaps Pompilia is thinking (so to speak) of the moment in *Paradise Lost* when Adam makes Raphael blush by asking whether the angels have sex, and Raphael replies that they do, and that it is better than the human sort. But Raphael's explanation is that since the angels are incorporeal, their 'union' is unobstructed by the 'exclusive bars' of the body (viii 622–9), and this is not quite what Pompilia has in mind. For her, human marriage is imperfect not because it is physical, but because its essence, which is indeed sexual attraction, is contaminated by *marriage-making*, the 'production' of marriage as the result of an economic process, a transaction involving money, social status, and the body. Perfect marriage is the result of a mutual 'knowing' (the word suggests both sexual and intellectual energy), an act which leaps over the grammatical tense of becoming: the angels 'are found / Married' as though this realisation of their new being had abolished the process which preceded it. No wonder earthly marriage seems 'counterfeit' to Pompilia; such transcendence is, truly, 'inimitable' in human time. But we are entitled to ask whether the poem endorses this exalted depreciation. After all Pompilia has a strong motive for wanting Caponsacchi, in particular, to subscribe to her view of marriage, since this will prevent him from even wishing to be married on earth and will save him for her in heaven. In fact Pompilia is going a step beyond Caponsacchi himself, who at the end of *his* monologue wistfully envisages a real, earthly marriage to Pompilia, even though he knows it to be an impossible fantasy – 'Mere delectation, meet for a minute's dream' (vi 2097). Pompilia uses 'we' in her lines to mean, ostensibly, 'everyone', 'human beings in general', but in ll. 1837–8 it comes close to meaning 'he and I'. The logic of Pompilia's argument is either that no one should marry at all, ever, or that those superior beings who perceive the inadequacy of earthly marriage should refrain from it, leaving the sordid business of 'marriage making' to the less sensitive. But logic is not at issue here; it almost never is where Browning's characters are concerned. Pompilia wants to marry Caponsacchi, and this is the only form of marriage in which she can imagine and utter her desire.

# CHAPTER 5
# *Politics*

## Browning's political attitudes

Most of Browning's political attitudes strike us as modern. He supported the emancipation of women. He was opposed to slavery, taking the side of the North in the American Civil War. Late in life, he championed Animal Rights in a series of poems attacking vivisection. In only one or two early and uncharacteristic works does he sound jingoistic,[1] and unlike Tennyson or Ruskin he never joined in the widespread Victorian glorification of war; nor did he acclaim the Empire. Almost the only issue on which he would now be called 'right-wing' was the Irish Question: according to his first biographer, Alexandra Orr, he was 'a passionate Unionist' (Orr 1891: 374).[2]

Many of these attitudes he held in common with his contemporaries of the intelligentsia, but in some he seems ahead of his time, or in a curious way out of tune with it. Orwell remarked that George Eliot and Dickens were almost the only Victorian writers who stuck up for the Jews: in fact Browning did so more consistently than either, arousing speculation that he must himself be Jewish.[3] For Orr, his feminism was if anything excessive. She notes that he 'was not, in the received sense of the word, chivalrous', and goes on:

1. The linked poems 'Home-Thoughts, from Abroad' and 'Home-Thoughts, from the Sea' are the principal examples: they were of course relentlessly anthologised.
2. There is no reason to doubt the word of this sober and scrupulous biographer, who was also Browning's close friend.
3. See in particular 'Holy-Cross Day' (1855) and 'Filippo Baldinucci on the Principle of Burial' (1876). Friends such as Mrs Orr and Frederick Furnivall showed what now seems almost a comic, or perhaps a sinister eagerness to prove that Browning was nevertheless not Jewish.

> Chivalry proceeds on the assumption that women not only cannot, but should not, take care of themselves in any active struggle with life; Mr. Browning had no theoretical objection to a woman's taking care of herself . . . he never quite understood that the strongest women are weak, or at all events vulnerable, in the very fact of their sex . . . (Orr 1891: 394–5)

Orr finds this attitude 'unconventional', and it is a word which takes us a long way towards understanding at least the tonality of Browning's politics. There is always something extreme, or unpredictable, as when he records having walked out of a dinner party because the host had been rude to his wife (Kelley xii: 1–2), or when Orr records how on the issue of the Irish Home Rule he broke with his old friend Gladstone (Orr 1891: 375). Unease at such intensities may be felt in Chesterton's characterisation of him as 'a *very strong* Liberal' (Chesterton: 86; my italics).

Some of this reflects the loudness and vehemence of Browning's later social persona, but I think it also expresses the complexities and compromises of his political development, which make it difficult to categorise him precisely. Of course, people tried. Both Chesterton and Orr call him a 'liberal', and he appears to confirm this designation by writing a poem called 'Why I am a Liberal' in 1877.[4] Before examining the position advanced in this poem, I must consider what the word 'liberal' would have meant to his contemporaries.

## What is a Liberal?

The word 'Liberal' itself, used as the name of a political position rather than a personal quality, is an index of the immense changes which took place in English politics in the nineteenth century. In the eighteenth century two parties, the Whigs and the Tories, divided the political spectrum. These labels originally represented the division between those who supported the dethronement of James II and his replacement by William of Orange – the Whigs – and those who opposed it – the Tories.[5] Both were aristocratic factions rather than

4. The poem was a contribution to a volume edited by Andrew Reid, called *Why I am a Liberal, Being Definitions of the Best Minds of the Liberal Party* (1885).

5. The story is much more tangled than I have space to detail, but religious differences should be mentioned: the Tories were much more hostile to the Puritan (=Dissenter: middle class) grouping of society than the Whigs.

parties in the modern sense, and the intellectual differences which originally distinguished them became very much less important than competition for power and patronage after the Hanoverian dynasty had established itself and extinguished Tory dreams of restoring the Stuarts. The nineteenth century saw the birth of modern party politics, symbolised by the mutation of the Whigs and Tories into Liberals and Conservatives, and their evolution of intellectual positions going beyond immediate factional interests.[6] Crudely, the Liberals stood for reform and a development towards equality, the Conservatives for the opposite. These boundary-lines were not very secure – as witness the passage of the 1867 Reform Act by a Conservative administration – but by 1876, when Trollope published *The Prime Minister*, the fifth in the Palliser series of political novels, it had become possible for him to ascribe something resembling a political ideology to his Liberal statesman Plantagenet Palliser:

> Equality would be a heaven, if we could attain it. How can we to whom so much has been given dare to think otherwise? How can you look at the bowed back and bent legs and abject face of that poor ploughman, who winter and summer has to drag his rheumatic limbs to his work, while you go a-hunting or sit in pride of place among the foremost few of your country, and say that all is as it ought to be? You are a Liberal because you know that it is not all as it ought to be, and because you would still march on to some nearer approach to equality; though the thing itself is so great, so glorious, so godlike, – nay so absolutely divine, – that you have been disgusted by the very promise of it, because its perfection is unattainable. (ch. 68)

Sentiments like this would have informed Browning's perception of himself, and others' perception of him, as a Liberal.

Such changes in Britain were functions of the larger change in European politics in the nineteenth century, changes initiated and symbolised by the formative event of modern history, the French Revolution. It is easy to suppose that because Britain went to war with revolutionary France in 1792 the French Revolution either had no effect in Britain, or was perceived only negatively. In fact there

6. When the Reform Act was passed in 1833, the words 'Liberal' and 'Whig' were still interchangeable as names for the party of Lord John Russell, the Prime Minister.

was and continued to be major support for it in the intelligentsia: Matthew Arnold, who attacked the Liberals and in many ways now looks a reactionary thinker, nevertheless regarded the Revolution not only as a formative but also a necessary and just event, and Carlyle and Dickens likewise represented it as an inevitable if disagreeable development. Because of the wars which followed, the full influence of the revolution was postponed in Britain, and when it came, it did so in a very different and arguably a diluted form. Yet the Reform Act of 1833, however cautious and pragmatic it looks now, in many ways was, and was undoubtedly *felt* to be, as momentous as its predecessor, and it marks the inception of the process which restructured English politics along ideological rather than factional lines. Palliser's statement has behind it the French commitment to equality, but the Reform Act had transformed equality from a revolutionary slogan into a conceivable ideal for a gradualist political philosophy.

## What is a Radical?

But if Browning had been asked to write a poem about his political position around the time of the Reform Act, he would probably have called it 'Why I am a *Radical*'. In one sense, 'Radical' could be seen as a notational variant on 'Liberal'. At the time of the Reform Act, and for some time after, it remained possible to see the Whigs/Liberals as an aristocratic party reluctantly driven towards reform by fear of revolution: indeed, it *was* partly that.[7] 'Radical' at that period was the term adopted by those who stood for a positively reforming politics, a politics of ideology rather than self-interest or fear. At the same time, it was more extreme than Liberalism ever became. English Radicalism at this period harboured the memory of the victims of the Peterloo massacre, the imprisonment of Horne Tooke for supporting the French Revolution, and beyond that the anarchism of Godwin's *Political Justice*. It was peculiarly the province of those who, alienated by class, religion or conviction from aristocratic politics, formed ideal visions of human liberty and equality and promoted political action

7. Bulwer-Lytton, for example, remarked that 'in England Liberal opinion did not favour the equalisation of rank and property' (Lytton: i 416). Parliamentary rejection of prototype Reform Bills caused considerable popular agitation and rioting.

towards these goals.[8] Shelley was a Radical, and much of what went into Browning's Radicalism at this time came to him from Shelley, and from surviving members of Shelley's circle such as Leigh Hunt. Browning was also friendly, during the early 1830s, with the Radical Unitarian preacher and editor W.J. Fox, to whom he offered his second poem, *Paracelsus*, explicitly as a Radical text:

> I shall affix my name & stick my arms akimbo; there are precious bold bits here & there, & the drift & scope are awfully radical, – I am 'off' for ever with the other side, but must by all means be 'on' with yours – a position once gained, worthier works shall follow. (Kelley: iii 134–5)

Similarly, in a letter of 1838 to another friend, Fanny Haworth, concerning his next poem *Sordello*, he spoke of his 'republicanism' (Kelley: iv 269), and in one of his best-known poems, 'The Lost Leader' (1845), he openly espoused the Radical cause in opposition to Wordsworth (the 'lost leader' of his title):

> Shakespeare was of us, Milton was for us,
> Burns, Shelley, were with us, – they watch from their graves!
> He alone breaks from the van and the freemen,
> He alone sinks to the rear and the slaves!
>
> (ll. 13–16)

Browning's 'us' here is complex. On the one hand, it represents a tradition of radical political thought which he identifies with Milton, Burns and Shelley. But the invocation of Shakespeare is accompanied by a distinction between those who, like the others, were 'with' or 'for' us, and a writer who was simply 'of' us. Some clue as to the meaning of this distinction emerges from a letter to John Ruskin:

> Shakespeare was *of* us – not *for* us, like Him of the Defensio; nor abreast with our political sympathies like the other two: I wish he had been more than *of* us. (1 Feb. 1858)[9]

8. Religious affiliation still played an important part in defining political tendencies: there was a strong polarisation during most of the nineteenth century between the Church of England (which was associated with the interests of the ruling class), and the various nonconformist or dissenting churches (which comprehended mainly the middle class and were associated with their reformist politics).

9. Published without editorial attribution as *A Letter from Robert Browning to John Ruskin* (Waco: Baylor Browning Interests, No. 17, n.p.).

It is apparent that Browning is referring here to *class*. Shelley ('Him of the Defensio', i.e. the *Defence of Poetry*) was '*for* us' in the sense that though not himself a member of the lower class – his family was aristocratic – he supported its claims; Shakespeare was *of* that class but (in Browning's view) not sufficiently radical in the sympathies expressed in his work to be thought of as being *for* it. As a middle-class dissenter Browning identifies himself as being, like his correspondent, 'of' as well as 'for us' (such conflation of the middle and lower classes was quite common during the period). Wordsworth's position in 'The Lost Leader' was determined by his renunciation of the Radicalism expressed in his initial support for the French Revolution and for William Godwin's *Political Justice* (1792), the great anarchist text of the Romantic period, a renunciation signalled by his adoption of Tory rhetoric and principles in *Letters to the Electors of Westmorland* (1814). His acceptance of the Poet Laureateship in 1843 was the more immediate cause of Browning's anger. As a court appointment, this post appeared to involve an implicit acceptance of monarchy, and in letters on the subject Browning mocked its ceremonial mummery, in particular the hilarious apparition of Wordsworth in a second-hand court dress which didn't fit (in contrast to EBB, who saw the laureateship rather as a symbol of wider social leadership to be inherited in due course by Browning himself):[10] the poem ends with a pointed reference to a very different kind of 'throne':

> Best fight on well, for we taught him, – come gallantly,
>    Strike our face hard ere we shatter his own;
> Then let him get the new knowledge and wait us,
>    Pardoned in Heaven, the first by the throne!
>
> (ll. 29–32)

The violence of the language of this passage ('fight . . . Strike . . . shatter') mirrors Browning's willingness, in this early period, to countenance actual physical violence in support of political ends. His plays, all written between 1837 and 1845, characteristically involve

10. 'Not that the Laureateship honored *him*, but that he honored it; & that, so honoring it, he preserves a symbol instructive to the masses, who are children & to be taught by symbols now as formerly . . . And wont the court laurel (such as it is) be all the worthier of *you* for Wordsworth's having worn it first?' (30 May 1845, Kelley: x 247).

some kind of revolutionary process and one or two of them condone violence as a legitimate or at least tolerated means: the third episode of *Pippa Passes*, for example, involves a debate between a young revolutionist and his mother about his plan to assassinate the Austrian Emperor, at the end of which he departs on that mission. It is made perfectly clear that this is a good thing to do: when Luigi wavers, Pippa is made to pass by singing a song which confirms and crystallises his resolution.[11] In 1845, we find a poem, 'Italy in England' in which a revolutionist blood-thirstily anticipates how

> I would grasp Metternich until
> I felt his red wet throat distil
> In blood thro' these two hands
> (ll. 121–3)

As late as 1855, in 'De Gustibus –', Browning imagines hearing with relish of an attempt to assassinate a Bourbon monarch, and implicitly approving of the hope that 'they have not caught the felons' (ll. 35–8).

In 'Why I Am a Liberal' Browning defines a very much less assertive political position:

> 'Why?' Because all I haply can and do,
> All that I am now, all I hope to be, –
> Whence comes it save from fortune setting free
> Body and soul the purpose to pursue,
> God traced for both? If fetters, not a few,
> Of prejudice, convention, fall from me,
> These shall I bid men, each in his degree
> Also God-guided – bear, and gaily too?
>
> But little or can do the best of us:
> THAT LITTLE IS ACHIEVED THROUGH LIBERTY.
> Who, then, dares hold – emancipated thus –
> His fellow shall continue bound? Not I,
> Who live, love, labour freely, nor discuss
> A brother's right to freedom. That is 'Why.'

In place of the 'us' of 'The Lost Leader' we meet here an 'I' who, 'free' himself, concludes that logically all others should be free as well. But

11. For a discussion of this episode from a different perspective, see pp. 90–4.

no kind of implementary action is envisaged: Browning himself has been 'set free' by 'fortune', and his assertion, 'But little do or can the best of us' seems to rule out or depreciate human intervention in fortune's allocations. The 'fetters' are no longer of social oppression but mental limitation ('prejudice, convention'), and they 'fall' without visible agency like leaves from a tree. The phrase 'each in his degree' is problematic, in that it implies either that some people are more God-guided than others, or that such guidance is in some way proportioned to or in collusion with the existing social hierarchy ('degrees'). The tortuous reasoning and vehement self-questioning seem a little tired, or reluctant; the phrase 'nor discuss / A brother's right to freedom' almost suggests indifference, and its tone contrasts markedly with Palliser's enthusiasm ('You are a Liberal because you know that it is not all as it ought to be'). Finally, the choice of the most 'closed' of poetic forms, the sonnet, confirmed by the last line's circuit back to the first, hardly seems to lend support to the claim to 'Liberty' which the poem states.

Browning's evolution from Radical to Liberal can be explained in various ways, the unfriendliest of which is Betty Miller's in her brilliant but tendentious biography. Miller clearly believes that after EBB's death Browning essentially sold out to London high society and forgot about his earlier Radicalism. There is some colour for this interpretation in the contrast between the social circles of his early and later years. The young Browning consorted with groups of young middle-class intellectual Radicals like himself,[12] but after his return to England in the 1860s he became a notorious social 'lion', willing to roar at any number of fashionable dinners and evening parties during the 'Season'. His early poems had been dedicated to Radical poets, such as Walter Savage Landor or Thomas Talfourd; *Balaustion's Adventure*, the first of his works to have been wholly conceived after his return to England, is dedicated to the Countess Cowper. Accounts of him in later life stress his powers as a raconteur, and his boisterous geniality; Henry James, another dedicated diner-out, devoted a short story ('The Private Life', 1893) to the puzzling split between this persona and his character as a poet.

12. In his excellent discussion of the 'Colloquials', as they were known, Maynard shows that most of its members were involved in trade or the law, and were 'by the standards of the time and in their own land, progressive in their views' (p. 105).

Miller evidently finds this transformation painful, and it is the case that it accompanied or was accompanied by the disappearance of overt political discourse from his poetry. He became embarrassed by the raw polemics of 'The Lost Leader', half-disclaiming its opinions and softening its attack upon Wordsworth by means of revisions to the text.[13] There is then a reading in which Browning simply became absorbed into the class he had previously distrusted and forgot or renounced his previous dislike of it. I do not think this is adequate, and I cite as contrary evidence a curious shadowy interchange which took place over thirty years between Browning and Edward Lytton Bulwer.

## Browning and the Lyttons

In 1842 Browning published what remains one of his most celebrated poems, 'My Last Duchess'. In it, an unnamed Duke narrates how he had his wife murdered because, in his judgement, she was too lavish with her sympathies, squandering on other people and things the 'smiles' which rightfully belonged to him. He emerges as a monster of pride, patriarchal rigidity and (not paradoxically) coldness or impotence. The phrase 'last Duchess' doesn't mean that the Duke has given up on marriage: quite the reverse. He tells his story to an envoy from a neighbouring Count who has been sent to negotiate terms for the Duke's *next* marriage.

In 1855 a poem called 'The Wife's Tragedy' appeared in a collection of poems by one 'Owen Meredith'. It echoes many phrases from Browning's poem and is clearly a response to it. Its speaker, an Earl this time, characterises his wife, who has left him for another man, as a shallow flirt unable to appreciate that his apparent coldness and neglect resulted from his patriotic commitment to social welfare and the 'labour' this entailed. We are given no reason to question these characterisations other than the Earl's extreme misogyny, which anyway seems to be a consequence of the wife's desertion and hence not criticised.

In 1876 Browning published 'A Forgiveness', one of his own favourite later poems.[14] The speaker (clearly aristocratic, though he

13. See Chapter 1, pp. 36–7 for details.

14. In answer to a request by Edmund Gosse to name 'Four Poems, of moderate length, which represent their writer fairly', he nominated 'A Forgiveness' in the 'narrative' class (Hood: 235).

does not give his name or rank) confesses to a priest that he murdered his wife. He had discovered that she was having an affair, though this was *not*, he claims, the immediate cause of his killing her. After his discovery, his wife declared her hatred for him, and he felt nothing but contempt for her; nevertheless he forced her to keep up the appearance of a happy marriage with him while he continued his 'work' (again unspecified but presumed to be of great national importance).[15] This 'work' was triumphantly completed three years later. At this point husband and wife had a final confrontation, in which the wife revealed that she had loved him all along, and had had the affair as revenge on him for his neglect of her. It is at this point that he killed her: by his perverse emotional logic, the fact that she still loved him released her from the ignominy of his contempt and indifference, and made her worthy of his hatred and revenge. This is the 'forgiveness' of the title. At the very end of the poem, the speaker reveals his knowledge that the priest to whom he is confessing was her lover, and stabs him through the grille of the confessional.[16]

These three poems represent a debate about the aristocratic principle, and it is a debate which exactly reflects the larger debate about the role of the aristocracy in political and social life which was in progress at this time. Browning's initial portrait of an aristocrat is of a man obsessed with rank, and a connoisseur: by a brilliant metonymy these two traits are fused and made to stand for each other, as the Duke's insistence on control of all around him is better satisfied by a portrait than a person:

> That's my last Duchess painted on the wall,
> Looking as if she were alive; I call
> That piece a wonder, now: Frà Pandolf's hands
> Worked busily a day, and there she stands.
> Will't please you sit and look at her? I said
> 'Frà Pandolf' by design, for never read
> Strangers like you that pictured countenance,
> The depth and passion of its earnest glance,
> But to myself they turned (since none puts by

15. It resembles the equally unspecified work which Norbert has performed for the Queen in 'In a Balcony'.
16. For a discussion of the speaker's psychology, and its relation to Browning's ideas about sexual hatred, see Karlin 1993: 203–8.

The curtain I have drawn for you, but I)
And seemed as they would ask me, if they durst,
How such a glance came there; so not the first
Are you to turn and ask thus.
(ll. 1–13)

And as his Duchess appears from behind the curtain when needed, to retire as punctually when the show is over, so the interlocutor, unidentified at this stage, finds himself being initiated into the ritual prescribed for 'Strangers' who 'to myself have turned' with their formulaic request: the Duke's 'Will't please you' has the force of a command. Just as the Duchess is the 'last' (i.e. latest) in a series, so the envoy is 'not the first' to ask about her: the Duke appropriates and stereotypes their identities, enforcing their subordination to his own.

In the first section of 'The Wife's Tragedy', called 'The Evening Before the Flight', the nameless Earl's wife reveals that she is leaving him for another man. The second section is spoken by the Earl, and is called 'The Portrait'. The second stanza reads as follows:

Years, years, years I have not drawn
  Back this curtain! there she stands
By the terrace on the lawn,
  With the white rose in her hands:

The echoes are too strong to miss (for the 'terrace' and the 'white' rose, see below) but Meredith's reading of the situation reverses Browning's. The Earl explains that he was 'vowed to life's broad duty' (st. xii) and this was the reason he seemed 'so calm, so cold', while actually full of 'heart's warmth' towards his wife (st. xxx). And he defines this 'duty' as that of the aristocracy towards the people:

'Mid the armies of Reform,
  To the People's cause allied,
We – the forces of the storm!
  We – the planets of the tide!
(st. xxvii)

The apparent illogicality of this outburst disappears when it is understood as a response to a covert *political* agenda in Browning's poem. For *his* Duchess is in effect a democrat:

She had
A heart . . how shall I say? . . too soon made glad,
Too easily impressed; she liked whate'er
She looked on, and her looks went everywhere.
Sir, 'twas all one! My favor at her breast,
The dropping of the daylight in the West,
The bough of cherries some officious fool
Broke in the orchard for her, the white mule
She rode with round the terrace – all and each
Would draw from her alike the forward speech,
Or blush, at least. She thanked men, – good; but thanked
Somehow . . I know not how . . as if she ranked
My gift of a nine hundred years old name
With anybody's gift.

(ll. 21–34)

The Duke's obsession with his lineage ('a nine hundred years old name'), which he regards as compromised by such indiscriminate radiance, is transformed in 'The Wife's Tragedy' into a legitimate 'ancient pride' (st. xiv) which is somehow coterminous with a paternalistic support for Reform: this section ends: 'I must toil. The People needs me: / And I speak for them tonight' (st. xlvii).

At this point, certain personal factors must be entered into the equation which produced these three poems. The first of these is that 'Owen Meredith' was actually Robert Lytton, who when 'The Wife's Tragedy' was published had become a close friend, even a sycophant, of Robert and Elizabeth Barrett Browning.[17] The second is that Lytton was the son of Edward Lytton Bulwer (now more usually referred to as Bulwer-Lytton), the popular novelist and poet. Politics never is an abstract collision of principles: the principles themselves are embodied in particular people and contingencies which continually modify their form and sometimes even determine it. Specifically, Browning's response to Lytton's response, 'A Forgiveness', only becomes fully intelligible when these contexts have been evaluated.

For Bulwer-Lytton was a member of the upper class (his aristocratic title as Baron Lytton dates from 1866) who had been a prominent Radical during the 1830s, entering Parliament in 1832 in support of the Reform Act. Indeed, he was credited by many, not least himself,

17. For details, see Harlan, ch. iii.

with having done as much as anyone to secure its passage;[18] he was instrumental in outlawing the iniquitous 'apprenticeship' system (really a continuation of slavery) in the West Indian plantations. His novels of this period, and his best-known play, *The Lady of Lyons*, were read as Radical texts, and do really contain some polemic against aristocratic pride on behalf of the peasantry.[19] But he wrote: 'I do not call myself a Radical, though I am generally called so', and he was a defender of the aristocratic principle. In his speech before the passage of the Reform Bill he spoke of 'the wholesome power of the aristocracy' and declared that after reform 'the legitimate and salutary influence of the aristocracy would remain' (Lytton: i 415, 416). This is precisely the position taken up by the Earl in 'The Wife's Tragedy', clearly modelled on the father whom Robert Lytton fanatically admired.

There is another side to Lytton's response to 'My Last Duchess', which is that in 1836 Bulwer-Lytton separated from his wife Rosina, Lytton's mother. The breach became a major source of scandal when in the late 1830s she began a long series of lawsuits against her husband, as well as pamphlet attacks on his (and later her son's) conduct. Lytton's Countess is clearly modelled on his mother. She is an adultress, and Rosina Bulwer had an affair with a Neapolitan Prince some time before the break-up of the marriage. She deserts her child, and Rosina Bulwer left Robert and his sister Emily with their father. She flees abroad, which is where Lytton's mother also ended up. Clearly, 'My Last Duchess' seemed to Lytton (consciously or unconsciously) to have been *based on his own parents*, and as a political 'reply' his poem envelopes a vindication of the aristocratic principle in a defence of his father's marital conduct.

By 1876, when he wrote 'A Forgiveness', Browning was thoroughly disillusioned with Robert Lytton, a feeling which seems to have been

18. His pamphlet, *Letter to a Late Cabinet Minister on the Present Crisis* (publ. Nov. 1834), was widely credited with having prevented the Tories from winning the General Election which shortly followed, an event that would have threatened reverse to the reforms put in place in the 1833 Reform Act. See Lytton: i 471–90.

19. In *Rienzi* it is the Italian aristocracy that is blamed for the downfall of the visionary (if rash and precipitate) popular leader Rienzi; in *The Lady of Lyons* the aristocratic Pauline is subjected to a complex revenge for a slight by the peasant Melnotte.

mutual.[20] And in 1873 Lord Lytton had died, facilitating Browning's reappraisal of the man who had been his rival for the title 'leading Radical writer' in the 1830s. Browning was one of a group assembled by the actor-manager William Macready to judge whether Bulwer-Lytton's *The Lady of Lyons* should be put on at Drury Lane. Browning was enthusiastic, but the play's success must have become painful when set against the repeated failure of his own. He may also have been made aware of the stand-offishness which caused Bulwer-Lytton to visit Macready only after all others, Browning included, had left, and of Bulwer-Lytton's ungracious response to his support.

If it is nevertheless unlikely that Browning had had Bulwer-Lytton's relations with his wife in mind when he wrote 'My Last Duchess', it seems clear that he did in 'A Forgiveness'. For his speaker's defence of his apparent neglect of his wife closely echoes that advanced by Robert Lytton's Earl. He too claims that he was too busy working to pay attention to her, and indeed uses the Earl's rather muddled argument that he neglected her on her own behalf.[21] In other respects, Browning's poem mirrors the Bulwer marriage more closely than Lytton had in 'The Wife's Tragedy'. Like Bulwer, his speaker tolerates his wife's adultery, and they live together for a while after it. But the rephrasing of Lytton's political argument is more central. There is no sign of devotion to the people in Browning's protagonist. Rather, he seems motivated by personal ambition, and his greatest triumph is to be visited by the king. His aristocratic commitment is not directly stressed, but is pervasive in the form of a personal pride based on the rigid code of honour of that rank. His reaction to his wife's adultery is initially to regard her as beneath contempt and to turn her into a non-person (refusing her request that he kill her, clearly on the grounds that she doesn't deserve it). When she reveals the complication that at the time of her adultery she still loved him his reaction is to upgrade his attitude from contempt into

20. In a letter to John Morley of 1875 Lytton scorns 'the ingrained vulgarity of Browning' (Harlan: 213).

21. More precisely: Lytton's Earl is muddled because he argues on the one hand that he was 'Toiling still to win for her / Honour, fortune, state in life' (st. xiii) immediately after claiming that 'Man's great business [was] uppermost / In my mind, not woman's beauty' (st. xii). For further discussion of the husband's use of this argument in 'A Forgiveness', see below, pp. 180–1.

hatred, and to reward her reinstatement into humanity by murdering her. His affection for the macabre weaponry from which he selects the fatal dagger recalls the original Duke's aestheticism, and like that constitutes a symbol of the combined elegance and violence which characterise aristocratic codes. What Browning seems to be implicitly saying is that Bulwer's early Radicalism never went very deep; that Robert Lytton's defence of him is therefore invalid; and that Bulwer therefore *is* very like the Duke in 'My Last Duchess'. Browning would have been conscious of Bulwer's consistent support for the Corn Laws, which 'England in Italy' denounces, and his mutation into a Tory in the 1850s. The equally implicit conclusion is: you have changed your politics; I have not.

It may be argued that hostility towards the aristocratic principle is not in itself especially Radical: Tennyson, a staunch imperialist, shared this attitude, and even Trollope, a devoted admirer of aristocracy, felt impelled to depict it as corrupt and exhausted in *The Way We Live Now* (1875), and to locate the principles of social energy elsewhere. But an analysis of Browning's relations with Lytton opens up two further topics which are connected to his critique of aristocratic values: the use of *history* to symbolise contemporary politics, and the *displacement* of political debate onto alternative sites.

## History and discursive displacement

Both these manoeuvres are foreshadowed in 'My Last Duchess', which Lytton evidently read not (only) as a historical study of a Renaissance character but as a contemporary political statement, and which, as we have seen, turns the Duke's aesthetic tastes into a metaphor for his politico-social attitudes. In this, it is characteristic of its period, both in the double displacement involved and in the use in particular of history as a way of distancing contemporary issues and giving them aesthetic shape. Literary use of history is probably never innocent of such intentions: Spenser's reworking of Romance materials in *The Faery Queen* and Shakespeare's representations of English and Roman history in his plays shadow Elizabethan and Jacobean politics while disclaiming overt commentary. But in the nineteenth century such a manoeuvre is both more pervasive and much stranger, since the censorship which part-motivated its use in earlier times no longer overtly existed except for drama. Yet Victorian writers of fiction and poetry largely eschew political commentary. Even Dickens, the most political of all, back-projects his statements into the past (admittedly not the distant past), and focuses his attacks on institutions rather than ideas. This may be interpreted as caution, but is more than that. The Victorian view of the past sees it not just as a mirror-image of the present, but as the site of the present's gestation, and therefore as standing in an evolutionary relation to it. But that very fact complicates and in a sense disables its status as a *metaphor* for the present, since evolution is always from the simple to the more complex, making the past always a less than perfect reflection of the present it gestates. We shall consider a number of poems from Browning's middle period in which this complication is addressed, bringing about a more radical displacement of political commentary onto other domains.

The first of these poems is the one which has perhaps recently replaced 'My Last Duchess' as Browning's most famous, 'Childe Roland to the Dark Tower Came'. In this poem, a knight tells how while on his quest for some nameless objective he allowed himself to be persuaded to 'turn aside' towards a Dark Tower at which he knows he will meet his death. He treks through a nightmare landscape filled with distorted natural forms and malign enginery, finally reaching the Dark Tower, where he blows his 'slug-horn' in defiant challenge of whatever it is that lurks inside. The poem bristles with unanswered questions. Who Childe Roland is, what his quest is for, why he deserts it, what has caused the devastation of the landscape he passes through, whether it is a real landscape or a *paysage intérieur*, what is in the Dark Tower, and what the outcome of his fight with it – all these questions are left unanswered, and the poem was received with widespread bewilderment which Browning steadfastly refused to dispel. As a result, various interpretations remain possible, the most interesting of which is perhaps that derived by Harold Bloom from Betty Miller's suggestion that the poem dramatises Browning's sense of having failed in the poetic mission he had undertaken. Miller cites Browning's general interest in crooks, frauds and failures as evidence for this interpretation, and Bloom has developed this reading into a more general commentary on Browning's sense of inferiority towards the Romantic poets generally and Shelley in particular. To these readings I would add a more specifically political one which is in fact in harmony with theirs but also accommodates the poem's simultaneously medieval and Victorian status. I interpret the poem as expressing a sense of having failed in a socio-political mission to involve poetry in contemporary society, and his choice of a romance vehicle for this failure as an ironic reflection both of the expectation that Victorian poets would undertake such subjects, as Tennyson did in *Idylls of the King*, and of the impossibility of making any kind of meaningful political statement out of them (as Tennyson believed he had in *Idylls of the King*).

In the romance sources on which Browning drew for 'Childe Roland', quest and combat represent the twin motifs of a civilising process. The Arthurian knight on his quest pursues not merely the specific giant or villain he is after, but the removal of the principle of evil from the world. He is locked into an inexorable code which defines the good, and characterises all its breakers as evil. Every quest, then, is in some sense the same quest, and every villain the same villain: the knights too become interchangeable protagonists of the code they inherit and represent. These patterns felt to Tennyson like inherently and eternally valid imperatives, and in his *Idylls* he sought to renovate them for modern use.[22] Browning's poem views all of them with alarm. In defecting from his quest Roland turns himself into a Bad Knight, yet the anti-quest for the Dark Tower (suicide) becomes during the course of the poem the quest itself. Similarly, his abandonment of solidarity with the other questers inverts into solidarity with those who have failed before him. And the anti-quest relays the stock motifs of the quest while inverting and ironising them. The unintelligibility of the landscape, of its origin and of its apotheosis, the Dark Tower, combine into a critique of the quest itself as a meaning-giving action. Roland has no precise idea of what he is looking for, only that he is looking: the landscape flows past him like a filmed backdrop while he effectively stands still (to confirm this, the reappearance of the sun at the poem's close recapitulates its reappearance at the beginning, suggesting that no time has elapsed during Roland's 'journey'). He witnesses the fossilised vestiges of combats whose nature and outcome have perished from the record. Yet his desire for quest and combat is so powerful that he tries to turn anti-quest into quest by blowing a challenge to its anti-objective, the Dark Tower. This culmination has been read as an existentialist

22. Though an elegiac, Götterdammerung-like pessimism implies that the Arthurian values are irretrievable – despite being characteristic of the Prince Consort.

self-recreation; but the refusal of the poem to confirm this reading by dramatising the conflict which would retrospectively shed meaning over the journey leaves also the possibility that it is an empty gesture, that there is *nothing in the Dark Tower* (or that Roland himself, or some alienated fragment of his psyche, is its inhabitant) and by extension that quest-combat is an empty or exhausted metaphor for social action.

Roland is a modern man exploring the possibility of reinvigorating the expression of social meaning through personal combat (becoming a 'childe': the 'e' is droppable), and finding it fail.[23] In the feudal order which nurtured the Arthurian legends power was personalised in ways which allowed the duel to represent its legitimate exercise, transforming a battle between two knights into the implementation of a civilising agenda. But in modern conditions the metaphor fails, in that the enemy is no longer personalised but semi-abstract. With the elimination of the Divine Right of kings and the redefinition of social power in terms of social contract, the revolution of 1688 as mediated by the political writings of John Locke had created the conditions in which power became an elusive essence incapable of reification. At least in such conditions the landed gentry remained as a vestigial personification of at least a practical manifestation of social power. But with the inexorable drift of financial power from land to capital in the nineteenth century even such vestigial reification became impossible or sentimental, for the capitalist is only an indefinitely replaceable joint in the elaborate, indecipherable networks of the elusive system in which he operates (hence the pathos of such figures as Merdle in Dickens's *Little Dorrit* and Melmotte in Trollope's *The Way We Live Now*, both swept away by the financial power they thought they could control). In such a situation the old model of combat for the right becomes outmoded because there is *nobody to fight*, and can only be renounced as it is by Claude in Clough's *Amours de Voyage* or reclaimed by the paradoxical gesture of embracing the resulting anonymity or self-loss, as the protagonist of Tennyson's *Maud* does by deciding to fight in the Crimean War.

There is a sense in which 'Childe Roland' too does this, but in

23. Compare Clough's feeble hero Claude, who during the Roman Revolution of 1848 'Dreamt of great indignations and angers transcendental, / Dreamt of a sword at my side and a battle-horse underneath me' (*Amours de Voyage* II iii 61–2).

another poem written at this time Browning mounts a critique even of this evacuated aggression. In 'Love Among the Ruins' an Italian peasant explains to a nameless tourist the nature of the ancient civilisation whose vestiges are traceable on the landscape in front of them. His interpretative confidence seems boundless, but the meaning he deduces is that there was no meaning, or only negative meaning, in the way of life thus teasingly (de-)inscribed. The poem is structured round the repeated contrast between the peaceful pastoral landscape and a violent and mercenary past which it simultaneously inherits and disowns:

Where the quiet-coloured end of evening smiles
  Miles and miles
On the solitary pastures where our sheep
  Half-asleep
Tinkle homeward thro' the twilight, stray or stop
  As they crop –

Was the site once of a city great and gay,
  (So they say)
Of our country's very capital, its prince
  Ages since
Held his court in, gathered councils, wielding far
  Peace or war.

(ll. 1–12)

The present landscape is made at once an expression of and a contrast to the ruined 'city great and gay' which historically precedes it: it 'does not even boast a tree' (l. 13) as though to memorialise the dedication to war which originally held sway there, but its 'plenty and perfection . . . of grass' (l. 25) hints at restoration of a fertility which the past contravened. The latter tendency reaches its culmination in the love-tryst which the speaker anticipates with 'a girl with eager eyes and yellow hair' who awaits him

In the turret, whence the charioteers caught soul
  For the goal,
When the king looked, where she looks now, breathless, dumb
  Till I come.

(ll. 57–60)

The poem famously ends with the affirmation that 'Love is best!', apparently simplifying the dialectic into a straightforward 'love–war' antinomy won by love, but there is a certain desperation about this commitment to the erotic, as though its disinheriting of its past somehow left it incomplete or maimed: conversely, the language of the love-encounter mimics the violence it apparently inverts:

> When I do come, she will speak not, she will stand,
>   Either hand
> On my shoulder, give her eyes the first embrace
>   Of my face,
> Ere we *rush*, ere we *extinguish sight and speech*
>   Each on each.
>
> (ll. 67–72; my italics)

In a related poem of this period, 'Two in the Campagna', the note of desperation is much stronger, and is again associated with the ghostly persistence of a lost or alienated past. The lovers wander over the Roman Campagna in an effort to connect the landscape ('The champaign with its endless fleece', l. 21) with its human history ('Rome's ghost since its decease', l. 25) and to participate in both through sexual intercourse: 'Let us be unashamed of soul, / As earth lies bare to heaven above' (ll. 32–3). But the endeavour fails:

> No. I yearn upward – touch you close,
>   Then stand away. I kiss your cheek,
> Catch your soul's warmth, – I pluck the rose
>   And love it more than tongue can speak –
> Then the good minute goes.
>
> (ll. 46–50)

The speaker attempts to integrate love into a triangular relation with, on the one hand the organic forces which possess and saturate the visible distances of nature, and on the other the human effort captured in its underlying strata (Rome); the attempt fails, and the lovers discover themselves to be as alienated from each other as both are from the place they are in. By inversion the failure of the past to survive in nature penetrates their sexual effort and nullifies its metaphysical success.

These actions are intimately intertwined with a contemporary politics whose relation to the past and to nature is just as ambiguous.

The Brownings witnessed the entry of Napoleon III into Paris and his inauguration of a régime which promised to 'save society'; but, like Childe Roland, Napoleon III was to find 'no vent in action' (to borrow the contemporary words of Matthew Arnold) for his social aims,[24] and became, in Browning's vision of him in *Prince Hohenstiel-Schwangau,* immobilised and incapable of inheriting the chivalric efficacy of his French predecessor Roland. And Browning was aware of the Great Exhibition of 1851 with its Rome-like ambition to express the confidence of Empire and manufacture the eternity of Englishness. The disintegrated civilisations of antiquity functioned at once as prototypes of this endeavour – the Great Exhibition featured archaeological relics – and prolepses of its failure to conquer time. The decline of Venice was similarly used by Ruskin as a covert critique of the arrogance of Empire.

It would seem that these poems announce Browning's disillusion with politics as doomed to fail, or to produce only brassy affirmations of an impossible conquest of mutability, but his simultaneous perception that the affirmation of survival in and through love – the 'moment, one and infinite' that the lovers enjoy in 'By the Fire-Side' – provides no true refuge from the wider social failure points to a subtler analysis of *sexual* politics than was common in the mid-Victorian period. Many Victorian writers regarded love, and the woman as the object of love, as providing a man with haven or shelter from a wider world which had lost direction, or coherence, or moral meaning. The most famous example is Matthew Arnold's 'Dover Beach', which ends:

> Ah, love, let us be true
> To one another! for the world, which seems
> To lie before us like a land of dreams,
> So various, so beautiful, so new,
> Hath really neither joy, nor love, nor light,
> Nor certitude, nor peace, nor help for pain;
> And we are here as on a darkling plain
> Swept with confused alarms of struggle and flight,
> Where ignorant armies clash by night.
>
> (ll. 29–37)

24. In Arnold's Preface to *Poems* (1853).

Such a gesture casts love-relationships as an alternative to a political and social world which has become unmanageable, a contrast which also informs the last sentence of Dickens's *Little Dorrit*:

> They went quietly down into the roaring streets, inseparable and blessed; and as they passed along in sunshine and shade, the noisy and the eager, and the arrogant and the froward and the vain, fretted, and chafed, and made their usual uproar.

Coventry Patmore's *The Angel in the House* (1854–63) elaborates this principle into a celebration of domesticity as the place to which the war-weary male turns to recover bliss and reproduce himself. It hardly needs saying that such a gesture depends upon a conception of gender difference which entraps the woman in social inaction and enslaves her to her image in the male ideal. Browning followed Shelley in feeling extreme mistrust for such a degradation. Shelley rejected marriage as an institution, on the grounds that it constrained the free development of both parties, but especially the woman. Browning's treatment of sexual relations is informed by the same anxiety. Of course, he himself famously got married and distanced himself from Shelleyan free love. (He was shocked and disillusioned when he learned, in the late 1850s, of the circumstances surrounding Shelley's desertion of his first wife, Harriet Westbrook.) But his letters to his future wife are filled with nervous assertions that he had originally planned not to marry, and as Miller and Karlin (1985) separately demonstrate, the question of who was to exercise power in their new relation was a source of constant anxiety to them both. The ideal is perfect interpersonal fusion, a possibility represented in poetry by Donne, whose work Browning intensely admired: 'By the Fire-Side', his most affirmative love-poem, alludes extensively to Donne's *The Exstasie* in passages like the following:

> My own, see where the years conduct!
>    At first, 'twas something our two souls
> Should mix as mists do: each is sucked
>    Into each now; on, the new stream rolls,
> Whatever rocks obstruct.
>
> Think, when our one soul understands
>    The great Word which makes all things new –
> When earth breaks up and Heaven expands –
>    How will the change strike me and you
> In the House not made with hands?

Oh, I must feel your brain prompt mine,
  Your heart anticipate my heart,
You must be just before, in fine,
  See and make me see, for your part,
New depths of the Divine!

(ll. 126–40)

But in 'Two in the Campagna', which may be read as a palinode to 'By the Fire-Side', the desire expressed in the last stanza dwindles to an impossible dream:

I would I could adopt your will,
  See with your eyes, and set my heart
Beating by yours, and drink my fill
  At your soul's springs, – your part, my part
In life, for good and ill.

No.

(ll. 41–6)

The 'No' is at once final and complex. It partly expresses the impossibility of extending the fusion experienced in sexual intercourse into the general world, or making it last beyond the moment of its occurrence. It also reflects the unease already present in 'By the Fire-Side' concerning power in love. The lover in this poem wants to fuse with his beloved, but on her terms: her brain is to prompt his, her heart anticipate his own, she 'must be just before' him in everything if they are to become one. This failure of synchronisation suggests that Browning finds it impossible to segregate the world of love from a larger public world in which the question would always be, who is to be master? In marriage, the obvious answer would be, the man, but he rejects this; yet in rejecting it he simply inverts it by giving the woman priority in a mirror-image of the traditional distribution.

When, therefore, in *The Ring and the Book* the husband-murdered heroine Pompilia expresses the hope that there will be, as biblically promised, no marriage in heaven, she does more than repudiate her husband-murderer, she dramatises Browning's continuing unease about marriage itself, an unease which in 'A Forgiveness' manifests itself as what amounts to a parody of the Victorian domestic ideal. The speaker says:

I ran life's race,
With the whole world to see, as only strains
His strength some athlete whose prodigious gains
Of good appal him: happy to excess, –
Work freely done should balance happiness
Fully enjoyed; and, since beneath my roof
Housed she who made home heaven, in heaven's behoof
I went forth every day, and all day long
Worked for the world.

(ll. 8–16)

Characteristic Victorian discontinuities beset this passage, as they had in Lytton's 'The Wife's Tragedy', a poem which, I have argued, Browning had in mind when composing 'A Forgiveness'.[25] The speaker struggles to position his wife at the centre of his life, but she keeps slipping to its edges. An athlete's work is self-dedicated and socially rewarded. It is not in her 'behoof' that he goes forth to labour, but that of the 'heaven' he makes her represent. It is unclear whether 'heaven' here represents a religious ideal in the name of which work might be undertaken, or a strictly secular sexual bliss to be 'balanced' by a corresponding amount of pain. And the phrase 'Worked for the world' implies that a second allegiance usurps the primacy of the first whenever he quits his heaven-haven of domestic peace.

In any case, it is all an illusion, since the wife is an adulteress.[26] Browning characteristically focuses not on the conventional culpability of her conduct, but on the legitimacy of her rebellion – the only one available to her – against the husband's narcissistic régime. His refusal to kill or even repudiate her paradoxically reinstates the power over her which her adultery threatened and institutes a second régime in which she becomes again his puppet, this time to be displayed publicly like the earlier Duke's Duchess in the interest of his political campaign: *she* now works on *his* behalf, as he had deluded himself he worked on hers. Her only resource, when that campaign concludes in triumph, is to demolish the premise on which her

25. See above, pp. 165–71.

26. Besides 'The Wife's Tragedy', 'A Forgiveness' combines elements of two poems which Browning owned, Coventry Patmore's *The Angel in the House*, and George Meredith's *Modern Love* (1862); in the latter an adulterous couple similarly perform the grim masquerade of love and harmony for social consumption.

servitude had been erected by telling him that she loved him when she betrayed him, and his response, as we have seen, is to concede her as much power as is necessary to make him feel obliged to kill her.

It is suggestive that the next poem in the *Pacchiarotto* collection is 'Cenciaja', a pendant to Shelley's drama *The Cenci*. In that play patriarchal power develops to the ultimate of paternal incest, and the woman, righting herself by murder, is condemned by the Pope and executed for her audacity. Browning's poem presents the inverse case of a man who murders his mother and gets away with it; his innocent brother is executed for complicity, as part of a corrupt deal between the Pope and Cardinal Aldobrandini, his 'nephew'; it turns out that Aldobrandini hated the innocent brother because they were rivals in love. The poem is virulently anti-Catholic as well as anti-patriarchal; at the end, Browning sarcastically quotes the pious 'chronicler' whose account he has used:

> 'God's justice, tardy though it prove perchance,
> Rests never till it reach delinquency.'
> Ay, or how otherwise had come to pass
> That Victor rules, this present year, in Rome?
> (ll. 296–300)[27]

The transition from sexual to social politics (similar in its abruptness to the mention of the Corn Laws at the end of 'England in Italy') suggests that Browning's exploration of the former not only remained radical, but exemplifies what I call the 'discursive displacement' of the political onto other domains, a displacement which following the crisis-poems of the early 1850s becomes the principal route for Browning's political self-expression. The fact of displacement is of course itself an element in the resulting equations, and for some commentators might even invalidate them, but there is another poem of this crucial period which illustrates that displacement is not the same as abandonment.

The only poem in *Men and Women* which features direct political comment is 'Old Pictures in Florence', in whose last lines Browning anticipates the liberation of Italy from Austrian rule:

27. Browning alludes to the Papacy's loss (in 1870) of the last vestiges of its temporal power over the city of Rome, and its confinement to the Vatican by decree of King Victor-Emmanuel, ruler of the newly-united kingdom of Italy.

Shall I be alive that morning the scaffold
  Is broken away, and the long-pent fire
Like the golden hope of the world unbaffled
  Springs from its sleep, and up goes the spire –
As, 'God and the People' plain for its motto,
  Thence the new tricolor flaps at the sky?[28]

In his support for Italian unification and independence Browning resembled many other English intellectuals of his time. His wife was a particularly strong enthusiast for the cause, devoting almost a whole collection, *Poems Before Congress* (1860), to propaganda on its behalf. By comparison Browning seems almost tepid, and a kind of evolutionary quietism ('Shall I be alive?') might be seen to underlie the confidence expressed in this stanza, whose fulfilment the end of 'Cenciaja' salutes. But 'Old Pictures' attempts a displacement of political onto *aesthetic* discourses in which the latter authorises and underwrites the former in a radical equation. The rising of 'the spire' from its 'scaffold' concludes an architectural metaphor based on Giotto's unfinished campanile, mentioned at the beginning of the poem as its motive, whose completion is made coterminous and simultaneous with the achievement of an Italian republic, connecting past with present in an ultimately irreversible genetic sequence. And between the first appearance of the campanile in stanza ii and its apotheosis as a libertarian symbol at the poem's end Browning positions an extended and apparently digressive history of early Italian art which, on inspection, proves to provide the symbolic content of the (r)evolutionary process itself.

The word is actually used at l. 157: 'The worthies began a revolution', but it is used in reference to the early Italian painters referred to in the title, who are represented as spiritual republicans rejecting the implicitly monarchical and oppressive régime of Greek art. Greek art is oppressive because in seeking perfection it condemned its beholders to experience their inevitable lack of it:

You would fain be kinglier, say than I am?
  Even so, you would not sit like Theseus.
You'd fain be a model? the Son of Priam
  Has yet the advantage in arms' and knees' use.
(ll. 97–100)

28. For Browning's revisions to these lines in proof, see Chapter 1, pp. 28–9.

Such imagery mirrors the slavery with which it historically coexisted, teaching that 'to submit is the worsted's duty' (l. 108); the Renaissance was revolutionary in the sense that whatever its social forms it was implicitly egalitarian and democratic in its art:

> Growth came when, looking your last on them all,
> You turned your eyes inwardly one fine day
> And cried with a start – What if we so small
> Are greater, ay, greater the while than they!
> (ll. 113–16)

The aesthetic flaws of early Italian art represent not incompetence but what Browning in the *Essay on Shelley* called 'perfection in imperfection', and as a result it *stays alive*: Browning imagines its painters continuing to haunt Florence in anticipation of their works' completion, a completion which he displaces onto the political level by contemporanising and comparing it with coming Italian liberation. Whereas the civic past depicted in 'Love Among the Ruins' is as doomed as it is misguided, the past in art survives as an evolution which serves as the template for an equivalent possibility on the political level. In that sense it is not a *figure for* (so displacement of) revolution but an (evolutionary) *anticipation of* it. Browning's displacement of political discourse in this poem, then, is hardly evasive or escapist. Indeed, he emphasises not the fixity but the mutability of art, as frescos 'peel and drop' under the neglect of successive generations of Italians; such mutability, however, is part of what transforms art into a living metaphor for politics rather than an escape from it, and contrasts with the immobility with which art is associated and which it imposes in 'My Last Duchess'.

This displacement of meaning into the future has repercussions for the reader–writer relationship, which Browning like his Romantic predecessors politicises. Eighteenth-century aestheticians followed Locke in supposing that linguistic meaning could only subsist by a general social agreement, which meant in effect that the writer could only mirror back to the reader the reader's existing thoughts, placing each in a passive relation to the other, and ensuring that literature would confirm the existing social arrangements on which its intelligibility was made to depend. Wordsworth noted that the result, far from the democracy it superficially mimicked, was doubly autocratic: the poet tyrannising over the reader by coming forward 'in the character of a man to be looked up to, a man of genius and authority', while the reader reciprocally forbids him to stray from 'certain known habits of association' at peril of being marginalised as unintelligible. Wordsworth compares such a reader to 'an Indian Prince or General, stretched on his Palanquin and borne by his Slaves': since 'Genius is the introduction of a new element into the intellectual universe', the reader ought to 'exert himself' to meet it.[29] In 'A Poet's Epitaph', Wordsworth puts it that 'you must love him, ere to you / He will seem worthy of your love' (43–4), by which he means that the reader must leap out of their known habits of association' on an impulse of trust in or love of the poet, making it possible for both to take up a position outside the existing social order and its ideology.

When Ruskin complained about the unintelligibility of one of his poems, Browning asked in reply, 'Is the business of [poetry] to tell people what they know already[?]' (Appendix B, p. 258); to a more sympathetic correspondent, W.G. Kingsland, he wrote:

> I am heartily glad I have your sympathy for what I write. Intelligence, by itself, is scarcely the thing with respect to a new book – as Wordsworth says (a little altered), 'you must like it before it be worthy of your liking'. (27 Nov. 1868, Hood: 128)

Like falling in love, reading should encounter and recognise 'A novel grace and a beauty strange' and the reader undergo the reciprocal change which recognition induces and presupposes. Such a position mobilises the poem–reader relation and gives it revolutionary possibilities. In 'Old Pictures in Florence' Browning says of Greek art-works, 'To-day's brief passion limits their range' while for Renaissance ones 'It seethes with the morrow . . . and more' (ll. 121–2). For him the reading of his poetry is positioned in the kind of future from which such comparisons become possible, a future to which the poetry itself. is simultaneously past. In reading the poem, the reader alters towards the state of *being able to read it*, which achieved marks a change both in them and in the poem which caused the change. Whereas a neo-classical work and its reader remain in principle unaltered through all readings (which therefore amount to a single

29. Preface and Appendix to *Lyrical Ballads* (Mason: 58, 89); 'Essay Supplementary to the Preface' [to the *Poems* of 1815] in Hayden: ii 946–7.

reading) a Browning poem is designed to be read *twice*, and to have changed in between in time with the change it has induced in its reader(s).

Thus Shelley's achievement is described as 'so drawing out, lifting up, and assimilating this ideal of a future man, thus descried as possible, to the present reality of the poet's soul already arrived at the higher state of development', and in 'Popularity', ironically the poem to whose 'unintelligibility' Ruskin took exception:

> My poet holds the future fast,
> Accepts the coming ages' duty,
> Their present for this past.
> (ll. 13–15)

Browning is fond of imagining a future to which the present becomes past ('By the Fire-Side'), or a past whose future is the present ('A Death in the Desert'); both are figures for the use of time as a mode of space in which self-repositioning through further reading is made possible. In 'By the Fire-Side' the same sequence of events appears twice, as if read two different ways with deepening enlightenment in the future in which rereading is predicated; Paracelsus appeals for vindication to 'the child of aftertime' (contemporary → future readers of Browning's poem); in *The Ring and the Book*, Pompilia appeals from contemporary listeners who misinterpret her relation with the priest Caponsacchi to future ones to whom it will be intelligible, and in particular to her own son, who, in the Christmas scene analysed in Chapter 3 (pp. 78–80) was supposed to become her and her supposed parents' prop in future life:

> I fancy him grown great,
> Strong, stern, a tall young man who tutors me,
> Frowns with the others 'Poor imprudent child!
> Why did you venture out of the safe street?
> Why go so far from help to that lone house?
> Why open at the whisper and the knock?'
> (vii 214–19)

In book x of the poem, the Pope both looks back to imagine Euripides responding to his reading of his plays (ll. 1667 ff.), and forward to Browning's reading of *his* deeds in turn in the distant future (i.e. the present). In dramatic monologues the act of reading is internalised in the form of the interlocutor's silent witness – silent, but nevertheless the determinant as it is the determiner of the speaker's meaning. The monologues are usually arranged to reflect this relation in the positioning of a speaker who is older than his interlocutor ('Bishop Blougram's Apology', 'Clive') or socially superior to him ('My Last Duchess') transforming him into an impersonation of the future towards which the speaker looks for his meaning.

One of Browning's last poems centrally engages this slippage, and reconnects it to the political sphere from which it originated. In 'Parleying with Charles Avison' he 'reads' (that is, plays) the eighteenth-century composer's 'Grand March' from the standpoint of his own time – a time which includes 'Brahms, / Wagner, Dvorak, Liszt' (ll. 99–100), adding all the associated changes in harmonic, melodic and structural practice that have made Avison's original tune seem to him naïve and elementary:

> I sprinkle my reactives, pitch broadcast
> Discords and resolutions, turn aghast
> Melody's easy-going . . .
>
> Sharps and flats,
> Lavish at need, shall dance athwart thy score
> When ophicleide and bombardon's uproar
> Mate the approaching trample, even now
> Big in the distance – or my ears deceive –
> Of federated England, fitly weave
> March-music for the Future!
>
> (ll. 301–3, 383–9)

The (player-)reader can change the work, contemporanising it with himself (the ophicleide and bombardon were nineteenth-century instruments) and then projecting a 'Future' beyond that present in which a *political* apotheosis meets the *artistic* apotheosis towards which the music tends ('federated England' implies an anarchistic or Owenite delegation of central power to semi-autonomous regions or communities). But then this Future rejoins the Past which it completes as Avison's tune is given Elizabethan harmonies and next fitted to a celebratory anthem (by Browning) in praise of the Puritan revolutionary Pym. This gesture looks back to the origins of Browning's own politics – his family came from a Puritan background and his library contained many Puritan pamphlets – and the historical continuity he discerns between the general past and future becomes also a figure for the continuity of his personal political radicalism.

# CHAPTER 6
# *Philosophy*

## Whose idea is this?

The main difficulty in discussing Browning's philosophy is the nature of the evidence. Because the overwhelming majority of his poems take the form of dramatic monologues, the words and thoughts of his invented characters usually conceal his own. He himself put it in these terms in a famous outburst to EBB: 'you speak out, *you*, – I only make men & women speak' (13 Jan. 1845, Kelley: x 22), adding, that although he finds writing in her fashion 'bleak melancholy work' he is 'going to try'. And try he did. *Christmas Eve and Easter Day* (1850), the first new work he published after their marriage, consists of two poems about visions or dreams of Christ which Browning tells us he himself has had, and many subsequent poems introduce his own point of view. In *Men and Women* only 'The Guardian-Angel', 'Memorabilia', 'Old Pictures in Florence', 'De Gustibus – ', and 'One Word More' may be understood as personal statements, but Browning also makes forays into dramatic monologues by attaching epilogues to 'Bishop Blougram's Apology' and 'The Statue and the Bust' in which he gives his own views on character and story:

> For Blougram, he believed, say, half he spoke. . . .
> He said true things, but called them by wrong names.
> (ll. 979, 995)

> Do your best, whether winning or losing it,
> If you choose to play – is my principle!
> Let a man contend to the uttermost
> For his life's set prize, be it what it will!
> (ll. 240–3)

In the 'Epilogue' to his next collection, *Dramatis Personae*, he appears under the name 'Third Speaker', in *The Ring and the Book* he speaks both book i and book xii, and after this poem it is quite common for collections and single-poem publications to appear with a 'Prologue' and/or an 'Epilogue'. *La Saisiaz*, published in 1878, represents his most extended appearance under his own name since *Christmas Eve and Easter Day*.

It is necessary, however, to be cautious in approaching these examples. Of *Easter Day* EBB wrote to Mrs Jameson: 'I have complained of the *asceticism* in the second part, but he said it was "one side of the question" ' (4 May 1850, Kenyon: i 449). In 'One Word More' he claims that all the other poems of *Men and Women*, presumably including the ones mentioned above as containing some personal statement, are the utterances of his 'fifty men and women' rather than himself. In every case, such works invariably mimic an actual speaking voice, and in some instances address an implied or actual interlocutor, making them sound very like the dramatic monologues they supposedly displace. *La Saisiaz* begins:

> Dared and done: at last I stand upon the summit, Dear and True!
> Singly dared and done; the climbing both of us were bound to do.

He addresses Annie Egerton Smith, whose death the poem memorialises: although the subject of the poem is the abstract theological question of the immortality of the soul, her 'participation' in the ensuing debate localises its reflections to their immediate temporal and topographical occasion ('the summit'); Browning's eventual affirmation of his belief in personal immortality is placed in a framework of merely human, potentially irrational hope rather than philosophical certainty. And even within that framework hope cannot become equivalent to assurance. Browning reflects that because the public may take his 'Fame' as a voucher for *any* opinions, true or false, rational or prejudiced, he may put forward, he must emphasise that what he has to offer is no more than the 'sorriest of conclusions': 'Well? He at least believed in Soul, was very sure of God.' The statement evades full subjective commitment by being produced in the third person, and sounds as though it has been extorted ('Well?'); it does not amount to an unequivocal claim that the soul survives after death; and in his epilogue, supposedly composed later, Browning can say only that he '*Found* the chain I *seemed* to forge there, flawless till it reached your grave' (l. 608; my italics). Seeming is not believing.

Similar analyses could be performed for all the poems which appear to offer Browning's own ideas, yet it seems unsatisfactory to conclude that nothing can be said about his mind. Early commentators assumed that something could, and although such confidence now looks naïve and pre-formalist, it was not necessarily misguided. Without exactly encouraging such endeavours, Browning can't be said to have forbidden them. When people asked him what particular poems meant, he usually fobbed them off, as for example when in response to a suggestion that 'Childe Roland' meant 'he who endures to the end shall be saved' he responded: 'Yes, something like that.' Yet in at least one letter to F.J. Furnivall he admitted implanting his own ideas in some poems:

> all that seems *proved* in Darwin's schemes was a conception familiar to me from the beginning: see in *Paracelsus* the progressive development from senseless matter to organized, until man's appearance (*Part* v). Also in *Cleon*, see the order of 'life's mechanics', – and I daresay in many passages of my poetry: for how can one look at Nature as a whole and doubt that, wherever there is a gap, a 'link' must be 'missing' – through the limited power and opportunity of the looker? But go back and back, as you please, *at* the back, as Mr. Sludge is made to insist, you find (*my* faith is constant) creative intelligence, acting as matter but not resulting from it. (11 Oct. 1881, Peterson: 34)

Note, however, the curiously circuitous phrasing: 'as Mr Sludge is made to insist . . . *my* faith is constant', which simultaneously concedes that the character is his mouthpiece and treats it as an independent being whose view just happens to coincide with his own.

To Margaret Moscheles he later offered the following account:

> Well, of the Poetry. You are to remember that it comprises all the views of life, from various points, taken in the course of time, – now a long one. When you speak of 'Paracelsus' – written fifty years or more ago – as 'Christmas Eve' was, almost forty – you should understand that they contain only partial endeavours at the truth, – & that only in the whole of my work may be expected to appear a genuine interpretation of the truth. The nearer you get to the end of my work, the more discernable ought to be its *guess* at what, I believe, it is not consistent with the nature of man that we should absolutely know.
> (24 Nov. 1887, ABL MS)

He seems to concede here that ideas can be drawn from his writings, but there is a contradiction, in that on the one hand such ideas must be sought 'in the whole of my work' and on the other hand they are to be found in 'the end of my work', that is his later work, where, still, they amount to no more than his '*guess* at what . . . it is not consistent with the nature of man that we should absolutely know'. Either way, as with *La Saisiaz*, certainty is not available, and Browning again seems embarrassed at the expectation that he might provide it.

I shall try to bear in mind all these qualifications in giving an account of Browning's ideas, or more accurately, the ideas with which his work was preoccupied. For as the idiom of his speakers' language stays the same,[1] so there is substantial consistency between the thoughts ascribed to them, and those thoughts are frequently philosophical in character. Indeed his poems show a philosophical zest and complexity of mind unparalleled in post-Renaissance English poetry. Renaissance poets such as Fulke Greville, Sir Philip Sidney and Henry More were happy to introduce abstract ideas into their work, and Browning particularly admired the poetry of 'revered and magisterial Donne', who was even more deeply immersed in philosophy (particularly Platonic and scholastic).[2] In the late seventeenth and eighteenth centuries there was a reaction against such complexities, a reaction still present in Hazlitt's remark in his essay on Byron in *The Spirit of the Age* (1825) that 'We like metaphysics . . . but not to see them making flowery speeches, nor dancing a measure in the fetters of verse' (Howe: xi 76). In *Sordello* Browning parodies this line of thought when Naddo objects to the philosophical character of Sordello's poetry:

> now you're a bard, a bard past doubt,
> And no philosopher; why introduce
> Crotchets like these? fine, surely, but no use
> In poetry – which still must be, to strike,
> Based upon common sense . . .
>
> (ii 788–92)

1. See on this topic Chapter 2, pp. 47–9.
2. There was a copy of More's *Philosophical Poems* in Browning's library. The reference to Donne is from *The Two Poets of Croisic* (1878), l. 924.

The nature of *Sordello* itself, with its convoluted philosophical digressions, bears witness to what we are clearly supposed to regard as the fallaciousness of Naddo's argument, and by extension the anti-intellectual tendency of Augustan poetry. Here is a sample:

> The common sort, the crowd,
> Exist, perceive; with Being are endowed,
> However slight, distinct from what they See,
> However bounded: Happiness must be
> To feed the first by gleanings from the last,
> Attain its qualities, and slow or fast
> Become what one beholds; such peace-in-strife
> By transmutation is the Use of Life,
> The Alien turning Native to the soul
> Or body – which instructs me; I am whole
> There and demand a Palma; had the world
> Been from my soul to a like distance hurled
> 'Twere Happiness to make it one with me –
> Whereas I must, ere I begin to Be,
> Include a world, in flesh, I comprehend
> In spirit now; and this done, what's to blend
> With? Nought is Alien here – my Will
> Owns it already; yet can turn it still
> Less Native, since my Means to correspond
> With Will are so unworthy 'twas my bond
> To tread the very ones that tantalize
> Me now into a grave, never to rise –
> I die then! Will the rest agree to die?
> (iii 159–81)

The lavish use of capitals ('Being', 'See', 'Happiness', 'Will') points to the abstract sense in which the vocabulary is being used, and Sordello's speculative self-constructions are equally abstract: he imagines himself first as a member of 'the common sort, the crowd' (ll. 1–11), and establishes the grounds on which such a mode of being might achieve 'Happiness', only to distinguish a mode he identifies as his own (ll. 11–23), dominated by the 'Will' and concerned to negotiate an ultimate comprehensiveness in which perception unites its object with its origin in consciousness. Most of Browning's speakers think similarly in terms of alternative models of themselves and their interactions with the not-self, and are in that sense philosophers. Mr Sludge, for example, argues first that his ghosts were faked, but next that they might have been real: both cases are logically developed and defended at great length. In *La Saisiaz* Browning deduces the actual state of humanity from a series of speculative premises, each adding a term to the one before until they compile the minimum equation which will account for the conditions of life.

It is not entirely obvious where this analytical-speculative turn of mind came from.[3] The obvious answer, that Browning read a lot of philosophy, is hard to prove. The vocabulary of the above passage, for example, suggests an acquaintanceship with the philosophy of Kant, Hegel and even Schopenhauer, but Browning denied any direct knowledge of German thought, and although it might have been routed to him by journal articles, conversation and/or other mediators it seems most profitable to begin with the philosophers he can be shown to have read. His library affords three immediate candidates, Plato, Aristotle and Locke.

Of these, Aristotle seems to have been the least important. Browning never refers to him in letters, and citations of him in the poetry are put into the mouths of compromised characters such as Festus in *Paracelsus* and the lawyers in *The Ring and the Book*.[4] In *Pauline*, by contrast, the speaker directly refers to a time when 'I lived with Plato and had the key of life', and further citations are put in the mouths of Browning's two 'biggest' speakers, Don Juan, who shows detailed acquaintance with his thought, and Balaustion, who expresses profound admiration of his character as a man.[5] Locke too is mentioned in the poetry, and parts of his thought are closely paraphrased in *La Saisiaz*, as we shall see.[6] But I suggest that a fourth figure be added, that of Coleridge. Coleridge shared in the odium

3. The modern term would be 'hypothetico-deductive', meaning that rather than inductively 'learning from the facts' the thinker introduces a hypothesis from which the facts may be deduced.

4. In 'Development' (1889) he speaks of reading Aristotle's *Ethics*, but comments: ''tis a treatise I find hard / To read aright now that my hair is grey' (ll. 109-10).

5. *Fifine at the Fair*, in which Don Juan speaks, is Browning's longest 'conventional' dramatic monologue; *Balaustion's Adventure* and *Aristophanes' Apology*, both spoken by Balaustion herself, amount to 8416 lines in all.

6. Locke appears in 'Mr. Sludge, "the Medium" ', ll. 589–90, where he is ranked with Milton and Homer. His rival, Hobbes, and his successors, Hume and Berkeley, by contrast, are never mentioned.

attached to Wordsworth's defection from the radical cause, and is never directly referred to in Browning's poetry, but the suggestion that Browning did not read him or was not influenced by him is quite untenable, as I have already demonstrated (see chapter 1, pp. 10–14).[7]

The following discussion will place Browning's ideas in a sequence he himself might have used. I begin with his theories concerning the innate endowment of the human entity, consciousness and perception. Next, I examine his theories of the primary reagents with that entity, the world, both human and natural. Then I consider his theory of God and Christ. The other topic I shall be concerned with is his theory of the poet and of poetry, but I found this so intertwined with the others as to be inseparable from them. Like other Romantic and post-Romantic writers, Browning was pressingly concerned with what the poet is and what is poetry, for reasons that will emerge, and many of his poems may be read as symbolic narratives of the creative process.

## The self as subject

> 'Tis the first Act of the Mind, when it has any Sentiments or *Ideas* at all, to perceive its *Ideas* . . . (Locke: IV i §4)

> a spirit is that, which is its own object, yet not originally an object, but an absolute subject for which all, itself included, may become an object . . . (Coleridge, *Biographia Literaria*: ch. xii)

> I am made up of an intensest life,
> Of a most clear idea of consciousness
> Of self – distinct from all its qualities,
> From all affections, passions, feelings, powers . . .
> (*Pauline* [1833], ll. 268–71)

> I profess
> To know just one fact – my self-consciousness, –
> 'Twixt ignorance and ignorance enisled . . .
> (*Parleying with Francis Furini* [1887], ll. 350–2)

The last two quotations come from opposite ends of Browning's career, indicating the consistency of his adherence to the post-Cartesian promotion of self-being to primacy among the objects of

7. In addition to these, who are all in some sense formal philosophers, I consider figures who might be called 'underground' philosophers, that is, representatives of occult or unorthodox intellectual traditions. Browning

knowledge. Before Descartes, philosophers had assumed the existence of God as the primary – that is, intuitive or self-evident – foundation of all knowledge. Descartes asked himself, not what he *knew*, but what he *could not doubt* without self-contradiction, and discovered that the answer could only be his own existence, or more precisely, the existence of the mind which doubts and in witnessing its doubt also realises the impossibility of doubting the existence of what doubts. Hence his famous epigram 'cogito ergo sum' (I think [am thinking], therefore I exist [am existing]). All other knowledge, including knowledge of God, is not self-evident in this sense and therefore has to be *proved*. Subsequent philosophy, in particular the British empiricist tradition whose representative in Browning's library was Locke, characteristically begins from this premise, which Browning too accepts. His formulations however add an element, or more properly, an emphasis that probably came to him from Coleridge: that the mind, in perceiving itself, simultaneously perceives its self-perception and is thus *self-conscious* (this is assumed but not stated in Descartes' formulation; Locke alludes to it but gives it no special emphasis). The reasons for this refinement, and for Browning's insistence on it, will emerge later.

The next question is: how does such a mind come to know anything else? Two radically divergent answers to this question were available in the intellectual traditions Browning inherited, and before considering Browning's position I shall describe these. They are the Idealist (Platonic) and the empiricist (Lockeian) theories of knowledge. Both take for granted what some extremer philosophies dispute, that we perceive things; the question is, how do we come to know anything more about them? The Platonic answer is: by a prior mental familiarity with them; the empiricist answer is: by experience of them, as organised in memory.

In Plato's philosophy the things we see are characterised as imperfect copies of their absolute archetypes, which he calls 'Forms'.

---

was deeply interested in such traditions. The epigraph to *Pauline* is taken from the preface to Heinrich Cornelius Agrippa's *De Occulta Philosophia*, first published 1531, an undated edition of which was, with other of Agrippa's works, in Browning's father's library; *Paracelsus* is based on the life, work and thought of the alchemist of that name; *Sordello* contains a long passage derived from one of the Gnostic gospels which, though excluded from the official biblical canon, constitute a major source for subsequent occult traditions.

The rabbit I see is a corrupted representation of the Form Rabbit. And that is how I know it is a rabbit: the Form Rabbit is already in my mind, enabling me to 'recognise' the empirical rabbit by *reminiscence* (I 'remember' it, or rather its ideal or transcendent essence). I come to know about things other than my own existence because my mind already contains their perfect archetypes. Perception is recollection.

There are many problems in this argument (how many Forms are there? Can there actually be more than one? If a new thing is made, such as a washing-machine, does a new Form Washing-Machine come into being, in which case how was it already in my mind?), but most pressing for the philosophical tradition is the supposition it entails that the contents of the world already in some sense exist in the mind.

This is what Locke radically disputes, arguing, as the central premise of his philosophy, that there are no innate ideas in the mind at all: my mind at birth was a clean slate ('tabula rasa'), and the knowledge I have of things is a result of my perception of them during the period of experience. More precisely, the mind has (must have) within it an innate capacity for organising percepts into classes, thereby coming to know that the rabbit I perceive belongs to the category Rabbit: that category, however, is not native to my mind as a pre-existing absolute type, but is rather my generalisation from rabbits I have known.

This formulation solves some of the problems of the Platonic theory of knowledge, but introduces others at the same time. In particular, there is the question, how can I know that I perceive the same rabbit as someone else? Since my knowledge of the world is not derived from a universal mental archetype, but constructed from a sequence of perceptions that I, and I alone, have had of it, there is no obvious way in which I can verify that anyone else knows it in the same way. This problem dominates the issue of language. Self-evidently, I and my interlocutor use the same word, 'rabbit'. But do we mean the same thing by this word? There is no way of proving that we do, and Locke notes, as we shall see, that it is at least possible that language, by means of which we apparently become privy to each others' thoughts, merely disguises the irreconcilability of the divergent worlds of perception that we inhabit.

In *Paracelsus*, Paracelsus begins by taking up an extreme Platonic position:

> Truth is within ourselves; it takes no rise
> From outward things, whate'er you may believe:
> There is an inmost centre in us all,
> Where truth abides in fulness; and around,
> Wall within wall, the gross flesh hems it in,
> Perfect and true perception – which is truth;
> A baffling and perverting carnal mesh
> Which blinds it, and makes error: and, '*to know*'
> Rather consists in opening out a way
> Whence the imprison'd splendour may dart forth,
> Than in effecting entry for the light
> Supposed to be without.
>
> (i 738–49)

This is an extreme version of Platonic dualism.[8] The 'truth' hidden in the mind emanates from a higher order of being than that occupied by the material world (the 'baffling and perverting carnal mesh'), and 'knowledge' is to be acquired not by perception of 'the light / Supposed to be without', but from contemplating the already-perfect formations of the mind itself.[9] *Sordello* clarifies that this must mean

8. Browning inherits the besetting problem of Western metaphysics, perhaps of all metaphysics, the conflict between monism and dualism. Broadly, monism is the belief that the universe contains one kind of thing only, dualism that there are two kinds of thing in it. The best-known exponents of monism are *pantheists*, who hold that all things, material and spiritual, are but inflections of a single universal substance; dualism contends that God, or more broadly spiritual or abstract or mental things, is irreconcilable with matter and has to be counted as the product of a different, 'higher' order of being. The most extreme form of dualism is Gnosticism, in which it is suppposed that God created the human soul, while Satan created the human body and the rest of the material creation. St Augustine's brilliant refutation of Gnosticism in his *Confessions* encouraged the adoption of a compromise position within the Christian tradition: God must have created everything there is, but the material part (which includes all evil) exists at a lower level than the spiritual and is in conflict with it. But other traditions persisted, and the Romantic period saw a revival of monism in the form of a natural pantheism uniting humanity at once with the natural world and with the divine principle inherent in that world.

9. The historical Paracelsus provides a precedent for this conception: 'The strength of this mystery of Nature is hindered by our bodily structure, just as if one were bound in a prison with chains and fetters. From this the

that the contents of the world are always already present in consciousness: he

> Proclaims each new revealment born a twin
> With a distinctest consciousness within
> Referring still the quality, now first
> Revealed, to their own soul; its instinct nursed
> In silence, now *remembered* better, shown
> More thoroughly, but not the less their own;
> (i 525–30; my italics)

This brings out the Platonic basis of Browning's thought, at least in this phase: when Sordello 'perceives' something outside himself, he treats it not as a new thing, but as 'remembered' from its prior mental archetype, and in the *Essay on Shelley* the 'subjective poet' is described as

> impelled to embody the thing he perceives, not so much with reference to the many below as to the one above him, the supreme Intelligence which apprehends all things in their absolute truth . . . Not what man sees, but what God sees – the *Ideas* of Plato, seeds of creation lying burningly on the Divine Hand – it is toward these that he struggles. (Appendix A, p. 247)

And he seeks them 'in his own soul', the domain in which their uncorrupted essences dwell. It is, however, Coleridge who provides the clearest and most radical statement of this position when in 'Dejection: an Ode' he argues:

> And would we aught behold, of higher worth,
> Than that inanimate cold world allowed
> To the poor loveless ever-anxious crowd,
> Ah! from the soul itself must issue forth
> A light, a glory, a fair luminous cloud
> Enveloping the Earth –
> (ll. 50–55)

Coleridge here anticipates Sordello's distinction between himself and 'the common sort' (see above, p. 191), implying that the poet

---

mind is free' (cited in Woolford and Karlin: i 146).

possesses some special faculty which they lack, enabling him to 'remember' the absolute Forms of objects which they are obliged to encounter in a different and darker way. They can perceive, and possess enough self-consciousness to know that they are 'distinct from what they See', but they develop knowledge solely with reference to the raw objects of perception themselves, with which they strive to interfuse:

> one character
> Denotes them through the progress and the stir;
> A need to blend with each external charm,
> Bury themselves, the whole heart wide and warm,
> In something not themselves; they would belong
> To what they worship – stronger and more strong
> Thus prodigally fed – that gathers shape
> And feature, soon imprisons past escape
> The votary framed to love and to submit
> Nor ask, as passionate he kneels to it,
> Whence grew the idol's empery.
> (*Sordello* i 505–15)

Coleridge puts Browning's argument in a way which usefully draws out its implications:

> The wise only possess ideas; the greater part of mankind are possessed by them . . . When once the mind . . . has abandoned its free power to a haunting impulse or idea, then whatever tends to give depth and vividness to this idea or indefinite imagination, increases its despotism, and in the same proportion renders the reason and free will ineffectual.
> ('Lecture xi', *A Course of Lectures* [1818], in Coleridge: i 190)[10]

The 'common sort' are *imprisoned* and *enslaved* by the object of their attention and find themselves as a result unable to think themselves away from it: they sacrifice their *freedom*. But this is also the case with those whom in the *Essay on Shelley* Browning categorises as 'objective poets', that is, those who unlike the 'subjective' to which Shelley (and Sordello) belong, endeavour to 'reproduce things external' rather than

10. The volume of *Literary Remains* in which these lectures were published appeared in 1836, when Browning was writing *Sordello*, so his focus on this issue could plausibly derive from Coleridge's expression of it.

refer these to their originals in the poet's mental thesaurus. Browning focuses this possibility in a comment to Thomas Kelsall on the poetry of Thomas Lovell Beddoes, in which he detects 'imperfect developments' resulting 'from Beddoes' predominating desire, in the first stage of his artistry, to deliver himself of what was absorbingly & exclusively interesting to him at the time'. Unable to turn 'his attention to other subjects of thought and feeling', he finds himself 'prevented somehow from venting these, and so goes round and round them, ends in the exclusive occupation of his soul with them' (22 May 1868, ABL MS). A slightly different version of this kind of tunnel vision is attributed to the poet Eglamor who in *Sordello* is called 'Sordello's opposite', and described as considering 'Verse a temple-worship' and himself as the willing slave of a 'fancy' appearing to him from without:

> every time
> He loosed that fancy from its bonds of rhyme,
> Like Perseus when he loosed his naked love,
> Faltering; so distinct and far above
> Himself, these fancies! He, no genius rare,
> Transfiguring in fire or wave or air
> At will, but a poor gnome that, cloistered up,
> In some rock-chamber with his agate cup,
> His topaz rod, his seed-pearl, in these few
> And their arrangement finds enough to do
> For his best art.
>
> (ii 209–19)[11]

Likewise, the 'objective poet' is described as inhabiting 'some sunken and darkened chamber of imagery' in which 'by amorous diligence . . . he had rendered permanent by art whatever came to diversify the gloom'. He becomes absorbed in whatever casual object waylays him and thus incapacitated from seeing 'the whole', because that is only available to those who can emancipate themselves from the immediate in the fashion described by Hazlitt:

> No subject can come amiss to him, and he is alike attracted and alike indifferent to all – he is not tied down to any one in

11. For discussion of this passage as it relates to Browning's conception of his own poetry, see Chapter 4, p. 144.

> particular – but floats from one to another, his mind every where finding its level, and feeling no limit but that of thought . . .
>
> (Hazlitt, 'On the Qualifications Necessary to Success in Life', *The Plain Speaker* [1826], in Howe: xii 199)

The subjective poet, then, is enabled by his Platonic capabilities to remain *free* where others become imprisoned and enslaved, and Sordello too stresses this benefit:

> So, range, my soul! Who by self-consciousness
> The last drop of all beauty dost express –
> The grace of seeing grace, a quintessence
> For thee . . .
>
> (ii 405–8)[12]

In effect, we have a Platonic and a neo-Lockeian epistemology laid side by side and ascribed to different types of mind. And, so far, the Platonic subjective type seems to have it all its own way. Where the objective suffers dependence upon its object, a dependence that destroys its existential liberty, the subjective can 'range' across all things without becoming absorbed in any one of them. And, according to Coleridge, this freedom corresponds with the possibility of poetry itself. Coleridge argues that what he calls the 'primary imagination' is the self-consciousness which distinguishes general humanity from everything except God.[13] The 'secondary imagination' is a faculty peculiar to poets (the word has a broader sense than usual) who, with aid of the 'conscious will', are able to break up the empirical sequence of things-perceived and position them within the new order of the poem. That is, they can free themselves from the bondage of the material order of perceptions, and the determinate sequence of their encounters with it, and create a new one: they *realise* the self-consciousness which they share with all humanity in an active form, while, as Sordello sees it, the 'common sort' seek to submerge their self-consciousness in the external world.

12. In the *Poetical Works* of 1888–9, Browning altered 'my soul' to 'free soul', which makes the point with even more emphasis.

13. 'The primary Imagination I hold to be the living power and prime agent of all human perception, and as a repetition in the finite mind of . . . the infinite I AM' (*Biographia Literaria*, ch. xiii).

Browning's development of this argument, however, constitutes a critique in which the apparent pre-eminence of the subjective type of mind/poet is progressively dismantled, and by default the objective comes into play as a necessary corrective.

## The selfish subject

> Between the operations of the mind which . . . I have called *solitary*, and those I have called *social*, there is this very remarkable distinction, that, in the solitary, the expression of them by words, or any other sensible sign, is accidental. They may exist, and be complete, without being expressed, without being known to any other person. But, in the social operations, the expression is essential. They cannot exist without being expressed by words or signs, and known to the other party.
>
> (Thomas Reid, 'Of the Nature and Obligation of a Contract', *Essays on the Active Powers of Man* [1788], in Hamilton: 664)

> Ah, but to find
> A certain mood enervate such a mind,
> Counsel it slumber in the solitude
> Thus reached nor, stooping, task for mankind's good
> Its nature . . .
>
> (*Sordello* i 553–7)

In the *Essay on Shelley* Browning argues that a subjective poet like Shelley 'selects that silence of the earth and sea in which he can best hear the beatings of his individual heart, and leaves the noisy, complex yet imperfect exhibitions of nature in the manifold experience of man around him'. Such self-sufficiency raises the question of why such a mind should find it necessary to engage with reality at all, as for example by writing poetry. Some ingredient other than self-consciousness needs to be added to the equation to account for such an impulse, and the comment on Sordello's 'mind' in the quotation above suggests that it will be a *moral* impulse to 'task for mankind's good / Its nature'. Similarly, Browning lays great stress in the *Essay on Shelley* on the excellence of Shelley's moral nature, with the implication that his 'sympathy with the oppressed' was the motivation of his poetry (Pettigrew and Collins: i 1008).

But in *Sordello* a quite different account of poetic motivation emerges. Sordello writes poetry to at once achieve and express his 'mastery' over both his human audience and general nature, and as such a desire can be directly deduced from the Platonic theory of knowledge without additional ingredients it proves more plausible, and much more problematic, than the admixture of a commitment to 'mankind's good'. The desire for mastery is not, however, restricted to the domain of poetry; in fact it emerges by default from a more extravagant desire to take possession of reality itself.

The passage from *Pauline* quoted above (p. 193) goes on to argue that the mind's 'consciousness / Of self' is

> linked in me, to self-supremacy,
> Existing as a centre to all things,
> Most potent to create, and rule, and call
> Upon all things to minister to it;
> And to a principle of restlessness
> Which would be all, have, see, know, taste, feel, all –
> This is myself; and I should thus have been,
> Though gifted lower than the meanest soul.
>
> (ll. 273–80)

This posits that alongside self-consciousness ('Primary Imagination') the poet's mind includes in its latent endowment what Browning calls 'self-supremacy', the desire to incorporate and rule all the modes of being represented in its perception ('secondary imagination'; but l. 280 implies that this wish is not unique to poets). It cannot tolerate the thought that anything outside itself is thereby also outside its control, and seeks to overcome otherness by transforming it into an inflection of its own consciousness. Self-consciousness, that is, leads to or includes the desire to incorporate all other modes of being. Needless to say, this is an impossible project:

> I grow mad
> Well-nigh, to know not one abode but holds
> Some pleasure – for my soul could grasp them all,
> But must remain with this vile form.
>
> (ll. 614–17)

Sordello, too, recognises that even though his 'Will' possesses the whole world, there is no way he can 'turn it . . . Native', because his 'Means to correspond / With Will are so unworthy' (iii 175–8). And in 'Cleon', this recognition becomes the ground of a critique of self-consciousness itself, as being responsible for an existential impasse. Cleon too takes the position that it is self-consciousness that distinguishes man from the rest of the material creation, and imagines how this might be represented as a benefit:

> by making each
> Grow conscious in himself – by that alone.
> All's perfect else: the shell sucks fast the rock,
> The fish strikes through the sea, the snake both swims
> And slides; the birds take flight, forth range the beasts,
> Till life's mechanics can no further go –
> And all this joy in natural life, is put,
> Like fire from off Thy finger into each,
> So exquisitely perfect is the same.
> But 'tis pure fire – and they mere matter are;
> It has them, not they it: and so I choose,
> For man, Thy last premeditated work
> (If I might add a glory to this scheme)
> That a third thing should stand apart from both,
> A quality arise within the soul,
> Which intro-active, made to supervise
> And feel the force it has, may view itself,
> And so be happy.
>
> (ll. 197–214)

This is not, however, the true position, since through self-consciousness

> we have discovered ('tis no dream –
> We know this, which we had not else perceived)
> That there's a world of capability
> For joy, spread round about us, meant for us,
> Inviting us; and still the soul craves all,
> And still the flesh replies, 'Take no jot more
> Than ere you climbed the tower to look abroad!
> Nay, so much less, as that fatigue has brought
> Deduction to it.' We struggle – fain to enlarge
> Our bounded physical recipiency,
> Increase our power, supply fresh oil to life,
> Repair the waste of age and sickness. No,
> It skills not: life's inadequate to joy,
> As the soul sees joy, tempting life to take.
>
> (ll. 237–50)

This development derives in the first instance from the Platonic theory of knowledge, but also extends it. Derives from it in the sense that if, as Plato posits, all objects of perception are already latent in the mind, the mind is clearly in some sense superior to them, and such superiority is already a kind of control over them.[14] Extends it, in the sense that where Plato's dualism led him to argue that this meant that the mind should strive to emancipate itself from the imperfect shows of material things, and rise towards a perfect intuition of the absolute, Browning seems to want the world of perception itself, in all its materiality, to literally be added to the mind. This implies a non-Platonic, potentially monistic valuation of the material world, and the presence of this in Browning's metaphysics may be understood as a modification of Lockeian materialism in the light of Romantic organicism. The material world, for Locke, contains no innate spiritual dimension; it is simply an order of substance as to whose metaphysical status no account need be given; but in Romantic philosophy it became admissible to argue that the material order is itself spiritual; that all things, including the body of the perceiver and his mind, are inflections of a universal substance which is identical to God; that the visible universe is the body of God, and God present in and as all things. This is the philosophy known as Romantic pantheism, and it marks the rehabilitation of monism as a feasible theory of being after the dualism of the Christian and Cartesian traditions. Its most famous expression came in Wordsworth's 'Tintern Abbey', where Wordsworth detects behind the material display 'A motion and a spirit, that impels / All thinking things, all objects of all thought, / And rolls through all things' (ll. 100–2); but Coleridge too claimed that all modes of being were 'parts and proportions of one wondrous whole' ('Religious Musings', l. 128).

This is the position advanced at the end of *Paracelsus*:

> God tastes an infinite joy
> In infinite ways – one everlasting bliss,
> From whom all being emanates, all power

14. Many of the occult traditions seized upon this possibility, Paracelsus for example arguing that 'SPECULATION is when a man speculates and imagines within himself, and thereby his imagination is united with heaven', simultaneously coming to know 'many things: future, present, and past, all arts and sciences'.

> Proceeds; in whom is life for evermore,
> Yet whom existence in its lowest form
> Includes; where dwells enjoyment there is He!
> . . . Thus He dwells in all,
> From life's minute beginnings, up at last
> To man . . .
>
> (v 628–33, 666–8)

Paracelsus here totally contradicts his earlier assertion that it was in the mind alone that 'truth' was to be found: rather, truth would seem to be distributed equally across all inhabitants of the material plane, since God is invested indiscriminately in all and all therefore equally attest and disclose his being. This is the metaphysic which underlies the objective poet's concern with material things: each is and all are separately and collectively perfect, since each includes and is included by God; therefore knowledge may legitimately pursue its perfection through study of them.

This possibility is confirmed by passages in which Browning appears to endorse Paracelsus's version of Romantic pantheism, in particular the last lines of the 'Epilogue' to *Dramatis Personae*, in which the 'Third Speaker' attempts to rebut the argument that God's 'Face' – his identity or felt presence – has somehow ebbed from the universe or was never there at all:

> That one Face, far from vanish, rather grows,
> Or decomposes but to recompose,
> Become my universe that feels and knows!

The idea that God could 'grow', 'decompose' and 'recompose' synchronises his being with the organic processes which he simultaneously sponsors as their originator. This is presumably what Browning means by saying in his letter about Sludge (p. 189) that behind material things 'you find . . . creative intelligence, acting as matter but not resulting from it': God is incarnate and manifest in the universe, but as its cause rather than its result.

According to Paracelsus, 'God is the perfect poet', meaning that only in him is self-consciousness is compatible with personal ubiquity, self-investment in every possible object of perception; on discovering the impossibility of implementing its felt universality by literal incorporation of all things, the human 'Will' turns to poetry as affording an equivalent possibility: that is, what the poet's body cannot materially appropriate may, by being included in his *poem*, become his property in another sense. Sordello writes poetry in order to achieve this surrogate form of control over the objects of his perception. In him, 'the common sort' will

Perceive
What I could do, a mastery believe,
Asserted and established to the throng
By their selected evidence of Song
Which now shall prove whate'er they are, or seek
To be, I am – who takes no pains to speak,
Change no old standards of perfection, vex
With no strange forms created to perplex,
But mean perform their bidding and no more,
At their own satiating-point give o'er,
And each shall love in me the love that leads
His soul to its perfection.

(ii 429–40)

In his poetry, Sordello proposes to comprise all possible varieties of his human audience, and by extension all things whatsoever; his appetite for ubiquity will thereby be satisfied without any tax on his body, since poetry becomes a substitute body in which the 'will's' universal cravings may be satisfied. Again, Browning remarks in the *Essay on Chatterton* on 'the tendency of certain spirits to subdue each man by perceiving what will master him, by straightway supplying it from their own resources, and so obtaining, as tokens of success, his admiration, or fear, or wonder' (Woolford and Karlin: ii 499).

This conception of poetry derives in part from Plato's critique of poetry, as put forward by Socrates in the *Ion*, which is concerned precisely with the question of the extent and kind of the poet's knowledge. Ion is a 'rhapsode' (effectively a poet), and Socrates playfully demands to know what kind of knowledge poetry can comprise. He argues that there is in fact no way in which poetry can really incorporate the kinds of knowledge it claims to transmit, for when it deals with, for example, the art of war, it is inferior to the general, and when it deals with the science of medicine it is inferior to the doctor, and so on:

just as I picked out for you passages in the *Iliad* and the *Odyssey* which belong to the prophet, the doctor, and the fisherman, you

> pick out for me, since you know Homer better than I do, passages which belong to the rhapsode and his art – things which the rhapsode ought to be able to examine and criticise better than other people.
>
> *Ion.* In my view, Socrates, that means everything. (Plato: 48)

Ion perceives (perhaps: he's not depicted as very bright) that Socrates is on the way to denying that poetry can communicate any kind of knowledge at all, and that the only way to bypass this limitation is to propose that the poet knows everything, that poetry is absolute and universal knowledge. Socrates has no difficulty in dismantling this hyperbole, but it is as if Sordello were engaged in trying to implement Ion's claim by arguing that the poet really can become 'everything', that is, incorporate not only all disciplines, with their associated routes to knowledge, but also all other modes of being, with their posited essences, inside his poetry.

We have then a motive to write, but it encounters two immediate problems: the problem of language and the problem of communication. The problem of language is that as (in some sense) a material instrument language proves incapable of embodying the 'perception' the poet requires it to express; the problem of communication is that if the poet and his audience occupy different planes of being and approach reality in different ways, it is not clear how he will be able to present his 'perception' to them in a form which they can understand. Both problems, or rather Browning's perception that they *are* problems, derive from Locke's critique, developing its darker tendency towards a denial of the possibility of a shared knowledge.

Locke's theory of knowledge puts language at two removes from reality. In the first instance, we can have no certainty that the ideas we form of things correspond to them in any way. But when we give names to our ideas – put them into language – we double the difficulty, since there is equally little correspondence between those ideas and the names we substitute for them:

> we *may not* think (as perhaps usually is done) that [ideas] are exactly the Images and *Resemblances* of something inherent in the subject; most of those of Sensation being in the Mind no more the likeness of something existing without us, than the Names, that stand for them, are the likeness of our *Ideas*, which yet upon hearing, they are apt to excite in us. (Locke: II viii §7)

There is no 'natural connexion . . . between particular articulate Sounds and certain *Ideas*, for then there would be but one Language amongst all Men; but by a voluntary Imposition . . . such a Word is made arbitrarily the Mark of such an *Idea*' (III ii §1). And when we try with the aid of words to communicate our ideas to others, the situation gets worse. To do this people both 'suppose their Words to stand also for the Reality of Things' (III i §5) and 'suppose their Words to be marks of *Ideas* in the Minds also of other Men, with whom they communicate' (III ii §4). But, warns Locke:

> every Man has so inviolable a Liberty, to make Words stand for what *Ideas* he pleases, that no one hath the Power to make others have the same *Ideas* in their Minds, that he has, when they use the same Words, that he does. (III ii §8)

He concludes that

> the signification of Words, in all Languages, depending very much on the Thoughts, Notions, and *Ideas* of him that uses them, must unavoidably be of great uncertainty, to Men of the same Language and Country. (III ix §22)

In his summary, he explicitly suggests that language, or at least its apparent interpersonal currency, is fraudulent:

> 'Tis true, the names of Substances would be much more useful, and Propositions made in them much more certain, were the real Essences of Substances the *Ideas* in our Minds, which those words signified. And 'tis for want of those real Essences, that our Words convey so little Knowledge or Certainty in our Discourses about them: And therefore the Mind, to remove that Imperfection as much as it can, makes them, by a secret Supposition, to stand for a Thing, having that real Essence, as if thereby it made some nearer approaches to it. (III x §18)

In conversation we pretend that joint reference to its 'real Essence' enables us to mean the same thing when we say rabbit;[15] but we do not, and the communication we construct is hallucinatory.

Sordello turns to poetry to transmit and vindicate his spiritual supremacy over his audience by comprising all their thoughts, but finds language an insuperable barrier:

15. Locke's example is 'Gold'.

Because perceptions whole, like that he sought
To clothe, reject so pure a work of thought
As language: Thought may take Perception's place
But hardly co-exist in any case,
Being its mere presentment – of the Whole
By Parts, the Simultaneous and the Sole
By the Successive and the Many.

(ii 589–950)

Like the body, language proves incapable of embodying the mind's idea because whereas that is eternal and infinite language is bound to temporality ('the Successive and the Many'). This scepticism about the capabilities of language prevails across Browning's oeuvre, as characteristically in the Pope's monologue in *The Ring and the Book*, where he attacks 'this vile way by the barren words / Which, more than any deed, characterize / Man as made subject to a curse' (x 348–5).

Similarly, Sordello finds himself unable to believe that when he puts his ideas into language his audience can reverse the process and convert his language back into his ideas:

Then how divine the cause
Such a performance should exact applause
From men if they have fancies too?

(ii 147–9)[16]

If (as Locke argued) each mind arrives privately at its sense of things by an association of ideas unique to itself, it is impossible, or extremely unlikely, that any given linguistic 'performance' should evoke the same ones in any others. In *La Saisiaz* Browning repeats this argument in a slightly different form for himself:

But, as knowledge, this comes only – things may be as I behold,
Or may not be, but, without me and above me, things there are;
I myself am what I know not – ignorance which proves no bar
To the knowledge that I am, and, since I am, can recognize
What to me is pain and pleasure: this is sure, the rest – surmise.
If my fellows are or are not, what may please them and what
pain, –
Mere surmise: my own experience – that is knowledge, once
again!

(ll. 258–64)

16. 'Then how divine' means 'Then how can I discover'.

Self-evidently, his reluctance to dogmatise to his audience about 'the soul and future life' derives from this abyss of uncertainties.

Two hypothetical solutions to this problem appear in Browning's work. Sordello postulates that while unable to grasp his 'perception' his audience may have managed to find 'a beauty separate' in his poetry itself, as verse (ii 150–1). This would imply the existence of a separate and presumably universal *aesthetic* quality, independent of the process of transmission which so damages original 'perception'. That he nevertheless goes on to attempt to communicate his 'perceptions whole' indicates that this solution is unsatisfactory, and Browning's statement to Ruskin that the poet's task 'is all teaching' indicates that it did not satisfy him either, though its existence in his thought establishes a precedent for what later became known as 'Aestheticism'. The second possibility is that the poet can in some mysterious way project his will *independently of his poem*, compelling other, differently constituted minds to recognise the inner meaning his words cannot directly deliver.

This curious possibility becomes most explicit in some draft notes Browning attached to *Sordello* when he was trying to rewrite it in the 1850s (the attempt was abandoned). Prominent among these notes is a whole series which introduce the concept of *mesmerism* into the poem's aesthetics. These are associated with Sordello's poetic attempts, and relate to the process by which his poems affect – or fail to affect – his audience.[17] Thus, when Sordello wonders how the verse which attempts to express *his* perception can affect others 'if they had fancies too', Browning added the marginal comment, 'not knowing yet what it was – mesmerism'. This points to the possibility that the poet's 'will', his desire to express himself and achieve 'self-revealment', might in this instance have by-passed the text itself, and lodged itself by a projective action directly in the minds of his auditors, as William Pitt's 'will', according to Hazlitt, 'was surcharged with electrical matter like a Voltaic battery; and all who stood within its reach felt the full force of the shock'.[18] The oratorical gestures by which a Pitt commun-

17. See *Sordello* (in Woolford and Karlin, vol. i) ii 71n., 141–60n., 168–9n., 317n., 355n., 402n., 415n., 998n.

18. 'On the Difference between Writing and Speaking', *The Plain Speaker* (1826) in Howe: xii 269. Browning's interest in this phenomenon may have been stimulated by Balzac's *Louis Lambert* (1832–3), which had a profound influence on *Paracelsus* and *Sordello*. Lambert conceives that,

icates his feelings are introduced into a theory of the literary text, making it possible for a reader's response to a text to be controlled by its author despite his empirical absence through distance or death.

The problem with this proposal, if we suppose it to be serious, is that it depends upon the poet's will-to-power over his readers. And it cannot even afford satisfaction in its original terms. Cleon points out what is obvious enough, that the 'mastery' achieved in this surrogate fashion is quite unreal, and therefore deeply unsatisfying:

> Because in my great epos I display
> How divers men young, strong, fair, wise, can act –
> Is this as though I acted? if I paint,
> Carve the young Phoebus, am I therefore young?
> Methinks I'm older that I bowed myself
> The many years of pain that taught me art!
> (ll. 285–90)

This difficulty is surmounted in two ways in Browning's poetry, both of which involve its transposition to the plane of ethics. The first is his casting of much of his work in the form of a satire upon egotism. The second is his invocation of a very different, *empathetic* account of the poetic impulse, an account which again derives from a combination of Platonic and Romantic sources.

Browning's dramatic monologues characteristically exhibit will-to-power in their speakers. I have shown (p. 167) how at the beginning of 'My Last Duchess' the speaker sets about taking control of his auditor, and this is characteristic; indeed it is essential if the convention by which the interlocutor in a dramatic monologue never speaks is to seem anything other than arbitrary. The interlocutor of 'Mr. Sludge, "the Medium" ', the ludicrously named 'Hiram H. Horsefall', resorts to violence in his attempt to wrest control away from the speaker – he tries to strangle him, to take away his power of speech, that is, his power *in* speech, his hegemony over the poem's linguistic space:

---

on the strength of 'Mesmer's discovery, so important and still so little appreciated', 'the Will could, by a concentrating movement of the inner self, gather itself together; then, by another movement, be projected outside [the self] . . . Thus the whole force of a man would have the capacity to act on other people' (our transl.). See *Sordello* ii 71n. in Woolford and Karlin: i 467.

'Get up?'
You still inflict on me that terrible face?
You show no mercy? – Not for Her dear sake,
The sainted spirit's, whose soft breath even now
Blows on my cheek – (don't you feel something, sir?)
You'll tell?
Go tell, then! Who the devil cares
What such a rowdy chooses to . . .
Aie – aie – aie!
Please, sir! your thumbs are through my windpipe, sir!
Ch – ch!

(ll. 10–18)

Needless to say the attempt fails, as indeed the poem's form, in which the interlocutor's words only appear when the speaker quotes them, has already predicted. Granted the opportunity to justify himself, Sludge argues his way towards a reversal of this moment, bringing his confession round to the moment when his hegemony was challenged:

But I, do I present you with my piece,
It's 'What, Sludge? When my sainted mother spoke
The verses Lady Jane Grey last composed
About the rosy bower in the seventh heaven
Where she and Queen Elizabeth keep house, –
You made the raps? 'Twas your invention that?
Cur, slave and devil' – eight fingers and two thumbs
Stuck in my throat!
Well, if the marks seem gone,
'Tis because stiffish cock-tail, taken in time,
Is better for a bruise than arnica.

(ll. 1470–9)

Sludge quotes words we have never heard ('What Sludge? etc.') but in a new context in which their power has leaked away into the interlocutor's remorseful withdrawal of his assault: we are clearly asked to insert a gesture or expression of concern into the space between 'Stuck in my throat' and 'Well, if the marks seem gone', and by making that gesture the interlocutor not only concedes the strength or at least fascination of Sludge's arguments but also cedes linguistic primacy to him and validates the form of the poem. But this is also to knuckle under to what Sludge readily admits is his own inviolable selfishness:

> What do I know or care about your world
> Which either is or seems to be? This snap
> Of my fingers, sir! My care is for myself;
> Myself am whole and sole reality
> Inside a raree-show and a market-mob
> Gathered about it: that's the use of things.
> (ll. 906–11)

In *The Ring and the Book*, Guido Franceschini elaborates this egomania into a social theory.

> I say that, long ago, when things began,
> All the world made agreement, such and such
> Were pleasure-giving profit-bearing acts,
> But henceforth extra-legal, nor to be:
> You must not kill the man whose death would please
> And profit you, unless his life stop yours
> Plainly, and need so be put aside:
> Get the thing by a public course, by law,
> Only no private bloodshed as of old!
> All of us, for the good of every one,
> Renounced such licence and conformed to law:
> Who breaks law, breaks pact, therefore, helps himself
> To pleasure and profit over and above the due,
> And must pay forfeit, – pain beyond his share:
> For pleasure is the sole good in the world . . .
> (xi 515–29)

Such a system assumes absolute selfishness as the human norm, and imagines social institutions as arising solely to set pragmatic limits to people's egotism. For Guido, murdering Pompilia was not an immoral act – there is no morality beyond the imperative to pleasure – but simply an illegal one, and his punishment is therefore not a moral retribution but mere social revenge. There is a weird sense in which his orgy of carnage, killing not just his wife, but her parents too, represents the dark underside of the subjective poet's will-to-power, just as Sludge's spiritualistic masquerades attempt to control not only (in the first instance) his audience but the larger reality which his spirit-world gathers into itself:

> You find you're in a flock
> Of the youthful, earnest, passionate – genius, beauty,

Rank and wealth also, if you care for these,
And all depose their natural rights, hail you,
(That's me, sir) as their mate and yoke-fellow,
Participate in Sludgehood – nay, grow mine,
I veritably possess them – banish doubt,
And reticence and modesty alike!
Why, here's the Golden Age, old Paradise
Or new Eutopia! Here is life indeed,
And the world well won now, yours for the first time!
(ll. 1423–33)

Sludge conceives that the spirit-world into which he has inserted all the historical characters he has ventriloquised affords him control over them: they 'participate in Sludgehood' in the sense that they become part of himself ('grow mine').

This sounds so like the configuration by which the subjective poet considers the objects of his perception to be mere imperfect replicas of their prototypes within his mind that it comes as no surprise when Sludge compares his fictions to poetry – more broadly, literature – itself:

And all this might be, may be, and with good help
Of a little lying shall be: so, Sludge lies!
Why, he's at worst your poet who sings how Greeks
That never were, in Troy which never was,
Did this or the other impossible great thing!
He's Lowell – it's a world, you smile and say,
Of his own invention – wondrous Longfellow,
Surprising Hawthorne! Sludge does more than they,
And acts the books they write: the more's his praise!
(ll. 1434–42)

It was presumably the fear of having such a reading applied to his own poetic impulses which led Browning to embrace, but also to revise, the more self-sacrificial approach to reality that he attributes to the objective poet. This ethical reading of the position appears as early as *Pauline*, where the speaker feels and/or expresses 'remorse' for the 'selfishness' which accompanies, if it is not identical with, the 'self-supremacy' he seeks, but claims simultaneously to be capable of self-abnegation:

Nought makes me trust in love so really,

> As the delight of the contented lowness
> With which I gaze on souls I'd keep for ever
> In beauty – I'd be sad to equal them;
> I'd feed their fame e'en from my heart's best blood,
> Withering unseen, that they might flourish still.
> (ll. 554–9)

It is intriguing that at that stage of his life Browning evidently struck at least one friend as being selfish in this sense. Opposite the above passage his friend Sarah Flower wrote in the margin of her copy: 'true to the perfected soul but not of yours RB, alas' (Maynard: 384), and opposite 'My selfishness is satiated not' (l. 601) she wrote 'true!'. And to J.S. Mill, who wrote an unpublished review of *Pauline* which Browning saw, 'this writer seems to me possessed with a more intense and morbid self-consciousness than I ever knew in any sane human being', adding, 'if he once could muster a hearty hatred of his selfishness, it would GO'.[19] The 'absolute independence' of which Browning boasted to EBB, and his reiterated unease about the confinements of marriage, clearly derive from what has to be called his egotism, and many commentators have felt uneasy about the form this assumed in later statements. In 'At the "Mermaid" ' Shakespeare is made to say:

> Have you found your life distasteful?
> My life did and does smack sweet.
> Was your youth of pleasure wasteful?
> Mine I saved and hold complete.
> (ll. 73–6)

And *La Saisiaz*, as we have seen, grounds this indifferentism in Lockeian principle: 'If my fellows are or are not, what may please them and what pain, – / Mere surmise: my own experience – that is knowledge, once again!' (ll. 263–4). It is against this background that Browning struggles to formulate an experience of *empathy* which he derived in the first instance from the Romantics, and at greater distance from Plato.

19. For the full text of this 'review', and Browning's reaction to it, see Woolford and Karlin: i 17–18.

## The selfless subject

> While the former darts himself forth, and passes into all the forms of human character and passion, the one Proteus of the fire and flood; the other attracts all forms and things to himself, into the unity of his own ideal. All things and modes of action shape themselves anew in the being of Milton; while Shakespeare becomes all things, yet for ever remaining himself.
>
> (Coleridge, *Biographia Literaria*, ch. xv)

> He tried to associate himself with the secret working of this natural world, and to identify so completely with its passive obedience, as to fall under the despotic and preserving law which governs instinctive beings.
>
> (Balzac, *The Wild Ass's Skin* [1831], ch. 51; our transl.)[20]

> It is doubtless an entirely peculiar privilege of his genius, that he had the power of absolutely and sensibly losing himself in the object, whatever it was, to which, at any particular point of time, his attention was directed, whether it were man, beast, bird or plant: nay, that he, to a certain extent, transformed himself in imagination into the very thing itself.
>
> (Müller's *Characteristics of Goethe*, cited Woolford and Karlin: i 184)

In his letter about Thomas Lovell Beddoes' poetry Browning accuses Beddoes of lacking 'insight into and sympathy with characters quite different from his own' (22 May 1868, ABL MS; see also above, pp. 30 and 199). This is more than his technical deficiency as a dramatist. In Romantic accounts such as Coleridge's above, it is indeed the dramatist who 'becomes all things, yet for ever remaining himself', but his capacity so to do is viewed simultaneously as giving an *epistemological* and a *moral* superiority over anyone who, like Beddoes, refuses to think beyond 'what was absorbingly & exclusively interesting to him at the time'. To forsake one's own subjective centre and become invested in that of another, whether 'man, beast, bird, or plant', is in the weak sense a necessary preliminary to all knowledge, in a stronger sense an act of altruism or self-sacrifice on behalf of that other, and in the strongest sense of all it involves participation in the unity of existence itself, at which point it passes seamlessly into organicism.

20. For an analogy betwen this passage of Balzac's novel and lines 716–28 of *Pauline*, see Woolford and Karlin: i 71.

The tradition of thought founded by Locke logically denies the possibility, or at least the objective reality, of any self-identification with another being, on the same premise which questioned the possibility of any genuine communication. In the Romantic and Victorian periods the Utilitarian thinkers maintained this position, but alongside it in the eighteenth century had already emerged a 'sympathetic school' whose members argued that as *feeling* was a distinguishing trait of human nature, so *sympathetic* feeling was necessary, as the Irish poet James Arbuckle put it, 'to enforce our Duty upon us, not only by Reason, but by Passion and powerful Inclination' (Arbuckle: 33–4). In Adam Smith's *Theory of Moral Sentiments*, sympathy is enlarged from this supplementary role to a constitutive one. Our moral nature is based on our capacity to understand the sensations of others, and '[a]s we have no immediate experience of what other men feel, we can form no idea of the manner in which they are affected, but by conceiving what we ourselves should feel in the like situation' (Smith: 2).

All English Romantic thinking was influenced by this position, but most of all, perhaps, that of Hazlitt, Shelley and Keats. Hazlitt argues that moral issues should not be subjects of rational calculation:

> Suppose, for instance, that in the discussions on the Slave-Trade, a description to the life was given of the horrors of the *Middle Passage* (as it was termed) – that you saw the manner in which thousands of wretches, year after year, were stowed together in the hold of a slave-ship, without air, without light, without food, without hope, so that what they suffered in reality was brought home to you in imagination, till you felt in sickness of heart as one of them, could it be said that this was a prejudging of the case, that your knowing the extent of the evil disqualified you from pronouncing sentence upon it, and that your disgust and abhorrence were the effects of a heated imagination? No.
>
> ('On Reason and Imagination', *The Plain Speaker* [1826], in Howe: xii 47)

A transition is visible here from Smith's notion of *sympathy* as a process in which we imagine what we would feel in *another's* situation, to its Romantic intensification into *empathy* (Einfühlung), where one is imaginatively transformed *into the other person*. From hearing a description of the slave trade, Hazlitt's imagined reader passes to specular apprehension of it ('you saw') out of which arises sympathy ('what they suffered in reality was brought home to you in imagination'), immediately followed by empathy ('you felt in sickness of heart as one of them'). The effect of this progression is to invalidate rational calculation as a basis for moral thinking, and Shelley, in the *Defence of Poetry*, by giving the name 'love' to the concept of sympathy/empathy, makes it the primary constituent of the moral nature itself:

> The great secret of morals is love; or a going out of our nature, and an identification of ourselves with the beautiful which exists in thought, action, or person, not our own. A man, to be greatly good, must imagine intensely and comprehensively; he must put himself in the place of another and of many others; the pains and pleasures of his species must become his own. (Brett-Smith: 33)

And this argument points directly to a justification of *poetry* as capable of 'enlarging the circumference of the imagination' and thereby 'strengthening the faculty which is the organ of the moral nature'. For Keats it is more than a justification, it is, as he wrote to Richard Woodhouse, a definition of the 'poetical Character itself':

> A Poet is the most unpoetical of any thing in existence; because he has no Identity – he is continually in for – and filling some other Body – The Sun, the Moon, the Sea and Men and Women who are creatures of impulse are poetical and have about them an unchangeable attribute – the poet has none; no identity – he is certainly the most unpoetical of all God's Creatures.
> (27 Oct. 1818, Rollins: i 387])[21]

Browning was evidently aware of this tradition by the time he wrote *Pauline*, since several passages concern the speaker's desire to enter other consciousnesses than his own, and in one instance to go further, and identify with the organic animate in nature:

> I can live all the life of plants, and gaze
> Drowsily on the bees that flit and play,

21. For another reference to the passage from the *Defence of Poetry*, see ch. 4, p. 118, where Keats's letter is also discussed; see n. 3 in that chapter for Browning's possible (in our view likely) familiarity with unpublished letters of Keats.

Or bare my breast for sunbeams which will kill,
Or open in the night of sounds, to look
For the dim stars; I can mount with the bird,
Leaping airily his pyramid of leaves
And twisted boughs of some tall mountain tree,
Or rise cheerfully springing to the heavens –
Or like a fish breathe in the morning air
In the misty sun-warm water – or with flowers
And trees can smile in light at the sinking sun,
Just as the storm comes – as a girl would look
On a departing lover – most serene.
(ll. 716–28)

But the movement here is incomplete: rather than *becoming* a plant, he passes into an intermediate state in which he at once knows what it might be like to be a plant and retains the human status implied in 'bare my breast'; to 'mount *with* the bird' does not achieve identity with it, as to be '*like* a fish' is not the same as actually being one; and the final image dissolves all the role-playing back into a specifically human scene and set of concerns. And in 'Two in the Campagna', he finds a 'wound' or chasm between himself and both his loved one and general nature.[22] But such limits do not invalidate the enterprise altogether, and *Fifine at the Fair* shows how it might be possible, in a double movement, both to become and yet not become the object of one's perception. Don Juan, the speaker of the poem, argues that

No creature's made so mean
But that, some way, it boasts, could we investigate,
Its supreme worth: fulfils, by ordinance of fate,
Its momentary task, gets glory all its own,
Tastes triumph in the world, pre-eminent, alone.
(ll. 339–43)

This takes account of the Lockeian assertion that each human experience differs, but capitalises on it rather than capitulating to it by making that difference, and the resulting infinite diversity of things, a source of value.[23] But Don Juan imagines that this existential

22. For further discussions of this poem, see pp. 132–3 and 179.

23. Browning was also probably drawing upon the historical Paracelsus's principle of 'separation', a principle which produces what Walter Pagel

isolationism will be superseded by a desire to unite with some other being:

each soul, just as weak
Its own way as its fellow, – departure from design
As flagrant in the flesh, – goes striving to combine
With what shall right the wrong, the under or above
The standard: supplement unloveliness by love.
– Ask Plato else!

(ll. 679–84)

The allusion is to Plato's doctrine of love, most famously advanced in the *Symposium*, where Socrates describes how in the first instance the lover experiences the desire to unite himself with the object of his affection, but in the process passes from worldly to spiritual beauty and finally to ultimate knowledge. Browning here plays off one part of Plato's philosophy, that part which he uses in defining the subjective poet, against another which by foreshadowing Romantic empathy came to imply for him an opposite, objective self-immersion in the object. By doing so, he allows Plato to 'answer' Locke, though at the price of exposing what is represented as a contradiction in Plato's thought.

Such overcoming of isolation is an aesthetic as much as an ethical or metaphysical objective. In book ii of *Paracelsus*, Aprile, a 'subjective' poet of Sordello's type, longs to join the opposing class: 'I would love infinitely and be loved . . . Every passion sprung from man, conceived by man, / Would I express' (ll. 368, 381–2). And Don Juan too moves the debate in this direction:

---

calls 'a "decentralising" tendency' which ' "differentiates" and infinitely divides the world' (Pagel: 36). Paracelsus himself put it that after Creation 'no mixture of the Elements continued fast united, but every Element betook it selfe to its own free power without dependence on another' (cited in Woolford and Karlin: i 106). Paracelsus's extreme individualism may be illustrated by his argument that when the differentiation of mankind ceases, and the next man to be born proves to be a repetition of some previous one, the world will come to an end.

– Ask Plato else! And this corroborates the sage,
That Art . . .
Must fumble for the whole, once fixing on a part
However poor, surpass the fragment, and aspire
To reconstruct thereby the ultimate entire.
Art, working with a will, discards the superflux,
Contributes to defect, toils on till, – *fiat lux*, –
There's the restored, the prime, the individual type!
(ll. 684–5, 689–94)

This is an attempted synthesis of the contending elements in Browning's philosophy through an enacted fusion of objective and subjective approaches. The artist seeks not to abolish but to celebrate the infinite varieties of existence, and he does this by – in the first instance – 'loving' a particular example of it. His first movement is therefore outward, towards the inner being of the object of his loving contemplation; he identifies with it, deferring his own interests to it. But because he remains conscious of an 'ultimate' from which the empirical object or person deviates, that love obliges him to seek to perfect it by reuniting it with the Form it represents. He therefore 'improves' it, but in its own interest, since in doing so he 'restores' its transcendent architecture without obliterating it as an 'individual'. The phrase 'individual type' registers the strain of this equation, since its terms pull in opposite directions, 'individual' towards the Lockeian-empirical perception of infinite difference between minds/objects, 'type' towards the Platonic preference of the 'one' over the 'many', the absolute over the particular, the Form over its corrupted image.

This balancing-act between opposed alternatives is reflected in the process by which a dramatic monologue speaker is initially represented as a compromised, often criminal character ('a part / However poor') but then gradually extended beyond its seemingly incorrigible limits. The resulting 'lyrical element', as Robert Langbaum calls it, is essential to the attempted synthesis (Langbaum: 182). Don Juan himself is a reprobate philanderer whose monologue offers, in the first instance, a justification of his adulteries to his wife Elvire (as Mr Sludge starts off by confessing to one of his dupes that he faked the supernatural apparitions of his séances). But in each instance the low motive, and the soiled or inadequate character, drops away to be replaced by astonishingly beautiful and compelling passages of metaphysical speculation. Langbaum argues that such passages remain, or should remain, true to the character, and that Browning's monologues test and affirm the capacity of a character to remain true to itself, but that is true, I think, in a rather complex sense. Browning sympathises with the character, strives to enter and comprehend its viewpoint, but in doing so he improves upon his original by imagining *the best possible argument* for its misdeeds, and then going beyond excuse-making towards a universal vision in which the latter dwindle into insignificance. This is the moment in which the character is 'restored' to its 'type', but that is not sufficient, it must simultaneously remain 'individual', so at the end of the poem the character reverts to its characteristic nature and conduct, Sludge curses his interlocutor and plans more and better swindles, Juan slides off for his rendezvous with Fifine, Prince Hohenstiel-Schwangau ruefully reflects that he has failed to carry out any of the magnificent gestures he has just been rehearsing in fantasy. Such tackings reflect, but also overcome, the strain of Browning's creative equation; they also capitalise on precisely the problem Sordello found insurmountable, the problem that language inhabits the medium of time and cannot transcend it.

## The Christian synthesis

So far, I have discussed Browning's thought with little or no reference to what most of his contemporaries saw as its most important aspect, the religious. The title of Henry Jones's *Browning as a Philosophical and Religious Teacher* indicates the inseparability of Browning's religion from his philosophy in Victorian perceptions of him and much subsequent work, some of it very good, has been done on that side of his thinking.[24] Apart from a certain rather ambiguous hostility to Catholicism, natural in one who was brought up as a Dissenter, Browning was tolerant and latitudinarian in his religious attitudes: he defended the Jews, used a Persian (presumably Muslim) speaker for one of his late collections of doctrinal statements (*Ferishtah's Fancies*), and throughout his life remained interested in occult and mystical traditions. The tracing in detail of these contributions is a fascinating study, but here I have space only to consider the relation of

24. William Whitla's *The Central Truth: The Incarnation in Browning's Poetry* (Toronto 1963) is the best discussion yet undertaken.

Browning's religious thought to the philosophical issues I have identified.

Browning remained true to his Lockeian roots in insisting that the existence of God, of Christ, and of related issues such as the reality of an afterlife, must come second to the primary *datum*, 'my own experience'. A late speaker, Francis Furini, remains faithful to this imperative: 'self-consciousness' is 'Knowledge', while whatever came 'before' him, his 'Cause', is 'styled God' ('Parleying with Francis Furini' [1887] 350–3). If I exist, as I find I do, then something must have caused me to exist, and the name 'God' may be attached to that cause without, in the first instance, further doctrinal entanglements. But if God created me, then he must have created everything else, must, therefore, be absolute Power: 'thus blend / I, and all things perceived, in one Effect' (ll. 360–1). The idea of God allows the mind to objectify itself into a feature of 'the universe', a step already anticipated in the self-beholding which allowed it to affirm its own existence: in that sense, Browning follows Coleridge in perceiving God as ultimate self-consciousness, and human self-consciousness as the imperfect echo of that absolute condition. So if I exist, to perceive myself, God must too, in order to perceive me. But Christ? It is not immediately evident how *his* existence could be deduced along these lines, and to affirm its necessity Browning turns in the first instance to the ethical sphere. God is Power, and human self-consciousness, especially when intensified into 'self-supremacy', mirrors that power. But Power cannot be the only ingredient of deity, since human beings possess another faculty not inherent in the idea of Power, the faculty of Love. And if, as Browning evidently felt, the ideas of Power and Love are in some sense contradictory, then in order to manifest Love, God must split in two, giving birth to Christ as the sundered fragment of his being through which his Love may find expression.

This is a highly unorthodox, if not heterodox, if not frankly heretical position.[25] Chesterton brilliantly argues that it might be said

25. Browning was not alone in his time in finding difficulty in reconciling the first two persons of the Trinity. Christina Rossetti, a more obviously devout Christian than Browning, notes the danger that we may 'feel towards the Divine Son as if he alone was our Friend, the Divine Father being our foe; as if Christ had not only to rescue us from the

to involve God feeling jealous of the human capacity for Love, and seeking to emulate it through his incarnation as Christ.[26] So strange was such a thesis that most contemporaries, Chesterton apart, chose to ignore it and to focus instead on the strictly ethical elements of Browning's religious thought. For my purposes, what is interesting is the extent to which it replicates the philosophical dilemma which I have already outlined. If God, the type of Power, corresponds to the subjective poet, Christ as the type of Love corresponds to the objective and Browning's theology, like his metaphysics and his poetics, proves to be dialectical in structure.

But since God *is* Christ the dialectic reaches synthesis, and that synthesis lies at the heart both of Browning's Christology and of his poetics. God is 'the perfect poet' in the sense that he is in the first instance a *subjective* poet who can achieve what his human equivalent inevitably lacks, absolute self-presence in any conceivable form of being. But in Christ Browning perceives a figure which, as it must be understood both as divine and as human, furnishes an exemplary synthesis of subjective and objective kinds of knowledge in a mode comprehensible to the human. His approach is characteristically oblique : in 'Saul', 'Cleon' and 'An Epistle . . . of Karshish' a speaker gains an intuition of God's relation to humanity by meditating on the meaning of the Christian Incarnation; in 'A Death in the Desert' we 'meet' an actual witness of that Incarnation, the apostle St. John. Such displacements reflect the extent to which Christ is in the process of being *metaphorised* in the individual human mind, which in turn reflects his status *as* a metaphor. That is, Christ may be seen as a trope through which the relation of the divine to the human, the infinite to the finite, is made humanly thinkable. He represents an *idea* with the help of which human beings are enabled to think more coherently about themselves as at once material and spiritual agents.

The best example of this metaphorising process is probably

---

righteous wrath of His Father but to shelter us from His enmity' (*Letter and Spirit*, 1883).

26. 'If man has self-sacrifice and God has none, then man has in the Universe a secret and blasphemous superiority. And this tremendous story of a Divine jealousy Browning reads into the story of the Crucifixion' (Chesterton: 18).

'Karshish'. As an 'Arab Physician' Karshish would be technically a pagan or perhaps a Platonist,[27] and the poem narrates how he encounters Christianity for the first time, some thirty years after the death of Christ. He encounters it, however, not as a theology but in the form of a clinical experience. During the course of a visit to Judaea he is introduced to one Lazarus, a 'madman' who claims that, years earlier, he died and was resurrected by someone whom Karshish calls a 'learned leech [doctor]' (l. 247; he clearly does not know Christ's name). Lazarus further claims that while he was dead he experienced heaven, and Karshish notes that as a result of this supposed foretaste of the afterlife Lazarus has become a misfit in the earthly life to which his resurrection has returned him, no longer able to live by its values or to fit its temporal jurisdiction into his recollection of the eternity to which he was so prematurely introduced.

As a scientist Karshish regards all this as madness, and he discusses the 'mania – subinduced / By epilepsy' (ll. 79–80) which he diagnoses as its clinical cause. But as a human being (and, perhaps, as a Platonist) he cannot help being fascinated by the possibility of its truth, because he perceives that if true it would profoundly alter human intuitions about God. For if the 'learned leech' was, as Lazarus claims, an emanation or materialisation of God himself, the idea of God itself immediately alters:

> The very God! think, Abib; dost thou think?
> So, the All-Great, were the All-Loving too –
> So, through the thunder comes a human voice
> Saying, 'O heart I made, a heart beats here!
> Face, my hands fashioned, see it in myself.
> Thou hast no power nor may'st conceive of mine,
> But love I gave thee, with Myself to love,
> And thou must love me who have died for thee!'
> The madman saith He said so: it is strange.
> (ll. 304–12)

Ethically, God becomes complete in Christ because through Christ he manifests the love which humanity recognises in itself, but not in an

27. Since he has an occult master, probably the latter: most occult traditions were inspired by Plato.

'All-Great' creator. A God of power, for Browning as for Shelley, is a moral monster, as the subjective poet also perhaps is; a God of love would have not only to love, but to manifest love, to represent it, and Christ is that representation, a representation which offers itself to the paraphrase which Karshish then puts into the mouth of God, synchronising God with human time, human thought and human speech. God's supposed utterance stands for his *thinkability* within the temporal domain: discourse about God becomes possible when God is imagined as capable of discourse, that is, of relaying his being in a speech like human speech. Christ is God's 'Word', his utterance, validating the human word and human poetry. Without the Christ-metaphor there can be no meaningful discourse about God: more radically, neither God nor the human could be thought without Christ's mediation. Humanity is made up of divine and material elements. In the figure of Christ, these elements become capable of synthesis, and the synthesis becomes the route through which the idea of God is made thinkable, existence comprehensible and poetry writable.

In one of Browning's most remarkable poems, 'Caliban upon Setebos', the instrumentality of Christ for the creation of thought is anticipated by a speaker who as a 'primitive' is in the process of formulating the grounds of his own being. Caliban does this by splitting off a part of his own nature and naming it 'Setebos', an objectification of his own cruel and vindictive impulses. In a kind of fixed economy of retribution Caliban imagines Setebos as inflicting upon him the deprivations and pain which he in turn inflicts on the creatures around him on Prospero's island. But he is revolted by his own nightmare theology, and expresses his contempt for it by a further self-projection into a figure which he calls 'the Quiet', a calm, contemplative, remote and morally neutral agency. Neither of these projections corresponds directly to Christ. Setebos is a god of hatred, the Quiet a god of indifference. But Caliban's creation of both registers his failure to be satisfied by either, and as both are self-representations so equivalently Christ becomes a more 'advanced' human self-projection in which the compassion lacking in Caliban is objectified. Such representation is what makes thought possible, and Caliban illustrates the inseparability of theology from thought. Thought, self-consciousness and an idea of deity become in this poem mutual sponsors, and grounds of the possibility of language.

When David in Browning's other great Christological poem 'Saul' has completed his prophesy of Christ he finds the reality round him utterly transformed:

> I know not too well how I found my way home in the night.
> There were witnesses, cohorts about me, to left and to right,
> Angels, powers, the unuttered, unseen, the alive – the aware –
> I repressed, I got through them as hardly, as strugglingly there,
> As a runner beset by the populace famished for news –
> Life or death. The whole earth was awakened, hell loosed with
> her crews;
> And the stars of night beat with emotion, and tingled and shot
> Out in fire the strong pain of pent knowledge: but I fainted not.
> For the Hand still impelled me at once and supported –
> suppressed
> All the tumult, and quenched it with quiet, and holy behest,
> Till the rapture was shut in itself, and the earth sank to rest.
> Anon at the dawn, all that trouble had withered from earth –
> Not so much, but I saw it die out in the day's tender birth;
> In the gathered intensity brought to the grey of the hills;
> In the shuddering forests' new awe; in the sudden wind-thrills;
> In the startled wild beasts that bore off, each with eye sidling still
> Tho' averted, in wonder and dread; and the birds stiff and chill
> That rose heavily, as I approached them, made stupid with awe!
> E'en the serpent that slid away silent, – he felt the new Law.
> The same stared in the white humid faces upturned by the
> flowers;
> The same worked in the heart of the cedar, and moved the
> vine-bowers.
> And the little brooks witnessing murmured, persistent and low,
> With their obstinate, all but hushed voices – E'en so! it is so.
> (ll. 313–35)

Here the idea of Christ is made to sponsor a universal organic awareness. David discovers that nature is not an alien system but of a similar being with his own, or rather through the Christ-metaphor he *makes* it so, and discovers, as a result, that his human duality casts a double shadow towards the divine ('Angels, powers, the unuttered, unseen') and the natural ('birds . . . made stupid with awe!'). In this way, the idea of Christ becomes a way of entertaining a theory of being which is at once monistic and dualistic. Coleridge describes

> the instinct, in which humanity itself is grounded: that by which, in every act of conscious perception, we at once identify our being with that of the world without us, and yet place ourselves in contra-distinction to that world. (Rooke: i 497)

This is the ground on which mental existence is erected, and by which poetry itself becomes possible. In theological terms, Christ is the self-objectification through which God beholds himself, and God and Christ are at once identical and antithetical embodiments of celestial being. Similarly, human poets both project their being into the external world, look back at the self which only such self-projection can identify, and finally return to themselves.

It is the paradoxical, intricate and unstable character of this equation that forces Browning to pass it through so many forms and repeat it so frequently, to embody it in both the material of his poetry and in its structures.[28] For the dramatic monologue intrinsically makes Browning at once identify with a token fragment of 'the world without' while by making it over into the alien domain of the poem he withdraws from it, as the reader also must. The epilogues attached to 'Bishop Blougram's Apology' and 'The Statue and the Bust' make this last move explicit and mandatory, and their very clumsiness becomes a sign of the intensity of the involvement developed during the course of the monologue, an involvement of which the fact of monologue itself is the immediate token. Later monologues such as 'Mr. Sludge "the Medium" ' and *Fifine at the Fair* eschew such direct intervention but continue to insist on the necessity of withdrawal, and conversely the precedent necessity of identification, by causing the speaker himself to dissolve the bond of sympathy established

28. The paradoxical elements in Browning's thought, and its poetic implementation, make him peculiarly suitable for deconstructive reading. Such a reading would note the ubiquity of contradiction in my account but then claim that the moment when the paradoxes become unbearable deconstructs the apparent approach to synthesis. I prefer to think in terms of an element of 'Romantic Irony' – the ineffableness and inexpressibility of synthesis – together with a dialectical element – the continuous resolution of synthesis into thesis to which an antithesis as continuously then appears. These elements lie at the heart of Romanticism, and have made it peculiarly susceptible to deconstruction; but deconstruction as a reconstituted Platonism arguably falsifies them by imposing its own negative agenda.

during the course of the poem: Sludge savagely curses Hiram H. Horsefall and looks forward to fleecing the English, Juan goes out looking for a prostitute. Such moral retractions blend into their counterparts, the poet's withdrawal from the object he has exalted and the reader's halt at the text's end.

So Browning's philosophy and theology prove to be inseparable from his poetics: each dovetails into both the others, or rather, all three are interchangeable symbols in the dialectic of his creative thought. No other poet of his period, or perhaps of any period, achieves such a synthesis, even if, or perhaps especially because, it always comes apart exactly when it reaches unification.

# CHAPTER 7
## *Studying Browning*

In this chapter we consider only those aspects of secondary material on Browning that seem unlikely to date. This makes it very basic. We have not attempted, for example, a comprehensive account of criticism of him: this would take up a lot of space and become obsolete almost before it was published. Instead, we provide a brief account of the most significant scholarly work currently available, followed by a short history of Browning's reputation.

### Editions

At the present time, three major editions of Browning's poetry are in progress: the Ohio/Baylor, edited by Roma King *et al.*, the Oxford, edited by Ian Jack *et al.*, and the Longman, edited by John Woolford, Daniel Karlin, and Joseph Phelan. All are in multiple volumes, as serious editions of Browning have to be, but each differs from the other two in certain important particulars. Ohio/Baylor is the most comprehensive, since it aims to include not only published and unpublished poems, plays and acknowledged prose, but the *Life of Strafford*, to which Browning certainly contributed, but in which his share cannot reliably be identified.[1] Oxford confines itself to works which are uncontroversially Browning's, including prose works. Longman includes poetry and prose but omits plays written for the stage.

The textual policies of the three editions also differ. This is most complex in the case of Ohio/Baylor, because of its changes of editorship. It has always been committed to the last authorially-supervised edition, that of 1888–9; but early editors reserved the right to alter the text where they saw fit, and scholarly misgivings over

1. Curiously, there seems to be no intention to present Browning's introduction to the sermons of Thomas Jones (1884), which though slight is not without interest.

some of the resulting decisions led to the adoption of a much stricter policy after volume iv. It is consequently difficult to see how the edition can be self-consistent unless and until earlier volumes are re-edited in conformity with the policy now in place. Like Ohio/Baylor, Oxford takes the 1888–9 text, but treats it with altogether more circumspection; in addition, some poems with an unusually complex publication history are given in parallel texts: *Pauline*, for example, in the texts of 1833 and 1888–9, *Paracelsus* in its manuscript and final state. As a result of this policy, Oxford will probably be the longest of the three editions. Longman takes the first published state of a given poem as its copy-text.

These differing textual policies reflect the ongoing contemporary debate about what may be regarded as the 'best text' of a given work. Oxford and Ohio/Baylor take the traditional position that the last authorially-supervised text represents the author's 'final intentions' and is therefore authoritative; Longman reflects recent questioning of this concept on the grounds that a 'work' is a mobile event whose reshapings in successive editions respond to external and internal change – in the historical situation, the audience for whom it is designed, and in the life of the author. Such a concept leads naturally to a preference for presenting *all* textual states of a work in electronic hypertext, but a volume edition must prioritise one such state, and we regard the first publication as representing the work's most active engagement with its historical moment. A more substantial discussion of this issue may be found in Chapter 1.

All these editions incorporate textual variants, so in principle each gives a textual history of the works it includes. Oxford and Ohio/Baylor include all variant readings, including punctuational changes; Longman includes changes of wording, but omits punctuational changes except where they clearly affect the sense or are of interest for other reasons. As a result of this policy and its exclusion of the stage-plays, Longman will be the shortest of the three editions.

A complication has arisen with Michael Meredith's recent discovery that the 1870 and 1875 reissues of the *Poetical Works* of 1868, previously supposed to be reprints, were in fact revised. As the most recent starter, Longman has been able to incorporate their changes, as Oxford has begun to do; Longman also provides variants from volumes of selections, which were also revised by Browning.

All three editions include annotation. That of Ohio/Baylor is the briefest, and it is placed at the end of each volume. Oxford and

Longman provide headnotes giving composition and publication history, and essential information about the given poem, supplemented by annotations placed beneath or alongside the passages of text to which they refer. Longman is the most comprehensively annotated, as its series' rationale demands, but Oxford annotation is substantial.

This is not the place to offer judgements on these editions, since as editors of one of them we can scarcely claim to be objective. In practice, since all are expensive, students are unlikely to buy them, and library copies may be consulted to settle the question of which is best at what (though their differing textual policies put them in a complementary as well as a competitive relation). The Penguin/Yale edition, edited by John Pettigrew, Thomas Collins and Richard Altick, is more likely to be bought, since it is comprehensive and compact (three volumes). Its text is sound, its annotation useful if necessarily very light. Two reservations must be borne in mind when using it. First, it contains a textual inconsistency, in that volumes I and III use the final text of 1888–9, but volume II, which is devoted to *The Ring and the Book*, uses the first edition text.[2] Secondly, it includes a number of poems which have been proved not to be by Browning, but by EBB. These are: 'Transcriptions from the "Anacreonta"' numbers I–X (number XI is his), 'She was fifteen – had great eyes' and 'Aeschylus' Soliloquy'. It would seem urgent that both these difficulties should be met by a corrected reissue of the Penguin/Yale: until that is done, it remains an extremely useful but imperfect edition.

The alternative, for complete editions, are the various double-column editions available second-hand. Most, though not all, of these are based on the 1888–9 text, and are perfectly reliable, if rather difficult to read because of their cramped format and small type. The 1888–9 edition itself, either in 17-volume or 8-volume bindings, is common in secondhand bookshops, and often very reasonably priced, like the earlier 6-volume edition of 1868 (not of course complete). The 1863 and 1849 editions are very rare. First

2. This reflects its publishing history. The edition of *The Ring and the Book*, edited by Richard Altick, was the first to be published, and at that stage was a freestanding volume. The remaining poetry was then edited by Pettigrew and Collins, and published separately; only subsequently were the three volumes gathered together as a single set.

edition copies of some later poems are also obtainable at reasonable rates, but the best known are difficult to find and pricey.

Victorian selections from Browning's poetry are not difficult to acquire, but only those made by Browning himself are of serious interest in the first instance. In practice, this means the selections of 1872 and 1880 and their reissues. They are not necessarily compilations of what Browning considered his best poems, but as he makes clear in his preface to *1872*, involve thematic groupings: it is a fascinating exercise to try to work out their rationale. Collaterally, Browning's selections from the poetry of EBB, avowedly constructed on the same principle, give interesting insights not only into how he read her poetry, but more generally into the kind of implicit logic he favoured in poetic juxtaposition.

## Letters

A gigantic project to publish all surviving letters of Browning is currently in progress: *The Brownings' Correspondence*, edited originally by Philip Kelley and Ronald Hudson, but after Hudson's death by Kelley and Scott Lewis. The edition has so far reached fourteen volumes and the year 1846: it is projected to comprise forty volumes as a whole.

The reason for this immense bulk is indicated by the series title: it includes the complete correspondence of both Browning and EBB. This decision has aroused some controversy, especially when early volumes, covering the years before they knew each other, contained masses of letters by her and almost none by him. But now that the series has covered the courtship correspondence, the soundness of the editors' decision has decisively emerged. Theirs is not the first edition to print the complete love-letters: indeed, both complete and selected editions of the letters of this period have, for obvious reasons, followed this policy. But this is the first edition in which their letters to other correspondents have been laid alongside their letters to each other, complicating, but also enriching, the picture which emerges. And because our information about Browning for the years of the marriage is quite largely derived from her letters to her huge circle of correspondents, future volumes will provide the most complete possible picture of both.

The texts of the letters and datings of undated ones are as definitive as such things can be, and there is also substantial annotation, which is especially good on biographical matters. Particularly useful additional features are the presentation of supplementary materials such as letters about Browning and EBB by other people, and the inclusion of all known reviews of their work. The indexes could be fuller: it would be useful, for example, to differentiate citations of given persons, books, etc., in Browning's letters, EBB's letters and editorial notes. But overall this is one of the great works of letter-editing, and students of Browning are fortunate to have it.

Until this project is complete, study of Browning's letters must be supplemented by attention to existing, incomplete collections. Kintner's edition of the courtship correspondence is not, we think, altogether superseded by Kelley and Lewis, since it possesses an intensity of focus which their scheme necessarily dissipates. Daniel Karlin's selection is based on the MSS and corrects Kintner's often imperfect text, and provides a convenient, if necessarily synoptic, picture of this celebrated episode. Other volumes of Browning letters are many, so I include here only those which are of particular interest. Browning varied his letter-writing style in proportion to his intimacy with his correspondents, and their mental powers: hence many of his letters, especially in later years, are acts of social politeness rather than revelations of anything very interesting. The most fascinating, and exasperating, is his correspondence with Julia Wedgwood, published in 1937 in an edition by Richard Curle, and it is worth taking a little space to describe this. It falls into two halves. The first, covering the years 1864–5, amounts to a period of courtship on his part and alarmed yet fascinated retreat on hers: there is a tradition in the Wedgwood family that it culminated in a rejected proposal of marriage on his part. The second half of the corres- pondence, between 1867 and 1870, covers the period during which *The Ring and the Book* was completed and published, and is dominated by that poem: Browning sends the volumes as they come out and she sends back comments, on which he then comments in turn, in his most extensive discussion of his own poetry outside the courtship correspondence with EBB. What is exasperating is the probability that the correspondence is not complete, and the fact that because the manuscripts used by Curle have disappeared, there is no way of correcting his palpably defective text.

Two other collections of letters to female correspondents are of interest: those to Isa Blagden and to Sarah FitzGerald. Blagden was a close friend of both Brownings in Florence, and after EBB's death she and Browning tried to keep up an undertaking to write to each other once a month. Browning, a reluctant correspondent, clearly found this difficult, and his letters are heavily padded with gossip (he loved gossip); but they do contain some important discussions of poetry, his own and that of others.[3] The correspondence with FitzGerald covers the last part on his life, from 1876 to 1889, and gives it useful insights into the pattern of Browning's reading of books and journals, with the occasional comment on his own poetry. The most important collection of letters to a male correspondent also belongs to later years. Frederick Furnivall founded the Browning Society amongst his multifarious other activities such as working on the Oxford English Dictionary, and came to be on friendly though never fully intimate terms with Browning. He frequently wrote seeking information about Browning's poetry, which Browning, rather reluctantly, generally gave: his comments are snippets rather than extended discussions, but they are of interest. William Peterson's *Browning's Trumpeter*, which contains these letters, is a model of scholarly editing.

Other useful collections include G. Hudson, *Browning to his American Friends*, his correspondence with the circle of Americans with whom he and EBB became acquainted in Florence in the 1850s; P. Landis, *Letters of the Brownings to George Barrett*, his and EBB's correspondence with the only one of her brothers who became Browning's friend; and M. Meredith, *More Than Friend*, his late correspondence with one of the most important friends of his later years, Katherine Bronson. David DeLaura has collected a substantial and very interesting series of letters between the Brownings and John Ruskin, and Thomas Collins gives his correspondence with Tennyson (see Bibliography).

The best general collections of Browning's letters remain T.L. Hood, *The Letters of Robert Browning* and W.C. DeVane and K.L. Knickerbocker, *New Letters of Robert Browning*. Both have very useful annotation, which cannot be said of, in particular, Curle.

3. The volume containing these letters (McAleer 1951), has long been out of print: there would be a case for incorporating EBB's letters to Blagden in an expanded reissue.

## Diaries and memoirs

It is always interesting to see what a writer's contemporaries thought of him, and there are plenty of memoirs and diaries in which opinions of Browning, anecdotes about him, and records of his conversation are preserved. Two diaries head the list. These are by Alfred Domett and William Allingham, the first a friend of Browning's earlier years who renewed his friendship with him on returning to England in 1872 (see Chapter 3), the second an Irish poet on close terms with many of the best-known figures of his time and thus able to provide a comparative estimate of Browning's personality. Of the memoirs, the most interesting is Edmund Gosse's *Robert Browning: Personalia*, which relates to the period of Browning's friendship with Gosse in the 1880s. Anne Ritchie's *Records of Tennyson, Ruskin and Browning* is a well-written and engaging memoir (*Red Cotton Night-Cap Country* is dedicated and addressed to her).

## Reference books

William Clyde DeVane's *A Browning Handbook* remains the most important single reference-book on Browning's works. It arranges the poems in order of collection publication (not necessarily the most helpful scheme) and offers varying amounts of biographical and source materials. It is not always reliable – especially in its comments on textual matters – but its scholarship is of a breadth that has never been surpassed. Three Victorian handbooks may be mentioned here, as not having been altogether superseded by DeVane. First there is Alexandra Orr's *A Handbook to the Works of Robert Browning*, the successive editions of which were expanded to include his last works as they came out, and revised in the light of his comments. The *Handbook* is less interesting than might have been expected, partly because of Orr's curious classification of the poems, but it remains of use. Secondly there is Edward Berdoe's *The Browning Cyclopaedia*. Berdoe like Orr and Furnivall was a member of the Browning Society, and his *Cyclopaedia* is a work of devoted, but often unreliable, scholarship. It is arranged on a simple alphabetic system and affords some useful information and, in its comments on or summaries of poems, interesting insight into how Browning was read at this period. The third of these Victorian handbooks, G.W. Cooke's *A Guide-Book to the Poetic and Dramatic Works of Robert Browning*, is in many ways the best, but it is also the hardest to find, at least in England. Again organised alphabetically, this is a work of admirable scholarship, not all of which is superseded by DeVane, and it is certainly more comprehensive than Orr and more reliable than Berdoe.

Modern reference-books are headed by Philip Kelley and Betty Coley's monumental *The Browning Collections: a Reconstruction*. The starting-point for this compilation was the 1913 Sotheby sale of Browning's son's effects; but Kelley and Coley have gone to enormous lengths to supplement the rather rudimentary information given by the sale catalogue with material from other sources. The result is the most comprehensive and valuable research aid yet produced. Of greatest interest to the Browning scholar will perhaps be section E, 'Manuscripts of Robert Browning', which gives a brief description and current location for every known manuscript at the date of publication, but the most remarkable scholarship has gone into section A, 'The Brownings' Library', which lists all known volumes owned by either Browning or EBB, including a large number discovered by Kelley himself in Brighton Library. Inscriptions are usually noted and sometimes transcribed, and with the help of these it is often possible to determine whether a given book originally belonged to Browning or to EBB or to both: a project to transcribe his inscriptions as part of a larger portrait of his mind and methods could easily be built on Kelley and Coley's work, and should be. A minor criticism is that the grounds for ascribing a book to the Brownings' library when that book was not individually listed in the Sotheby catalogue are not usually given; it would also have been interesting to learn the price at which the Sotheby books and manuscripts were sold (for this information, see Woolford 1972).

Other sections of Kelley and Coley include likenesses of both poets (F, G), 'Works of Art, Household and Personal Effects' (H), and interestingly, works both of Browning's father and his son Pen (J, K). These are likely to be of more interest to the specialist than to the student.

The concordance to Browning's poetry compiled by Broughton and Stelter in 1924–5 was subsequently republished in 1970, and may be found in libraries: it is textually reliable, but limited by the edition upon which it is based, which incorporates among unpublished items only those presented in Kenyon 1914. The Chadwyck-Healey database of English poetry, currently available on CD-ROM, provides the possibility of a concordance for Browning as for the other poets it includes, together with many other facilities for textual search and analysis.

## Bibliographies

There is currently no single comprehensive bibliography of Browning, but the situation is not too desperate, since there exists a series of partial bibliographies which add together into a reasonably complete picture. The first bibliography of substance was compiled by Broughton, Northup and Pearsall and published in 1949; the revised 1953 edition was republished in 1970. It contains many errors and omissions but remains valuable for the years it covers. William Peterson's continuation of Broughton *et al.* differs in that it includes EBB, but it helpfully reproduces its predecessor's classification, as does the continuation in turn of Peterson which is to be found in the annual volumes of *Browning Institute Studies* (1970–90) and subsequently in *Victorian Literature and Culture* (compiled by Sandra Donaldson). It is to be hoped that these bibliographies can be blended, perhaps in the form of an updatable electronic text.

These bibliographies all aim to be comprehensive, and, although they provide some commentary, they do not evaluate the materials they list. More evaluative discussions may be found in the annual volumes of *The Year's Work in English Studies*, and an annual number of *Victorian Poetry* includes a survey of Browning criticism for each year (recently the work of John Maynard, and authoritative). Philip Drew also provides a useful survey.

## Biographies

There are plenty of biographies of Browning but no perfect one. This is partly due to the extreme and extremely different views of him, which range from Chesterton's bluff optimist to Miller's migraine-dogged neurotic. The most balanced, and in some ways the best biography, Alexandra Orr's, was also the first. Her access to his letters was limited, and she passed over some of the more problematic aspects of his life, such as his alleged proposal to Lady Ashburton, in silence; but her close friendship with him did not lead her to produce a hagiography, but rather a shrewd and well-informed appraisal. Chesterton's biography, as a biography, is negligible, though it should be read for its brilliant and still-pertinent critical insights. Griffin and Minchin's *Life* is the next significant extension of knowledge, though it is rather dull in itself; Betty Miller's *Portrait* is the reverse of dull, and remains essential reading. It contains a good deal of real scholarship, and sets out to depict Browning as a closet neurotic, his marriage as a failure, and his later life as an exercise in social climbing. Making this case involves much strained argumentation, and some actual abuse of materials, but there is enough in it to mean that subsequent biographers cannot ignore it.

The best and most original biography since Miller, perhaps the best biography of Browning yet produced, is John Maynard's *Browning's Youth.* This puts meticulous research into fluent and readable narration, with much fascinating detail about the family, interests, education, friends and girl-friends of Browning's early years: its only drawback is that it stops in the early 1840s. Daniel Karlin's *The Courtship of Robert Browning and Elizabeth Barrett* is as much a critical study as a biography, but it contains much useful biographical detail, and its cross-readings between poems, letters and life are innovatory and illuminating. Of others, both Maisie Ward's and Irvine and Honan's contain useful further information, especially on the later years, but neither adds much to the picture of Browning himself, though attention should be drawn to Ward's *The Tragi-Comedy of Pen Browning*, a fascinating study of the Brownings' son. Apart from Clyde Ryals', which however is critical rather than scholarly, the many other biographies are in the main of negligible interest and importance.

## Journals

The Brownings are fortunate in having had no less than four scholarly journals devoted to them. The first of these was *Browning Society Notes*, a revival of *The Browning Society's Papers*, published by the Browning Society from 1881 to 1891. Much very interesting work has appeared in it: its current editor is Michael Meredith. The second of the four is Baylor University's *Studies in Browning and his Circle*, which is more variable, but with some good contributions: its current editor is Roger Brooks. The Browning Institute's *Browning Institute Studies* takes the form of an annual volume, and is probably the most significant of the established journals: it has recently changed its title to *Victorian Literature and Culture*, under the joint editorship of John Maynard and Adrienne Munich, with the expanded focus such a title indicates. Articles on the Brownings also appear regularly in journals such as *Victorian Poetry* and *Victorian Studies*.

## Criticism

The history of Browning criticism is a roller-coaster ride. Few major poets have been so controversial not only in their lifetime but after their death. The sequence in both instances has been peak-trough-peak, and I begin with the first peak, which came with the publication of *Paracelsus* in 1835. This was a decided success, though the poem was never a best-seller. The more radical journals welcomed it, and even the Tory press was gracious. In part, this reception owed something to Browning's powerful friends Leigh Hunt (in whose *London Journal* a very favourable review appeared), John Forster (who reviewed it twice) and William Fox, but approval extended well beyond this circle, and was maintained in most later references to the poem in journals and books.

But such references took on a decidedly double edge, for until the publication of *The Ring and the Book, Paracelsus* was frequently cited not only as Browning's greatest poem, but also as his only intelligible one. After a mixed though not damning reception of his first play *Strafford* in 1837 came the publication of *Sordello* in 1840, and with it an eclipse of Browning's reputation that for a long time threatened to be permanent. The poem was declared unreadable, unintelligible and ludicrous in its style and narrative structure. It plunged Browning, not into obscurity, but notoriety; and while the obloquy was lightened by the odd favourable review of some numbers of *Bells and Pomegranates* and *Christmas Eve and Easter Day*, and by the admiration of the Pre-Raphaelite Brotherhood, especially Dante Gabriel Rossetti, the mainly hostile reception of *Men and Women* in 1855 confirmed that the entire period from 1840 to 1864 must be regarded as the first trough in Browning's reputation.

John Woolford has discussed elsewhere the reasons for the better receptions of *Dramatis Personae* (1864) and *The Ring and the Book* (1868–9).[4] The latter in particular marked the second peak of Browning's career, and established his position as Tennyson's rival for the title 'greatest living poet'. Or rather, it established him as 'next

4. See Woolford 1982, pp. 109–145; and Woolford, 1988, pp. 173 ff.

poet' after Tennyson, because in the years that followed he never repeated the success of *The Ring and the Book*, and was frequently taken to task for supposedly reverting to the perverse obscurities of *Sordello*.[5] He himself became increasingly angry about his still-equivocal critical reputation, and began attacking his reviewers in print. During this period, however, the reading of him by which his reputation was to be kept high was steadily evolving. This reading involved conceding that his writing was often hasty, obscure and rough, but claiming that he was a great teacher, and should be read and valued as that. Browning himself shows unease about this supposition in *La Saisiaz*, and in *The Inn Album* he imputes it to the villainous Elder Man, who remarks of an entry in the album: 'That bard's a Browning; he neglects the form: / But oh, the sense, ye gods, the weighty sense!' (ll. 17–18). But whatever reservations he may have had, his reputation endowed him with the éclat of a prophet and religious leader: John Woolford remembers coming across his grandfather's copy of the 1880 *Selections*, and wondering how many other works of poetry would have been allowed into the small library of a working-class Primitive Methodist household. Most of the books about him which began to appear from the 1860s onwards treat his poetry as a kind of Bible requiring exegesis, and this attitude (in both England and America) largely persisted until at least the First World War, and can still be found.

What then happened – the second great trough of Browning's reputation – has to be understood in part as a reaction against the hyperboles of the previous generation, but there is more to it than that. Browning became, for the Cambridge School critics in England and a little later the American New Critics, a pawn in a larger game: specifically, the discrediting of nineteenth-century poetry as a whole as flawed and inadequate.

In very general terms, the great critical movements of the 1920s and 1930s were formalistic in their tendencies. They rejected the biographical emphasis of Victorian criticism in favour of the quasi-scientific analysis of the work as a linguistic event. This led indirectly to a preference for poetry of great surface complexity, and

5. *Balaustion's Adventure* (1871) and *Dramatic Idyls* (1879) were well received, but other poems of the 1870s, such as *Fifine at the Fair* (1872) and *Red Cotton Night-Cap Country* (1873) evoked a decidedly more mixed response.

the rehabilitation of the long-ridiculed 'Metaphysical' poets. It also led to, or resulted from, a comprehensive rejection of Romantic and post-Romantic poetry as being too subjective to produce the properly-objective, richly-complex work which results when, as Eliot said of Donne, the poet 'feel[s his] thought as immediately as the odour of a rose' (Eliot: 287).

Browning's position in relation to this change of critical paradigm is a complex one – so complex, in fact, that it became necessary to pretend that it was absolutely simple. His *reputation* opened him to all the standard charges. His admirers had claimed that it was the ideas in his work rather than its form that mattered; that is, they posited his subjectivity as an indispensable supplement or key to his writing, opening the latter to objection that it was not internally complete. And that subjectivity in turn was attacked by, most influentially, F.R. Leavis, as naïve and crass. On the basis of perhaps having seen *The Barretts of Wimpole Street* and heard Browning described as an optimist – it is difficult to believe he had read much of the poetry – Leavis accused him of lacking 'an adult sensitive mind' and concerning himself only with 'simple emotions and sentiments' (Leavis: 20), and the assumption that his creative personality was inadequate in ways which then reappeared in and diminished the poetry has remained widespread.[6]

The notion of Browning as a breezy simpleton seems almost perverse when one considers how complex much of his writing is, and how much he admired and was influenced by the great icon of both the Cambridge School and New Criticism, John Donne. Indeed, Leavis was conscious that Browning didn't fit the Procrustean bed set up for him, and rather uneasily dismissed what he described as his 'exercise of certain grosser cerebral muscles'. This comment concedes that Browning, like Donne, could and did think in verse, but argues or implies that his impoverished subjectivity fatally impaired both the thought itself and its embodiment in the poetry.

When Robert Langbaum undertook to rescue Browning from the obloquy with which he had been mainly treated between 1920 and 1950, it was by incorporating him into the ambit of New Criticism

6. An exception must be made here for Ezra Pound, a lifelong admirer of Browning, who tirelessly recommended him to his friends (including Eliot) and was, especially during his early career, profoundly influenced by him. On this, see Woolford 1992.

rather than questioning the bases of New Criticism itself. Langbaum argued that Browning's 'philosophy', the complexities of thought which his poetry delivers, is itself part of the poetry not of the poet, and may therefore be counted into the work's array of forms rather than assigned to the writer as a person beyond it. This argument motivates Langbaum's focus on the dramatic monologues. In them, we encounter thought, but it is the thought of a dramatised character rather than of Browning, and Langbaum claims that the resulting gap between the speaker and the poet is the site for a constitutional ambiguity which makes such poems as complex and ambiguous as Donne's or Marvell's: the complexity resides not in the thought itself, though that may be separately complex, but in the tension between 'sympathy' and 'judgment' which the form establishes. The emphasis on the *reader* which this account puts forward represents a move away from formalism, anticipating later developments while retaining the best elements of New Criticism.

This brilliant book may be the most important event in Browning criticism so far. It rehabilitated Browning not simply for New Criticism, but for the schools which have followed New Criticism, principally Bloomian influence-theory in the 1970s and 1980s, post-structuralism in the 1980s, and New Historicism in the 1990s. For while each of these schools has tended to quarrel with the others, and all attack New Criticism, none has questioned the importance which Langbaum established for Browning. This may be a way of saying that much New Criticial methodology seeps into the work of these schools; but it would be as reasonable to argue that Browning has proved highly adaptable: Park Honan's *Browning's Characters*, Bloom's constantly-renewed attentions to 'Childe Roland to the Dark Tower Came' and 'Thamuris marching', Herbert Tucker's excellent *Browning's Beginnings*, Loy Martin's Marxist study *Browning's Dramatic Monologues and the Post-Romantic Subject*, David Shaw and Warwick Slinn's more phenomenological and Hegelian discussions, represent widely different perspectives which their subject seems effortlessly to accommodate. He could also stand up to a good feminist and/or New Historical discussion.[7] It looks as though the peak-trough-peak sequence may have reached a plateau, as the infinite reinterpretability

7. The most interesting study to appear so far is Viscusi 1984. The one book-length feminist study (Brady 1988) is weakened by an inattention to historical context resulting from Brady's universalisation of feminism itself.

of Browning's work provides materials which future changes of critical approach are unlikely to exhaust.

# APPENDIX A
## *Extract from Browning's* Essay on Shelley

See Chronology, 1852. This extract starts from the second paragraph of the essay. It contains Browning's major critical statement of the distinction between the 'objective' and the 'subjective' poet, and concludes with his assertion of Shelley's pre-eminence. The remainder of the essay has a more biographical focus. The complete essay is available in Pettigrew and Collins (i 1001–13) and the Ohio/Baylor edition (v 137–51), and is forthcoming in the Oxford and Longman editions. The text is that of the first printing.

Doubtless we accept gladly the biography of an objective poet, as the phrase now goes; one whose endeavour has been to reproduce things external (whether the phenomena of the scenic universe, or the manifested action of the human heart and brain) with an immediate reference, in every case, to the common eye and apprehension of his fellow men, assumed capable of receiving and profiting by this reproduction. It has been obtained through the poet's double faculty of seeing external objects more clearly, widely, and deeply, than is possible to the average mind, at the same time that he is so acquainted and in sympathy with its narrower comprehension as to be careful to supply it with no other materials than it can combine into an intelligible whole. The auditory of such a poet will include, not only the intelligences which, save for such assistance, would have missed the deeper meaning and enjoyment of the original objects, but also the spirits of a like endowment with his own, who, by means of his abstract, can forthwith pass to the reality it was made from, and either corroborate their impressions of things known already, or supply themselves with new from whatever shows in the inexhaustible variety of existence may have hitherto escaped their knowledge. Such a poet is properly the ποιητηζ, the fashioner; and the thing fashioned, his poetry, will of necessity be substantive, projected from himself and distinct. We are ignorant what the inventor of 'Othello' conceived of that fact as he beheld it in completeness, how he accounted for it, under what known law he registered its nature, or to what unknown law he traced its coincidence. We learn only what he intended we should learn by that particular exercise of his power, – the fact itself, – which, with its infinite significances, each of us receives for the first time as a creation, and is hereafter left to deal with, as, in proportion to his own intelligence, he best may. We are ignorant, and would fain be otherwise.

Doubtless, with respect to such a poet, we covet his biography. We desire to look back upon the process of gathering together in a lifetime, the materials of the work we behold entire; of elaborating, perhaps under difficulty and with hindrance, all that is familiar to our admiration in the apparent facility of success. And the inner impulse of this effort and operation, what induced it? Did a soul's delight in its own extended sphere of vision set it, for the gratification of an insuppressible power, on labour, as other men are set on rest? Or did a sense of duty or of love lead it to communicate its own sensations to mankind? Did an irresistible sympathy with men compel it to bring down and suit its own provision of knowledge and beauty to their narrow scope? Did the personality of such an one stand like an open watch-tower in the midst of the territory it is erected to gaze on, and were the storms and calms, the stars and meteors, its watchman was wont to report of, the habitual variegation of his every-day life, as they glanced across its open roof or lay reflected on its four-square parapet? Or did some sunken and darkened chamber of imagery witness, in the artificial illumination of every storied compartment we are permitted to contemplate, how rare and precious were the outlooks through here and there an embrasure upon a world beyond, and how blankly would have pressed on the artificer the boundary of his daily life, except for the amorous diligence with which he had rendered permanent by art whatever came to diversify the gloom? Still, fraught with instruction and interest as such details undoubtedly are, we can, if needs be, dispense with them. The man passes, the work remains. The work speaks for itself, as we say: and the biography of the worker is no more necessary to an understanding or enjoyment of it, than is a model or anatomy of some tropical tree, to the right tasting of the fruit we are familiar with on the market-stall, – or a geologist's map and stratification, to the prompt recognition of the hill-top, our land-mark of every day.

We turn with stronger needs to the genius of an opposite tendency – the subjective poet of modern classification. He, gifted like the objective poet with the fuller perception of nature and man, is impelled to embody the thing he perceives, not so much with reference to the many below as to the one above him, the supreme Intelligence which apprehends all things in their absolute truth, – an ultimate view ever aspired to, if but partially attained, by the poet's own soul. Not what man sees, but what God sees – the *Ideas* of Plato, seeds of creation lying burningly on the Divine Hand – it is toward these that he struggles. Not with the combination of humanity in action, but with the primal elements of humanity he has to do; and he digs where he stands, – preferring to seek them in his own soul as the nearest reflex of that absolute Mind, according to the intuitions of which he desires to perceive and speak. Such a poet does not deal habitually with the picturesque groupings and tempestuous tossings of the forest-trees, but with their roots and fibres naked to the chalk and stone. He does not paint pictures and hang them on the walls, but rather carries them on the retina of his own eyes: we must look deep into his human eyes, to see those pictures on them. He is rather a seer, accordingly, than a fashioner, and what he produces will be less a work than an effluence. That effluence cannot be easily considered in abstraction from his personality, – being indeed the very radiance and aroma of his personality, projected from it but not separated. Therefore, in our approach to the poetry, we necessarily approach the personality of the poet; in apprehending it we apprehend him, and certainly we cannot love it without loving him. Both for love's and for understanding's sake we desire to know him, and as readers of his poetry must be readers of his biography also.

I shall observe, in passing, that it seems not so much from any essential distinction in the faculty of the two poets or in the nature of the objects contemplated by either, as in the more immediate adaptability of these objects to the distinct purpose of each, that the objective poet, in his appeal to the aggregate human mind, chooses to deal with the doings of men, (the result of which dealing, in its pure form, when even description, as suggesting a describer, is dispensed with, is what we call dramatic poetry), while the subjective poet, whose study has been himself, appealing through himself to the absolute Divine mind, prefers to dwell upon those external scenic appearances which strike out most abundantly and uninterruptedly his inner light and power, selects that silence of the earth and sea in which he can best hear the beating of his individual heart, and leaves the noisy, complex, yet imperfect exhibitions of nature in the manifold experience of man around him, which serve only to distract and suppress the working of his brain. These opposite tendencies of genius will be more readily descried in their artistic effect than in their moral spring and cause. Pushed to an extreme and manifested as a deformity, they will be seen plainest of all in the fault of either artist, when subsidiarily to the human interest of his work his occasional illustrations from scenic nature are introduced as in the earlier works of the originative painters – men and women filling the foreground with consummate mastery, while mountain, grove and rivulet show like an anticipatory revenge on that succeeding race of landscape-painters whose 'figures' disturb the perfection of their earth and sky. It would be idle to inquire, of these two kinds of poetic faculty in operation, which is the higher or even rarer endowment. If the subjective might seem to be the ultimate requirement of every age, the objective, in the strictest state, must still retain its original value. For it is with this world, as starting point and basis alike, that we shall always have to concern ourselves: the world is not to be learned and thrown aside, but reverted to and relearned. The spiritual comprehension may be infinitely subtilised, but the raw material it operates upon, must remain. There may be no end of the poets who communicate to us what they see in an object with reference to their own individuality; what it was before they saw it, in reference to the aggregate human mind, will be as desirable to know as ever. Nor is there any reason why these two modes of poetic faculty may not issue hereafter from the same poet in successive perfect works examples of which, according to what are now considered the exigences of art, we have hitherto possessed in distinct individuals only. A mere running-in of the one faculty upon the other, is, of course, the ordinary circumstance. Far more rarely it happens that either is found so decidedly prominent and superior, as to be pronounced comparatively pure: while of the perfect shield, with the gold and the silver side set up for all comers to challenge, there has yet been no instance. Either faculty in its eminent state is doubtless conceded by Providence as a best gift to men, according to their especial want. There is a time when the general eye has, so to speak, absorbed its fill of the phenomena around it, whether spiritual or material, and desires rather to learn the exacter significance of what it possesses, than to receive any augmentation of what is possessed. Then is the opportunity for the poet of loftier vision, to lift his fellows, with their half-apprehensions, up to his own sphere, by intensifying the import of details and rounding the universal meaning. The influence of such an achievement will not soon die out. A tribe of successors (Homerides) working more or less in the same spirit, dwell on his discoveries and reinforce his doctrine; till, at unawares, the world is found to be subsisting wholly on the shadow of a reality, on sentiments diluted from passions, on the tradition of a fact, the convention of a moral, the straw of last year's harvest. Then is the imperative call for the appearance of another sort of poet, who shall at once replace this intellectual rumination of food swallowed long ago, by a supply of the fresh and living swathe; getting at new substance by breaking up the assumed wholes into parts of independent and unclassed value, careless of the unknown laws for recombining them (it will be the business of yet another poet to suggest those hereafter), prodigal of objects for men's outer and not inner sight, shaping for their uses a new and different creation from the last, which it displaces by the right of life over death, – to endure until, in the inevitable process, its very sufficiency to itself shall require, at length, an exposition of its affinity to something higher, – when the positive yet conflicting facts shall again precipitate themselves under a harmonising law, and one more degree will be apparent for a poet to climb in that mighty ladder, of which, however cloud-involved and undefined may glimmer the topmost step, the world dares no longer doubt that its gradations ascend.

Such being the two kinds of artists, it is naturally, as I have shown, with the biography of the subjective poet that we have the deeper concern. Apart from his recorded life altogether, we might fail to determine with satisfactory precision to what class his productions belong, and what amount of praise is assignable to the producer. Certainly, in the face of any conspicuous achievement of genius, philosophy, no less than sympathetic instinct, warrants our belief in a great moral purpose having mainly inspired even where it does not visibly look out of the same. Greatness in a work suggests an adequate instrumentality; and none of the lower incitements, however they may avail to initiate or even effect many considerable displays of power, simulating the nobler inspiration to which they are mistakenly referred, have been found able, under the ordinary conditions of humanity, to task themselves to the end of so exacting a performance as a poet's complete work. As soon will the galvanism that provokes to violent action the muscles of a corpse, induce it to cross the chamber steadily: sooner. The love of displaying power for the display's sake, the love of riches, of distinction, of notoriety, – the desire of a triumph over rivals, and the vanity in the applause of friends, – each and all of such whetted appetites grow intenser by exercise and increasingly sagacious as to the best and readiest means of self-appeasement, – while for any of their ends, whether the money or the pointed finger of the crowd, or the flattery and hate to heart's content, there are cheaper prices to pay, they will all find soon enough, than the bestowment of a life upon a labour, hard, slow, and not sure. Also, assuming the proper moral aim to have produced a work, there are many and various states of an aim: it may be more intense than clear-sighted, or too easily satisfied with a lower field of activity than a steadier aspiration would reach. All the bad poetry in the world (accounted poetry, that is, by its affinities) will be found to result from some one of the infinite degrees of discrepancy between the attributes of the poet's soul, occasioning a want of correspondency between his work and the verities of nature, – issuing in poetry, false under whatever form, which shows a thing not as it is to mankind generally, nor as it is to the particular describer, but as it is supposed to be for some unreal neutral mood, midway between both and of value to neither, and living its brief minute simply through the indolence of whoever accepts it or his incapacity to denounce a cheat. Although of such depths of failure there can be no question here we must in every case betake ourselves to the review of a poet's life ere we determine some of the nicer questions concerning his poetry, – more especially if the performance we seek to estimate aright, has been obstructed and cut short of completion by circumstances, – a disastrous youth or a premature death. We may learn from the biography whether his spirit invariably saw and spoke from the last height to which it had attained. An absolute vision is not for this world, but we are permitted a continual approximation to it, every degree of which in the individual, provided it exceed the attainment of the masses, must procure him a clear advantage. Did the poet ever attain to a higher platform than where he rested and exhibited a result? Did he know more than he spoke of?

I concede however, in respect to the subject of our study as well as some few other illustrious examples, that the unmistakeable quality of the verse would be evidence enough, under usual circumstances, not only of the kind and degree of the intellectual but of the moral constitution of Shelley: the whole personality of the poet shining forward from the poems, without much need of going further to seek it. The 'Remains' – produced within a period of ten years, and at a season of life when other men of at all comparable genius have hardly done more than prepare the eye for future sight and the tongue for speech – present us with the complete enginery of a poet, as signal in the excellence of its several adaptitudes as transcendent in the combination of effects, – examples, in fact, of the whole poet's function of beholding with an understanding keenness the universe, nature and man, in their actual state of perfection in imperfection, – of the whole poet's virtue of being untempted by the manifold partial developments of beauty and good on every side, into leaving them the ultimates he found them, – induced by the facility of the gratification of his own sense of those qualities, or by the pleasure of acquiescence in the short-comings of his predecessors in art, and the pain of disturbing their conventionalisms, – the whole poet's virtue, I repeat, of looking higher than any manifestation yet made of both beauty and good, in order to suggest from the utmost actual realisation of the one a corresponding capability in the other, and out of the calm, purity and energy of nature, to reconstitute and store up for the forthcoming stage of man's being, a gift in repayment of that former gift, in which man's own thought and passion had been lavished by the poet on the else-incompleted magnificence of the sunrise, the else-uninterpreted mystery of the lake, – so drawing out, lifting up, and assimilating this ideal of a future man, thus descried as possible, to the present reality of the poet's soul already arrived at the higher state of development, and still aspirant to elevate and extend itself in conformity with its still-improving perceptions of, no longer the eventual Human, but the actual Divine. In conjunction with which noble and rare powers, came the subordinate power of delivering these attained results to the world in an embodiment of verse more closely answering to and indicative of the process of the informing spirit, (failing as it occasionally does, in art, only to succeed in highest art), – with a diction more adequate to the task in its natural and acquired richness, its material colour and spiritual transparency, – the whole being moved by and suffused with a music at once of the soul and the sense, expressive both of an external might of sincere passion and an internal fitness and consonancy, – than can be attributed to any other writer whose record is among us. Such was the spheric poetical faculty of Shelley, as its own self-sufficing central light, radiating equally through immaturity and accomplishment, through many fragments and occasional completion, reveals it to a competent judgement.

# APPENDIX B

## *Ruskin's letter to Browning about* Men and Women, *and Browning's reply*

The text of Ruskin's letter is from DeLaura; the text of Browning's reply is from Collingwood: i 199–202. Since much of the debate concerns a detailed reading of 'Popularity', this poem is reprinted following the two letters.

Denmark Hill
2nd December 1855

Dear Mr Browning

I know you have been wondering that I did not write, but I could not till now – and hardly can, now: not because I am busy – nor careless, but because I cannot at all make up my mind about these poems of yours: and so far as my mind *is* made up, I am not sure whether it is in the least right. Of their power there can of course be no question – nor do you need to be told of it; for everyone who *has* power of this kind, knows it – *must* know it. But as to the Presentation of the Power, I am in great doubt. Being hard worked at present, & not being able to give the cream of the day to poetry – when I take up these poems in the evening I find them absolutely and literally a set of the most amazing Conundrums that ever were proposed to me. I try at them, for – say twenty minutes – in which time I make out about twenty lines, always having to miss two, for every one that I make out. I enjoy the twenty, each separately very much, but the puzzlement about the intermediate ones increases in comfortlessness till I get a headache, & give in.

Now that you may exactly understand the way I feel about them – I will read, with you, one poem – as I read it to myself, with all my comments and questions. I open at Random – Cleon? – no – that's not a fair example being harder than most. The twins? – no – I have made out that – (except the fifth stanza) – so it is not a fair example on the other side being easier than most. Popularity? – yes, that touches the matter in hand.

Stand still, true poet that you are
I know you; – let me try and draw you:

(Does this mean: literally – stand still? or where was the poet figuratively going – and why couldn't he be drawn as he went?) Some night you'll fail us? (Why some *night*? – rather than some day? – 'Fail us.' Now? Die?) When afar you Rise – (Where? – Now?) remember &c. (very good – I understand. My star, God's glowworm. (Very fine. I understand and like that.) Why ^ extend that loving hand.

(Grammatically, this applies to the Poet, the ellipsis of 'Should He' at ^ throws one quite out – like a step in a floor which one doesn't expect.

Yet locks you safe. How does God's hand lock him; do you mean – keeps him from being seen? – and how does it make him safe. Why is a poet safer or more locked up than anybody else? I go on – in hope. 'His clenched hand – – beauty' – very good – but I don't understand why the hand should have held close so long – which is just the point I wanted to be explained. Why the poet *had to be* locked up.

'My poet holds the future fast.' How? Do you mean he anticipates it in his mind – trusts in it – I *don't* know if you mean that, because I don't know if poets *do* that. If you mean that – I wish you had said so plainly.

That day the earths feastmaster's brow. Who is the earths F.? An Angel? – a [*sic*] Everybody?

The chalice *raising*. This, grammatically, agrees with '*brow*', and makes me uncomfortable. Others, &c. very pretty I like that. 'Meantime I'll draw you.' Do you mean – his Cork? – we have not had anything about painting for ever so long – very well. *Do* draw him then: I should like to have him drawn very much.

I'll say – 'a fisher – &c.'.

Now, where *are* you going to – this is, I believe pure malice against *me*, for having said that painters should always grind their own colours.

Who has not heard – – merchant sells. Do you mean – the silk that the merchant sells Raw – or what do you want with the merchant at all.

'And each bystander.' Who are these bystanders – I didn't hear of any before – Are they people who have gone to see the fishing?

'Could criticise, & quote tradition.'

Criticise what? the fishing? – and why should they – what was wrong in it? – Quote tradition. Do you mean about purple? But if they made purple at the time, it wasn't tradition merely – but experience. – You might as well tell me you heard the colourmen in Long-Acre, quote tradition touching their next cargo of Indigo or cochineal.

'Depths – sublimed.' I don't know what you mean by 'sublimed'. Made sublime? – if so – it is not English. To sublime means to evaporate dryly, I believe and has participle 'Sublimated'.

'Worth scepter, crown and ball' – Indeed. Was there ever such a fool of a King? – You ought to have put a note saying who.

'Yet there's', &c. Well. I understand that, & it's very pretty.

Enough to furnish Solomon, &c.

I don't think Solomons spouse swore – at least not about blue-bells. I understand this bit, but fear most people won't. How many have noticed a blue-bells stamen?

'Bee to her groom' I don't understand. I thought there was only one Queen-bee and *she* never was out o'nights – nor came home drunk or disorderly. Besides if she does, unless you had told me what o'clock in the morning she comes home at, the simile is of no use to me.

'Mere conchs – [art?].' Well, but what has this to do with the Poet. Who 'Pounds' *him*? – I don't understand –

World stand[s] aloof – yes – from the purple manufactory, but from Pounding of Poets? – does it? – and if so – who distils – or fines, & bottles them.

'Flasked & fine.' Now *is* that what you call painting a poet. Under the whole & sole image of a bottle of Blue, with a bladder over the cork? The Arabian fisherman with his genie was nothing to this.

Hobbs, Nobbs, &c. paint the future. Why the future. Do you mean *in* the future.

Blue into their line? I don't understand; – do you mean Quote the Poet, or write articles upon him – or in his style? And if so – was this what God kept him *safe* for? to feed Nobbs with Turtle. Is this what you call Accepting the future ages duty. – I don't understand.

'What porridge'? Porridge is a Scotch dish, I believe; typical of bad fare. Do you mean that Keats had bad fare? But if he had – how was he kept safe to the worlds end? I don't understand at all!!!!!!!

Now, that is the way I read, as well as I can, poem after poem, picking up a little bit here & there & enjoying it, but wholly unable to put anything together. I can't say I have really made out any one yet, except the epistle from the Arabian physician, which I like immensely, and I am only a stanza or so out with one or two others –

in by the fireside for instance I am only *dead* beat by the 41–43, and in fra Lippo – I am only fast at the grated orris root, which I looked for in the Encyclopaedia and couldn't find; and at the There's for you – give me six months – because I don't know *What's* for you.[1]

Well, how far all this is as it should be, I really know not. There is a stuff and fancy in your work which assuredly is in no other living writer's, and how far this purple of it *must* be within this terrible shell; and only to be fished for among threshing of foam & slippery rocks, I don't know. There are truths & depths in it, far beyond anything I have read except Shakespeare – and truly, if you had just written Hamlet, I believe I should have written to you, precisely this kind of letter – merely quoting your own Rosencrantz against you – 'I understand you not, my Lord.' I cannot write in enthusiastic praise, because I look at you every day as a monkey does at a cocoanut, having great faith in the milk – hearing it rattle indeed – inside – but quite beside myself for the Fibres. Still less can I write in blame. When a man has real power, God only knows how he can bring it out, or ought to bring it out. But, I would pray you, faith, heartily, to consider with yourself, how far you can amend matters, & make the real virtue of your work acceptable & profitable to more people.

For one thing, I entirely deny & refuse the right of any poet to require me to pronounce words short and long, exactly as he likes – to require me to read a plain & harsh & straightforward piece of prose. 'Till I felt where the fold-skirts (*fly*, redundant) open.' Then, once more, I prayed; as a dactylic verse, with skirts! for a short syllable Foldskĭrts flў – 'as tremendous a long monosyllable as any in the language' and to say, 'Wunce-mur-y' – prayed, instead of 'once more I'.[2]

And in the second place, I entirely deny that a poet of your real dramatic power ought to let *himself* come up, as you constantly do,

1. Ruskin alludes to 'An Epistle . . . of Karshish, the Arab Physician', 'By the Fire-Side', and 'Fra Lippo Lippi'; in the latter poem the 'grated orris-root' comes at l. 351 (for Browning's riposte see below, p. 259) and 'There's for you' at l. 345. Browning does not explain this phrase; it may mean that Lippi is handing out money, though he has already done so at l. 28, or it may be equivalent to 'That will show you!'

2. Ruskin objects to the metre of 'Saul', l. 20: 'Till I felt where the foldskirts fly open. Then once more I prayed'.

through all manner of characters, so that every now and then poor Pippa herself shall speak a long piece of Robert Browning.

And in the third place, your Ellipses are quite Unconscionable: before one can get through ten lines, one has to patch you up in twenty places, wrong or right, and if one hasn't much stuff of one's own to spare to patch with! You are worse than the worst Alpine Glacier I ever crossed. Bright, & deep enough truly, but so full of Clefts that half the journey has to be done with ladder & hatchet.

However, I have found some great things in you already, and I think you must be a wonderful mine, when I have real time & strength to set to work properly. That bit about the Bishop & St Praxed, in the older poems, is very glorious. Rossetti showed it me. In fact, I oughtn't to write to you yet, at all, but such is my state of mind at present and it may perhaps be well that you should know it, even though it may soon change to a more acceptant one, because it most certainly represents the feelings of a good many more, besides myself, who ought to admire you & learn from you, but can't because you are so difficult.

Well – there's a specimen for you of my art of saying pleasant things to my friends.

I have no time left, now, for any unpleasant ones – so I must just say goodbye and beg you to accept, with my dear M^rs^ Browning, the assurance of my exceeding regard & respect.

Ever most faithfully Yours,
J Ruskin

PARIS, Dec. 10th, '55

My dear Ruskin, – for so you let me begin, with the honest friendliness that befits, – You never were more in the wrong than when you professed to say 'your unpleasant things' to me. This is pleasant and proper at all points, over-liberal of praise here and there, kindly and sympathetic everywhere, and with enough of yourself in even – what I fancy – the misjudging, to make the whole letter precious indeed. I wanted to thank you thus much at once, – that is, when the letter reached me; but the strife of lodging-hunting was too sore, and only now that I can sit down for a minute without self-reproach do I allow my thoughts to let go south-aspects, warm bedrooms, and the like, and begin as you see. For the deepnesses you think you discern, – may they be more than mere blacknesses! For the hopes you entertain of what may come of subsequent readings, – all success to them! For your bewilderment more especially noted – how shall I help *that*? We don't read poetry the same way, by the same law; it is too clear. I cannot begin writing poetry till my imaginary reader has conceded licences to me which you demur at altogether. I *know* that I don't make out my conception by my language; all poetry being a putting the infinite within the finite. You would have me paint it all plain out, which can't be; but by various artifices I try to make shift with touches and bits and outlines which *succeed* if they bear the conception from me to you. You ought, I think, to keep pace with the thought tripping from ledge to ledge of my 'glaciers', as you call them; not stand poking your alpenstock into the holes, and demonstrating that no foot could have stood there; – suppose it sprang over there? In *prose* you may criticise so – because that is the absolute representation of portions of truth, what chronicling is to history – but in asking for more *ultimates* you must accept less *mediates*, nor expect that a Druid stone-circle will be traced for you with as few breaks to the eye as the North Crescent and South Crescent that go together so cleverly in many a suburb. Why, you look at my little song as if it were Hobbs' or Nobbs' lease of his house, or testament of his devisings, wherein, I grant you, not a 'then and there', 'to him and his heirs', 'to have and to hold', and so on, would be superfluous; and so you begin: – 'Stand still, – why?' For the reason indicated in the verse, to be sure – *to let me draw him* – and because he is at present going his way, and fancying nobody notices him, – and moreover, 'going on' (as we say) against the injustice of that, – and lastly, inasmuch as one night he'll fail us, as a star is apt to drop out of heaven, in authentic astronomic records, and I want to make the most of my time. So much may be in 'stand still'. And how much more was (for instance) in that 'stay!' of Samuel's (I. xv. 16). So could I twit you through the whole series of your objurgations, but the declaring my own notion of the law on the subject will do. And why, – I prithee, friend and fellow-student, – why, having told the Poet what you read, – may I not turn to the bystanders, and tell them a bit of my own mind about their own stupid thanklessness and mistaking? Is the jump too much there? The whole is all but a simultaneous feeling with me.

The other hard measure you deal me I won't bear – about my requiring you to pronounce words short and long, exactly as I like. Nay, but exactly as the language likes, in this case. *Foldskirts* not a trochee? A spondee possible in English? Two of the 'longest monosyllables' continuing to be each of the old length when in junction? Sentence: let the delinquent be forced to supply the stone-cutter with a thousand companions to 'Affliction sore – long time he bore', after the fashion of 'He lost his life – by a pen-knife' – 'He turned to clay – last Good Friday', 'Departed hence – nor owed six-pence', and so on – so would pronounce a jury accustomed from the nipple to say lord and landlord, bridge and Cambridge, Gog and Magog, man and woman, house and workhouse, coal and charcoal, cloth and broadcloth, skirts and foldskirts, more and once more, – in short! Once *more* I prayed! – is the confession of a self-searching professor! 'I stand here for law!'

The last charge I cannot answer, for you may be right in preferring it, however unwitting I am of the fact. I *may* put Robert Browning into Pippa and other men and maids. If so, *peccavi*: but I don't see myself in them, at all events.

Do you think poetry was ever generally understood – or can be? Is the business of it to tell people what they know already, as they know it, and so precisely that they shall be able to cry out – 'Here you should supply *this* – *that*, you evidently pass over, and I'll help you from my own stock'? It is all teaching, on the contrary, and the people hate to be taught. They say otherwise, – make foolish fables about Orpheus enchanting stocks and stones, poets standing up and being worshipped, – all nonsense and impossible dreaming. A poet's affair is with God, to whom he is accountable, and of whom is his reward: look elsewhere, and you find misery enough. Do you believe people understand *Hamlet*? The last time I saw it acted, the heartiest applause of the night went to a little by-play of the actor's own – who, to simulate madness in a hurry, plucked forth his handkerchief and flourished it hither and thither: certainly a third of the play, with no end of noble things, had been (as from time immemorial) suppressed, with the auditory's amplest acquiescence and benediction. Are these wasted, therefore? No – they act upon a very few, who react upon the rest: as Goldsmith says, 'some lords, my acquaintance, that settle the nation, are pleased to be kind'.

Don't let me lose *my* lord by any seeming self-sufficiency or petulance: I look on my own shortcomings too sorrowfully, try to remedy them too earnestly: but I shall never change my point of sight, or feel other than disconcerted and apprehensive when the public, critics and all, begin to understand and approve me. But what right have *you* to disconcert me in the other way? Why won't you ask the next perfumer for a packet of *orris*-root? Don't everybody know 'tis a corruption of *iris*-root – the Florentine lily, the *giaggolo*, of world-wide fame as a good savour? And because 'iris' means so many objects already, and I use the old word, you blame me! But I write in the blind-dark and bitter cold, and past post-time as I fear. Take my truest thanks, and understand at least this rough writing, and, at all events, the real affection with which I venture to regard you. And 'I' means my wife as well as

Yours ever faithfully,
Robert Browning.

## *Popularity*

1

Stand still, true poet that you are,
  I know you; let me try and draw you.
Some night you'll fail us. When afar
  You rise, remember one man saw you,
Knew you, and named a star.

2

My star, God's glow-worm! Why extend
  That loving hand of His which leads you,
Yet locks you safe from end to end
  Of this dark world, unless He needs you –
Just saves your light to spend?

3

His clenched Hand shall unclose at last
  I know, and let out all the beauty.
My poet holds the future fast,
  Accepts the coming ages' duty,
Their present for this past.

4

That day, the earth's feast-master's brow
  Shall clear, to God the chalice raising;
'Others give best at first, but Thou
  For ever set'st our table praising, –
Keep'st the good wine till now.'

5

Meantime, I'll draw you as you stand,
   With few or none to watch and wonder.
I'll say – a fisher (on the sand
   By Tyre the Old) his ocean-plunder,
A netful, brought to land.

6

Who has not heard how Tyrian shells
   Enclosed the blue, that dye of dyes
Whereof one drop worked miracles,
   And coloured like Astarte's eyes
Raw silk the merchant sells?

7

And each bystander of them all
   Could criticise, and quote tradition
How depths of blue sublimed some pall,
   To get which, pricked a king's ambition;
Worth sceptre, crown and ball.

8

Yet there's the dye, – in that rough mesh,
   The sea has only just o'er-whispered!
Live whelks, the lip's-beard dripping fresh,
   As if they still the water's lisp heard
Through foam the rock-weeds thresh.

9

Enough to furnish Solomon
   Such hangings for his cedar-house,
That when gold-robed he took the throne
   In that abyss of blue, the Spouse
Might swear his presence shone

10

Most like the centre-spike of gold
   Which burns deep in the blue-bell's womb,
What time, with ardours manifold,
   The bee goes singing to her groom,
Drunken and overbold.

11

Mere conchs! not fit for warp and woof!
  Till art comes, – comes to pound and squeeze
And clarify, – refines to proof
  The liquor filtered by degrees,
While the world stands aloof.

12

And there's the extract, flasked and fine,
  And priced, and saleable at last!
And Hobbs, Nobbs, Stokes and Nokes combine
  To paint the future from the past,
Put blue into their line.

13

Hobbs hints blue, – straight he turtle eats.
  Nobbs prints blue, – claret crowns his cup.
Nokes outdares Stokes in azure feats, –
  Both gorge. Who fished the murex up?
What porridge had John Keats?

# Bibliography

*The place of publication is London unless otherwise stated.*


Allingham, H. and Radford, D. (eds), *William Allingham, a Diary*, 1907.

Altick, R. (ed.), *The Ring and the Book*, Harmondsworth 1971.

Arbuckle, James, *Hibernicus's Letters: a Collection of Letters and Essays on Several Subjects*, 2 vols, 1729.

Augustine, St. transl. R.S. Pine-Coffin, *Confessions*, Harmondsworth, 1961.

Berdoe, E., *The Browning Cyclopaedia*, 1892.

Bloom, H. and Munich, A. (eds), *Robert Browning: a Collection of Critical Essays*, 1987.

Bloom, H., *A Map of Misreading*, Oxford 1975.

Brady, A.P., *Pompilia: a Feminist Reading of Robert Browning's The Ring and the Book*, Athens, Ohio 1988.

Brett-Smith, H.F. (ed.), *The Four Ages of Poetry* [etc.], 1972

Broughton, L.N. and Stelter, B.F., *A Concordance to the Poems of Robert Browning*, 4 vols, New York 1924–5, repr. 1970.

Broughton, L.N., Northup, C.S. and Pearsall, R.B., *Robert Browning: a Bibliography*, 1830–1950, New York 1953.

Carr, C. (ed.), *Harriet Hosmer: Letters and Memories*, 1913.

Chadwyck-Healey Database of English Poetry, 1994.

Chesterton, G.K., *Robert Browning*, 1903.

Coleridge, H. N. (ed.), *Literary Remains of Samuel Taylor Coleridge*, 4 vols, 1836–9.

Collingwood, W. G. *Life and Work of John Ruskin*, 2 vols., 1893.

Collins, T.J., *The Brownings to the Tennysons*, Waco, Texas 1971.

Cooke, G.W., *A Guide-Book to the Poetic and Dramatic Works of Robert Browning*, Boston and New York 1894.

Culler, A.D., 'Monodrama and the Dramatic Monologue', *PMLA* xc (1975), 366–85.

Curle, R. (ed.), *Robert Browning and Julia Wedgwood: a Broken Friendship as Revealed in their Letters*, 1937.

Davies, H.S., *Browning and the Modern Novel*, Hull 1962.

DeLaura, D. (ed.), 'Ruskin and the Brownings: Twenty-five Unpublished Letters', *Bulletin of the John Rylands Library* liv, 1972, 314–56.

DeVane, W.C. and Knickerbocker, K.L. *New Letters of Robert Browning*, 1951.
DeVane, W.C., *A Browning Handbook*, 2nd edn, New York 1955.
Donner, H.W. (ed.), *The Browning Box: or, the Life and Works of Thomas Lovell Beddoes, as Reflected in Letters by his Friends and Admirers*, Oxford 1935.
Drew, P., *An Annotated Critical Bibliography of Robert Browning*, 1990.
Eliot, T.S., *Selected Essays*, 1951.
Gosse, E., *Robert Browning: Personalia*, 1890.
Griffin, W.H. and Minchin, H.C., *The Life of Robert Browning*, 1910; 2nd edn 1938.
Grigson, G., *The Englishman's Flora*, 1958.
Hamilton, W. (ed.), *The Works of Thomas Reid, D.D.*, Edinburgh 1846.
Harlan, A.B., *Owen Meredith*, New York 1946.
Hayden, J. O. (ed.), *William Wordsworth: The Poems*, 2 vols., 1977.
Honan, P. and Irvine, W., *The Book, the Ring and the Poet*, 1975.
Honan, P., *Browning's Characters: a Study in Poetic Technique*, New Haven 1961.
Hood, T.L. (ed.), *The Letters of Robert Browning*, 1933.
Horsman, E.A. (ed.), *The Diary of Alfred Domett 1872–1885*, Oxford 1953.
Howe, P. P. (ed.), *The Complete Works of William Hazlitt* (Centenary Edition), 21 vols., 1930–4.
Hudson, G.R. (ed.), *Browning to his American Friends*, 1965.
Jack, I.R.J. *et al.* (eds), *The Poetical Works of Robert Browning*, Oxford 1981–.
Karlin, D.R. *The Courtship Correspondence 1845–1846; Robert Browning and Elizabeth Barrett: a Selection*, Oxford 1989.
Karlin, D.R., *Browning's Hatreds*, Oxford 1993.
Karlin, D.R., *The Courtship of Robert Browning and Elizabeth Barrett*, Oxford 1985.
Kelley, P. *et al.* (eds), *The Brownings' Correspondence*, Winfield, Kansas 1984–.
Kelley, P. and Coley, B., *The Browning Collections: a Reconstruction*, Winfield, Kansas 1984.
Kenyon, F.G. (ed.), *New Poems by Robert and Elizabeth Barrett Browning*, 1914.
Kenyon, F.G. (ed.), *The Letters of Elizabeth Barrett Browning*, 2 vols, 1898.
King, R. *et al.* (eds), *The Complete Works of Robert Browning*, Ohio and Waco, Texas 1969–.
Kintner, E., *The Letters of Robert Browning and Elizabeth Barrett Browning 1845–1846*, Cambridge, Mass. 1969.
Landis, P., *Letters of the Brownings to George Barrett*, Urbana, Ill. 1958.
Langbaum, R., *The Poetry of Experience*, 1957.
Leavis, F.R., *New Bearings in English Poetry: a Study of the Contemporary Situation*, 1932.
Locke, J., *An Essay Concerning Humane Understanding*, 3rd edn, 1695.
Lytton, V.A.G.R., *The Life of Edward Bulwer, First Lord Lytton*, 2 vols, 1913.
Martin, L.D., *Browning's Dramatic Monologues and the Post-Romantic Subject*, Baltimore 1985.

Mason, M. (ed.), *Lyrical Ballads*, 1992.

Maynard, J., *Browning's Youth*, Cambridge, Mass. 1977.

McAleer, E.C., *Dearest Isa: Robert Browning's Letters to Isabella Blagden*, Austin, Texas, 1951.

McAleer, E.C., *Learned Lady: Letters from Robert Browning to Mrs Thomas Fitzgerald* 1876–1889, Cambridge, Mass. 1969.

Meredith, M. (ed.), *More than Friend: the Letters of Robert Browning to Katherine de Kay Bronson*, Waco, Texas and Winfield, Kansas 1985.

Meredith, M., 'Learning's Crabbed Text: Reconsideration of the 1868 Edition of Browning's Poetical Works', *Studies in Browning and His Circle* xiii, 1985, 97–107.

Miller, B., *Robert Browning: a Portrait*, 1952.

Orr, A.S., A *Handbook to the Works of Robert Browning*, 7th edn, 1896.

Orr, A.S., *Life and Letters of Robert Browning*, 1891.

Pagel, W., *An Introduction to Philosophical Medicine in the Era of the Renaissance*, New York 1958.

Peterson, W.S. (ed.), *Browning's Trumpeter: the Correspondence of Robert Browning and Frederick J. Furnivall 1872–1889*, Washington D.C. 1979.

Peterson, W.S., *Robert and Elizabeth Barrett Browning: an Annotated Bibliography*, 1951–1970, New York 1974.

Pettigrew, J. and Collins, T.J., *Robert Browning: the Poems*, 2 vols, Harmondsworth 1981.

Plato, *Ion*, transl. D.A. Russell, in Russell and M. Winterbottom (eds), *Ancient Literary Criticism*, Oxford, 1972.

Proust, M., transl. C.K. Scott Moncrieff and T. Kilmartin, *Remembrance of Things Past*, Harmondsworth 1981.

Ritchie, A.T., *Records of Tennyson, Ruskin and Browning*, 1893.

Rollins, H.E. (ed.), *The Letters of John Keats*, 2 vols, Cambridge, Mass. 1958.

Rooke, B.E. (ed.), *The Friend* (Collected Works of Samuel Taylor Coleridge, vol. iv), 2 vols., 1969.

Rossetti, C., *Letter and Spirit*, 1883.

Rossetti, W.M., *Ruskin: Rossetti: Pre-Raphaelitism*, 1899.

Ryals, C., *The Life of Robert Browning: a Critical Biography*, Oxford 1993.

Shaw, W.D., *The Dialectical Temper*, New York 1968.

Slinn, E.W., *Browning and the Fictions of Identity*, 1982.

Smith, A., A *Theory of Moral Sentiments*, 2nd edn, 1762.

Tucker, H.F., *Browning's Beginnings: the Art of Disclosure*, Minneapolis 1980.

Viscusi, R., ' "The Englishman in Italy": Free Trade as a Principle of Aesthetics', *Browning Institute Studies* xii, 1984, 1–29.

Ward, M.J., *Robert Browning and his World*, 2 vols, 1967–9.

Ward, M.J., *The Tragi-Comedy of Pen Browning 1849–1912*, New York, 1972.

Whitla, W., *The Central Truth: the Incarnation in Browning's Poetry*, Toronto 1963.

Woolford, J. (ed.), *Browning, Ruskin, Swinburne*, vol. vi of *Sale Catalogues of the Libraries of Eminent Persons*, gen. ed. A.N.L. Munby, 1972.

Woolford, J., 'Periodicals and the Practice of Literary Criticism 1855–1964' in J. Shattock and M. Wolff (eds), *The Victorian Periodical Press*, Leicester 1982.

Woolford, J., *Browning the Revisionary*, 1988.

Woolford, J. and D. R. Karlin (eds), *The Poems of Browning*, vol. i (1826–1840) and vol. ii (1840–1846), 1991.

Woolford, J., ' "What's Left for Me to Do?": Pound, Browning and the Problem of Poetic Influence' in A. Gibson (ed.), *Pound in Multiple Perspective*, Basingstoke 1992, pp. 8–39.

# *Chronology*

| Year | Life and work of Robert Browning (includes summary details of Elizabeth Barrett Browning) | Births, Deaths, and selected publications of other writers | Political, economic and social history |
|---|---|---|---|
| 1806 | (6 *March*) Birth of Elizabeth Barrett Moulton-Barrett (EBB). | Birth of John Stuart Mill. Walter Scott (b. 1771), *Ballads and Lyrical Pieces*. | (January) Death of Pitt. 'Ministry of all the Talents': Grenville (Tory) Prime Minister, Fox (Whig) Foreign Secretary.(*September*) Death of Fox. |
| 1807 | | Birth of Henry Wadsworth Longfellow. Byron (b. 1788), *Hours of Idleness*. George Crabbe (b. 1754), *Poems*. Anne-Louise-Germaine Necker (Mme de Staël, b. 1766), *Corinne*. William Wordsworth (b. 1770), *Poems in Two Volumes*. | Portland Prime Minister. General election: Tory victory. Slave trade (but not slavery itself) abolished in British territories. Robert Southey (b. 1774) given government pension. |

| | | | |
|---|---|---|---|
| 1808 | | Johann Wolfgang von Goethe (b. 1749), *Faust, Part One*. Scott, *Marmion*. | Peninsular War begins. |
| 1809 | The Barrett family moves to Hope End, Herefordshire. | Birth of Charles Darwin, Edward FitzGerald, William Gladstone, Edgar Allan Poe, Alfred Tennyson. Byron, *English Bards and Scotch Reviewers*. Goethe, *Elective Affinities*. | Perceval Prime Minister. Bribery Act restricts sale of Parliamentary seats. Wellesley becomes Duke of Wellington after victory of Talavera. Foundation of *Quarterly Review* as Tory rival to *Edinburgh Review* (founded 1802). |
| 1810 | | Birth of Margaret Fuller, Elizabeth Stevenson (Gaskell). Crabbe, *The Borough*. Mme de Staël, *De l'Allemagne*. Scott, *The Lady of the Lake*. Southey, *The Curse of Kehama*. | George III's mental incapacity recurs (permanently). Strikes in response to economic policy. |
| 1811 | | Birth of William Makepeace Thackeray. Jane Austen (b. 1775), *Sense and Sensibility*. Goethe, *Poetry and Truth* (autobiographical writings, to 1832). | Prince of Wales becomes Prince Regent. First Luddite attacks in Nottingham. |

| | | | |
|---|---|---|---|
| 1812 | (*7 May*) Birth of Robert Browning, son of Robert Browning and Sarah Anna Browning (née Wiedemann), in Camberwell, then a rural village to the south of London. Browning's father, whose family originally came from Dorset, is a clerk in the Bank of England, a mild, tolerant man interested in art and books; he had broken with his own father by refusing to take part in the management of slave plantations in the West Indies. Browning's mother, of Scottish-German descent, is a devout Nonconformist, who loves gardening and music. The family has connections with the worlds of shipping and international finance (Browning's half-uncles, William and Reuben, work for Rothschild's, William in the Paris office) and is relatively cosmopolitan and liberal in culture and outlook; careers at different times envisaged for Browning include diplomacy and the law. | Birth of Charles Dickens, Edward Lear. Byron, *Childe Harold's Pilgrimage*, cantos I and II. Crabbe, *Tales in Verse*. | Napoleon invades Russia; 'victory' at Borodino followed by disastrous retreat from Moscow. Widespread economic distress in England (wheat price reaches nineteenth-century high); Luddite riots; 'frame-breaking' made a capital offence. Perceval assassinated; Liverpool Prime Minister. War with United States. Formation of Baptist Union. Central London streets first lit by gas. |

| | | | |
|---|---|---|---|
| 1813 | | Austen, *Pride and Prejudice*. Byron, *The Bride of Abydos; The Giaour*. Coleridge (b. 1772), *Remorse*. Scott, *Rokeby*. Percy Bysshe Shelley (b. 1792), *Queen Mab*. Southey, *Life of Nelson*. | Victory in Peninsular War; British army enters France. Foundation of Methodist Missionary Society. East India Company monopoly ended. Southey appointed Poet Laureate. Wordsworth appointed Stamp Distributor for Westmorland. |
| 1814 | Birth of Sarianna, Browning's only sibling. | Austen, *Mansfield Park*. Byron, *The Corsair; Lara*. Scott, *Waverley*. Wordsworth, *The Excursion*. | Defeat of France; Napoleon abdicates and goes into exile on island of Elba; restoration of Louis XVIII. Peace with United States. Stephenson builds steam locomotive. Foundation of *New Monthly Magazine* in opposition to radical *Monthly Magazine* (founded 1796). |
| 1815 | | Birth of Anthony Trollope. Jeremy Bentham (b. 1748), *Chrestomathia*. Byron, *Hebrew Melodies*. Scott, *The Lord of the Isles; Guy Mannering*. Wordsworth, *Poems* (collected); *The White Doe of Rylstone*. | Napoleon returns from Elba; the '100 days' end with defeat at Waterloo and exile to island of St Helena. Congress of Vienna frames European political settlement. Corn Law restricts import of foreign grain. |
| 1816 | | Birth of Charlotte Brontë. Austen, *Emma*. Byron, *Childe Harold's Pilgrimage*, canto III; *The Prisoner of Chillon*. Coleridge, *Christabel; Kubla* | Severe economic depression. Agitation for reform (Hampden Clubs); Spa Fields riot. |

| | | | |
|---|---|---|---|
| 1816 | | *Khan; The Pains of Sleep.* Thomas Love Peacock (b. 1785), *Headlong Hall.* Scott, *The Antiquary; Old Mortality.* Shelley, *Alastor.* | |
| 1817 | | Birth of G(eorge) H(enry) Lewes. Death of Jane Austen, Mme de Staël. Byron, *The Lament of Tasso; Manfred.* William Cobbett (b. 1762), *A Grammar of the English Language.* Goethe, *Italian Journey.* William Hazlitt (b. 1778), *The Round Table; Characters of Shakespeare's Plays.* John Keats (b. 1795), *Poems.* Thomas Moore (b. 1779), *Lalla Rookh.* Shelley, *Laon and Cythna* revised and publ. 1818 as *The Revolt of Islam.* Southey, *Wat Tyler* (early radical play, publ. by his enemies). | Pentrich rising in Derbyshire. Habeas Corpus suspended. Act banning seditious meetings passed. Foundation of *Blackwood's Magazine.* |
| 1818 | | Birth of Emily Brontë, Karl Marx. Austen, *Northanger Abbey* and *Persuasion* (posthumous publ.). Byron, *Beppo; Childe Harold's Pilgrimage,* canto IV. Coleridge, *Sibylline Leaves, Biographia Literaria.* | General election: Tory victory. Habeas Corpus restored. |

| | | |
|---|---|---|
| | *Hazlitt, A View of the English Stage; Lectures on the English Poets.* Keats, *Endymion.* Peacock, *Rhododaphne; Nightmare Abbey.* Scott, *Rob Roy.* Mary Wollstonecraft Shelley (b. 1797), *Frankenstein.* | |
| 1819 | Birth of Arthur Hugh Clough, Mary Ann Evans (George Eliot), Charles Kingsley, Herman Melville, John Ruskin, Walt Whitman. Byron, *Don Juan*, cantos I–II, *Mazeppa.* Cobbett, *Journal of a Year's Residence in the United States.* Crabbe, *Tales of the Hall.* Goethe, *East-West Divan.* Hazlitt, *A Letter to William Gifford; Lectures on the English Comic Writers.* B.W. Proctor ('Barry Cornwall', b. 1787), *Dramatic Scenes.* Scott, *Ivanhoe.* Shelley, *Rosalind and Helen; The Cenci; The Mask of Anarchy* (response to Peterloo Massacre, suppressed until 1832). Wordsworth, *Peter Bell; The Waggoner.* | Birth of (future Queen) Victoria and (future Prince Consort) Albert. Stamford Raffles takes Singapore. Peterloo Massacre, Manchester. Passing of the 'Six Acts' to suppress radicalism. Telford begins building the Menai suspension bridge. |

| | | | |
|---|---|---|---|
| 1820–6 | Attends Peckham School as weekly boarder, first at the lower school run by the Misses Ready, then the upper school run by their brother, the Rev. Thomas Ready. Receives a thorough, conventional, middle-class education. An epigram lampooning Ready is among his earliest surviving verse, but so is a boyish tribute to him. Alfred Domett later quotes Browning reciting verses on the 'undiluted misery' of his schooldays, but this seems somewhat exaggerated. | | |
| 1820 | (*March*) EBB's *The Battle of Marathon* privately printed. | Birth of Anne Brontë, Friedrich Engels. Byron, *Don Juan*, cantos III–IV. John Clare (b. 1793), *Poems Descriptive of Rural Life and Scenery*. Washington Irving (b. 1783), *The Sketch-Book*. Moore, *Irish Melodies*. Peacock, 'The Four Ages of Poetry' (essay in *Ollier's Literary Miscellany*; prompted Shelley's *Defence of Poetry*). Proctor, *Marcian Colonna*. Shelley, *Prometheus Unbound*. Southey, *Life of Wesley*. Wordsworth, *The River Duddon; Miscellaneous Poems*. | Death of George III. Accession of George IV. General election: Tory victory. Cato Street conspiracy to murder government exposed; leaders executed. Bill to enable George IV to divorce Queen Caroline. Launch of first iron steamship. |

| | | | |
|---|---|---|---|
| 1821 | | Birth of Gustave Flaubert. Death of Keats. Thomas Lovell Beddoes (b. 1803), *The Improvisatore*. Bentham, *Elements of the Art of Packing, as applied to Special Juries; On the Liberty of the Press*. Byron, *Cain*; *Don Juan*, cantos V–VIII; *Marino Faliero*; *Sardanapalus*; *The Two Foscari*. Clare, *The Village Minstrel*. Goethe, *Wilhelm Meister's Travels* (transl. Carlyle, 1827). Hazlitt, *Table-Talk*. Scott, *Kenilworth*. Shelley, *Epipsychidion*; *Adonais*. Southey, *A Vision of Judgement*. | Greek War of Independence. Death of Napoleon. Failure of George IV's divorce plans. Queen Caroline barred from attending coronation. Foundation of *Manchester Guardian* (weekly to 1855, then daily). |
| 1822 | | Birth of Matthew Arnold. Death of Shelley. Beddoes, *The Bride's Tragedy*. Byron, *Don Juan*, cantos IX–XII; *The Vision of Judgement* (satirising Southey, above). Irving, *Bracebridge Hall*. Peacock, *Maid Marian*. Stendhal (pseudonym of Henri Beyle, b. 1783), *De l'amour*. Shelley, *Hellas*. Wordsworth, *Ecclesiastical Sketches* (later *Ecclesiastical Sonnets*). | |

| | | | |
|---|---|---|---|
| 1823–4 | First becomes acquainted with Eliza and Sarah Flower, wards of the Rev. William Johnstone Fox, Unitarian minister and radical in politics, editor of the *Monthly Repository*, in which some of Browning's earliest poems will be published. Browning later refers to Fox as his 'literary father'. In later 1820s he is romantically attached to Eliza Flower. | | |
| 1823 | | Birth of Coventry Patmore. Byron, *The Age of Bronze; The Island; Werner*. Hazlitt, *Liber Amoris*. Charles Lamb (b. 1775), *Essays of Elia*. Scott, *Quentin Durward.* Shelley, *Posthumous Poems* (ed. Mary Shelley). Stendhal, *Racine et Shakespeare.* First English transl. (Edgar Taylor) of tales collected by brothers Grimm. | Foundation of Irish Catholic Association. Prison Reform Act. Charles Macintosh invents waterproof garment. |
| 1824 | | Birth of (William) Wilkie Collins. Death of Byron. Byron, *The Deformed Transformed.* Thomas Carlyle (b. 1795), transl. Goethe, *Wilhelm* | Death of Louis XVIII. Accession of Charles X. In England, Combination Acts against trade unions repealed. Foundation of Society for the |

| | | | |
|---|---|---|---|
| | | *Meister's Apprenticeship*. Cobbett, *History of the Protestant 'Reformation' in England and Ireland*. James Hogg (1770–1835), *The Private Memoirs and Confessions of a Justified Sinner*. Letitia Landon ('L.E.L.', b. 1802), *The Improvisatrice*. Walter Savage Landor (b. 1775), *Imaginary Conversations of Literary Men and Statesmen* (to 1829). Scott, *Redgauntlet*. | Prevention of Cruelty to Animals (later Royal Society). Foundation of *Westminster Review*. |
| 1825 | | Carlyle, *Life of Schiller*. Hazlitt, *The Spirit of the Age*. Hemans, *Poetical Works; Lays of Many Lands*. Thomas Hood (b. 1799), *Odes and Addresses to Great People*. Landon, *The Troubadour*. | Catholic Relief bill fails in House of Lords. Opening of Stockton and Darlington Railway. |
| 1826–8 | Leaves Ready's school and continues his education at home, with tutors in music, drawing, and French; other activities include riding (at reckless speed), fencing, boxing, and dancing. Writes a volume of poems (*Incondita* = 'mere trifles') but subsequently destroys | | |

| | | | |
|---|---|---|---|
| 1826–8 | them; two ('The Dance of Death' and 'The First-Born of Egypt') survive as copies in a letter of Sarah Flower dated 31 May 1827, where she states that Browning wrote them at 14 years of age. | | |
| 1826 | Browning's cousin, James Silverthorne, gives him Shelley's *Miscellaneous Poems*, a pirated edition issued in this year by the radical publisher William Benbow. He had possibly already encountered Shelley's work through Eliza Flower. The Benbow volume contains shorter poems taken mainly from the authorised *Posthumous Poems* of 1824. Browning heavily annotates and marks the volume; in 1878 he erases many of his comments and adds an embarrassed preface. Under Shelley's influence, he becomes for a brief period vegetarian and expresses scepticism about the literal truth of Christianity, bringing him into conflict with his parents, especially his mother. Sarah Flower records her faith being | Benjamin Disraeli (b. 1804), *Vivian Grey* (sequel 1827). Hazlitt, *The Plain Speaker*. Mary Shelley, *The Last Man*. | General election: Tory victory. Deed of settlement for new University of London (built in 1827, officially opened in 1828) admitting dissenters to higher education. Foundation of Zoological Society of London. |

| | | | |
|---|---|---|---|
| | shaken in arguments about religion with him. His political opinions are also strongly affected. A close friend, Joseph Arnould, later alludes to this period of Browning's life as one in which 'Shelley was his God'. Browning's idealisation of Shelley is confirmed in succeeding years by accounts of his life in biographies and memoirs written by friends such as Leigh Hunt, but disillusionment sets in with his discovery of Shelley's treatment of his first wife: see below, 1858. Publication of EBB's *An Essay on Mind*. | | |
| 1827 | | Bentham, *The Rationale of Evidence*. Edward Bulwer-Lytton (b. 1803), *Falkland*. Clare, *The Shepherd's Calendar*. Disraeli, *Popanilla*. Hood, *The Plea of the Mid-summer Fairies*. John Keble (b. 1792), *The Christian Year*. Landon, *The Golden Violet*. Tennyson, *Poems by Two Brothers*. | Liverpool resigns as Prime Minister; Canning succeeds him but dies soon afterwards; Goderich Prime Minister. Reform of criminal law by Peel: fewer capital offences, redefinition of property law. Foundation of Society for the Diffusion of Useful Knowledge. |

| | | | |
|---|---|---|---|
| 1828 | (*October*) Enrols in newly founded London University for classes in Latin, Greek, and German (as a Nonconformist or Dissenter he could not have gone to Oxford or Cambridge). (*October*) Death of EBB's mother. | Birth of George Meredith, Dante Gabriel Rossetti. Bulwer-Lytton, *Pelham*. Hemans, *Records of Woman*. Irving, *Life and Voyages of Christopher Columbus*. Landon, *The Venetian Bracelet*. | Goderich resigns; Wellington Prime Minister. Repeal of Test and Corporation Acts allows religious liberty to dissenters. Thomas Arnold becomes headmaster of Rugby School. Foundation of the *Athenaeum* and the *Spectator*. |
| 1829 | (*May*) Leaves London University, 'an event as painful as it was unexpected' according to his father. Begins private tuition in Italian from Angelo Cerutti, a political exile, grammarian and philosopher. | Honoré de Balzac (b. 1799), *Les Chouans*. Cobbett, *Advice to Young Men; The Emigrant's Guide*. Hood, *The Dream of Eugene Aram*. Irving, *Conquest of Granada*. Peacock, *The Misfortunes of Elphin*. | Catholic Emancipation bill passed. Peel creates new London police force. Stephenson's *Rocket* wins Liverpool and Manchester Railway competition. Foundation of King's College, London. |
| 1830 | Member of 'The Set' or 'The Colloquials', an informal literary and debating society of young men; contributes skits and epigrams to the group's amateur magazine, *The Trifler*. Close friendships with some members (Alfred Domett, Joseph Arnould, Christopher Dowson) develop over course of next decade. | Birth of Christina Rossetti. Death of Hazlitt. Bentham, *Constitutional Code*. Bulwer-Lytton, *Paul Clifford*. Cobbett, *Rural Rides*. Hemans, *Songs of the Affections*. Victor Hugo (b. 1802), *Hernani*. Charles Lyell, *Principles of Geology*. Moore (ed.), *Letters and Journals of Lord Byron*. Stendhal, *Le Rouge et le Noir*. Tennyson, *Poems, Chiefly Lyrical*. | 'July Revolution' in France. Charles X abdicates. Accession of Louis-Philippe. In England, death of George IV. Accession of William IV. General election indicates support for parliamentary reform. Agricultural labourers' riots in south of England. Wellington resigns; Grey forms Whig administration. Opening of Liverpool and Manchester Railway (marred by the running over of the statesman William |

| | | | |
|---|---|---|---|
| | | | Huskisson at the opening ceremony). Foundation of *Fraser's Magazine*. |
| 1831 | | Birth of William Hale White (Mark Rutherford). Balzac, *La peau de chagrin*. Disraeli, *The Young Duke*. Peacock, *Crotchet Castle*. Poe, *Poems*. Hugo, *Les Feuilles d'automne; Notre-Dame de Paris*. | Beginnings in Italy of 'Risorgimento' ('resurrection' or 'rebirth'), the period of agitation and struggle for national unity and independence from Austria. In England, defeat of first Reform bill. General election strengthens reform majority in Commons. Second Reform bill rejected in Lords; riots in Bristol, Nottingham, and other places. Darwin begins voyage to South America as naturalist on H.M.S. *Beagle*. Foundation of British Association for the Advancement of Science. |
| 1832 | (*August*) Mr Barrett forced to sell Hope End; Barrett family move to Sidmouth. (*22 October*) Browning sees Edmund Kean acting Richard III at Richmond, and conceives 'a foolish plan which occupied me mightily for a time, and which had for its object the enabling me to assume & realise I know not how many different | Birth of Charles Dodgson (Lewis Carroll). Death of Bentham, Crabbe, Goethe, Scott. Balzac, *Louis Lambert*. Bulwer-Lytton, *Eugene Aram*. Disraeli, *Contarini Fleming*. Goethe, *Faust, Part Two*. Irving, *The Alhambra*. Harriet Martineau (b. 1802), *Illustrations of Political Economy* (to 1834). Mary Russell | Third Reform bill passes Commons but delayed in Lords; Grey resigns. Constitutional crisis and public disturbances (the 'Days of May'). Wellington fails to form a government; Grey resumes office and secures passage of Reform Act in Lords. General election: landslide victory for Whigs. |

| | | | |
|---|---|---|---|
| 1832 | characters; – meanwhile the world was never to guess that . . . the respective Authors of this poem, the other novel, such an opera, such a speech &c &c were no other than one and the same individual' (prefatory note in Mill's copy of *Pauline*: see below). *Pauline*, the first (and only) product of the 'foolish plan', is probably written in the autumn and winter of this year. Around this time, Browning finally decides to dedicate himself to poetry, refusing to follow a conventional career; he persuades his parents, initially reluctant, to support him. | Mitford (1787–1855), *Our Village*. Proctor, *English Songs*. George Sand (pseudonym of Lucile-Aurore Dupin, baronne Dudevant, b. 1804), *Indiana*. Shelley, *The Mask of Anarchy* (publ. by Leigh Hunt). Tennyson, *Poems* (dated 1833). Fanny Trollope (1780–1863), *Domestic Manners of the Americans*. | |
| 1833 | (*March*) *Pauline* published anonymously by Saunders & Otley; publication paid for by Browning's aunt, Mrs Christiana Silverthorne (mother of James). Browning presents copies to Fox, who writes an encouraging review himself in the *Monthly Repository* and secures brief notices in other journals (some | Balzac, *Eugénie Grandet; Le médecin de campagne*. Bulwer-Lytton, *England and the English*. Disraeli, *Alroy*. Lamb, *Last Essays of Elia*. Martineau, *Poor Laws and Paupers Illustrated* (to 1834). Sand, *Lélia*. | Slavery abolished in British territories. Factory Act provides for inspection of factories. First state grants to churches for building schools. Marriages permitted in Nonconformist chapels. Keble's sermon, *National Apostasy*, initiates the Oxford Movement, whose theological and social ideas are developed in *Tracts for the Times* by Keble, Newman, R.H. |

favourable, some not). Fox gives a copy to John Stuart Mill, who offers to review it in the liberal *Examiner*, which refuses, and in *Tait's Magazine*, where a dismissive one-line mention has already appeared. Mill annotates his copy and returns it to Fox, who in turn passes it back to Browning. Mill's comments include the statement that the writer of the poem has 'a more intense and morbid self-consciousness than I ever knew in any sane human being' and interprets it as a personal confession. Browning writes responses to some of Mill's annotations and a 'preface' which describes the 'foolish scheme' of which the poem was a product (see above). No copy of *Pauline* is sold at the time of publication. Browning retrieves the unbound sheets from the publisher and subsequently destroys them. Apart from occasional mentions in magazines by indiscreet friends, and episodes such as D.G. Rossetti's discovery of the poem in 1847 (see below), knowledge

Froude and others (hence the other name for the Oxford Movement, the Tractarian Movement).

| | | | |
|---|---|---|---|
| 1833 | of it is confined to Browning's immediate circle for 35 years; the prospect of unauthorised publication eventually obliges him to reprint it in *Poetical Works*, 1868 (see below). (*May*) Publication of EBB's *Prometheus Bound* (see below, 1850). | | |
| 1834 | (*March–June*) Travels overland to St Petersburg as unpaid secretary to the Chevalier George de Benkhausen, on a mission to negotiate a loan by Rothschild's to the Russian government. The following year Browning applies for a diplomatic post in a British government mission to Persia, but is turned down. Impressions of Russian landscape reappear over forty years later in 'Ivàn Ivànovitch' (*Dramatic Idyls*, 1879). (*Summer*) Begins writing *Sordello*, whose composition (with several interruptions and changes of conception) will take over five years. (*August*) Meets a young French aristocrat, Amédée de Ripert-Monclar, who becomes a close friend and stimulates his interest | Birth of William Morris. Death of Coleridge. Death of Lamb. Balzac, *La recherche de l'absolu; Le père Goriot*. Bulwer-Lytton, *The Last Days of Pompeii*. Disraeli, *The Revolutionary Epic*. | Grey resigns; Melbourne briefly Prime Minister, then resigns; Peel forms minority administration. Dorset agricultural labourers (the 'Tolpuddle martyrs') transported for taking illegal oath to join a Union. Poor Law Amendment Act. Houses of Parliament destroyed by fire. Hansom cabs first appear in London. |

| | | | |
|---|---|---|---|
| | in French literature and history; he and Monclar join the newly-formed Historical Institute of Paris. Monclar suggests Paracelsus as subject for a poem, but then retracts the suggestion on grounds that there is no love-interest; despite this, Browning begins work on *Paracelsus* in September, finishing it the following March. Again solicits help from Fox, this time prior to publication, and stressing the poem's political radicalism; this enables Fox to persuade the publisher Effingham Wilson to take it (though not at financial risk; Browning's father pays for publication of this and every subsequent volume, except *Strafford*, up to the last number of *Bells and Pomegranates* in 1846). | | |
| 1835 | (*August*) Publication of *Paracelsus*, with dedication to Monclar and preface explaining Browning's 'novel' dramatic method of presenting 'any phenomenon of the mind or passions': 'instead of having recourse to an external machinery of incidents . . . | Death of Cobbett, Hemans. Bulwer-Lytton, *Rienzi*. Clare, *The Rural Muse*. Hugo, *Les Chants du crépuscule*. Landon, *The Vow of the Peacock*. Thomas Noon Talfourd (1795–1854), *Ion*. Wordsworth, *Yarrow Revisited; Guide to the Lakes*. | General election: Tories make some gains, but Peel resigns when defeated on Irish Church issue. Whigs resume office; Melbourne Prime Minister. |

| | | | |
|---|---|---|---|
| 1835 | I have ventured to display somewhat minutely the mood itself in its rise and progress'. The poem is favourably reviewed by Fox, John Forster, and Leigh Hunt, and strongly impresses a number of already-established figures (e.g. EBB, Walter Savage Landor, the actor-manager William Charles Macready, Harriet Martineau, the lawyer and playwright Thomas Noon Talfourd). Important personal friendships with some of these follow, especially, in this period, Forster and Macready; through Macready Browning also meets Euphrasia Fanny Haworth, who becomes his closest female friend before his marriage. (*December*) Barrett family move to Devonshire Place, London. | | |
| 1836 | (*Spring*) Helps Forster complete his *Life of Strafford*, publ. under Forster's name alone but with substantial contributions by Browning. (*August*) Abandons *Sordello* to write his own | Bulwer-Lytton (ed.), *Literary Remains of William Hazlitt.* Carlyle, *Sartor Resartus.* Coleridge, *Literary Remains* (4 vols, to 1839). Landor, *A Satire on Satirists; Pericles and Aspasia.* Dickens, | Louis Napoleon, nephew of Napoleon, leads abortive insurrection. In England, tithe Commutation Act ends practice of tithe payment in kind. Foundation of London Working Men's Association. |

| | | | |
|---|---|---|---|
| | play *Strafford*. (*November*) Finishes *Strafford*; Forster, who acts throughout as Browning's adviser and sponsor, delivers the MS to Macready. Over the winter of 1836–7 Macready struggles to get the play into theatrical shape and is pessimistic about its chances; Forster and Browning quarrel at intervals over Forster's interventions. | *Sketches by Boz*. Ralph Waldo Emerson (b. 1803), *Nature*. Birth of W(illiam) S(chwenk) Gilbert. Irving, *Astoria*. John Henry Newman (b. 1801), *Lyra Apostolica*. | Return of Darwin to England. |
| 1837 | (*1 May*) *Strafford* published by Longman; on the same day produced at Covent Garden with Macready in the title role and Helen Faucit (later Lady Martin) as Lucy; closes after five performances. The play's mixed reception in the theatre and lukewarm critical reception (including an unenthusiastic review by Forster) deter Browning from immediately pursuing his theatrical ambitions; he turns instead to completing *Sordello*. | Birth of Algernon Charles Swinburne. Balzac, *Illusions perdues* (3 vols, to 1843). Bulwer-Lytton, *Ernest Maltravers*. Carlyle, *The French Revolution*. Dickens, *Pickwick Papers*. Disraeli, *Henrietta Temple*; *Venetia*. Nathaniel Hawthorne (b. 1804), *Twice-Told Tales*. Martineau, *Society in America*. | Death of William IV. Accession of Queen Victoria. General election: Whig victory. Civil registration of births, marriages, and deaths begins. |
| 1838 | (*April*) Barrett family move to 50 Wimpole Street. (*April–July*) First trip to Italy, by sea to Trieste, then Venice | Death of Landon. Balzac, *Splendeurs et misères des courtisanes* (4 vols, to 1847). Bentham, *Collected Works* (to | Louis Napoleon, *Idées napoléoniennes* publ. in London, advocating fulfilment of Napoleon's social reforms. Publ. of |

| | | | |
|---|---|---|---|
| 1838 | and the surrounding countryside, including Treviso, Bassano, Vicenza, and Padua, all significant locations for *Sordello*; intends to 'finish my poem among the scenes which it describes', but does not in fact do so. Most important of all, first sight of 'delicious Asolo', the little town near Venice which will be the setting for *Pippa Passes*, and remains Browning's talismanic Italian place, haunting his memory until his return forty years later and reappearing at last in his final volume, *Asolando.* Returns to England overland and down the Rhine to Antwerp. (*June*) Publication of EBB's *The Seraphim*. (*August*) EBB moves to Torquay to recuperate from illness. | 1843). Bulwer-Lytton, *The Lady of Lyons.* Carlyle, *Critical and Miscellaneous Essays*. Dickens, *Oliver Twist.* Hugo, *Ruy Blas*. Landon, *Flowers of Loveliness*. Mill, 'Bentham' (essay in *London and Westminster Review*). Poe, *Narrative of Arthur Gordon Pym*. Robert Surtees (b. 1803), *Jorrocks' Jaunts and Jollities*. Thackeray, *Yellowplush Papers*. | People's Charter with six points for democratic reform. Anti-Corn Law League founded by Manchester businessmen. Irish Poor Law Amendment Act. National Gallery opened in London on present site. Foundation of Public Record Office. |
| 1839 | (*Exact date unknown*) Meets John Kenyon, an old schoolfriend of his father, who becomes a close friend and warm admirer and supporter of his poetry. Through Kenyon Browning becomes better acquainted with Wordsworth, Landor, and other literary | Birth of Walter Pater. Balzac, *Béatrix*. Bulwer-Lytton, *Richelieu.* Darwin, *Journal* of his voyage on the *Beagle*. Dickens, *Nicholas Nickleby*. Hazlitt, *Sketches and Essays* (posthumous collection). Hood, *Hood's Own*. Longfellow, *Hyperion; Voices of the* | Chartist National Convention. Melbourne resigns, but Queen Victoria resists replacement of some ladies-in-waiting with Tory nominees and Peel refuses to form a government; Melbourne resumes office. Rejection of Chartist petition leads to riots; |

| | | | |
|---|---|---|---|
| | figures; Kenyon is also one of the few people who knows EBB personally and will later play a crucial role in bringing the two poets together (see below, 1842 and 1844). (*26 May*) Tells Macready he has finished *Sordello*; the final date for correction of proofs is nearly a year later, in February 1840. (*September*) Submits his second play, *King Victor and King Charles*, to Macready, who rejects it. | *Night*. Martineau, *Deerbrook.* Shelley, *Poetical Works* (ed. Mary Shelley). Stendhal, *La Chartreuse de Parme*. Thackeray, *Catherine*. | attempted rising at Newport suppressed. 'Opium War' with China; capture of Hong Kong. |
| 1840 | Meets Tennyson, whose writing he already knows and admires. (*March*) Publication of *Sordello*. The first review, in the *Spectator*, sets the tone: 'What this poem may be in its extent we are unable to say, for we *cannot* read it. Whatever may be the poetical spirit of Mr Browning, it is so overlaid in *Sordello* by digression, affectation, obscurity, and all the faults that spring, it would seem, from crudity of plan and a self-opinion which will neither cull thoughts nor revise composition, that the reader – at least a reader of our | Birth of Thomas Hardy. Balzac, *La Rabouilleuse*. Bulwer-Lytton, *Money*. Carlyle, *Chartism*. Mill, 'Coleridge' (essay in *London and Westminster Review*) Poe, *Tales of the Grotesque and Arabesque*. Shelley's *Defence of Poetry* publ. (written 1821). Thackeray, *A Shabby Genteel Story*; *The Paris Sketch Book*. | Reinterment of Napoleon's remains in the Invalides, Paris. Louis Napoleon leads a second abortive insurrection, is sentenced to life imprisonment. Britain assumes sovereignty over New Zealand. Establishment of Penny Post. Botanical Gardens opened at Kew. Foundation of Percy Society for the publ. of old English lyrics and ballads. Foundation of the London Library. |

1840 stamp – turns away.' Browning's reputation for wilful obscurity lasts for a quarter of a century and the poem becomes the butt of numberless jokes and anecdotes. His great poem's total failure is a trauma from which, in some ways, Browning never recovers; his attitude to his readers and critics, and his relationship with them, are permanently scarred. (*April*) Has, or has suggested to him, the idea of publishing his work in a series of cheap paper-bound pamphlets, to which he eventually gives the title of *Bells and Pomegranates*. (*April–September*) Submits a third play, *The Return of the Druses*, to Macready; revises it and re-submits it; Macready finally rejects it in September. (*July*) Death of EBB's brother Edward ('Bro') in a boating accident at Torquay; she blames herself for asking him to stay with her, and suffers a severe mental and physical breakdown. (*December*) Browning family moves from Camberwell to New Cross, Hatcham, in Surrey, Browning's home until his marriage.

| | | | |
|---|---|---|---|
| 1841 | (*April*) Publication of *Pippa Passes*, no. 1 of *Bells and Pomegranates*, by Moxon who will publish the remainder of the series. (*September*) Submits yet another play, *A Blot in the 'Scutcheon*, to Macready, who, pressured by Forster, reluctantly accepts it before his move from the Haymarket to Drury Lane in December. (*September*) EBB returns from Torquay to Wimpole Street; she lives in seclusion, seeing very few people but corresponding with many and continuing to write and publish. | Balzac, *Une Ténébreuse Affaire*. Carlyle, *On Heroes and Hero-Worship*. Dickens, *Master Humphrey's Clock*; *Barnaby Rudge*; *The Old Curiosity Shop*. Emerson, *Essays*. Longfellow, *Ballads*; *Poems on Slavery*. Martineau, *The Hour and the Man*. Poe, 'The Murders in the Rue Morgue' (publ. in *Graham's Magazine*). | General election: Tory victory; Peel Prime Minister. Severe economic depression and revival of Chartism. Newman, *Tract XC* on the incompatibility of the 39 Articles of the Church of England with Catholic theology. Foundation of *Punch*. |
| 1842 | (*March*) Publication of *King Victor and King Charles*, no. 2 of *Bells and Pomegranates*. John Kenyon (see above, 1839) offers to introduce him to EBB, but she declines for reasons of ill-health and shyness. (*April*) Alfred Domett (see above, 1830) emigrates to New Zealand. (*July*) Publication of review (ostensibly) of a book on Italian Renaissance poet Torquato Tasso in *Foreign Quarterly Review*; Browning's article turns into apologia for the life | Birth of Arthur Sullivan. Death of Stendhal. Balzac begins publ. of collected works (17 vols, to 1848) under generic title *La Comédie humaine*. Dickens, *American Notes*. Macaulay, *Lays of Ancient Rome*. Sand, *Consuelo*. Tennyson, *Poems* (two volumes; revised selection of 1830 and 1832 with new poems). Wordsworth, *Poems, Chiefly of Early and Late Years; including The Borderers, a Tragedy*. | Second Chartist petition rejected, again leading to widespread disturbances. Mine owners banned from employing women and children underground. Edwin Chadwick, *Report on the Sanitary Condition of the Labouring Poor*. |

1842 and work of Thomas Chatterton, eighteenth-century forger of the pseudo-medieval 'Rowley' poems. The work is known to Browning scholars as the *Essay on Chatterton* and is, apart from the *Essay on Shelley* (see below, 1852) Browning's only work of critical prose. (*June*) Publication of EBB's *The Greek Christian Poets* in the *Athenaeum*. (*July–September*) Publication of EBB's review of an anthology, *The Book of the Poets* and of Wordsworth's recent *Poems*, in the *Athenaeum*; later repr. by Browning as one essay, *The Book of the Poets*; EBB's only published works of criticism apart from her anonymous contributions to Horne's *New Spirit of the Age* (see below, 1844). (*November*) Publication of *Dramatic Lyrics*, no. 3 of *Bells and Pomegranates*; Browning had been persuaded by Moxon to include a volume of shorter poems in the series. Among the poems are 'My Last Duchess', 'Waring' (based on Alfred Domett), and 'The Pied Piper of Hamelin' (included at the last minute

| | | | |
|---|---|---|---|
| | because the printers found themselves short of material). | | |
| 1843 | (*January*) Publication of *The Return of the Druses*, no. 4 of *Bells and Pomegranates*. (*February*) Publication of *A Blot in the 'Scutcheon*, no. 5 of *Bells and Pomegranates*; on the same day the play is finally produced at Drury Lane, after protracted and acrimonious disagreements between Browning and Macready over proposed cuts and casting; closes after three performances. Browning blames Macready for wrecking the play and their friendship ends, though there will be a formal reconciliation in the 1860s. Opens negotiations with Macready's main rival, the actor-manager Charles Kean, son of Edmund Kean (see above, 1832), who offers him £500 for a new play; begins *Colombe's Birthday*. | Birth of Henry James. Carlyle, *Past and Present*. Dickens, *A Christmas Carol*, *Martin Chuzzlewit* (to 1844). Hood, *The Bridge of Sighs*; *The Song of the Shirt*. Richard Hengist Horne, *Orion* (the 'Farthing Epic'). Ebenezer Jones (1820–60), *Studies of Sensation and Event*. Thomas Babington Macaulay (b. 1800), *Critical and Historical Essays*. Mill, *System of Logic*. Ruskin, *Modern Painters* , vol. 1 (vol. 2 1846, vols 3–4 1856, vol. 5 1860). Death of Southey. Surtees, *Handley Cross*. Thackeray, *Irish Sketch Book*. | The *Economist* founded to promote free trade. United Free Church of Scotland formed. Wordsworth appointed Poet Laureate. |
| 1844 | EBB contributes anonymous articles and suggestions for Horne's survey of contemporary literature and culture, A | Birth of Gerard Manley Hopkins, Friedrich Nietzsche. Balzac, *Modeste Mignon*. Dickens, *The Chimes*. | Factory Act limits working hours for women and children in textile mills. Royal Commission on Health of Towns. |

| | | |
|---|---|---|
| 1844 | *New Spirit of the Age*. (*March*) Browning reads *Colombe's Birthday* to Kean and his wife. Kean says he likes the play but wants to defer production until the following year, and asks Browning not to publish it meanwhile; Browning refuses and publishes the play in April as no. 6 of *Bells and Pomegranates.* He never again writes for the stage. (*July–December*) Travels by sea to Naples; on this second Italian journey visits Rome and Florence; returns to England overland. (*August*) Publication of EBB's *Poems* including 'Lady Geraldine's Courtship', which contains a flattering reference to Browning's poetry: 'from Browning some "Pomegranate," which, if cut deep down the middle, / Shows a heart within blood-tinctured, of a veined humanity'. (*December*) On his return, reads 'Lady Geraldine's Courtship', perhaps drawn to his attention by John Kenyon (see above, 1839), who encourages him to write directly to EBB. | Disraeli, *Coningsby*. Emerson, *Essays (Second Series)*. Horne, A *New Spirit of the Age*. Patmore, *Poems*. Thackeray, *The Luck of Barry Lyndon*. |

| | | | |
|---|---|---|---|
| 1845 | (*10 January*) Writes first letter to EBB: 'Dear Miss Barrett, I love your poems with all my heart . . . I do, as I say, love these books with all my heart – and I love you too . . .' EBB replies warmly ('Such a letter from such a hand!') and correspondence continues. (*20 May*) Browning makes first visit to EBB in Wimpole Street. He writes her a declaration of love which she rejects, returning his letter and asking him to destroy it; the relationship, however, survives. (*Summer*) EBB comments on poems to be included in Browning's forthcoming volume, beginning with 'The Flight of the Duchess'. She also reveals to Browning significant details of her own life (especially the trauma she suffered after the death of her brother: see above, 1840) and tells him about her father's character and the peculiar conditions of domestic life in Wimpole Street, including his refusal to countenance the idea of any of his children marrying. (*Autumn*) In the aftermath of Mr Barrett's effectively | Death of Hood. Carlyle, *Oliver Cromwell's Letters and Speeches*. Disraeli, *Sybil*. Engels, *The Condition of the Working Class in England*. Fuller, *Woman in the Nineteenth Century*. Lear, *A Book of Nonsense*. Lewes, *A Biographical History of Philosophy* (to 1846). Longfellow, *The Belfry of Bruges*. Poe, *The Raven; Tales*. | Maynooth controversy (over state aid to an Irish Catholic seminary). Beginning of Irish potato famine. Parliamentary crisis over repeal of Corn Law. Newman's conversion to Catholicism. Tennyson awarded Civil List pension of £200. |

1845 forbidding EBB to travel to Italy for the winter, Browning renews his declarations of love and EBB declares her love for him in return. (*November*) Publication of *Dramatic Romances and Lyrics*, no. 7 of *Bells and Pomegranates*, and the second collection of shorter poems following *Dramatic Lyrics*; includes 'How They Brought the Good News from Ghent to Aix', 'The Lost Leader', 'Home-Thoughts, from Abroad', 'The Tomb at St Praxed's' ['The Bishop Orders His Tomb at Saint Praxed's Church'], 'The Laboratory', and 'The Flight of the Duchess'.

1845–6 (*Winter*) Browning and EBB begin to make plans to marry and live in Italy. Their correspondence is running at several letters each day and they meet twice or three times a week; the frequency of both letters and visits is kept a secret from Mr Barrett, but becomes known to other members of the Barrett family; EBB confides fully

| | | | |
|---|---|---|---|
| | in her two sisters, Henrietta and Arabel, but not in her six brothers. | | |
| 1846 | (*February*) Publication of two plays, *Luria* and *A Soul's Tragedy*, together as no. 8 of *Bells and Pomegranates*. (*9 September*) Mr Barrett announces that the Barrett family is to leave Wimpole Street while the house is cleaned and re-painted; EBB writes to Browning asking what they should do. (*10 September*) Browning replies: 'We must be *married directly* and go to Italy.' (*12 September*) Marriage by special licence of Browning and EBB at St Marylebone Church; the two witnesses are EBB's maid, Elizabeth Wilson, and Browning's cousin, James Silverthorne (see above, 1826, 1833). After the wedding Browning and EBB return to their respective homes and continue to correspond while making final arrangements for their journey to Italy. (*19 September*) The Brownings leave England and travel to Le Havre; from there they make their way to Paris, | Balzac, *La cousine Bette*. Dickens, *Pictures from Italy*. George Eliot, transl. of Strauss's *Life of Jesus*. Fuller, *Papers on Literature and Art*. Hawthorne, *Mosses from an Old Manse*. Keble, *Lyra Innocentium*. Melville, *Typee*. Sand, *La Mare au diable*. | Louis Napoleon escapes from prison and goes to England. Repeal of Corn Law. Tory party split; Peel resigns; Russell Prime Minister of Whig (Liberal) administration. Standard railway gauge introduced. National pupil–teacher training scheme established. Liverpool Sanitary Act passed (first appointment of a town medical officer of health). |

| | | | |
|---|---|---|---|
| 1846 | arriving on 21 September. In Paris they meet a close friend of both, the art historian Anna Jameson, who accompanies them on the remainder of their journey through France and Italy to Pisa, where they arrive 14 October. They find lodgings in the Collegio Ferdinando, where they live until April 1847. Despite repeated attempts at reconciliation in the years that follow, Mr Barrett refuses all further communication with his daughter and never forgives her; her brothers, at first offended by the secrecy of the marriage, are eventually reconciled. | | |
| 1847 | (*March*) EBB miscarries. (*April*) The Brownings move to Florence. Browning receives a letter from D.G. Rossetti asking if *Pauline*, which Rossetti had come across by accident in the British Museum Library, is by him, and replies that it is; he meets Rossetti on his visit to England in 1851 and their friendship lasts until the publication of *Fifine at the Fair* in | Balzac, *Le cousin Pons*. Anne Brontë, *Agnes Grey*. Charlotte Brontë, *Jane Eyre*. Emily Brontë, *Wuthering Heights*. Disraeli, *Tancred*. Melville, *Omoo*. Tennyson, *The Princess*. Trollope, *The Macdermots of Ballycoran*. | General election: Liberal victory. Sharp rise in price of wheat leads to last food riots in England. |

| | | | |
|---|---|---|---|
| | 1872 (see below). (*July–October*) First period of residence at Casa Guidi in Florence. (*October–May*) Residence in Piazza Pitti, Florence. | | |
| 1848 | (*May*) Return to Casa Guidi, which becomes their permanent home (with long intervals of travel to other parts of Italy, to France and England) for the rest of their married life. In Florence the Brownings form friendships with Frederick Tennyson and T.A. Trollope (brothers of the poet and novelist respectively), with the poet and future Viceroy of India Robert Lytton, and with several American residents and visitors: Nathaniel Hawthorne, Margaret Fuller, William Wetmore Story, Harriet Hosmer, and Hiram Powers. Both the Brownings support the cause of Italian independence from Austria, though EBB puts a trust in France, and in particular Louis Napoleon, which Browning does not share. EBB's strong belief in spiritualism in the 1850s also brings her into conflict with Browning. | Death of Emily Brontë. Anne Brontë, *The Tenant of Wildfell Hall*. Clough, *The Bothie of Tober-na-Vuolich.* Dickens, *Dombey and Son*. Engels and Marx, *The Communist Manifesto*. Gaskell, *Mary Barton*. Mill, *Principles of Political Economy*. Richard Monckton Milnes (1809–85), *Life, Letters, and Literary Remains of John Keats*. Newman, *Loss and Gain*. Poe, *Eureka.* Sand, *La Petite Fadette*. Thackeray, *Vanity Fair; The Book of Snobs*. Trollope, *The Kellys and the O'Kellys* | The 'year of revolutions' in Europe (France, Italy, Hungary). In France, fall of monarchy: Louis-Philippe abdicates and the Second Republic is formed amid bloody rioting in Paris. Louis Napoleon elected deputy to National Assembly, then President of the Republic. In Italy, republican uprisings defeated in Rome, Florence, Turin, and Venice. In England, Chartist meeting at Kennington Common disperses peacefully. Public Health Act sets up General Board of Health. First meetings of the 'Pre-Raphaelite Brotherhood', led by John Everett Millais, D.G. and W.M. Rossetti, William Holman Hunt, and Thomas Woolner. |

| | | | |
|---|---|---|---|
| 1849 | (*January*) Publication of *Poems* in two volumes, the first collected edition of Browning's poetry, containing heavily revised versions of *Paracelsus*, *Pippa Passes*, and other works, but omitting *Strafford* and *Sordello*. The publisher is no longer Moxon, but Chapman & Hall (whose decision to take on Browning may have been influenced by the fact that he came in a package with his much more saleable wife). From this point on Browning no longer pays for the publication of his work, though it will be a long time before he gains any substantial income from it. (*8 March*) Birth of the Brownings' only child, Robert Wiedemann Barrett Browning (later nicknamed 'Penini' or 'Pen'). (*18 March*) Death of Browning's mother. Browning suffers terribly, in part because he had not seen her since leaving England and because she had died without being aware of the birth of her grandchild. (*Summer*) At Bagni di Lucca, EBB shows Browning her sonnets on their | Death of Beddoes, Anne Brontë, Poe. Arnold, *The Strayed Reveller*. Clough, *Ambarvalia.* Charlotte Brontë, *Shirley*. Emerson, *Poems*. Macaulay, *History of England*, vols 1 and 2. Martineau, *History of the Thirty Years' Peace*. Melville, *Mardi; Redburn*. Ruskin, *Seven Lamps of Architecture*. | Formation of Christian Socialist movement led by Kingsley, F.D. Maurice, and others. Foundation of Bedford College for women. |

| | | | |
|---|---|---|---|
| | courtship, which he persuades her to publish in her forthcoming collection as *Sonnets from the Portuguese*. | | |
| 1850 | (*March*) Publication of EBB's *Poems*, a collected edition including revised versions of earlier poems, *Sonnets from the Portuguese* and other new poems, and a new translation of *Prometheus Bound*. (*April*) Publication of *Christmas Eve and Easter Day*, Browning's first new work since his marriage; the two poems are an attempt both to write more according to EBB's principles, and to appeal to a topical interest in religious debate; but after an initial surge coinciding with the Easter period sales of the volume fall off. (*July*) EBB's second miscarriage; there are no subsequent pregnancies, though she continues to hope for a daughter. | Birth of Robert Louis Stevenson. Death of Balzac, Margaret Fuller, Wordsworth. Beddoes, *Death's Jest-Book* (posthumous publ.). Carlyle, *Latter-Day Pamphlets*. Dickens, *David Copperfield*. Emerson, *Representative Men*. Hawthorne, *The Scarlet Letter*. Kingsley, *Alton Locke*. Melville, *White-Jacket*. Sand, *François le champi*. Tennyson, *In Memoriam*. Thackeray, *Pendennis*. Wordsworth, *The Prelude* (posthumous publ.) | Pope establishes new Catholic bishoprics in England (so-called 'Papal Aggression'). Publication of the Pre-Raphaelite journal *The Germ* (4 nos only). Dickens starts journal, *Household Words* (to 1859). Tennyson appointed Poet Laureate. |
| 1851 | (*May–June*) Trip to Venice, then on to Paris, where they remain until late July. (*May*) Publication of EBB's *Casa Guidi Windows*. (*July–September*) Trip | Death of Mary Shelley. Carlyle, *Life of John Sterling*. Hawthorne, *The House of the Seven Gables*. Kingsley, *Yeast*. Longfellow, *The Golden Legend*. | Louis Napoleon seizes power in *coup d'état*, dissolves National Assembly, and is elected President for a ten-year term. In England, Ecclesiastical Titles Act |

| | | | |
|---|---|---|---|
| 1851 | to London, where Browning renews friendships with Tennyson, Carlyle and others; the Brownings return to Paris in late September. (*August*) Publication in *Revue des Deux Mondes* of detailed and appreciative article on Browning's poetry by French critic Joseph Milsand; Browning and Milsand later meet and become close friends, a friendship which endures until Milsand's death in 1887. (*November*) Browning learns of his father's relationship with a widow, Mrs Von Müller, which has ended in an engagement from which Mr Browning now wishes to withdraw. He gives his son a misleading account of the relationship and in particular does not mention the numerous love-letters he has written to Mrs Von Müller. Both Browning and his father write to Mrs Von Müller, Mr Browning formally breaking off the engagement; the result is a breach of promise suit which causes Browning deep pain and mortification. (*December*) The | Henry Mayhew (1812–87), *London Labour and the London Poor* (to 1852). Melville, *Moby Dick*. Meredith, *Poems*. Ruskin, *Stones of Venice*, vol. 1 (vols 2–3 1853); *Pre-Raphaelitism*. | (preventing Catholic bishops from adopting British titles) passed but not enforced; repealed 1871. Great Exhibition. Religious census (the only one ever taken in Britain). |

| | | | |
|---|---|---|---|
| | Brownings witness Louis Napoleon's *coup d'état* and argue over its justification (EBB for, Browning against). | | |
| 1852 | (*January*) Publication of a collection of letters supposedly by Shelley, with an 'Introductory Essay' by Browning, his only formal work of literary criticism besides the *Essay on Chatterton* (see above, 1842). However, all but two of the letters are revealed to be forgeries, and the volume is almost immediately withdrawn from sale. Browning's essay is referred to by Browning scholars as the *Essay on Shelley*. (*February*) The Brownings meet the French novelist George Sand, whom EBB has long admired; Browning is considerably cooler towards both the writer and her Bohemian coterie, but goes to see Sand on several other occasions. (*July*) Trip to London. Browning's father loses the breach of promise suit and Mrs Von Müller is awarded damages of £800; since he cannot pay such a sum, Mr | Birth of George Moore. Death of Thomas Moore. Arnold, *Empedocles on Etna, and Other Poems*. Hawthorne, *The Blithedale Romance*. Hugo, *Napoléon le petit*; *Histoire d'un crime* (not publ. until 1877). Melville, *Pierre*. Newman, *Discourses on the Scope and Nature of University Education* (eventually publ. in 1873 as *The Idea of a University*). Harriet Beecher Stowe (1811–96), *Uncle Tom's Cabin*. Tennyson, *Ode on the Death of the Duke of Wellington*. Thackeray, *Henry Esmond*. | In France, final dissolution of Second Republic and beginning of Second Empire: Louis Napoleon assumes title of Emperor Napoleon III. In England, Liberal government resigns; Derby forms minority Tory administration, but is defeated over Disraeli's budget and resigns; Aberdeen forms coalition of Liberals and Peelite Tories with Gladstone as Chancellor. |

| | | | |
|---|---|---|---|
| 1852 | Browning is forced to leave England. Browning returns to Paris in mid-July with his father and sister, who live there until Mr Browning's death in 1866; Browning returns to England after finding his father lodgings. (*October*) The Brownings return to Paris, and after a brief stay travel back to Casa Guidi. | | |
| 1853 | (*February*) Writes to Milsand: 'I am writing – a first step towards popularity for me – lyrics with more music and painting than before, so as to get people to hear and see'; these will form part of *Men and Women* ('music and painting' refers to qualities of style, i.e. lyrical and descriptive writing, not subject matter, though *Men and Women* does contain poems about musicians and painters). | Arnold, *Poems*. Charlotte Brontë, *Villette*. Dickens, *Bleak House*. Eliot, transl. of Feuerbach's *Essence of Christianity*. Gaskell, *Cranford*; *Ruth*. Hugo, *Les Châtiments*. Kingsley, *Hypatia*. Landor, *Imaginary Conversations of Greeks and Romans*. Lewes, *Comte's Philosophy of the Sciences*. Martineau (transl.), *The Philosophy of Comte*. Surtees, *Mr Sponge's Sporting Tour*. Thackeray, *The English Humourists of the Eighteenth Century*. | Marriage of Napoleon III with Eugénie de Montijo. Failure of negotiations between Britain and Russia over Turkish territorial issue; mobilisation of navy in Dardanelles. Northcote-Trevelyan *Report on Civil Service* criticises patronage and advocates reform. |

| | | | |
|---|---|---|---|
| 1854 | | Dickens, *Hard Times*. Patmore, *The Angel in the House* (subsequent vols to 1863). Sand, *Histoire de ma vie* (4 vols to 1855). Tennyson, 'Charge of the Light Brigade'. | Britain and France declare war on Russia (Crimean War). Charge of the Light Brigade at battle of Balaclava. Florence Nightingale (1820–1910) leads contingent of nurses to Scutari and begins campaign for reform of army medical provision. |
| 1855 | (*June–July*) Trip to Paris. (*July–October*) Trip to London. (*July*) The Brownings, who strongly disagree about the truth of spiritualist phenomena, attend a séance conducted by the famous American medium D.D. Home, later the model for Browning's Mr Sludge. (*September*) First meeting with Ruskin. (*October*) Return to Paris. (*November*) Publication of *Men and Women* in two volumes; Browning had been working on the poems of this collection since 1852, and has high hopes of its success. The fifty poems of the original collection include 'Love Among the Ruins', 'Fra Lippo Lippi', 'A Toccata of Galuppi's', 'Childe Roland to the Dark Tower Came', | Death of Charlotte Brontë. Arnold, *Poems, Second Series*. Gaskell, *North and South*. Irving, *Life of George Washington* (to 1859). Kingsley, *Westward Ho!* Lewes, *Life and Works of Goethe*. Longfellow, *Song of Hiawatha*. Macaulay, *History of England*, vols 3 and 4. Melville, *Israel Potter*. Tennyson, *Maud*. Thackeray, *The Newcomes*. Trollope, *The Warden*. Whitman, *Leaves of Grass* (enlarged and revised eds 1856, 1860, 1867, 1871, 1889, 1892). | Aberdeen coalition resigns; Palmerston forms Liberal administration. Stamp duty on newspapers abolished. Foundation of *The Daily Telegraph*. |

| | | | |
|---|---|---|---|
| 1855 | 'Bishop Blougram's Apology', 'Andrea del Sarto', 'Cleon', 'Two in the Campagna', and 'A Grammarian's Funeral'; at the last moment Browning adds a dedicatory poem to EBB at the end of the volume, 'One Word More'. But the volume fails both critically and commercially, and Browning is bitterly disappointed and hurt. Signs of the revival in his reputation (especially among the Pre-Raphaelites, led by D.G. Rossetti) are as yet invisible to him. | | |
| 1856 | (*June*) Trip to London. (*October*) Return to Paris, then travel back to Casa Guidi. (*November*) Publication of EBB's *Aurora Leigh*. (*December*) Death of John Kenyon; his legacy of £11,000 makes the Brownings financially secure for the rest of their lives. | Birth of (Henry) Rider Haggard, Oscar Wilde. Emerson, *English Traits*. Hugo, *Les Contemplations*. Melville, *Piazza Tales*. Meredith, *The Shaving of Shagpat*. Newman, *Callista*. | End of Crimean War (Treaty of Paris). |
| 1857 | (*April*) Death of Mr Barrett. | Birth of George Gissing. Charles Baudelaire (1821–67), *Les Fleurs du mal*. Charlotte Brontë, *The Professor*. Dickens, *Little Dorrit*. Flaubert, | Indian Mutiny (finally suppressed 1858). General election: Liberal victory. Foundation of Science Museum. |

| | | | |
|---|---|---|---|
| | | *Madame Bovary*. Gaskell, *Life of Charlotte Brontë*. Thomas Hughes (1822–96), *Tom Brown's Schooldays*. Kingsley, *Two Years Ago*. Melville, *The Confidence Man*. Ruskin, *Political Economy of Art*. Trollope, *Barchester Towers*. | |
| 1858 | (*July–October*) Trip to France (Paris and Normandy). Browning meets a friend of Shelley and of his first wife Harriet Westbrook, the bookseller Thomas Hookham, who tells him the true story of Shelley's treatment of her and shows Browning some of Harriet's letters. Browning is devastated, though his opinion of Shelley's poetry remains high. | Arnold, *Merope*. Carlyle, *History of Frederick the Great* (6 vols, to 1865). Clough, *Amours de Voyage*. Dickens, *Dombey and Son*. Eliot, *Scenes of Clerical Life*. Thomas Jefferson Hogg (1792–1862), *Life of Shelley*. Kingsley, *Andromeda*. Longfellow, *The Courtship of Miles Standish*. Morris, *The Defence of Guinevere*. Peacock, *Memoirs of Shelley* (in origin a review of Hogg and Trelawney). Edward Trelawney (1792–1881), *Recollections of the Last Days of Shelley and Byron*. Trollope, *The Three Clerks; Doctor Thorne; The Bertrams*. | Palmerston's government falls; Derby forms minority Tory administration. Political restrictions on Jews removed. Property qualification for MPs abolished. Launch of Brunel's steamship, the *Great Eastern*. |

| | | | |
|---|---|---|---|
| 1859 | The Brownings give refuge to W.S. Landor after Landor's quarrel with his family; Browning looks after Landor's domestic arrangements until his death in 1864. | Death of Irving, Macaulay. Arnold, *England and the Italian Question*. Darwin, *Origin of Species*. Dickens, *A Tale of Two Cities*. Eliot, *Adam Bede*. FitzGerald, *The Rubáiyát of Omar Khayyám* (anon.; revised 1868, 1872, 1879). Hugo, *La Légende des siècles* (to 1883). Meredith, *The Ordeal of Richard Feverel*. Mill, *On Liberty*; *Thoughts on Parliamentary Reform*. Ruskin, *The Two Paths*. Samuel Smiles (1812–1904), *Self-Help*. Tennyson, *Idylls of the King*: 'Enid', 'Vivien', 'Eliane', and 'Guinevere'. Thackeray, *The Virginians*. Trollope, *The West Indies and the Spanish Main*. | France declares war on Austria and intervenes in Italian conflict as ally of Piedmont. Despite a series of victories, Napoleon III signs peace of Villafranca which stops short of achieving Italian independence but which secures Nice and part of Savoy for France. Garibaldi calls on Italians to take up arms. In England, general election: Derby's minority government remains in power, but falls shortly afterwards; Palmerston resumes office. Dickens starts weekly journal, *All the Year Round*. |
| 1860 | (*March*) Publication of EBB's *Poems Before Congress*. Death of Anna Jameson (see above, 1846). (*June*) On a market stall in Florence, Browning finds the 'Old Yellow Book', the bundle of printed and manuscript documents which later form the basis of *The Ring and the Book*. (*November*) Death of EBB's sister Henrietta. | Collins, *The Woman in White*. Eliot, *The Mill on the Floss*. Emerson, *The Conduct of Life*. Hawthorne, *The Marble Faun*. Ruskin, *Unto this Last*. Trollope, *Castle Richmond*. Publication of *Essays and Reviews*, a collection of essays on religion from a liberal or Broad Church standpoint; condemned the following year by a | Britain and France declare in favour of Italian independence and unification. Garibaldi liberates Sicily and joins forces with Victor-Emmanuel, king of Sardinia-Piedmont. In England, debate between Bishop Wilberforce and T.H. Huxley over Darwin's ideas. Foundation of *Cornhill Magazine*. |

| | | | |
|---|---|---|---|
| | | meeting of bishops and by the General Synod in 1864. | |
| 1861 | (*29 June*) Death of EBB at Casa Guidi; she is buried in the Protestant Cemetery in Florence. (*1 August*) Browning leaves Florence, to which he never returns, and after a short stay in France travels to London, arriving 27 September. His usual pattern from now is to spend the autumn and winter in London, and to take long summer holidays in Scotland or abroad. Gradually, over the next quarter of a century, his poetry becomes more successful and widely known, and he is established as one of the great men of letters of the period and a social 'lion'; accordingly his social circle widens and becomes more worldly. In the London 'season', the great passion of the last years of his life is music: see 'The Founder of the Feast' (1884) a sonnet honouring the music publisher and impresario Arthur Chappell, where Browning remembers music 'poured by | Death of Clough. Arnold, *On Translating Homer*. Eliot, *Silas Marner*. Dickens, *Great Expectations*. Mill, *Considerations on Representative Government*. Francis Turner Palgrave (1824–97, ed.) *The Golden Treasury* (second series 1897). Peacock, *Gryll Grange*. Charles Reade (1814–84), *The Cloister and the Hearth*. D.G. Rossetti, *The Early Italian Poets*. Thackeray, *Lovel the Widower*. Trollope, *Framley Parsonage*. | Unification of Italy as kingdom under Victor-Emmanuel. American Civil War. Death of Prince Albert. |

| | | | |
|---|---|---|---|
| 1861 | perfect ministrants, / By Hallé, Schumann, Piatti, Joachim'. (*August*) Begins regular correspondence with Isa Blagden, one of his and EBB's closest friends in Florence, which lasts until her death in 1873. | | |
| 1862 | (*February*) Elected to membership of Athenaeum Club. (*March*) Publication of EBB's *Last Poems*, collected by Browning and dedicated by him to 'grateful Florence'. (*May*) Moves to 19 Warwick Crescent, his London home until 1887. (*December*) Publication of *Selections* (dated 1863 on title page), the contents of which had been chosen by Browning's friends John Forster and B.W. Proctor; it is favourably reviewed and signals the beginning of Browning's critical rehabilitation. | Collins, *No Name*. Flaubert, *Salammbô*. Hugo, *Les Misérables*. Meredith, *Modern Love*. C. Rossetti, *Goblin Market*. Thackeray, *The Adventures of Philip*. Trollope, *Orley Farm; North America*. Queen Victoria, *Leaves from a Journal of Our Life in the Highlands*. | 'Cotton famine' in Lancashire as a result of American Civil War. Albert Memorial designed by Gilbert Scott. |
| 1863 | (*Spring*) First meeting with Julia Wedgwood. (*May–July*) Publication of *Poetical Works* in three volumes, including a revised *Sordello*, also favourably reviewed. In this edition | Death of Thackeray. Gaskell, *Sylvia's Lovers*. Hawthorne, *Our Old Home*. Kingsley, *The Water-Babies*. Landor, *Heroic Idylls*. Longfellow, *Tales of a Wayside Inn*. Mill, *Utilitarianism*. | Foundation of Football Association. |

| | | | |
|---|---|---|---|
| | Browning redistributes the poems of *Dramatic Lyrics*, *Dramatic Romances and Lyrics*, and *Men and Women* into the categories 'Lyrics', 'Romances' and 'Men and Women' (which now consists of only 12 poems, not all of them from the original collection). This format is retained with minor changes in the *Poetical Works* of 1868 and 1888–9. Chapman & Hall delay publication of Browning's new volume in order to take advantage of increased sales. | Ernest Renan (1823–92), *Vie de Jésus*, first vol. of his *Histoire des origines du Christianisme*. Thackeray, *Roundabout Papers*. | |
| 1864 | (*April*) Meets Julia Wedgwood again and begins corresponding with her and meeting her regularly. Though Browning probably never proposes marriage to her, this relationship is the closest he comes to it after EBB's death. (*May*) Publication of *Dramatis Personae*, including 'James Lee', 'Rabbi Ben Ezra', 'A Death in the Desert', 'Caliban Upon Setebos', 'A Likeness', and 'Mr Sludge, "the Medium"'. Later in the year a second edition is required, for the first time in Browning's career. | Death of Clare, Hawthorne, Landor, Surtees. Newman, *Apologia pro Vita Sua*. Tennyson, *Enoch Arden*. Thackeray, *Denis Duval* (posthumous publ.). Trollope, *The Small House at Allington; Can You Forgive Her?* | Gladstone's declaration in favour of further parliamentary reform. Foundation of Manchester Reform Union. Meeting of the First International in London. Opening of Metropolitan Railway. Foundation of Early English Texts Society. |

| | | | |
|---|---|---|---|
| 1865 | (*March*) Julia Wedgwood writes to Browning breaking off their relationship because of rumours that she wanted to marry him. Browning promises to send her *The Ring and the Book* when it is finished 'next year' (in fact it takes a further three years). | Birth of Rudyard Kipling, W(illiam) B(utler) Yeats. Death of Gaskell. Arnold, *Essays in Criticism*. Carroll, *Alice's Adventures in Wonderland*. Dickens, *Our Mutual Friend*. Mill, *Auguste Comte and Positivism*. Ruskin, *Sesame and Lilies*. Swinburne, *Atalanta in Calydon*; *Chastelard*. Whitman, *Drum-Taps*. | General election: Liberal victory. Death of Palmerston; Russell Prime Minister, promises further reform. Foundation of Reform League. Opening of Atlantic telegraph cable. Foundation of the *Fortnightly Review*. |
| 1866 | (*June*) Death of Browning's father in Paris. Sarianna moves to London and lives with Browning until his death. Browning is 'profoundly discontented' with his publisher, Chapman & Hall. | Death of Keble. Collins, *Armadale*. Eliot, *Felix Holt*. Gaskell, *Wives and Daughters*. Hugo, *Les Travailleurs de la mer*. Kingsley, *Hereward the Wake*. Melville, *Battle-Pieces and Aspects of the War*. Newman, *The Dream of Gerontius*. C. Rossetti, *The Prince's Progress*. Ruskin, *Crown of Wild Olive*; *Ethics of the Dust*. Swinburne, *Poems and Ballads*. Trollope, *The Belton Estate*. | Fenian unrest in Ireland; Habeas Corpus suspended there. Russell's government split over reform and falls; Derby Prime Minister of minority Tory administration, with Disraeli leader in Commons. Growth of agitation for reform: Hyde Park riots. Marquis of Queensbury codifies rules of boxing. Foundation of Amateur Athletic Association. Foundation of *Contemporary Review*. |
| 1867 | (*June*) Oxford University awards Browning an honorary M.A. (*October*) Balliol College (the Master, Benjamin Jowett, is a friend) makes Browning an | Arnold, *On the Study of Celtic Literature*. Carlyle, *Shooting Niagara*. Marx, *Das Kapital*. Mill, *Inaugural Address at the University of St.* | Second Reform Act passed. Factory Act, Extension Act and Agricultural Gangs Act provide greater protection for female and child labour. Fenian disturbances in |

| | | | |
|---|---|---|---|
| | honorary Fellow. Browning wants his son, Pen, to enter Balliol and he is given intensive tutoring in Greek and Latin. | *Andrews*. Swinburne, *A Song of Italy*. Trollope, *The Last Chronicle of Barset*; *The Claverings*. | England; outbreaks of anti-Irish sentiment. Joseph Lister pioneers antiseptic surgery. |
| 1868 | John T. Nettleship, *Essays on Robert Browning's Poetry*, dedicated to Browning. See also 1889. (*April*) Pen fails his matriculation at Oxford, but Browning decides that he should try again in the autumn. (*Spring*) Publication of *Poetical Works* in six volumes by Browning's new publisher, Smith, Elder. This is the first collection to include *Pauline*, with a preface in which Browning states that he acknowledges the poem as his 'with extreme repugnance' and does so only to avert the threat of a pirated edition. (*Spring*) Thomas Kelsall, literary executor of Thomas Lovell Beddoes, sends Browning his collection of Beddoes' manuscripts, which Browning examines and returns; in 1872, when Kelsall dies, he bequeaths the manuscripts to Browning, who in turn | Collins, *The Moonstone*. Eliot, *The Spanish Gypsy*. Morris, *The Earthly Paradise* (to 1870). Swinburne, *William Blake*. | Derby resigns; Disraeli Prime Minister. General election: Liberal victory. Disraeli resigns; Gladstone Prime Minister. Foundation of Royal Historical Society. Foundation of Press Association. |

1868 (1883) gives them to Edmund Gosse. (*June*) EBB's sister Arabel Barrett, the only one of her siblings to whom Browning had been close, dies in his arms. (*October*) Jowett tells Browning that Pen is unlikely to pass his matriculation at Balliol. (*November*) Publication of first volume of *The Ring and the Book*, containing books i–iii. Books iv–vi were published in December, books vii–ix in January 1869, and books x–xii in February. The poem (at over 21,000 lines the longest single work by a major poet in the language) is widely reviewed, generally with acclaim, and sells well; it finally establishes Browning's contemporary reputation. Browning sends advance copies to Julia Wedgwood and corresponds with her about the poem's morality and aesthetics, but their personal relationship is not renewed; Browning tells her he 'underwent great pain' from its sudden ending. Jowett writes to Browning asking him if he would accept nomination to the Rectorship of St Andrew's University,

| | | | |
|---|---|---|---|
| | the first of many such requests over the next two decades; Browning declines them all. | | |
| 1869 | (*January*) Pen enters Christ Church, Oxford, after passing an easier matriculation than the one required by Balliol. (*March*) Browning is presented to Queen Victoria in the company of Carlyle, the historian George Grote, and the geologist Charles Lyell. (*September*) Is attracted to Louisa, Lady Ashburton, but when she proposes marriage tells her that his 'heart [is] buried in Florence' and that if he accepted it would only be for Pen's sake. Lady Ashburton lets it be known that *she* refused *his* proposal, and a bitter estrangement takes place (Lady Ashburton's version of events gains widespread belief and still circulates today). | Arnold, *Culture and Anarchy*. R.D. Blackmore (1825–1900), *Lorna Doone*. Carroll, *Phantasmagoria.* Clough, *Poems and Prose Remains* (incl. *Dipsychus and the Spirit*). Flaubert, *L'Education sentimentale.* Gilbert, *Bab Ballads*. Hugo, *L'Homme qui rit*. Mill, *On the Subjection of Women.* Henry Crabb Robinson (1775– 1867), *Diaries*. Ruskin, *The Queen of the Air*. Tennyson, *Idylls of the King*: 'The coming of Arthur', 'The Holy Grail', 'Pelleas and Ettarre', and 'The Passing of Arthur'. Trollope, *Phineas Finn; He Knew He Was Right.* | Church of Ireland disestablished. Foundation of Girton College for women, first at Hitchin, then (1873) transferred to Cambridge. |
| 1870 | | Death of Dickens. Dickens, *The Mystery of Edwin Drood.* Disraeli, *Lothair*. Emerson, *Society and Solitude*. | Franco-Prussian War; France defeated; siege of Paris. Doctrine of Papal Infallibility propounded. Elementary |

| | | | |
|---|---|---|---|
| | | Newman, *A Grammar of Assent*. D.G. Rossetti, *Poems*. Trollope, *The Vicar of Bullhampton*. | Education Act provides for local 'board schools' but elementary education not yet compulsory. Married Women's Property Act. Introduction of competitive entrance examinations to Civil Service (except Foreign Office). |
| 1871 | (*March*) Publication in *Cornhill Magazine* of 'Hervé Riel', founded on a legendary exploit by a French sailor; Browning took the unusual step (for him) of publishing his work in a magazine in order to raise money for the relief of the starving citizens of Paris in the aftermath of the Franco-Prussian war. (*August*) Publication of *Balaustion's Adventure*, a narrative poem incorporating a 'transcript' (translation) of Euripides' *Alcestis*; it proves one of his most popular poems, reaching several editions. (*December*) Publication of *Prince Hohenstiel-Schwangau, Saviour of Society*, a long dramatic monologue spoken by a fictitious statesman based on Napoleon III. | Arnold, *Friendship's Garland*. R.W. Buchanan (1841–1901), 'The Fleshly School of Poetry' (attack on D.G. Rossetti publ. under pseudonym of 'Thomas Maitland' in *Contemporary Review*). Darwin, *Descent of Man*. Hardy, *Desperate Remedies*. Lear, *Nonsense Songs*. Ruskin, *Fors Clavigera* (to 1878). Swinburne, *Songs before Sunrise*. Tennyson, *Idylls of the King: 'The Last Tournament'*. Trollope, *Ralph the Heir*. Whitman, *Democratic Vistas; Passage to India*. | Capitulation of France and armistice with Prussia. Napoleon III deposed and goes into exile in England; Third Republic proclaimed. Paris refuses to lay down arms; the Commune (March–May) is bloodily suppressed by French army. In England, Trade Union Act legalises unions. University Tests Act abolishes religious test for entry to Oxford and Cambridge. Establishment of FA Cup competition. Bank holidays introduced in England and Wales. |

| | | | |
|---|---|---|---|
| 1872 | (*January or February*) First meets Mrs Sarah Anna FitzGerald, who becomes a close friend and correspondent in the late 1870s and 1880s. (*February*) Alfred Domett returns to England from New Zealand; his friendship with Browning is resumed, but at a less intense level. (*May*) Publication of *Selections from the Poetical Works*, dedicated to Tennyson; together with the second volume published in 1880, these became the standard selected editions of Browning's poetry and were many times reissued. (*June*) Publication of *Fifine at the Fair*, according to Browning himself the 'most metaphysical and boldest' poem he had written since *Sordello*, and of whose 'reception by the public' he is 'very doubtful' – with reason. The poem is a failure, and also causes a breach with D.G. Rossetti, who is convinced it contains an attack on him in collusion with R.W. Buchanan (see column 2, 1871). (*June*) Pen fails his examinations at Oxford and leaves without taking his degree. | Samuel Butler (1835–1902), *Erewhon*. Carroll, *Through the Looking-Glass and What Alice Found There*. Darwin, *The Expression of the Emotions in Man and Animals*. Eliot, *Middlemarch*. Hardy, *Under the Greenwood Tree*. Hugo, *L'Année terrible*. Lear, *More Nonsense*. Longfellow, *Three Books of Song*. Nietzsche, *Birth of Tragedy*. C. Rossetti, *Sing-Song*. D.G. Rossetti, 'The Stealthy School of Criticism' (reply to Buchanan publ. in *Athenaeum*: see above). Tennyson, *Idylls of the King*: 'Gareth and Lynette'. | Ballot Act (voting by secret ballot). |

| | | | |
|---|---|---|---|
| 1873 | (*May*) Publication of *Red Cotton Night-Cap Country*, based on a contemporary *cause célèbre* involving suicide and a disputed will, about which Browning had read the previous year while on holiday in Normandy. The poem is delayed by the publisher's legal worries about possible grounds for libel; Browning changes the names of characters and locations in proof. | Death of Bulwer-Lytton, Mill. Arnold, *Literature and Dogma*. Hardy, *A Pair of Blue Eyes*. Hugo, *Quatrevingt-treize*. Mill, *Autobiography* (posthumous publ.). Pater, *Studies in the History of the Renaissance*. Trollope, *The Eustace Diamonds*. | Gladstone resigns after defeat of Irish University bill; Disraeli refuses to form government: Gladstone resumes office. Judicature Act consolidates courts in England and Wales into single system. Ashanti War. |
| 1874 | (*Spring*) Pen begins studying painting under Jean Arnould Heyermans in Antwerp. He later studies sculpture in Paris in Rodin's studio. From this period Browning energetically and uncritically fosters Pen's career as an artist, using his influence to get his friends to view (and buy) his work, which is mediocre at best. His devotion is repaid for a while by Pen's industry and moderate success. After his marriage (see 1887) Pen turns his attention and talent to restoring and redecorating Palazzo Rezzonico in Venice, and after Browning's death his career as an artist ceases. | Death of Proctor, Sand. Eliot, *The Legend of Jubal*. Flaubert, *La Tentation de Saint Antoine*. Hardy, *Far From the Madding Crowd*. Lewes, *Problems of Life and Mind* (to 1879). Swinburne, *Bothwell*. James Thomson ('B.V.', 1834–82), *The City of Dreadful Night*. Trollope, *Phineas Redux*. | General election: Tory victory. Disraeli Prime Minister. Royal Commission on labour laws. Factory Act reduces working week to 56½ hours. Public Worship Act to curb ritualism in Church of England. |

| | | | |
|---|---|---|---|
| 1875 | (*April*) Publication of *Aristophanes' Apology*, a sequel to *Balaustion's Adventure*, and like it containing a 'transcript' of a play by Euripides, this time the *Heracles*. After *The Ring and the Book* and *Sordello*, the poem is Browning's longest (5711 lines). (*November*) Publication of *The Inn Album*, a melodrama of erotic intrigue with a violent *dénouement*, admired by Swinburne as a 'sensation novel in verse'. | Gilbert and Sullivan, *Trial by Jury*. James, *A Passionate Pilgrim*. Lewes, *On Actors and the Art of Acting*. Longfellow, *The Masque of Pandora*. Swinburne, *George Chapman*. Tennyson, *Queen Mary*. Trollope, *The Way We Live Now*. Whitman, *Memoranda during the War*. | Public Health Act. Charles Stewart Parnell (1846–91) elected MP for Meath and becomes leader of Irish Home Rule party. |
| 1876 | (*July*) Publication of *Pacchiarotto and How He Worked in Distemper: with Other Poems*, Browning's first collection of shorter poems since *Dramatis Personae*. The title poem contains a savage attack on his critics, and in particular Alfred Austin (later Poet Laureate in succession to Tennyson); the volume also includes 'House' (a rejection of confessional poetry), 'Hervé Riel' (see above, 1871), 'A Forgiveness', and 'Filippo Baldinucci on the Privilege of Burial', a powerful satire on anti-semitism. | Death of Martineau. Carroll, *The Hunting of the Snark*. Eliot, *Daniel Deronda*. Emerson, *Letters and Social Aims*. Hardy, *The Hand of Ethelberta*. James, *Roderick Hudson*. Melville, *Clarel*. Morris, *Sigurd the Volsung*. Swinburne, *Erectheus*. Tennyson, *Harold*. Trollope, *The Prime Minister*. Whitman, *Two Rivulets*. | Queen Victoria becomes Empress of India. Disraeli made Earl of Beaconsfield. First International disbanded. Telephone invented by Alexander Graham Bell. |

| | | | |
|---|---|---|---|
| 1877 | (*September*) Sudden death of Annie Egerton Smith, on holiday in the Alps with Browning and Sarianna. (*October*) Publication of *The Agamemnon of Aeschylus*, with a preface defending Browning's method of translation, one which is 'literal at every cost save that of absolute violence to our language'. Browning agrees to the publication of EBB's letters to R.H. Horne in order to give financial help to Horne, an old literary acquaintance; this is the only instance in which he allows biographers access to such materials. | Flaubert, *Trois Contes*. Gilbert and Sullivan, *The Sorcerer*. James, *The American*. Lear, *Laughable Lyrics*. Martineau, *Autobiography*. Meredith, *On the Idea of Comedy* (lecture; publ. 1897). Patmore, *The Unknown Eros*. Trollope, *The American Senator*. | Prisons Act brings all prisons under Home Office control. Foundation of National Liberal Federation. Foundation of the Society for the Protection of Ancient Buildings. Foundation of the *Nineteenth Century* (journal). All-England Lawn Tennis Championship first played at Wimbledon. |
| 1878 | (*May*) Publication in one volume of *La Saisiaz*, a philosophical elegy for Annie Egerton Smith, and *The Two Poets of Croisic*, a contrastingly comic poem about two obscure local figures from the village in Brittany where Browning spent several summers. (*September*) Revisits Asolo for the first time since 1838. | Death of G.H. Lewes. Gilbert and Sullivan, *H.M.S. Pinafore*. Hardy, *The Return of the Native*. James, *The Europeans; Watch and Ward* (serialised 1871). Swinburne, *Poems and Ballads, Second Series*. Trollope, *Is He Popenjoy?* | Afghan War (to 1879). Foundation of Salvation Army. Roman Catholic hierarchy restored in Scotland. |

| | | | |
|---|---|---|---|
| 1879 | (*April*) Publication of *Dramatic Idyls*, a volume of short and medium-length poems, mostly dramatic monologues but all with a strong narrative focus ('Martin Relph', 'Ivàn Ivànovitch', 'Ned Bratts'); the volume is well reviewed and popular, and its reception encourages Browning to publish a second collection the following year. The use of the term 'Idyl' in the title annoyed Tennyson; though the spelling was (deliberately?) different from Tennyson's *English Idylls* or *Idylls of the King*, it is likely that Browning was aware that he was challenging the Laureate on his own ground. | Arnold, *Mixed Essays*. Eliot, *Impressions of Theophrastus Such*. Gilbert and Sullivan, *The Pirates of Penzance*. James, *Daisy Miller; An International Episode; The Madonna of the Future; Hawthorne*. Meredith, *The Egoist*. Trollope, *Thackeray*. | Zulu War. Foundation of Irish National Land League with Parnell as president. Newman created a Cardinal. Thomas Edison perfects electric light. |
| 1880 | (*June*) Publication of *Dramatic Idyls*, *Second Series*, including 'Clive', 'Echetlos', and 'Pan and Luna'. (*October*) First meeting, in Venice, with Katharine de Kay Bronson, perhaps the closest woman friend of the last decade of his life. | Death of Eliot, Flaubert. Disraeli, *Endymion*. Gissing, *Workers in the Dawn*. Hardy, *The Trumpet-Major*. James, *Confidence*. Longfellow, *Ultima Thule*. Tennyson, *Ballads*. Trollope, *The Duke's Children*. | General election: Liberal victory. Gladstone Prime Minister. Parnell's policy of 'boycotting' landlords begins in Ireland as part of agitation for Home Rule. |

| | | | |
|---|---|---|---|
| 1881 | (*October*) First meeting of the Browning Society, founded by F.J. Furnivall and Emily Hickey. Browning's reaction is a mixture of pleasure, amusement and embarrassment. | Death of Carlyle, Disraeli. Posthumous publ. of Carlyle's *Reminiscences*, ed. J.A. Froude. Gilbert and Sullivan, *Patience*. Hardy, A *Laodicean*. James, *Washington Square*; *The Portrait of a Lady*. C. Rossetti, A *Pageant*; *Called to be Saints*. D.G. Rossetti, *Ballads and Sonnets*; *Poems*. Swinburne, *Mary Stuart*. Trollope, *Dr Wortle's School*; *Ayala's Angel*. White (Mark Rutherford), *The Autobiography of Mark Rutherford*. Wilde, *Poems*. | Habeas Corpus again suspended in Ireland. Irish Land Act. Parnell briefly imprisoned. |
| 1882 | (*June*) Awarded honorary degree of D.C.L. by Oxford University. At the degree ceremony in the Sheldonian Theatre, a red cotton night-cap is lowered from the gallery onto Browning's head; the student joker is let off at Browning's intercession. | Death of Darwin, Emerson, Longfellow, D.G. Rossetti. Arnold, *Irish Essays and Others*. Gilbert and Sullivan, *Iolanthe*. Hardy, *Two on a Tower*. Longfellow, *In the Harbor*. Nietzsche, *The Gay Science*. Swinburne, *Tristram of Lyonesse*. Whitman, *Specimen Days and Collect*. | Parnell and Gladstone agree on Home Rule policy. Phoenix Park murders in Dublin. Married Women's Property Act extends 1870 legislation. Foundation of Society for Psychical Research. Publ. of *Dictionary of National Biography* begins. |

| | | | |
|---|---|---|---|
| 1883 | (*March*) Publication of *Jocoseria*, a collection of shorter poems which, as the title implies, is more miscellaneous in form and tone than the two series of *Dramatic Idyls*. Includes the much-parodied lyric 'Wanting is – what?', 'Donald' (an attack on deer-stalking, one of his son's favourite pastimes), 'Ixion', and one of the most moving of his late love-lyrics, 'Never the Time and the Place'. The volume is well reviewed and popular, and runs to several editions. | Moore, *A Modern Lover*. Nietzsche, *Thus Spake Zarathustra*. Stevenson, *Treasure Island.* Trollope, *Mr Scarborough's Family; An Autobiography* (both posthumous publ.). Queen Victoria, *More Leaves*. | |
| 1884 | (*April*) Awarded honorary degree of LL.D. by Edinburgh University. (*November*) Publication of *Ferishtah's Fancies*, philosophical and didactic poems ('The Melon-Seller', 'Two Camels', 'A Bean-Stripe: also Apple-Eating') using the eponymous Persian sage as mouthpiece. The Prologue to the volume ('Pray, Reader, have you eaten ortolans / Ever in Italy') is a witty comment on his poetics, and the Ferishtah poems | Death of Horne. Gilbert and Sullivan, *Princess Ida*. Gissing, *The Unclassed.* Morris, *Chants for Socialists*. Tennyson, *The Falcon; The Cup; Becket*. | Third Reform Act. Foundation of Fabian Society. Publ. of first part of *New English Dictionary (Oxford English Dictionary)*, conceived 1858. Foundation of Society of Authors. Tennyson made a hereditary peer. |

| | | | |
|---|---|---|---|
| 1884 | alternate with short lyrics including 'Round us the wild creatures', 'Man I am and man would be, Love', and 'Verse-making was least of my virtues'. | | |
| 1885 | Alexandra Orr, *A Handbook to the Works of Robert Browning*, publ. with Browning's consent if not active collaboration; several subsequent editions. (*November*) Negotiates for the purchase of Palazzo Manzoni in Venice, but the deal eventually falls through. (*December*) Refuses the presidency of the newly-formed Shelley Society. | Death of Hugo. Richard Burton (1821–90), unexpurgated version of *Arabian Nights* (to 1888). Gilbert and Sullivan, *The Mikado*. Rider Haggard, *King Solomon's Mines*. Meredith, *Diana of the Crossways*. Moore, *A Mummer's Wife*. Pater, *Marius the Epicurean.* C. Rossetti, *Time Flies.* Swinburne, *Marino Faliero.* Tennyson, *Tiresias; Idylls of the King*: 'Balin and Balan'. White (Mark Rutherford), *Deliverance.* | Gladstone resigns; Salisbury forms Tory administration. Discovery of radio waves. Invention of internal combustion engine. Foundation of Shelley Society. |
| 1886 | Arthur Symons, *An Introduction to the Study of Browning.* | Frances Hodgson Burnett (1849–1924), *Little Lord Fauntleroy.* Gissing, *Demos; Isabel Clarendon.* Hardy, *The Mayor of Casterbridge.* Hugo, *La Fin de Satan* (posthumous publ.). James, *The Bostonians; The Princess Casamassima*. Kipling, *Departmental Ditties*. Nietzsche, | Salisbury resigns; Gladstone Prime Minister. Irish Home Rule Bill splits Liberal party and government falls. General election: Tory victory. Salisbury Prime Minister. Mass demonstration of unemployed in Trafalgar Square followed by riots. Foundation of Indian National Congress. |

| | | | |
|---|---|---|---|
| | | *Beyond Good and Evil.* Arthur Rimbaud (1854–91), *Les Illuminations.* Ruskin, *Praeterita*, vol. 1 (vol. 2 1887, vol. 3 1888–9). Stevenson, *Dr Jekyll and Mr Hyde; Kidnapped.* Tennyson, *Locksley Hall Sixty Years After.* | |
| 1887 | (*January*) Publication of *Parleyings with Certain People of Importance in Their Day*. The figures with whom the poet 'parleys' are all from the seventeenth and eighteenth centuries, and all (as the title implies) obscure or of lesser fame; but all are of personal importance to Browning, often associated with early memories: the Dutch-born physician, social philosopher and satirist Bernard de Mandeville (1670–1733), author of *The Fable of the Bees*; the Italian Jesuit historian Daniello Bartoli (1609–85), whose *De' simboli trasportati al morale* had been edited by Browning's old Italian tutor, Angelo Cerutti; the poet Christopher Smart (1722–71), less | Arnold, *Kaiser Dead.* Arthur Conan Doyle (1859–1930), *A Study in Scarlet* (first Sherlock Holmes story). Gilbert and Sullivan, *Ruddigore.* Gissing, *Thyrza.* Rider Haggard, *She; Allan Quatermain.* Hardy, *The Woodlanders.* Nietzsche, *The Genealogy of Morals.* Pater, *Imaginary Portraits.* White (Mark Rutherford), *The Revolution in Tanner's Lane.* | Queen Victoria's Golden Jubilee. Demonstrations and riots of unemployed in Trafalgar Square and Hyde Park. |

1887 obscure today than in Browning's time, whose *Song to David* was one of Browning's favourite poems; the Whig statesman George Bubb Dodington (1691–1762), through whom Browning attacks Disraeli; the Florentine painter Francesco Furini (*c.* 1600–49), known chiefly for his nudes; Gerard de Lairesse (1641–1711), the Dutch painter and writer on art whose treatise *The Art of Painting* is a crucial source for many of Browning's landscapes and descriptions (especially 'Childe Roland'); and Charles Avison (*c.* 1710–70), organist and minor composer, whose 'Grand March' is printed at the end of the poem with lyrics celebrating Browning's hero John Pym, one of the leaders of the Parliamentary opposition to King Charles I. The collection constitutes, as has been often remarked, an oblique autobiography or apologia. (*June*) Forced to move from Warwick Crescent and takes up final London residence at 29 DeVere Gardens in

| | | | |
|---|---|---|---|
| | Kensington. (*October*) Marriage of Pen Browning and Fannie Coddington, a wealthy American woman; the marriage lasts until two years after Browning's death, after which the couple separate. | | |
| 1888 | (*April*) Publication of final *Poetical Works*, in 16 volumes appearing monthly (to July 1889). (*Summer*) Pen and Fannie Browning buy Palazzo Rezzonico in Venice. | Death of Arnold, Lear. Arnold, *Essays in Criticism, Second Series*. Gissing, *A Life's Morning*. James, *The Aspern Papers; The Reverberator*. Kipling, *Plain Tales from the Hills*. Melville, *John Marr and Other Sailors*. Morris, *A Dream of John Ball*. Nietzsche, *The Antichrist*. Mary Augusta Ward (Mrs Humphrey Ward, 1851–1920), *Robert Ellesmere*. Whitman, *November Boughs*. Wilde, *The Happy Prince*. | |
| 1889 | (*12 December*) Publication of *Asolando*, Browning's last volume, dedicated to Mrs Bronson (see above, 1880) containing miscellaneous shorter poems in a variety of genres ('Prologue', 'Now', 'Bad Dreams', | Death of Collins, Hopkins (his poems not publ. until 1918). Charles Booth (1840–1916), *Labour and Life of the People*, later the multi-volume *Life and Labour of the People in London*. Carroll, *Sylvie and Bruno* | Formation of the Second (Socialist) International, based in Brussels. |

| | | |
|---|---|---|
| 1889 | 'Beatrice Signorini', 'Imperante Augusto Natus Est –', and 'Development'), and concluding with the famous 'Epilogue' in which Browning described himself as 'One who never turned his back but marched breast forward' and which has unduly influenced his subsequent reputation for (in the *DNB*'s words) 'unflinching optimism'. On the same day Browning dies in Palazzo Rezzonico in Venice, shortly after receiving news by telegram that *Asolando* had been favourably reviewed. (*31 December*) Buried in Poets' Corner, Westminster Abbey. Among early tributes and biographical and critical responses: Edmund Gosse, *Robert Browning: Personalia*; Henry James, 'Browning in Westminster Abbey' (later publ. in *English Hours*, 1905); Nettleship (see 1868), *Robert Browning: Essays and Thoughts*; William Sharp, *Life of Robert Browning*; Swinburne, *Sonnets on the Death of Browning* (all 1890); Orr, *Life and Letters of Robert Browning*; (vol. 2 1893). | Gilbert and Sullivan, *The Yeomen of the Guard*; *The Gondoliers*. James, *A London Life*. Nietzsche, *Twilight of the Idols*. Pater, *Appreciations*. Stevenson, *The Master of Ballantrae*. Swinburne, *Poems and Ballads, Third Series*. Tennyson, *Demeter*. Yeats, *The Wandering of Oisin*. |

| | | | |
|---|---|---|---|
| | Henry Jones, *Browning as a Philosophical and Religious Teacher* (both 1891). | | |
| 1890 | | Kipling, *Soldiers Three.* | Fall of Parnell after being named as co-respondent in O'Shea divorce case. William Morris starts Kelmscott Press. |
| 1891 | | Death of Melville. Gissing, *New Grub Street.* Hardy, *Tess of the D'Urbervilles.* Melville, *Timoleon.* Morris, *News from Nowhere.* Whitman, *Good-Bye, My Fancy.* Wilde, *The Picture of Dorian Gray; Lord Arthur Savile's Crime; Intentions* (incl. 'The Decay of Lying' and 'The Critic as Artist'); *The Soul of Man under Socialism.* | Death of Parnell. |
| 1892 | | Death of Tennyson. Gissing, *Born in Exile.* George and Weedon Grossmith, *The Diary of a Nobody.* Kipling, *Barrack-Room Ballads.* Tennyson, *The Foresters; The Death of Oenone* (posthumous). Wilde, *Lady Windermere's Fan.* Yeats, *The Countess Kathleen.* | |

| | | | |
|---|---|---|---|
| 1893 | | James, *The Private Life* (story based on Browning). Moore, *Esther Waters*. Wilde, *A Woman of No Importance; Salomé* (in French; English transl. 1894). | |
| 1894 | | Death of C. Rossetti. Yeats, *The Land of Heart's Desire.* | |
| 1895 | | Wilde, *An Ideal Husband; The Importance of Being Earnest.* | |
| 1896 | | Death of Patmore. Hardy, *Jude the Obscure.* | |
| 1898 | | Death of Carroll, Gladstone. Hardy, *Wessex Poems*. Wilde, *Ballad of Reading Gaol.* | |
| 1899 | | Yeats, *The Wind Among the Reeds.* | |
| 1900 | | Death of Ruskin. | |
| 1901 | | Hardy, *Poems of the Past and the Present.* | Death of Queen Victoria. |
| 1903 | Death of Sarianna Browning. | | |
| 1912 | Death of Pen Browning. | | |

| | |
|---|---|
| 1913 | Sale of Browning estate at Sotheby's in order to pay Pen's debts, resulting in dispersal of books, manuscripts, furniture, and memorabilia. |

# Index

Note: RB = Robert Browning. EBB = Elizabeth Barrett Browning. The chronology has been indexed not by the page number, but by the date e.g. C1864. The first column only of the chronology has been indexed.